THE TARGUMS AND
RABBINIC LITERATURE

42.50

THE TARGUMS AND RABBINIC LITERATURE

An Introduction to Jewish Interpretations of Scripture

JOHN BOWKER

Professor of Religious Studies
University of Lancaster

CAMBRIDGE UNIVERSITY PRESS

Cambridge
London   New York   Melbourne

Published by the Syndics of the Cambridge University Press
The Pitt Building, Trumpington Street, Cambridge CB2 1RP
Bentley House, 200 Euston Road, London NW1 2DB
32 East 57th Street, New York, NY 10022, USA
296 Beaconsfield Parade, Middle Park, Melbourne 3206, Australia

Library of Congress catalogue card number: 71–80817

ISBN 0 521 07415 0

First published 1969
Reprinted with corrections 1979

Printed in Great Britain at the
University Press, Cambridge

To Margaret

CONTENTS

CONTENTS

PREFACE

This book has two purposes. The first is to provide an introduction to the Aramaic Targums, which preserve some of the most basic and popular elements of Jewish biblical interpretation; the second is to show how the Targums form a part of Jewish exegesis in general, and thus the book is also intended to be a brief introduction to rabbinic literature.

The need for such a guide has become increasingly urgent, particularly for students of the New Testament who are unlikely to become specialists in the field of rabbinic thought and literature, but for whom a knowledge of both is now essential. It is, for example, significant how many recent studies of the Gospels have relied heavily on Jewish background material—it is only necessary to mention B. Gerhardsson (on the transmission of oral material in rabbinic Judaism and the possible bearing this might have on the transmission of the teaching of Jesus), W. D. Davies (on the Sermon on the Mount), and C. H. Dodd (on John) to indicate how indispensable a knowledge of Jewish material has become.

The intention of this book is to provide, in the simplest and most manageable form, an introduction to that material, taking into account recent work and discoveries. The introduction most widely available at the present time is that of H. L. Strack (*Introduction to the Talmud and Midrash*), which first appeared in 1887 and was last revised in 1924. It remains an important and extremely useful book, and to some extent (particularly in its summaries of work done before those dates) it has been presupposed in this book. But inevitably much work and research has been done since then, and a number of spectacular discoveries have been made of hitherto unknown material, reopening many questions in the study of early Judaism and of Christian origins; the Dead Sea Scrolls are the most obvious example of such discoveries, but they are by no means the only one: of conceivably equal importance in its own way is the discovery of a targum text which, although late in itself, may contain material going back to a date earlier than that of any previously known text, perhaps even *in origin* to the time of Jesus. Already much important work has been done making use of this and other Targum texts (as, for example, by R. le Déaut and M. McNamara on the New

ix

Testament, and by R. Bloch and G. Vermes), and there is no doubt that Targum material will now play an increasingly important part in the study both of early Judaism and of the New Testament.

It is of interest that Strack, in his *Introduction*, did not give an account of the Targums, although he was aware of their importance as repositories of Jewish traditions and exegesis. Conversely, this book concentrates primarily on the Targums because of the growing recognition of their importance. P. Kahle summarised their importance by saying: 'In the Palestinian Targum of the Pentateuch we have in the main material coming from pre-Christian times which must be studied by everyone who wishes to understand the state of Judaism at the time of the birth of Christianity. And we possess this material in a language of which we can say that it is very similar to that spoken by the earliest Christians. It is material the importance of which can scarcely be exaggerated.' (*The Cairo Geniza*, 1959, p. 208.) Even if this estimate itself turns out to be exaggerated, it is clear that the Targums deserve careful study and consideration. What, then, are the Targums? The Targums are interpretative translations of the Hebrew text of the Bible. Their interest and fascination lies in the crucial fact that they are not simple or literal translations of the text: they work into their translation an interpretation of what the text means. The reason for this is simple: in origin the Targums were closely connected with the synagogue. From its earliest days (before the fall of Jerusalem in A.D. 70) the synagogue existed primarily for the reading and exposition of scripture, but since many of those present had little or no knowledge of Hebrew, the public reading or reciting of the Hebrew text had to be accompanied by a translation, or *targum*, of it into the vernacular. The written Aramaic Targums are derived from those accompanying translations (*targums*) which were intended to explain the Hebrew text. It is because the purpose of the *targum* was to convey the meaning of the text to the assembled congregation that the *targums* could be so free in their interpretation. They provided a kind of 'running commentary' on the text. There was no fear that the sacred text was being altered or mishandled, because the text had already been read out. The purpose of the *targum* was to expound its meaning.

The *targum* was thus a part of the process through which scripture was expounded and taught in synagogue week by week. As the centuries went by, a traditional, though very loose, body of interpretation, a kind of 'targum-tradition', began to form, always extending and developing, but always having its roots in the past. The written Targums can best be understood as a sort of cross-section of that process, a point at which the developing tradition has been frozen for a moment and committed to writing. The written Targums are all related to each other and yet at the same time they are different from each other, each bearing witness to the state of the loose 'targum-tradition' at different points in its evolution and development.

The Targums, therefore, are of great importance. In the first place, since in origin they were connected with the synagogue, they help to show, in brilliantly concentrated form, what a verse of scripture may have meant to a Jewish synagogue congregation, and they show that the meaning was often far removed from the meaning intended by the Hebrew text. Secondly, since the written Targums come from different periods, ranging from the first to the seventh or eighth century, they reveal something of the long history of Jewish thought and exegesis. They are, therefore, indispensable for the study of Jewish thought in that period; they are equally important for the study of the Patristic period of the Church, since they frequently represent the other side of the Christian–Jewish debate. Christians tended to base their arguments against Judaism on verses of scripture, and the Targum-interpretation of those verses was often deliberately designed to exclude the Christian argument. There are particularly good examples of this in Genesis. Thirdly, since some of the interpretations in the recently discovered Targum (Neofiti I) go back to an early date, the Targums have become startlingly relevant to the New Testament and to the study of Jewish thought at the time of Jesus. The text of this Targum is shortly to be published, and it is certain to increase the discussion and study of the Targums greatly.

It will be seen that this book falls into two parts: the first part is an Introduction, which explains how Jewish biblical exegesis arose, and gives a brief description of the main works it produced; obviously, it cannot provide more than a brief summary, but it may perhaps help the non-specialist to understand the nature of Jewish literature in the early centuries of the Christian era, and enable him to find his way around in it with greater ease. The second part is intended to give some examples of Targum method and of the results it produced. It consists of a translation of a particular Targum for certain chapters of Genesis, together with a translation of selections from other Targums on the same passages—it is hoped that this will show something of the complex relationship which exists between the Targums. The translations are then followed by notes. The purpose of the notes is to show how the Targums arrived at their interpretation of a particular verse. The Targums often preserve (and this is their great value) interpretations of particular verses widely accepted elsewhere in Judaism, but they preserve those interpretations in a highly compressed and concentrated form. As a result it is frequently difficult to understand, at first sight, how the Targums reached their interpretation. The notes, therefore, consist largely of quotations from other Jewish (and occasionally from Christian or Jewish-Christian) works, where the exegesis and the arguments leading up to the Targum interpretations are given in greater detail. The importance of the notes is that they reveal at least something of the actual process of Jewish exegesis.

The Targum chosen for translation is the one known as Pseudo-Jonathan (Ps. Jon.). It was chosen, partly because it is the latest and most developed example of the 'Targum-tradition', showing what that tradition became in its most extended form, and also because in M. McNamara's view (*The New Testament and the Palestinian Targum . . .*, pp. 61 f.) it reveals the closest relationship of all Targums to the New Testament. The book of Genesis was chosen, chiefly because its stories were used and valued, not only in Judaism, but also in the New Testament and in early Christianity. Genesis provides a good basis for comparative study. On grounds of length and cost it proved impossible to translate the whole of the book; certain chapters were chosen, either because they are of doctrinal importance in Judaism and Christianity (for example, the Creation narratives, Gen. xxii and xlix) or because they are particularly revealing of Targum methods and material.

In writing this book, I owe a debt of gratitude far greater than I can express to three people in particular: to William Horbury who, at an early stage, checked and corrected the entire book; to Dr H. Knopf of Cambridge University Library, who read the Introduction and made extremely helpful criticisms and suggestions, and who also drew my attention to a number of recent articles which might otherwise have escaped my attention; and to Raphael Loewe, who read almost the whole of the final draft, and who made many important corrections and improvements. It is true to say that this book would never have been completed without their generous help. For the mistakes and imperfections that remain they are in no way responsible. I am also extremely grateful to Professor C. F. Evans, who read the Introduction, and to Miss Ilana Teplitzky, for help with modern Hebrew books. I would like to thank the libraries of Cambridge University and of the Cambridge Faculty of Divinity; by their willingness to issue books on loan the writing of this book was made much easier. Mrs J. Smith and Miss M. Gurley typed the book at various stages, and I am grateful for their skill and patience in dealing with a difficult manuscript. Finally my thanks go to my wife, who has given me much help and constant encouragement.

ACKNOWLEDGEMENTS

Generous grants, to assist in the publication of this book, have been made from the Bethune–Baker Fund and the Hort Memorial Fund. I would like to thank the Trustees of these Funds for this very great assistance.   J.B.

NOTE ON THE 1979 REPRINT

In making corrections for this reprint, I should like to thank those critics who identified errors or who suggested other interpretations. Above all, my thanks are due to R. le Déaut, who, with his customary attention to detail and immaculate scholarship, made important corrections. So far as the resetting of the type allowed, his corrections, and those of others, have been incorporated in this reprint.   J.B.

NOTE ON TRANSLITERATION

The main points of transliteration are:

א ’
ו v or w
ח ḥ
ע ‘
צ ẓ or ṣ

  Conventional spellings have not been standardised (e.g. Aboth, not 'Aboth); in quotations from other translations the form of transliteration has been left as it appears in the original (unless it might have proved confusing); and in common references א and ע have not been transliterated (Taan. not Ta‘an.). This means that there is no artificial uniformity: פ may appear as *f* or *ph*, final ת as *t* or *th*, the feminine singular as *-a* or *-ah*. None of these variants is likely to prove difficult to anyone with a knowledge of Semitic languages, whereas a standardisation might well have been confusing to a reader without such knowledge, since it would have changed the accepted and most familiar form of certain words.

NOTE ON BIBLIOGRAPHICAL REFERENCES

References to books and articles cited in the text and in the footnotes have usually been given in the shortest form possible. For full bibliographical details, see the bibliography.

ABBREVIATIONS

Act. Pil.	Acts of Pilate
Adv. Haer.	*Adversus Haereses*
Adv. Marc.	*Adversus Marcionem*
A.I.P.O.	*Annuaire de l'Institut de Philologie et d'Histoire Orientales de l'Université Libre de Bruxelles*
A.J.S.L.	*American Journal of Semitic Languages and Literature*
A.N.C.L.	Ante-Nicene Christian Library
Ant.	*Antiquities*
A.N.V.A.	*Avhandlinger utgitt av det Norske Videnskaps-Akademie, Oslo*
Apoc. Abr.	Apocalypse of Abraham
Apocr. and Pseudepigr.	*Apocrypha and Pseudepigrapha* (R. H. Charles)
Apol.	*Apology*
Aq.	Aquila
Arab. Vers.	Arabic Version
A.R.N.	Aboth deRabbi Nathan
Asc. Is.	Ascension of Isaiah
Ass. Mos.	Assumption of Moses
A.Z.	Abodah Zarah
B.	Babli or Babylonian (usually followed immediately by another abbr. which indicates a particular tractate in the Babylonian Talmud)
Bar.	Baruch
B.B.	Baba Bathra
Bek.	Bekoroth
Bem.	Bemidbar (Numbers)
Ber.	Berakoth
Ber.	Bereshith (Genesis)
Bet haMidr.	*Bet haMidrash*
Beẓ.	Beẓah
Bibl.	*Biblica*
B.J.R.L.	*Bulletin of the John Rylands Library*
B.M.	Baba Meẓia
B.M.	British Museum
B.O.	*Bibliotheca Orientalis*
B.Q. (K)	Baba Qamma
C.D.C.	The Damascus Rule (the Zadokite Fragment)
C.G.	Cairo Geniza (fragments)
Chron. Jer.	Chronicles of Jeraḥmeel
Cont. Ap.	*Contra Apionem*

C.P.J.	*Corpus Papyrorum Judaicarum* (V. Tcherikover)
C.U.P.	Cambridge University Press
De Abr.	*De Abrahamo*
De Civ. Dei.	*De Civitate Dei*
De Dec.	*De Decalogo*
De Gig.	*De Gigantibus*
De Joseph.	*De Josepho*
De Leg.	*De Legatione ad Gaium*
De Migr.	*De Migratione Abrahami*
De Mort.	*De Mortalitate*
De Opif. Mund.	*De Opificio Mundi*
De Post.	*De Posteritate Caini*
De Praem. et Poen.	*De Praemiis et Poenis*
De Sacr. Abel.	*De Sacrificiis Abelis et Caini*
De Sobr.	*De Sobrietate*
De Somn.	*De Somniis*
De Trin.	*De Trinitate*
De Vit. Mos.	*De Vita Mosis*
Deb.	Debarim (Deuteronomy)
Dial.	*Dialogue with Trypho*
D.J.D.	*Discoveries in the Judaean Desert*
D.S.S.	Dead Sea Scrolls
Eduy.	Eduyyoth
Ep. Arist.	*Epistle of Aristeas*
Ep. Barn.	Epistle of Barnabas
E.R.E.	*Encyclopedia of Religion and Ethics*
Erub.	Erubin
Evang. Quart.	*Evangelical Quarterly*
F.T.	Fragmentary Targum
Gen. Apoc.	Genesis Apocryphon
Gins.	Ginsburger's edition of the Fragmentary Targum
Gitt.	Gittin
Ḥag.	Ḥagigah
Hist. Jud.	*Historia Judaica*
Hor.	Horayoth
H.S.S.	*Harvard Semitic Studies*
H.T.R.	*Harvard Theological Review*
H.U.C.A.	*Hebrew Union College Annual*
H.U.C.P.	Hebrew Union College Press
Ḥull.	Ḥullin
In Ioann.	In Ioannem
J.	Jerushalmi or Jerusalem (indicating works of a Palestinian provenance, particularly in conjunction with another abbr. following immediately and indicating a particular tractate in the Palestinian Talmud)

J.A.O.S.	*Journal of the American Oriental Society*
J.B.L.	*Journal of Biblical Literature*
J.E.	*Jewish Encyclopedia*
J.J.G.L.	*Jahrbuch für jüdische Geschichte und Literatur*
J.J.L.P.	*Journal of Jewish Lore and Philosophy*
J.J.S.	*Journal of Jewish Studies*
J.N.E S	*Journal of Near Eastern Studies*
Journ. Rel.	*Journal of Religion*
J.Q.R.	*Jewish Quarterly Review*
J.S.S.	*Journal of Semitic Studies*
Jub.	Jubilees
Ker. Pet. Hom.	The Preaching of Peter
Ket.	Ketuboth
Kil.	Kilayim
Kit. alMaj.	Kitab alMajal
Leg. All.	*Legum Allegoriae*
LXX	Septuagint
M.	Mishnah (usually followed immediately by another abbr. which indicates a particular tractate in the Mishnah)
M.A.A.	*Mededeelingen der Koninklijke Akademie van Wetenschappen te Amsterdam*
Maas.	Maaseroth
Mas. Sof.	Masseket Soferim
Meg.	Megillah
Mek.	Mekilta
Men.	Menahoth
M.G.W.J.	*Monatsschrift für die Geschichte und Wissenschaft des Judentums*
Mid.	Middoth
Midr. haGad.	Midrash haGadol
Midr. Tann.	Midrash Tannaim
Midr. Teh.	Midrash Tehillim
M.Sh.	Maaser Sheni
M.T.	Massoretic Text
N.	Neofiti I
Naz.	Nazir
Ned.	Nedarim
N.T.	Novum Testamentum (also New Testament)
N.T.S.	*New Testament Studies*
Ohol.	Oholoth
Onq.	Onqelos
Or. Chr.	*Oriens Christianus*
P.A.	Pirqe Aboth
P.A.A.J.R.	*Proceedings of the American Academy of Jewish Research*

P.E.Q.	*Palestine Exploration Quarterly*
Pes.	Pesaḥim
Pesh.	Peshitta
Pes.K.	Pesiqta deRab Kahana
Pes.R.	Pesiqta Rabbati
P.R.E.	Pirqe deRabbi Eliezer
Ps. Clem. Hom.	Pseudo-Clement, *Homilies*
Ps. Jon.	Pseudo-Jonathan
1 QApoc.	Genesis Apocryphon
1 QH	The Thanksgiving Hymns
1 QpHab.	The Habakkuk Commentary
1 QM	The Wars of the Sons of Light against the Sons of Darkness
1 QS	Manual of Discipline
4 QFlor.	The Blessing of Jacob
4 QpNah.	The Nahum Commentary
4 QTest.	The 'Testimonia'
Qid.	Qiddushin
Qin.	Qinnim
Qoh.	Qoheleth (Ecclesiastes)
Quaes. Gen.	*Quaestiones et Solutiones in Genesin*
Quod Det.	*Quod Deterius Potiori Insidiari Solet*
R.	Rabbi, Rab
...R.	Rabbah (indicating a commentary in the Midrash Rabbah)
R.B.	*Revue Biblique*
R.E.J.	*Revue des Etudes Juives*
R.H.	Rosh haShanah
R.H.P.R.	*Revue d'Histoire et de Philosophie Religieuses*
Riv. d. Stud. Orient.	*Rivista degli Studi Orientali*
Rn.	Rabban
R.S.R.	*Recherches de Science Religieuse*
R.T.P.	*Revue de Théologie et de Philosophie*
R.V.	Revised Version
Sam. Pent.	Samaritan Pentateuch
San.	Sanhedrin
Shab.	Shabbath
Sheb.	Shebiith or Shebuoth
Shek.	Shekalim
Shem.	Shemoth (Exodus)
Shir.	Shir haShirim (Song of Songs)
Sib. Or.	Sibylline Oracles
Sifre Z.	Sifre Zuta
Slav.	Slavonic
Sot.	Sotah

S.T.	*Studia Theologica*
S.Th.U.	*Schweizerische Theologische Umschau*
Strom.	*Stromateis*
Stud. Patr.	*Studia Patristica*
Sukk.	Sukkah
Syr. Comm.	Syriac Commentary
T.	Tosefta (usually followed by a further abbr. indicating the tractate in the Tosefta)
T.J.	Targum Jerushalmi
1T.J.	Pseudo-Jonathan
2T.J.	Fragmentary Targum
T.O.	Targum Onqelos
Taan.	Taanith
Tam.	Tamid
Tan.d.El. (T.d.E.)	Tanna debe Eliyyahu
Tanḥ.	Tanḥuma
Tanḥ.B.	Tanḥuma in Buber's edition
Targ.	Targum
Teb. Yom.	Tebul Yom
Test. Abr.	Testament of Abraham
Test. Ash.	Testament of Asher
Test. Ben.	Testament of Benjamin
Test. Jud.	Testament of Judah
Test. Lev.	Testament of Levi
Test. Naph.	Testament of Naphtali
Test. Reub.	Testament of Reuben
Test. Zeb.	Testament of Zebulun
T.J. I	Pseudo-Jonathan
T.J. II	Fragmentary Targum
T.L. (Z)	*Theologische Literaturzeitung*
T.S.F. Bulletin	*Theological Students' Fellowship Bulletin*
Vay.	Vayyiqra (Leviticus)
V.T.	*Vetus Testamentum*
Vulg.	Vulgate
W.Z. d. Karl Marx-Univ.	*Wissenschaftliche Zeitschrift der Karl Marx-Univ. Leipzig*
Yad.	Yadaim
Yeb.	Yebamoth
Yom.	Yoma
Zab.	Zabim
Zad. Frag.	Zadokite Fragment
Z.A.W.	*Zeitschrift für die alttestamentliche Wissenschaft*
Z.D.M.G.	*Zeitschrift der deutschen morgenländischen Gesellschaft*
Zeb.	Zebahim
Z.N.W.	*Zeitschrift für die neutestamentliche Wissenschaft*
Z.R.G.	*Zeitschrift der Savigny-Stiftung für Rechtsgeschichte*

INTRODUCTION:
THE BACKGROUND OF
THE TARGUMS

1

TRANSLATION AND
INTERPRETATION

The word *targum* means in general 'translation' or 'interpretation', but in particular it is most often used to refer to the Aramaic versions of the Hebrew Bible.[1] The need for such versions arose early: Aramaic was the official language of the Persian empire, and it soon became a 'common language' in the Near East; it was not an entirely uniform language, since different areas and ages developed their own dialects.[2] The Jews accepted Aramaic without much difficulty, partly for practical reasons, but also because Aramaic and Hebrew are closely related to each other. The Jews never lost sight of the fact that Hebrew was the language of revelation,[3] and the Scrolls recovered from the Dead Sea area[4] indicate how important Hebrew remained, not least because of its use in legal and other documents; but Aramaic rapidly rivalled it as an ordinary spoken language. As early as the book of Nehemiah there is a lament that Hebrew is inadequately known,[5] and some later parts of the Bible are written in Aramaic.

Understanding of Hebrew was undermined not only by the spread of Aramaic but also by the fact that many Jews, both in the Dispersion and in Palestine, knew Greek and nothing else.[6] Moreover, in the

[1] See W. Bacher, *Die Terminologie der Tannaiten*, pp. 205 ff.

[2] For a brief summary of some of the main dialects as known at present, see J. A. Fitzmyer, *The Genesis Apocryphon of Qumran Cave I*, p. 20.

[3] Consider, for example, the attempts of the *Letter of Aristeas* to justify and to stabilise a translation of the O.T. into Greek; on Aristeas see p. 4 n. 1; and see also Pseudo-Jonathan on Gen. xi. 1.

[4] See p. 33.

[5] *In those days also saw I the Jews that had married women of Ashdod, of Ammon and of Moab: and their children spake half in the speech of Ashdod, and could not speak in the Jews' language* . . . (Neh. xiii. 23, 24).

[6] E. R. Goodenough has pointed out how seldom Aramaic appears in inscriptions coming from Palestine, and how much, therefore, Greek was the natural language of many Jews in Palestine: 'Aramaic, we judge from the inscriptions, remained important during the first Christian centuries in

Dispersion there was a constant contact between Jews and non-Jews. The need, therefore, arose to translate 'the books of the law of the Jews . . ., being written in Hebrew letters and language';[1] and it arose for two reasons, first, so that Jews themselves could understand their own scriptures,[2] and second so that non-Jews could understand them

Palmyra, Nabatea, and Babylonia, but practically nothing has survived in Aramaic from popular Palestine. On the contrary, the inscriptions show after the fall of Jerusalem almost as complete a victory of the Greek language in Palestine as in Rome' (Goodenough, *Jewish Symbols* . . ., II, 123). For a summary of Goodenough's general conclusions, see the Introduction, pp. 36 ff. For a summary of the languages of first-century Palestine, see M. Black, *An Aramaic Approach* . . . (1967), pp. 15 ff.

[1] *Ep. Arist.* 30. The *Letter of Aristeas* was written largely as propaganda to justify the Greek translations made at Alexandria. The Septuagint (LXX) is the Greek translation emanating from Alexandria, but its origin was more complicated than Aristeas allowed. Aristeas argued four things in particular: (i) Translation is a legitimate activity; the Alexandrian translation was authorised by the Jerusalem authorities (§§ 41–6), and six of the ablest men from each tribe were chosen for the task (they prove their wisdom in the 72 questions and answers, §§ 187–300). (ii) The Alexandrian translation is the best: *Ep. Arist.* shows an awareness of other attempts to translate Hebrew books into Greek (§ 314), but it argues that the version emanating from Alexandria is better than any other, because it is the product of consultation and co-operation (§ 302; note that despite unconscious assumptions to the contrary—for example, P. Kahle, *The Cairo Geniza*, p. 209—the legend that the translators worked separately, and that on examination their translations were found miraculously to agree in every way, is later—possibly Philo, *de Vit. Mos.* ii. 37; *Cohortatio ad Graecos*, 13; Irenaeus, *Adv. Haer.* iii. 21. 2. The later embellishment was taken up in Christianity because it enhanced the status of the translation still further. The Jews became suspicious of the Alexandrian translation because of its use by Christians, and they tried to produce other versions—the probable origin of the very literal Aquila, *c.* A.D. 130). (iii) Part of its purpose was to commend Judaism by increased understanding of it; although the completed translation was presented first to the Jewish community and only after that to the Pharaoh (§§ 308–12), it was, nevertheless, commissioned by and for the Pharaoh; this is equally clear in other parts of *Ep. Arist.*, which include an apology for Mosaic Law (§§ 128–71), and a description of Jerusalem (§§ 83–120). (iv) The Alexandrian version is a single translation (although in fact the LXX is a compound of distinct translations of different books or sections of books). *Ep. Arist.* comes probably from some time in the second half of the second century B.C. For the text see H. B. Swete, *An Introduction to the Old Testament in Greek*, pp. 499–574 (the text was edited by H. St. J. Thackeray); for a translation see R. H. Charles, *Apocr. and Pseudepigr.* II, 83–122 (the translation was by H. T. Andrews). See also A. J. F. Klijn, 'The Letter of Aristeas and the Greek Translation of the Pentateuch in Egypt'; V. Tcherikover, *C.P.J.* I, 43; H. G. Meechan, *The Letter of Aristeas.*

[2] The word 'scripture' should not be understood too formally at this early stage. Although the idea of 'scripture' was established, and some books (for

4

as well.[1] It follows that since the emphasis in translation was on understanding, there was a tendency right from the start to express meaning rather than to be scrupulously literal. Thus LXX frequently explained Hebrew words or phrases. For example, Urim and Thummim were 'explained' as ἡ δήλωσις καὶ ἡ ἀλήθεια;[2] Exod. iii. 14 became ἐγώ εἰμι ὁ ὤν. The most common changes were to avoid anthropomorphisms, as might be expected,[3] but LXX was also prepared to make alterations to avoid difficulties[4] and in the interests of doctrine.[5]

The tendency in translation to express meaning rather than to be literal was reinforced by the efforts of Jews in every generation to interpret scripture and apply it to their own situation and time. Scripture was the foundation of life, because it was the self-revealing of God, a particularly vital way in which he had made himself known. But scripture had been revealed in the past, and it was essential for one generation after another to penetrate its meaning. The methods by which this was done were very different: they ranged from the

example, the Pentateuch) were generally accepted as inspired or revealed, there was not yet a fixed canon: there were ideas of a canon of scripture but the edges of it were blurred. While the Pentateuch and Prophets were generally accepted, there was greater uncertainty about the later writings (*Ketubim*), the Hagiographa. An attempt to formulate the Jewish canon was made just before the fall of Jerusalem (A.D. 70), and again during the consolidation and re-organisation of Judaism at Yavneh and at Usha afterwards. See S. Zeitlin, 'An Historical Study of the Canonization of the Hebrew Scriptures'; W. D. Davies, *Christian Origins and Judaism*.

[1] To some extent Judaism was bound to be a 'missionary' religion, since it was widely believed (on the basis, particularly, of Isa. xl–lv) that a part of the vocation of Israel was to be 'a light to the Gentiles'. But it was disputed whether this involved actively encouraging proselytes, or whether it meant sustaining such a quality of life within the community that outsiders would inevitably be attracted to it. There were thus conflicting attitudes to proselytes and proselytism. See B. J. Bamberger, *Proselytism in the Talmudic Period*; W. G. Braude, *Jewish Proselytising* ...; P. Dalbert, *Die Theologie der hellenistisch-judischen Missionsliteratur*; I. Levi, 'Le prosélytisme juif'.

[2] Exod. xxviii. 26 (30).

[3] For example, *And they saw the God of Israel* ... (Exod. xxiv. 10) became 'And they saw the place where the God of Israel had stood ...'.

[4] See, for example, F.T. and notes on Gen. ii. 2.

[5] E.g. Prov. xi. 7. For a brief discussion of LXX as a translation see E. J. Bikermann, 'The Septuagint as a Translation'. For possible connections with the hermeneutic rules (Appendix II), see L. Prijs, *Jüdische Tradition in der Septuaginta*.

allegorical exegesis of Philo[1] to the popular 'retelling' of the Bible story which was not afraid to introduce entirely new material into the narrative.[2] The Dead Sea Scrolls provide good examples of the great variety in the methods of exegesis which were possible. The methods found in the Scrolls include verse by verse commentary (e.g. 1QpHab,[3] 4QpNah), extension of scripture by producing works purporting to come from biblical figures (e.g. Enoch, Moses, the XII Patriarchs), retelling of a biblical narrative (e.g. Jubilees, the Genesis Apocryphon), imitation of scripture, by producing works modelled on accepted scriptural books (e.g. 1QH, The Psalms of Joshua, The Prayer of Nabonidus), anthologising scripture, by collecting related passages and linking them together with brief notes and comments (e.g. 4QTest, the Messianic Anthology), and the application of Mosaic law to contemporary situations (e.g. the Commentary on Biblical Laws). All these methods of making the text of scripture relevant and meaningful to later generations were in use in Judaism generally, and were not confined to a group or groups (if any) which produced the Dead Sea Scrolls.

The fact that there was such diversity in method is important, because it helps to show how essential and fundamental the work of

[1] On Philo see the Introduction, p. 29. A typical example of Philo's exegesis is his comment on Gen. xxiv. 12–14 (*Quaes. Gen.* iv. 95): 'Why does the servant, beginning with the prospering of the journey, prophesy what is to come? (The question is based on LXX.) The literal meaning is that since the angel of God was his companion on the journey and was near by, he was perhaps enthused by him and began to be possessed. But as for the deeper meaning, they are types of God-loving characters, each of which the reason carefully examines and fully investigates. And when it finds that they are united, it rejoices at their being complete, as it hoped. Now, there are three types. One is being a virgin; the second, that she inclines the water-jar; and the third, that she gives (them) to drink. For the sign of a virgin is a pure and sincere intention, which honours the sincere and incorruptible nature without passion. Moreover, the inclining downwards of the water-jar (signifies) length of teaching and participation . . . He who in tasting desires to draw the measure of the water-jar is anxious not to spill it altogether on the ground, but lifts up the drink for the sharing (of it) and for love of man . . .'.

[2] This method of exegesis appears in the Bible itself: Chronicles is, in a sense, a 'retelling' of Samuel and Kings in order to express the insights and interests of a later generation. A good example of a work which 'retold' the biblical narrative is Pseudo-Philo, *The Biblical Antiquities*, part of which is translated in Appendix 1; see also p. 30 for a brief description.

[3] For an explanation of these abbreviations see p. 34.

exegesis was. Scripture, particularly Torah,[1] was the foundation of Jewish life, but differences (often very great differences) arose over its interpretation and application to life. The diversity of Judaism was very great at the time when Jesus was alive; in Palestine, for example, the rivalry between the Sadducees and the Pharisees was often intense (and Pharisaism itself contained different groups within it);[2] the seeds of the Zealot movement had already been sown and were about to flower in a disastrous demand for a more fervent expression of Jewish faith;[3] various sects were flourishing whose purpose was to purify the true believer within Israel,[4] and no doubt the Samaritans considered that they alone were the only faithful guardians of the law of Moses. Outside Palestine Jewish communities were constructing their own interpretations of Judaism, sometimes with very little reference to Jerusalem at all.[5] Yet all these groups were established on the same

[1] Torah is a word meaning 'instruction' or 'guidance', and it is the word used to refer to the first five books of the Bible, more usually known now as the Pentateuch. Thus in B.Ber. 5a there is a comment on Exod. xxiv. 12: '*I will give thee the tables of stone, and the law and the commandment, which I have written, that thou mayest teach them. Tables of stone* means the ten commandments, *the law* means scripture (i.e. the Pentateuch), *the commandment* means Mishnah (see pp. 46 f.), *which I have written* means the Prophets and the Writings (the remaining books of the Bible), *that thou mayest teach them* means gemara (see p. 64). The verse shows that all these things were given by God to Moses on Sinai.' Torah is sometimes translated as 'Law', but it is really 'guidance in life', which includes certain commands, but which also includes a great deal more general material as well (as in the book of Genesis). It is probably better to retain the word Torah and not to translate it at all.

[2] See especially L. Finkelstein, *The Pharisees*; essays in J. Z. Lauterbach, *Rabbinic Essays*; summaries in A. Finkel, *The Pharisees* . . . .

[3] On the Zealots see especially W. R. Farmer, *Maccabees, Zealots and Josephus*; M. Hengel, *Die Zeloten*.

[4] As, for example, the Essenes and the Therapeutae.

[5] E.g. Leontopolis, Alexandria, Dura-Europos (see the reports on the excavations, C. H. Kraeling and C. B. Welles; J. Neusner, *A History of the Jews in Babylonia*; 'Judaism at Dura Europos'; E. R. Goodenough, *Jewish Symbols*. It should be noted that J. L. Teicher concluded that two liturgical fragments found at Dura-Europos should probably be assessed as Christian, not Jewish; see J. L. Teicher, 'Ancient Eucharistic Prayers in Hebrew'. His views have not yet been argued through in detail. In a more recent analysis A. von Gerkan, 'Zur Hauskirche von Dura-Europos', has suggested (though, as he recognises, without absolute proof) that Christian occupation of Dura-Europos began in *c.* A.D. 175 and that the main decorations were added in the third century. On the diversity of 'non-rabbinic' Judaism, see also pp. 36–9.

foundation, the revelation entrusted by God to Moses on Sinai. Some groups were unwilling to extend the scope of revelation much further,[1] but all accepted Torah as God's fundamental guidance and instruction in life. Thus to a great extent the common ground of Judaism lay in the past, and the diversity of Judaism at the time of Jesus was a consequence of different (and at times rival) attempts to apply Torah in life. The task was to define, not what Judaism was (it was the community which God had called into being and to which he had entrusted Torah), but what Judaism ought to become. The question to be answered was what Judaism ought to be in the present as a consequence of what was known to have happened in the past. It was because the answers to that question differed so much that the diversity of Judaism was so great.[2] The fall of Jerusalem to the Romans and the failure of the Bar-Kokeba revolt[3] tended to eliminate many of the answers, but it was some time before one of them, the Pharisaic-Rabbinic interpretation, emerged as the prevailing definition of Judaism.[4]

The need to find ways of applying past revelation in the present was inescapable, since it was in that way, perhaps more than in any other, that the immediacy of God could be retained in Israel. It certainly had its effect on translation. Translation became a part of the attempt to make scripture meaningful in the present. This is already apparent in LXX; it is even more dramatically apparent in the Targums. The Targums, like LXX, followed the Hebrew text verse by verse, but they incorporated in their representation of the text a great deal of explanation and interpretation. Thus the text and its interpretation were woven together, and the interpretation often extended and amplified the text greatly. The Targums, therefore, lie half-way between the LXX (which incorporated interpretation but remained relatively close to the Hebrew text) and those works which set out to retell the biblical narrative in their own words, often for their own particular purposes; examples of the latter would be Jubilees, the Genesis Apocryphon, or Pseudo-Philo.[5] Those works followed the Hebrew narrative only very

[1] E.g. the Samaritans.
[2] There is a sense in which early Christianity was a part of that pattern: many parts of the N.T. are attempts to express what Judaism has become now that the Messiah, the Christ, has arrived.
[3] A.D. 132–5.
[4] For the continuing diversity of Judaism, see further pp. 36–9.
[5] On these, see pp. 30 f., 34.

roughly, and they were prepared to introduce incidents or comments to make the narrative more meaningful;[1] in addition, they made no attempt to represent the whole text, but concentrated on selected parts of it only. The Targums lie half-way between those two extremes: they make an attempt to represent the text verse by verse but at the same time they introduce into it extensive and often far-ranging interpretations. The reason for that half-way position is simple: the origin of the Targums is closely connected with the synagogue.

The process by which synagogues emerged in Judaism is difficult to trace in detail, since not enough direct evidence has survived. The problem is complicated by the fact that the word 'synagogue' means simply 'assembly', and on some occasions when the word is used it is hard to know whether it has a formal, technical sense or not. Indeed it is hard to know at exactly what stage a distinction between the general usage and the technical can be made. What does seem clear is that the origin of the synagogue in Judaea was closely connected with the *ma'amadoth*. The *ma'amadoth*[2] were divisions of the people throughout Judaea, which were intended to correspond to the twenty-four courses of the priests in the Temple. In this way all the people were involved in the duties and sacrifices of the Temple, even though they could not be present in Jerusalem. Each *ma'amad* assembled, when its turn came, to read passages of scripture corresponding to the sacrifices taking place in Jerusalem. It was from these 'assemblies' that 'synagogues' in Palestine[3] seem to have developed. If that is so, then the origin of the synagogue was closely connected with the reading of

---

[1] A good example would be the long story introduced in Pseudo-Philo vi, an entirely imaginative exercise making use of the common exegesis of Ur (of the Chaldees), which was based on the observation that Ur means 'a flame'; for this see Appendix I, and see also the Targum and notes on Gen. xi. 28.

[2] Literally 'places of standing'.

[3] Perhaps the earliest synagogue that can actually be dated is the one recently excavated at Masada (Masada is a high rock in the hilly country about 30 miles south of Jerusalem, on the western shore of the Dead Sea; it was there that Herod built a fortified palace, and there also that a remnant of Jews made a defiant and epic last stand against the Romans at the end of the first Jewish revolt in A.D. 72/3; the excavation of Masada began in October 1963 under the direction of Yigael Yadin). The building appears to have been in use as a synagogue *before* the last stand, i.e. before A.D. 73. For a brief but well-illustrated account see Y. Yadin, *Masada*, pp. 180–91, esp. pp. 187 ff.

Torah from its earliest days.[1] From these beginnings it developed into a place where Torah was read and studied in a much wider way, and that remained its function and purpose until the fall of Jerusalem. Before that time it does not seem to have been a 'house of prayer'. A house of prayer was unnecessary for the Jew living in Judaea: within certain limits of purification he could pray anywhere, and he had no need of a particular building. In the Diaspora the situation was slightly different: there, houses of prayer did exist[2] and they were apparently distinct from synagogues.[3] But the purpose of the synagogue in the Diaspora was the same as in Judaea, the reading and study of Torah. It was only after the fall of Jerusalem, when Temple services and sacrifices were no longer so possible, that the two were finally fused, and that the study of Torah was set in a liturgical context.[4]

[1] M.Taan. iv. 2 refers briefly to the *ma'amadoth* and gives the reason for them: 'What are the *ma'amadoth*? In accordance with what is written, *Command the children of Israel, and say unto them, My oblation, my food* (. . . *shall ye observe to offer unto me in their due season*) (Num. xxviii. 2). But how is a man's offering offered if he does not stand beside it? The first prophets established twenty-four courses, and for every course there was a *ma'amad* in Jerusalem, of priests, Levites and Israelites. When the time came for a course to go up, the priests and Levites went up to Jerusalem, and the Israelites belonging to that course assembled (the verb is from the same root as *kenesset*, the word which was used as the name of the formal synagogue; but like "synagogue" it can also be used in a non-technical sense) in their own town to read in the work (section) "In the beginning" (i.e. the opening section of Genesis).'

[2] Perhaps because of the greater proximity and threat of pagan festivals and idolatry.

[3] It is significant that Acts xvi. 13 ff. maintains the distinction. At the same time, there seems to have been some overlap, since Philo ascribes to προσευχαί a function similar to that of synagogues (*de Leg.* xxiii. 156), and in *de Vit. Mos.* ii. 216 he says of προσευκτήρια: 'The Jews every seventh day occupy themselves with the philosophy of their fathers. . . For what are our προσευκτήρια throughout the cities but schools of prudence . . . and every virtue by which duties to God and men are discerned and rightly performed.' Cf. also the important passage in *de Leg.* xl. 311 f. For an inscription in which the words *sunagoge* and *proseuche* are combined, see Tcherikover, *C.P.J.* 1, 253 (no. 138, l. 1). The fragment refers to a collective decision, taken at a formal meeting, but unfortunately too little of the fragment has survived for us to be sure exactly what was the decision or what was the real nature of the meeting. The fragment (from the first half of the first century B.C.) is headed: 'At the synagogue (assembly) in the *proseuche*.'

[4] On the origins of the synagogue see S. Zeitlin, *The Rise and Fall of the Jewish State*, 1, 179, 430; 'The Origin of the Synagogue'; 'The Tefillah, the Shemoneh Esreh'; S. B. Hoenig, 'Historical Inquiries . . .'; 'The Suppositious Temple Synagogue'. See also K. Hruby, 'La Synagogue dans la littérature rabbinique'.

It must of course be remembered that exact details of synagogues in Palestine before the fall of Jerusalem are almost impossible to establish, since so many buildings were destroyed in the two wars against Rome. Excavations of synagogue buildings dating from the second century A.D., as for example at Tiberias, show that there was great variety in worship and imagery. It is possible, therefore, that the distinctions outlined above may not have been so rigid as they appear in the literary sources. Practice often contradicts theory, but the sources certainly make it clear that there was some distinction. Yet it is equally true that E. R. Goodenough has found in the archaeological evidence proof that there was a divide between hellenised Judaism and rabbinic Judaism even in Palestine,[1] and it is essential to bear in mind the possibility of diversity in this field as much as in any other. A description of excavated synagogues can be found in Goodenough's *Jewish Symbols in the Greco-Roman Period.*

The fundamental purpose of the synagogue is very well summarised in a Greek inscription from Jerusalem, dating probably from the first century A.D.: 'Theodotos, son of Vettenos, priest and *archisynagogos*, built the synagogue for the reading of the Law and for the searching of the Commandments; furthermore, the Hospice and the Chambers, and the water installation for lodging of needy strangers. The foundation stone thereof had been laid by his fathers, and the Elders, and Simonides.'[2] Both Philo[3] and Josephus[4] emphasised the importance of the regular study of Torah in synagogue, and both say that Moses himself commanded it.[5] As Josephus put it, 'Moses appointed the Law to be

---

[1] Goodenough's views have been conveniently summarised by L. H. Feldman: 'He concludes that the pagan symbols found everywhere in Hellenistic Jewish art constituted a sub-rational *lingua franca* among Jews and non-Jews alike, just as the Greek language provided a rational bond among them, and that these symbols represent a kind of allegorization through art of the sort that Philo attempted through philosophy. Goodenough thus argues that there was a "popular", extra-Talmudic Judaism (the fact that these pagan symbols are found on synagogues shows that they represent communal attitudes) in opposition to normative Pharisaic Judaism' (Feldman, *Studies in Judaica*, p. 17 on Goodenough, *Jewish Symbols*). For a summary in Goodenough's own words see pp. 36 f.

[2] Text and translation in E. L. Sukenik, *The Ancient Synagogue of el-Ḥammeh.*

[3] References on p. 10 n. 3 above, and also *de Opif. Mund.* xliii. 128.

[4] *Cont. Ap.* ii. 175, *Ant.* xvi. 43.

[5] This is in accordance with popular tradition (see, for example, J.Meg. iv. 1), which was later to be much elaborated.

the most excellent and necessary form of instruction, ordaining, not that it should be heard once for all or twice or on several occasions, but that every week men should desert their other occupations and assemble to listen to the Law and to obtain a thorough and accurate knowledge of it . . .'.[1]

That passage from Josephus is important for another reason. It indicates the most important way in which Torah was presented to the congregation: it was through its public recitation.[2] The recitation of Torah eventually followed set lectionaries[3] and was governed by fairly precise rules.[4] But however regularly and carefully Torah was recited in synagogue it was little help if only a few people could understand it. By constantly confronting the believer with Torah the synagogue was, in a sense, confronting him with God, but that could scarcely be so if he understood little of what he heard. The practice, therefore, began of accompanying the recitation of the text with a translation, or *targum*, of it. The basic distinction between scripture-reading and targum-interpretation was described at a later time by Pes.R. 14*b*:

R. Judah b. Pazzi said: 'The verse, *Write thou these words*,[5] means that scripture was given in writing. But . . . *according to the mouth*[6] *of these words* means that the Targum was given orally.'[7] R. Judah b. Shalom said: 'Moses wanted Mishnah[8] to be written as well, but the Holy One, blessed be he, knew that the time would come when the nations would translate the Torah and read it in Greek, and that they would say, "These (the Jews) are not Israel". So the Holy One, blessed be he, said to Moses, "The time will come when the nations will say, We are Israel, we are the children of God, and Israel will say, We are the children of God." Since the scales are balanced evenly, God will say to the nations, "Why do you

---

[1] *Cont. Ap.* ii. 175.   [2] *Miqra.*

[3] See p. 72.

[4] For a summary of some of the principles governing the transmission of written and oral Torah, see B. Gerhardsson, *Memory and Manuscript*, and in this connection see esp. ch. 5, pp. 67–70.

[5] Exod. xxxiv. 27.

[6] R.V., *after the tenor of* . . . .

[7] If the targum was read from a scroll it might be confused with scripture by the onlooker; the reader of scripture had the scroll open before him because the text of scripture was invariable. The targums varied and were therefore given without reference to a written text, in order to avoid confusion between the two.

[8] Meaning here 'oral Torah', as opposed to 'written Torah'; the more technical meanings of Mishnah are described on pp. 46 f.

say that you are my children? I know only those who possess my secret,[1] they are my children." Then they will say, "What is your secret?" and God will answer, "It is Mishnah".'[2]

The translator was called *thargeman* or more usually *methurgeman* (sometimes in the form *methorgeman*).[3] The process of translation was described in M.Meg. iv. 4:[4] 'The reader of Torah is not to read less than three verses. He is to read to the *methurgeman* not more than one verse at a time, or in a reading from the Prophets[5] not more than three. If the three form three separate sections he reads them one by one.' Thus the *methurgeman* worked in close conjunction with the Hebrew text, and yet his purpose was to interpret the text, and make it meaningful to the congregation. That explains why the Targums lie half-way between straightforward translation and free retelling of the biblical narrative: they were clearly attached to the Hebrew text, and at times translated it in a reasonably straightforward way, but they were also prepared to introduce into the translation as much interpretation as seemed necessary to clarify the sense. It has already been pointed out briefly that there was no feeling that the text was being altered or changed, since the text had *already* been read: the purpose of the Targum was to make the text meaningful and to bring home its significance to the congregation. The written Targums, therefore,

---

[1] Or 'mystery', μυστήριον.

[2] On oral Torah as the 'mystery' of Israel, compare Tanh.B. ii. 116 f.: 'When the Holy One, blessed be he, wanted to give the Torah, he spoke it to Moses in order (*seder*), scripture, *mishnah*, *haggadah* and *talmud*, as it is written, *And God spake all these words* (Exod. xx. 1). He even made known what the student would ask his master (the emphasis was placed on "all".) . . . When Moses had learned it, the Holy One, blessed be he, said to him, "Go and teach my children". Moses said to him, "Lord of the universe, write it for your children". He said to him, "I wanted to give it to them in writing, but it was revealed before me that the time would come when the nations of the world would rule over them and claim Torah for themselves, and my children would then be like the nations of the world. So give scripture to them in writing, and *mishnah*, *haggadah* and *talmud* by mouth (*'al peh*) . . ., and they will distinguish between Israel and the nations of the world."' For anti-Jewish polemic based on the distinction between written and oral Torah see Ker. Pet. Hom. iii. 47. 1–4.

[3] See Pseudo-Jonathan on Gen. xlii. 23. For a summary of these uses, see J. Rabbinowitz, *Mishnah Megillah*, pp. 121–3.

[4] On the rules controlling the targum see also Tanh.B. i. 87 f., Tanh. Vay. 5.

[5] The reading from the Prophets is known as the *haftarah*. It is a kind of 'second lesson', read in conjunction with the passage from Torah chosen for the day; see also p. 73.

summarise the traditional and most widely accepted interpretations of scripture.[1]

It is, however, important to bear in mind the limitations of the present written Targums on the Pentateuch, if it is hoped to use them for evidence of early synagogue Judaism—as, for example, of the time of Jesus. It cannot simply be assumed that the surviving written Targums are identical with the earliest targums as actually rendered in synagogues throughout the Jewish world, or that there was one standard targum, rendered everywhere in the same form. In fact what seems probable is that attempts *were* made to standardise the Aramaic rendering, but that these attempts belong to the second or third centuries onward. There seems no doubt at all that these attempts to move towards a standard rendering drew on existing and far older traditions, but at present the evidence is lacking through which a *direct* connection might be established (as opposed to arguments of probability) between the existing written Targums and the targum as it might have been rendered in synagogue in the earliest days. What *can* be said is that the written Targums contain interpretative material which is known from other sources to go back to an early date, and that the Targum-tradition, although a developing one, is nevertheless a *tradition*—that is to say, it has continuity in itself. It is of interest that according to Sifre on Deut. § 161, the Targum is an object of study along with *Miqra* (scripture), *Mishnah* and *Talmud*, although otherwise references to targum-study are rare.[2]

Written Targums exist for all the biblical books (except for those which already contain substantial portions of Aramaic—Ezra, Nehemiah, and Daniel), but they come from widely different dates.[3] In their present form, the latest are those on the Hagiographa,[4] but this does

---

[1] It must be remembered that the *methurgeman* was not allowed to translate with complete freedom. There are a few notes of the *methurgeman* being corrected, and that perhaps explains why written recensions of the Palestinian Targum-tradition are independent and yet display a basic uniformity.

[2] A.R.N.B. xii refers to R. Aqiba studying Targum.

[3] For a detailed analysis of the Targum on Song of Songs, see R. Loewe, 'Apologetic Motifs in the Targum to the Song of Songs'.

[4] Since the completion of this book, the first part of the fourth volume of A. Sperber's *The Bible in Aramaic* has been finished. The two parts will offer a text and analysis of the Targums to the Hagiographa, and also introductory material to the other volumes. Sperber advances the argument that the so-called Targums on the Hagiographa in fact represent a transition from genuine

not mean that there were not earlier Targums on those books, which have failed to survive. A Targum on Job, for example, is mentioned in the first century A.D.[1] The earliest Targums are those on the Pentateuch and Prophets, as is to be expected since those were the books which were first read and expounded in synagogue.[2] In both cases Targum texts or fragments have survived which show considerable differences and variety. This indicates that there was no such thing as a single Aramaic translation: there was a continuous process of exegesis which produced traditions of interpretation in different areas of Judaism,[3] and the synagogue targums undoubtedly reflected that process. There was, therefore, no such thing as *the* Targum, only a Targum tradition, or perhaps more accurately Targum traditions.[4] The Targum texts (or fragments) that have survived are isolated moments extracted from a continuous process: they are, as it were, 'cross-sections' of an evolving tradition, revealing what the tradition

Targum method to *midrash* (see pp. 45 f.) on the various books; that is to say, they are commentaries on the books which at first sight resemble Targums, rather than genuine Targums as such.

[1] B.Shab. 115a: 'R. Jose said: "My father Ḥalafta was once visiting R. Gamaliel Berabbi at Tiberias. He found him sitting with Joḥanan the excommunicated holding the Targum on Job in his hand and reading it. He said, I remember R. Gamaliel, your grandfather, standing high up on the Temple Mount when the Targum on Job was brought to him . . ."' See also Mas. Sof. v. 15. A note at the end of LXX Job says: 'This was translated from a Syriac (i.e. Aramaic) book', though this may simply refer to the traditional identification of Job with the Edomite King Jobab (Gen. xxxvi. 33). In the light of these comments it is particularly interesting that one of the D.S.S. fragments is a part of a Targum on Job. On this see G. L. Harding, 'Recent Discoveries in Jordan'; C.-H. Hunzinger, 'Aus der Arbeit an den unveröffentlichten Texten von Qumran'; J. van der Ploeg, *Le Targum de Job de la Grotte II de Qumran*; A. S. van der Woude, 'Das Hiobtargum aus Qumran-Höhle XI'. See also R. le Déaut, *La Nuit Pascale*, p. 20, with further references.

[2] Traditionally Targums were thought to date back to the time of Ezra; see e.g. B.Meg. 3a, B.Ned. 37b.

[3] E.g. Babylonia and Palestine. There was a considerable overlap between these traditions, partly because of the interchange of scholars but also because much of the tradition as we now have it comes through Babylonian Judaism.

[4] This becomes increasingly clear the more Targum texts are discovered. So, for example, W. Baars commented on a Cairo Geniza fragment: 'The text, which shows variations from both Targum (Ps.-) Jonathan and the (so-called) Fragmentary Targum, testifies once more to the diversity of targumic texts circulated till a relatively late date' (Baars, 'A Targum on Exod. xv. 7–21 from the Cairo Geniza'). Only when the many different texts and fragments are published will it be possible to trace the different families and establish the relationships between them.

was at a particular time. It follows from this that although a Targum text may be late it will often contain a great deal of very early material.

The Targum texts and fragments on the Pentateuch mostly represent the Palestinian targum, but they represent that tradition of interpretation in very different forms. They fall into roughly five groups:

a. NEOFITI I. This is a manuscript discovered by Professor A. Diez Macho[1] in the Vatican Library and now published.[2] It is the only complete copy of a Palestinian Targum to the whole Pentateuch, and even so it drew on more than one version of the Palestinian Targum. It contains variant readings in the margin or between the lines, which Diez Macho described as follows: 'Each Palestinian Targum MS differs from the other MSS to a greater or lesser extent. This explains why the MS N (Neofiti I) exhibits on the margins (M) or between the lines (I) an impressive amount of variant readings, which betray at least three different original sources. The differences are differences of orthography, spelling, lexicography, grammar and of range of paraphrase.'[3] Diez Macho has claimed that Neofiti represents the Palestinian Targum at a very early stage; in his view it demonstrates that the Palestinian Targum is of pre-Christian origin even though Neofiti is a first or second century A.D. recension of it.[4]

In his article, 'The Recently Discovered Palestinian Targum', he put forward nine arguments for the antiquity of Neofiti I:

(i) '...In MS. N, we find many of the passages contrary to the official interpretation, taken from Geniza fragments of the Palestinian Targum.'[5] In other words it predates any official revision.

(ii) Some specific interpretations of later Targums are not found, in particular in the rendering of Deut. xxxiii. 11.[6]

(iii) Messianic passages used by Christianity are retained with a Messianic sense. At a later date they would have been given other interpretations.[7]

---

[1] See the bibliography, and also p. 28 n. 1.

[2] The text, with translations into major European languages, has been published as A. Diez Macho (ed.), *Neophyti I: Targum Palestinense—MS. de la Biblioteca Vaticana*, Madrid and Barcelona, 1968– .

[3] A. Diez Macho, 'The Recently Discovered Palestinian Targum ...', p. 237. For a careful description of the MS see M. F. Martin, 'The Palaeographical Character of Codex Neofiti I', and G. E. Weil, 'Le Codex Neophiti I ...'.

[4] Diez Macho, 'The Recently Discovered Palestinian Targum ...'.

[5] *Ibid.* p. 225, on the Geniza fragments, see below, section *c*.

[6] *Ibid.* p. 226.   [7] *Ibid.* pp. 226–7.

(iv) The study of the historical development of particular items of exegesis puts N into its proper place in sequence, and again indicates an early date; Diez Macho here referred to the work of G. Vermes.[1]

(v) Historical and geographical identifications, particularly in Gen. x.[2]

(vi) Negative evidence: interpretations known to be late do not appear.[3]

(vii) 'The text of N which, of course, was composed in Palestine, belongs to a time that the Greek language had penetrated deeply in the country: this can safely be inferred from many Greek and several Latin words which recur in the Aramaic text.'[4]

(viii) N.T. dependence on the Palestinian Targum as represented by Neofiti I.[5]

(ix) The reconstruction of the Hebrew text underlying Neofiti I.[6]

His arguments have been questioned by P. Wernberg-Møller[7] on the grounds that the material so far produced by Diez Macho does not prove his point. However, Wernberg-Møller was careful to point out that no final decision can be reached until the whole of Neofiti is published, and that in any case the antiquity of targum material can be established in other ways, even if Neofiti turns out to be later than Diez Macho supposes: 'The text-critical material presented by Macho is incapable of proving a pre-Massoretic, pre-Christian date of the Palestinian Targum ... My intention has not been to suggest that the Palestinian Targum—and all other Targums for that matter—are necessarily late. In the Judaean manuscripts we find a certain amount of Targumic material (this is the case in the non-biblical manuscripts 1QS, 1QpHab, and 1QH)[8]—a fact which suggests that the bulk of Targumic traditions was fixed by the time those writings were composed.'[9]

More recently M. McNamara has published the results of a detailed study of Neofiti I,[10] in which he set out to answer the following question: 'A question that yet remains to be solved is how much older than the Geniza fragments is the Palestinian Targum to the Pentateuch itself.

---

[1] *Ibid.* p. 227.
[2] *Ibid.* pp. 227–9.
[3] *Ibid.* pp. 229–30.
[4] *Ibid.* p. 230.
[5] *Ibid.* pp. 230–3.
[6] *Ibid.* pp. 233–6.
[7] 'An Inquiry into the Validity of the Text-critical Argument ...'
[8] For the meaning of the abbreviations, see pp. 34 f.
[9] Wernberg-Møller, *op. cit.* p. 330.
[10] 'Some Early Rabbinic Citations ...'

If it existed and was known in Palestinian Judaism one would expect to find some evidence of it in Palestinian writings, just as we find citations from Onqelos in the Babylonian Talmud.'[1] McNamara came to the following conclusions:

(i) 'Neofiti abides by all the rabbinic rules referring to Targumic renderings . . . Neofiti, as it now stands, appears to have received a rabbinic recension after c. 350 A.D. Pseudo-Jonathan, on the other hand, is not affected by these rabbinic rules . . . This text of the Palestinian Targum-tradition must have had a different history of transmission from Neofiti and other Palestinian Targum representatives.'[2]

(ii) 'Neofiti and Jewish liturgy: the close manner in which Neofiti adheres to the Mishnaic rules on targumic renderings . . . gives one the impression that in Neofiti we are in the presence of a text that was closely associated with the liturgy;[3] one that may well reflect the translation as it was actually given in the synagogues.'[4]

(iii) Rabbinic citations were drawn from the Palestinian Targum: 'In not a few, the relation with the form of the Palestinian Targum as represented by Neofiti is particularly noticeable.'[5]

(iv) 'These citations take us from the second (or first) century A.D. down to the end of the fourth, and show that in Palestine throughout these centuries various texts of the Palestinian Targum were cited . . . We may take these citations, then, as a strong indication that the Palestinian Targum as we now have it must have existed substantially in these early centuries.'[6]

(v) 'The early date of Neofiti: the close connection of the Mishnaic and other rabbinic texts with our present MS of Neofiti is particularly striking . . . Could it be that in Neofiti we have an official or semi-official text, one that would have taken in Palestinian Judaism the place that Onqelos[7] enjoyed in Babylon? Such a hypothesis would explain how closely the citations follow on Neofiti. It would also give a reason for

---

[1] 'Some Early Rabbinic Citations', p. 1.   [2] *Ibid.* p. 13.

[3] The connection of the Targums with the liturgy is not surprising in view of their use in synagogue. The Targums in fact include liturgical fragments (see for example R. le Déaut, *La Nuit Pascale*). Much progress has been made in recent years on Synagogue liturgies, largely as a result of material from the Cairo Geniza, and liturgical poetry forms an important part of the background to the Targums. For a brief summary see M. Black, *An Aramaic Approach . . .* (1954), pp. 240–4; (1967), pp. 305–9.

[4] McNamara, *op. cit.* p. 13.   [5] *Ibid.* p. 14.

[6] *Ibid.* p. 14.   [7] See below, section *d*.

the rabbinic recension that appears clear in Neofiti . . . and will explain why no Targum Onqelos citations appear in writings of Palestinian Jewish provenance.'[1]

(vi) Having summarised the arguments in favour of an early written form (or forms) of the Palestinian Targum-tradition, he then concluded: 'There is no reason whatever why this Targum should not have been Neofiti.'

At the same time, McNamara is unwilling to take Neofiti I back to quite so early a date as Diez Macho, not only because of the connections with the Tannaitic[2] period summarised above,[3] but also because of the fact that Neofiti I is the only extant Targum text which does not translate the 'forbidden passages': according to M.Meg. iv. 10 certain passages were not to be given a targum interpretation in synagogue for fear of causing offence: 'The story of Reuben is read out but not interpreted,[4] the story of Tamar is read out and interpreted,[5] the first story of the calf is read out and interpreted, and the second is read out but not interpreted.[6] The Blessing of the Priests[7] and the story of David[8] and of Amnon[9] are read out but not interpreted...' In most other extant Targum texts which cover those passages they are translated, but not in Neofiti I; this suggests that Neofiti I followed the Mishnaic ruling. That, however, in itself is not conclusive as to dating, since it is not known when those prohibitions were introduced, and it is in any case extremely likely that they are pre-Mishnaic; furthermore, it is always possible that Neofiti I represents an earlier text that has been brought into line with a subsequent ruling. Nevertheless, McNamara concluded: 'If one were to pass a provisional judgement on Neofiti I it would be that it represents a very old text of the Palestinian Targum that was familiar to Palestinian rabbis and was edited by them to bring it into line with the major points of halakah.[10] The basis of N. would then be very old, but its present recension would be from later and talmudic times. This judgement can only be provisional, but it is the one that seems to flow from the textual evidence.'[11]

---

[1] *Ibid.* p. 14.   [2] See p. 49.
[3] See also McNamara, *The New Testament and the Palestinian Targum . . .*, pp. 62 f.   [4] Gen. xxxv. 22.   [5] Gen. xxxviii. 13 ff.
[6] Exod. xxxii. 1–20 and xxxii. 21–5 and 35.
[7] Num. vi. 24–6.   [8] II Sam. xi. 2–17.
[9] II Sam. xiii. 1 ff.   [10] See pp. 43–7.
[11] McNamara, *op. cit.* p. 63.

From these arguments there seems little doubt that Neofiti I represents the Palestinian Targum-tradition at an early stage, but that its present form comes, most probably, from the third century. This conclusion is supported by the fact that the translation at least consulted, and perhaps was based on, a Greek version. Several of its idioms and grammatical curiosities seem to imply a Greek rather than Hebrew background, though not exclusively so.[1] This suggests that it was not a purely 'academic' exercise, but one which sought to convey the meaning of the text as well as rendering it with some accuracy. If this conclusion about the date is right, it means that the question of the possible relevance of Neofiti I to the New Testament is a difficult one. What seems clear is that its material is potentially of great importance, but that it should be used in conjunction with other material which will help to establish its position in the whole history of exegesis and interpretation.

Since the text of Neofiti I has been published, with an English translation, passages from Neofiti have not been translated in this book: it is now possible to make an extensive comparison with Pseudo-Jonathan, and the space saved has been able to be devoted to fuller notes than would otherwise have been possible. For examples of the way in which material from Neofiti and other Targums is being applied to N.T. problems, see the bibliography under R. le Déaut, M. McNamara and P. Nickels, and for a criticism see the bibliography under G. J. Cowling.

b. THE FRAGMENTARY TARGUM. Five texts have preserved fragments of the Palestinian Targum, but they represent two different recensions (or developments) of it: (i) The four texts V, B, N, L[2] have preserved between them just under a thousand verses of the Pentateuch. They have 863 verses in common, and although they show variations between each other, they are clearly derived from a single origin; that is to say, they represent the Palestinian Targum in one particular group. (ii) The text in P[3] also preserves fragments of the Palestinian Targum, but in a

---

[1] For a summary of some of the arguments which point in this direction, see G. J. Cowling, 'New Light on the New Testament?' For another explanation, see p. 17 (vii).

[2] Vaticanus 440, Bomberg Bible (1517), Nürnberg I, Leipzig I.

[3] Paris 110.

different recension (or evolution) of it.[1] Perhaps it may have started from something like the same original, but it has evolved quite separately from V, B, N, and L. The fragmentary Targum was published by M. Ginsburger in 1899,[2] but not with complete accuracy. M. C. Doubles, in a recent article, commented: 'I myself have prepared the texts originally published by Moses Ginsburger for republication, in the process of which about 2,000 errors have been discovered in Ginsburger's presentation of MSS Vaticanus 440 and Leipzig I.'[3]

c. THE CAIRO GENIZA FRAGMENTS.[4] Among the many manuscripts and fragments found in the Cairo Geniza there were some fragments from the Palestinian Targum. Some of them were published by P. Kahle,[5] others have been published subsequently[6] and a collected publication is intended.[7] The Geniza Fragments not only represent the Palestinian Targum in a different recension,[8] but they also differ among themselves: where the same verse has survived in two fragments, the two fragments may well represent the verse differently.[9] This again bears witness to the extremely fluid state of the Palestinian Targum. It seems likely that the Fragmentary Targum(s) was a deliberate attempt to preserve material which might otherwise have been lost when the Targum Onqelos (see p. 22) was established in Palestine as the more or less official Targum.

---

[1] This was noted by M. Ginsburger when he was working on his edition of the Fragmentary Targum (*Das Fragmententhargum*), and was also pointed out in his article, 'Die Fragmente des Thargum . . .' For a summary see M. C. Doubles, 'Palestinian Targum'.

[2] See the bibliography, and note especially the article by Ginsburger referred to above.

[3] M. C. Doubles, *op. cit.* p. 16.

[4] The Cairo Geniza was part of the synagogue in Old Cairo. The manuscripts discovered in it, some of incomparable importance, began to be published towards the end of the last century, and fragments still continue to appear. See P. Kahle, *The Cairo Geniza*, 2nd edn.

[5] *Masoreten des Westens*, vol. II.

[6] See the bibliography under A. Diez Macho, Y. Komlos, W. Baars.

[7] P. Kahle, *op. cit.* p. 201 note 2 and p. 205 note 2; M. C. Doubles, *op. cit.* p. 23.

[8] E.g. from that of V, B, N, L.

[9] For a summary, see M. C. Doubles, *op. cit.* pp. 21 f.

d. TARGUM ONQELOS. The usual view of Targum Onqelos is that it is an official Babylonian version of the Palestinian Targum.[1] This has been argued on three main grounds:

(i) The language of Onqelos is different; it is literary Aramaic. P. Kahle summarised: 'Concerning the language of Targum Onqelos,

[1] For a long time Babylonian and Palestinian Judaism existed side by side. Both communities produced their own texts and targums, as well as all the other products of Jewish biblical study (though it must, of course, be remembered that they have the Mishnah in common); so, for example, there is a Palestinian Talmud and a Babylonian Talmud (see pp. 64 ff.), both of which are based on the Mishnah. Texts may, therefore, be a product of either community or of both. To some extent texts can be distinguished by the pointing added to the consonants. (Pointing in Hebrew and Aramaic texts is the system of adding signs to a consonantal text in order to indicate the vowels, and to some extent the punctuation.) Pointing in the early centuries falls into four groups: (*a*) the old Babylonian tradition. This is characterised by pointing and accentuation marks above the line (supralinear, as opposed to Tiberian pointing which is below the line). The old Babylonian tradition is not a unity in itself, since it developed differently in the great Babylonian academies at Nehardea and Sura. (See especially the different Masoras on Targum Onqelos listed in A. Berliner, *Die Masorah zum Targum Onkelos nach Handschriften und unter Benutzung*.) Not a large number of Babylonian texts has survived, and some of those that have done so have been worked over by a later hand to make them conform to (later) Tiberian grammar. Great impetus was given to the study of the old Babylonian tradition by P. Kahle (*Der Masoretische Text, Masoreten des Ostens*), and since that time other examples of the Babylonian tradition have been unearthed, e.g. the Babylonian Onqelos discovered by A. Diez Macho in Vat. Hebr. 448 (see Diez Macho in *Homenaje a Millas-Vallicrosa*, I, Barcelona, 1954). But note that the presence of supralinear pointing in a manuscript does *not* necessarily mean that the manuscript represents the old Babylonian tradition; it may be a later text which has been given supralinear pointing: on this point, see (*d*) below, and also M. Martin's criticism of Sperber's edition of Targum Onqelos and of Stenning's edition of the Targum on Isaiah, in 'The Babylonian Tradition and Targum'. (*b*) Pre-Masoretic Palestinian Hebrew, better referred to as pre-Tiberian Hebrew or Palestinian punctuation. This was largely replaced by the Tiberian system, but a number of manuscripts have survived, both biblical and non-biblical. For a summary see Kahle, *The Cairo Geniza*, pp. 66 f. and A. Murtonen, *Materials for a non-Masoretic Hebrew Grammar*, I (1958). (*c*) The Tiberian system, which eventually prevailed and eliminated earlier systems. For a while the Tiberian and old Babylonian traditions existed side by side; they were for a time in two separate empires. Even when Babylonian Judaism began to decline, the Babylonian system and tradition lingered on (particularly in the Sephardi communities in Spain). But eventually the Tiberian system prevailed, and the Babylonian material which had been transferred to Palestine was brought into conformity with it. (Hence the texts which combine both systems, as for example the Sabbioneta Onqelos (A. Berliner, *Targum*

Gustaf Dalman—like others before him—is quite right in pointing out that it corresponds with neither the Aramaic dialect of the Babylonian Talmud, nor the Aramaic dialect of the Palestinian Talmud . . .' It is 'composed in a language which had become the official Aramaic language in the Persian Empire'.[1]

(ii) Onqelos was not highly regarded in Palestine; it did not replace the Palestinian Targum tradition until a much later time. It was not quoted, for example, in the Mishnah (though in view of the date of the Mishnah that is not very surprising), and it is extremely unlikely that it was quoted in the Palestinian Talmud. A. E. Silverstone, *Aquila and Onkelos*, gave J.Meg. iv. 1 and iv. 11 as examples, but these have not generally been accepted. This does not necessarily mean that Onqelos must have been composed in Babylonia; it may still be a Palestinian production which took root only in Babylonia, where it then received a characteristically Babylonian shape (as in the Babylonian MSS of Onqelos referred to on p. 22 n. 1).

(iii) Onqelos contains very little interpretation; except for obvious changes to avoid anthropomorphism, it stays close to the Hebrew text with scarcely any of the extensive haggadic interpretations of the Palestinian Targum-tradition.

Unfortunately, the position is not so clear as those arguments make it appear, and that is largely because the third of them is completely wrong. Onqelos contains a great deal of interpretative material, both haggadic and halakic,[2] much of which is the same as that in the Palestinian Targum. The extensive haggadah in Onqelos is not immediately obvious because it has been reduced and compressed, sometimes being limited to a single word, but a reference to the quotations from Onqelos in the second part of this book will reveal how extensive in fact it is.[3]

Onkelos).) From the ninth century onward the Tiberian system became the controlling system. (*d*) The Yemenite 'system'. Yemenite MSS represent the stage during which the Tiberian system was replacing the old Babylonian, hence they vary in form. In general they keep a supralinear punctuation but supply it to the Tiberian text tradition. Hence although Yemenite manuscripts look like old Babylonian, they are often in fact Tiberian.

[1] *Cairo Geniza*, p. 192.
[2] For the meaning of these terms, see p. 43.
[3] See G. Vermes, 'Haggadah in the Onkelos Targum', and my own article with more detail, 'Haggadah in the Targum Onqelos'. The extent to which Onqelos is connected with the Palestinian Targum cannot adequately be shown in translation. Often Onqelos uses exactly the same words in its translation

In some places the interpretations are linguistically identical with those in other known versions of the Palestinian Targum, but occasionally the interpretation in Onqelos appears to be independent; that is to say, there are places where the interpretations in Onqelos and in surviving recensions of the Palestinian Targum are different.[1]

The relationship of Onqelos to other Targums is thus extremely complicated. The situation is further confused by the fact that texts of different Targums have influenced each other: when Onqelos became the 'official' Aramaic Targum it influenced texts of the Palestinian Targum (before it replaced it), and it certainly influenced Pseudo-Jonathan.[2] But similarly the text of Onqelos was influenced by other Targums, especially by Pseudo-Jonathan.[3] What is certain is that the interpretations in Onqelos cannot be explained as later insertions. They are far too integral to the text, and often they are represented by a single, but all-revealing, word which depends on a more extensive interpretation in the background.[4]

The problem of Onqelos is that it is much closer to being a straight-forward translation than the other recensions of the Palestinian Targum, staying as it does much closer to the Hebrew text, and yet it contains abbreviated interpretations which seem to be a slightly variant form of the Palestinian Targum-tradition.[5] Onqelos, therefore, is something of a compromise, and perhaps it was deliberately intended to be so. A possible solution is that it was a deliberate attempt to make an Aramaic

of the Hebrew as other recensions of the Palestinian Targum, but leaves out the full interpretations. A comparison of Targum Onqelos, Fragmentary Targum and Ps. Jonathan on Gen. i is instructive from this point of view.

[1] This was also noticed by M. Z. Kadari, 'The use of d- Clauses in the Language of Targum Onkelos', p. 37. Kadari gave as examples Gen. iv. 23, xliv. 9, 17, 22, xlix. 24.

[2] See below, section e.

[3] See my article, 'Haggadah in the Targum Onqelos', pp. 63 f.

[4] The extent of Targum Onqelos' linguistic agreement with the Palestinian Targum-tradition makes it unlikely that the haggadic elements were introduced into a literal translation as a result of Babylonian editing—which was the conclusion reached, for example, by H. Barnstein, *The Targum of Onkelos* . . . .

[5] The Palestinian Targum-tradition, whatever stage it had reached at the time when Onqelos was produced, was not a translation: its purpose was to expound the Hebrew text as well as to represent it, as has been said above.

translation, and that it may well have been a part of the general attempt in Judaism from the second century A.D. onward to provide authoritative translations as a safeguard against Christian interpretations of scripture based on LXX. This would perhaps explain (and justify) the ascription of the Targum to Aquila (Onqelos),[1] and it would also explain the distinct nature of its Aramaic. At the same time, the translator(s) who produced Onqelos was well aware of the existing Palestinian Targum-tradition, and he not only based his translation on it, but was also prepared to incorporate its interpretations into his translation as being the proper meaning of the text.[2] This in itself would not determine

---

[1] Aquila produced a literal Greek version of the Bible during the second century A.D., which was intended by the Rabbis to replace the LXX in Judaism (the LXX having by then become the Christian Bible). According to J.Meg. i.11, J.Qid. i.1, Aquila was a proselyte (cf. the story in Epiphanius, *de Mens. et Pond.* §§ 14 f.) who became a pupil of R. Eliezer and R. Joshua (B.Meg. 3a; according to B.Qid. 59a it was R. Aqiba). In the Palestinian Talmud his name is spelt variously 'Aqilas, 'Aqilas, Qilas and 'Aqi'alas, but in the Babylonian Talmud it becomes Onqelos. It is B.Meg. 3a (based on J.Meg. i. 9) which ascribes the Targum under discussion to Onqelos: 'R. Jeremiah (but others say R. Ḥiyya b. Abba) said: "The Targum of the Pentateuch was made by the proselyte Onqelos from the instruction (lit. 'from the mouth of') R. Eliezer and R. Joshua."' The ascription to Aquila may be evidence that the Targum Onqelos comes from about the same period or that the literal Aquila version suggested the worthwhileness of a literal Aramaic version, or it may simply be that both were seen to be fairly literal representations of the Hebrew text. On the other hand, A. E. Silverstone made a detailed analysis of Aquila and Targum Onqelos, and came to the conclusion that the traditional ascription was justified (*Aquila and Onkelos*). He based his arguments particularly on agreements between Aquila and Targum Onqelos against LXX, and on agreements between Targum Onqelos and R. Aqiba (who was traditionally held to have been the teacher of Aquila). But Silverstone underestimated (and in fact virtually failed to consider) the agreements between Targum Onqelos and other recensions of the Palestinian Targum-tradition, and his arguments need to be reassessed with those agreements in mind. At the same time, some of the contacts pointed out by him between Aquila and Targum Onqelos remain important, however they are finally to be explained.

On Aquila, see Origen, *ad Africanum* 2, and E. R. Goodenough, *Jewish Symbols*, I, 17.

[2] This view has also been reached by G. J. Kuiper, in an unpublished thesis on the relationship between Ps. Jon. and Targ. Onq. M. Black has summarised Kuiper's conclusions: 'The results, which it is hoped will be published soon, have proved surprisingly interesting: Onkelos, while admittedly showing traces of Babylonian influence, appears nevertheless to have been an authoritative redaction of the same kind of Targum tradition as is preserved, still in its fluid state, in the Fragmentary Targum, the Geniza Fragments, Pseudo-Jonathan, and Targum Neofiti I.' (*An Aramaic Approach* . . . (1967), p. 42.)

whether Onqelos was produced in Babylon or Palestine, but in either case the lack of interest taken in the Targum in Palestine might have been because its compromise character was recognised; it included some haggadic interpretation, but not much, and so it could not hope to rival the Palestinian Targum on its own ground.

Onqelos may have been in existence in Babylonia before the end of the third century A.D., because it was apparently established and worked on in Nehardea, and Nehardea was temporarily destroyed in the second half of that century. For the text, see especially Sperber, *The Bible in Aramaic*.

e. PSEUDO-JONATHAN. This is a complete Targum to the whole Pentateuch, representing a Babylonian version of the Palestinian Targum-tradition in its most developed form. It is certainly quite late in its final form,[1] but since it rests on a tradition going back to pre-Christian times it includes very early material.[2] The value of Pseudo-Jonathan is that it frequently summarises the most usual and accepted rabbinic interpretations of the text, as well as others which are not otherwise known. Therefore, although Pseudo-Jonathan is a unified attempt to present a finished version of the Palestinian Targum, the interpretations contained within it may come from any period of Jewish exegesis, from the earliest times onward. It follows that each element of its interpretation has to be studied quite separately if its origin and antiquity are to be established. This can be done in two ways: (*a*) Within the Targum tradition itself; where the same verse appears in other recensions of the Targum it is possible to make a direct comparison and see how it is treated in each place. Here the publication of Neofiti I will be of immense value because it will reveal the complete Palestinian Targum at an earlier stage. (*b*) By comparison with other works of Jewish exegesis, both pre-Rabbinic and Rabbinic. (Evidence can also be gathered from Christian works which drew on or knew of the Jewish tradition.) Much work needs to be done in this field

[1] For example, on Gen. xv. 14 it mentions the names of Muhammad's wives as the wives of Ishmael, Ishmael being the father of the Arabs; cf. also the mention of Constantinople in Pseudo-Jonathan on Num. xxiv. 24, and of the six Orders of the Mishnah in Pseudo-Jonathan on Exod. xxvi. 9.

[2] It must also be remembered that Pseudo-Jonathan is not necessarily a static work, but that it may have been changed during the course of its transmission to keep it 'up to date'.

before a full history of the Targums can be written.[1] There is no doubt that what is needed is the publication of the known versions of the Palestinian Targum-tradition in synoptic form, but the cost might be prohibitive—though if it were done it might well throw important light on the methodology of the synoptic study of the Gospels. A few synoptic studies have already been made of brief passages, and the results have been most suggestive.[2]

The text of Pseudo-Jonathan according to B.M. MS Add. 27031 was published by M. Ginsburger in 1903, but with a number of mistakes or misprints—as in the case of his edition of Fragmentary Targum (see p. 21 above).

The name Pseudo-Jonathan arose as follows: Targums on the Prophets developed in much the same way as Targums on the Pentateuch; that is to say, originally there was no single targum but an evolving, developing tradition of targum-interpretation. Eventually a more or less official Targum was drawn up, corresponding to Onqelos but containing much larger elements of interpretation. As Onqelos was ascribed to Aquila so the Targum on the Prophets was ascribed to the maker of another Greek version, Theodotion. In Hebrew that is the name Jonathan. Jonathan was then identified as Jonathan ben Uzziel, a pupil of Hillel (B.Meg. 3 a). The Targum now known as Pseudo-Jonathan was originally called the Palestinian or Jerushalmi Targum, abbreviated as Targum J. The J was later misunderstood as an abbreviation for Jonathan. The addition of 'Pseudo' is a recognition of the mistake. The name Pseudo-Jonathan has been retained in this book because it is the most usual, and also because it avoids confusion: to call it the Palestinian Targum would confuse it with the general Palestinian Targum-tradition of which Targum texts are individual

---

[1] J. Heinemann, in a review of G. Vermes, *Scripture and Tradition*, queried the value of trying to establish the antiquity of Targum material. He argued that since the Targums are known to contain late material, the early date of any material can only be established by comparison with material from outside the Targums which can be dated. In that case, he asked, what is the value of the Targum material? But Heinemann missed the point which Vermes constantly repeats, that what is needed is to look at material in its greatest possible variety; only in that way can the history of its transmission begin to be unravelled. The review is in *Tarbiz*, xxxv (1965), 84–94 (in Hebrew). See also McNamara, *op. cit.* pp. 60–2.

[2] See e.g. R. le Déaut, *La Nuit Pascale*; P. Grelot, 'Les Targums du Pentateuque . . .'.

recensions or examples. The name Jerusalem Targum is better, so long as it is broken up, as in a common system of abbreviations, where TJ (Targum Jerushalmi) stands for the Palestinian Targum, 1TJ (or TJI) for Ps. Jon., 2TJ (or TJII) for the Fragmentary Targum. In order to make recognition of the different Targums more immediate and obvious, the following abbreviations have been employed in this book:

C.G.: Cairo Geniza Fragments
F.T.: Fragmentary Targum
N.: Neofiti I
Ps. Jon.: Pseudo-Jonathan
T.O.: Targum Onqelos

For particular studies or editions of the Targums, see the bibliography under Albeck, Baars, Barnstein, Bassfreund, Baumstark, Berliner, Bernhardt, Birkeland, Black, Bloch, Bowker, Brayer, Brownlee, Churgin, Corré, Cowling, Dalman, le Déaut, Dias, Diez-Macho, Doubles, Edelmann, Etheridge, Frankel, Friedmann, Geiger, Ginsburger, Goldberg, Goshen-Gottstein, Gottlieb, Greenup, Grelot, Hamp, Harding, Hausdorff, Hill, Hornik, Humbert, Hunzinger, Jansma, Kadari, Kahle, Karminka, Komlos, Lagarde, Loewe, Marmorstein, Martin, McNamara, Melamed, Mingana, Nickels, Peters, van der Ploeg, Praetorius, Rosenthal, Schelbert, Schmerter, Schoenfelder, Schulz, Silverstone, Singer, Speier, Sperber, Stauffer, Stenning, Stummer, Teicher, Vermes, Vööbus, Weil, Weinberg, Wernberg-Møller, Wieder, Wikgren, Winter, Wohl, van der Woude; and in reference works, Brederek.

For a brief survey of early (pre-nineteenth century) studies, see M. McNamara, *The New Testament and the Palestinian Targum . . .*, pp. 5–20.[1]

[1] Since this book was written an important article on Neofiti I has been published by D. Rieder ('On the Targum Yerushalmi in Neofiti I', *Tarbiz*, xxxviii, 1968, pp. 81–6 (Hebrew)). In this article, Rieder argues that the text in N. has suffered greatly in the course of transmission, particularly from careless copying; he suggests also that the Targumist made errors, and that the MS. must therefore be used with extreme caution. Among examples from the whole Pentateuch, the following passages from Genesis are discussed: Gen. i. 4, 10; vi. 8; xi. 2, 26; xxiv. 11, 55.

2
PRE-RABBINIC LITERATURE[1]

The antiquity of material in the Targums can often be established by
seeing whether the same interpretation occurs elsewhere, and therefore
the notes in this book contain references to other works, as explained in
the preface. Jewish pre-Rabbinic literature is too well known to require
a general introduction here, but for the sake of completeness a list of
authors and sources quoted in this book will be given, together with brief
information about them.

Philo

The date of Philo's birth is uncertain. J. Schwartz put it between 15
and 10 B.C.[2] Equally uncertain is the date of his death, though he must
have been alive in A.D. 39–40, since that was the date of the embassy to
Gaius. His exegesis of scripture was predominantly allegorical. He was
evidently concerned to commend Judaism to the Hellenistic world (of
which, living in Alexandria, he was a part) through the media of
Hellenism. But this should not be allowed to obscure the fact that
Philo was deeply and fundamentally Jewish.[3] What is particularly

---

[1] The phrase is used in a mainly chronological sense, meaning by 'rabbinic'
the period of the ascendancy of the rabbis after the fall of Jerusalem, though
obviously many individual rabbis were contemporaries of Philo or Josephus.
Pre-Rabbinic literature is as diverse as Judaism itself, and the phrase should
not be taken to imply that there was a unified body of tradition preceding
Rabbinic literature. Similarly, it does not mean that the writers or works
referred to were necessarily in sympathy with the Rabbinic position.

[2] 'Note sur la famille de Philon d'Alexandrie'.

[3] This is well illustrated in *de Migr*. xvi. 89–93: 'There are some who regard-
ing laws in their literal sense in the light of symbols of matters belonging to the
intellect, are over-punctilious about the latter, while treating the former with
easy-going neglect. Such men I for my part should blame for handling the
matter in too easy and off-hand a manner: ... It is true that receiving circumcision does indeed portray the excision of pleasure and all passions, and
the putting away of the impious conceit, under which the mind supposed that
it was capable of begetting by its own power: but let us not on this account
repeal the law laid down for circumcising ... If we keep and observe these, we
shall gain a clearer conception of those things of which these are the symbols.'

important for the purposes of this book is the possibility that Philo in his exegesis occasionally shows traces of 'Palestinian' interpretation; that is to say, it is possible that there are points of contact between Philo and the traditions which are to be found in Rabbinic works of exegesis (and eventually in Ps. Jon.). If this is so, it means that Philo might sometimes be an important witness to the antiquity of a particular item of interpretation, or at least can supplement our knowledge of what the interpretation was at an earlier time. Even if Philo's interpretation differs, it can show that a difficulty was recognised in a particular verse at his time. On the other hand, it must be remembered that the exact nature of Philo's relationship to the 'Palestinian tradition' is much disputed.[1]

The text and translation quoted in this book are those of the Loeb edition. For a useful summary of recent work on Philo see L. H. Feldman, *Studies in Judaica*.

Pseudo-Philo

This is a work of great importance in the study of early Jewish exegesis, even though it is relatively little known. It is a continuous history of Israel, extending in its present form from Adam to the death of Saul; it is probable that the original was longer. It follows the biblical narrative, but only very roughly. It makes extensive additions, often of stories without any basis in scripture,[2] and it has many omissions.

---

[1] Those who argue the closest connections are Y. Baer, 'The Ancient Hasidim . . .'; S. Belkin (see the entries in the bibliography); H. A. Wolfson, *Philo*. Some parallels were listed by L. Ginzberg, *Legends of the Jews*, notes and indices (vols. v–vii); but many of them are very doubtful; see also G. Allon, 'Studies in the Halakah of Philo'; E. E. Hallevy, 'External Haggadah in Shemoth Rabba', introd. to *Shemoth Rabbah*, pp. 38–44 (Hebrew). Against close connections are D. Daube, 'Rabbinic Methods of Interpretation . . .'; also a review of S. Belkin, *Philo and the Oral Law*; L. H. Feldman, 'The Orthodoxy of the Jews in Hellenistic Egypt'; E. R. Goodenough, *The Jurisprudence of the Jewish Courts in Egypt*; *By Light, Light*; also a review of H. A. Wolfson, *Philo*; I. Heinemann, *Philons griechische und jüdische Bildung*; S. Sandmel (see the bibliography); E. Stein, 'Allegorische Exegese des Philo aus Alexandreia'; and R. J. Z. Werblowsky, 'Philo and Zohar', criticising Belkin. See also J.-G. Kahn, 'Did Philo know Hebrew?' Much work on this difficult topic remains to be done.

[2] For example, in the stories of the Judges, xxv ff.; for the possible influence of Ps. Philo's version of Judg. xiii on Luke i see P. Winter, 'The Proto-Source of Luke'.

It has survived only in a Latin text, but it was argued by L. Cohn and M. R. James that the Latin text was a translation from Greek and that the Greek in turn was a translation from a Semitic original. It is generally agreed that the book dates from the first century A.D., probably after the fall of Jerusalem, but its traditions and legends may well go back much earlier. It is one of the earliest examples of continuous haggadic interpretation and it is an important witness to the antiquity of many traditions and to the early form of others.

The Latin text has been edited by Guido Kisch,[1] but because of conditions during the war his edition had to be based on a limited number of available texts, particularly the Admont MS. Kisch himself recognised these limitations, and this edition remains the best available. It contains a bibliography[2] and introduction, where the arguments about the date and origin are summarised. There is an English translation by M. R. James,[3] but that inevitably (because of its early date) was based on an even less critical text. The importance of Pseudo-Philo is so great that a translation of the passages connected with Genesis is provided in Appendix I, so that they may be compared with the interpretations of the Targums.

Josephus

Josephus was born A.D. 37–8, and died probably at some time after A.D. 100. Much of his surviving work is apologetic, either for himself and his conduct during the Jewish War, or for his understanding of Judaism itself. In the *Antiquities* Josephus retold the history of Israel from the Creation down to the procuratorship of Gessius Florus. His retelling of the biblical narrative shows many traces of the Palestinian tradition, and thus Josephus is a vitally important witness to the antiquity of many items in that tradition. A few parallels between Josephus and other Jewish writings on Genesis were given by J. Weill in his French translation of *Ant.* i–v.[4] Many more can be found in

---

[1] *Pseudo-Philo's Liber Antiquitatum Biblicarum.*

[2] To which add G. Kisch, 'A Note on the New Edition of Pseudo-Philo's Biblical Antiquities'; 'Postlegomena to the New Edition', providing addenda and corrigenda; A. Spiro, 'Samaritans, Tobiads and Judahites in Pseudo-Philo'; 'Pseudo-Philo's Saul and the Rabbis' Messiah ben Ephraim'; 'The Ascension of Phinehas'.

[3] M. R. James, *The Biblical Antiquities of Philo.*

[4] *Œuvres Complètes de Flavius Josephus*, ed. T. Reinach, vol. I.

L. Ginzberg, *Legends of the Jews*, vols. v–vii, and in the notes in the Loeb edition of Josephus, particularly the volumes translated by R. Marcus, who also pointed out some of the connections between Josephus and Targ. Jon. on the Prophets.[1] One of the best short introductions to Josephus in general still remains that of B. Niese, *E.R.E.* vii, 569–79. For a summary of recent work on Josephus see L. H. Feldman, *Studies in Judaica*, and see also the forthcoming *Bibliographie zu Flavius Josephus*, prepared by H. Schreckenberg.

Mention must also be made at this point of Josippon. Josippon is a Hebrew paraphrase of the *Jewish War*, which depended in part on Hegesippus, but which made numerous additions from Hebrew sources. S. Zeitlin[2] and A. A. Neuman[3] both hold that some of the material included in Josippon was drawn from early sources dating from before the fall of Jerusalem. The composition itself is late.[4]

The letter of Aristeas

For a summary of this, see p. 4.

Apocrypha and Pseudepigrapha

Under this heading come a large number of works, ranging in date from the third or second century B.C. down to the Middle Ages. Many individual works changed during their history, as, for example, when Jewish works were taken over by Christians and were made to conform more closely to the new faith. Other works show signs of having been repeatedly extended or 'brought up to date'. Thus I Enoch is like a snowball running downhill and gathering more and more material as it goes: in its final form it is almost an anthology. Apocrypha and Pseudepigrapha were popular both in Judaism and in Christianity, and they were, therefore, important vehicles of argument, encouragement and belief. Because of their anonymity (under the guise of attributed authorship) they were also an extremely useful vehicle for

---

[1] See also A. Mez, *Die Bibel des Josephus*; S. Rappaport, *Agada und Exegese bei Flavius Josephus*.

[2] 'Josippon.'

[3] 'Josippon and the Apocrypha'; see also Neuman, 'Josippon: History and Pietism'; 'A Note on John the Baptist and Jesus in Josippon'.

[4] See also Y. Baer, 'The Book of Josippon the Jew'; D. Flusser, 'The Author of the Book of Josippon'.

the ideas of those who stood outside the main streams of 'orthodoxy'. Amongst them, for example, can be found some of the few remaining traces of Jewish Christianity, though the traces are now very indistinct. It would be impossible to introduce each work separately in a work of this scope, and it would in any case be superfluous, since several introductions to these works exist already in English: see particularly O. Eissfeldt, *The Old Testament, An Introduction*, pp. 571–636, with good bibliographies; D. S. Russell, *The Method and Message of Jewish Apocalyptic*. The most convenient collection of translations is that of R. H. Charles (see the bibliography); for N.T. Apocrypha, to which occasional reference is made in this book, see E. Hennecke, *New Testament Apocrypha*, 2 vols.

The Dead Sea Scrolls

The scrolls found in different areas in the vicinity of the Dead Sea represent an enormous variety of material. At present no certain conclusions can be drawn about the provenance of the material, or about its connections, if any, with a sect at Qumran. It is not even possible yet to identify the sect of the sectarian documents with any finality; an identification with the Essenes is sometimes almost taken for granted but it cannot be regarded as conclusive yet. It is only just twenty years since work on the scrolls began, so it is not surprising that different theories and hypotheses abound. It will be a long time before they can be adequately tested and assessed. At the moment, the scrolls need to be used with great caution. Their date is not yet known, nor is it established to what extent they can be treated as a unity. Perhaps, however, the way in which conflicting conclusions can be drawn from the basic evidence of the scrolls should be regarded as a primary fact about them; and if the scrolls are to be connected with a sect which produced them, the sect should be understood as having changed its character considerably during the course of its history as different elements in Judaism attached themselves to it. It may be, in other words, that the evidence demands an evolutionary rather than a static solution. In that way the Zadokite, Zealot and Essene characteristics (which all appear in the scrolls) might be explained, without having recourse necessarily to a much later date. But although caution is undoubtedly wise, caution is not the same thing as abstinence, and some of the scrolls are certainly relevant to the Targums. In the present instance, the most relevant is the Genesis Apocryphon (1QApoc). Only parts of this scroll, which was one of the seven scrolls first found in Cave 1, have survived. It consists of stories of the patriarchs told in the first person, with many apocryphal additions.[1] Col. II is Lamech's account of the birth of Noah (Gen. v), Cols. XIX and XX are Abram's account of the descent into Egypt (Gen. xii), Cols. XXI and XXII cover Gen. xiii and xiv.

For a brief and well-organised introduction to the scrolls see M. Mansoor, *The Dead Sea Scrolls, A College Textbook and a Study Guide* (Leiden, 1964); a good translation is that of G. Vermes, *The Dead Sea Scrolls in English* (Pelican, 1962), though references are often difficult to track down in it; a convenient collection of some of the main texts is that of A. M. Habermann, *Megillot Midbar Yehuda* (Israel, 1959), which includes a Hebrew concordance. Its transcription of the texts is not entirely accurate; see, for example, a critical review, which makes several corrections, by S. B. Hoenig, *J.Q.R.* LI (1960), 72–8.[2]

The most usual abbreviations in references to the scrolls are those which start with a number identifying the cave in which the scroll or fragment was found, a letter identifying the area, and an abbreviation indicating the contents. Thus 1QIs[a] indicates the first scroll of Isaiah found in the first cave at Qumran. The most common abbreviations are:

DJD 1– . *Discoveries in the Judaean Desert*, 1 (O.U.P. 1955).

D.S.S. 1 and 11: *The Dead Sea Scrolls of St Mark's Monastery*, 1 and 11, New Haven, 1951.

1QS (or DSD): the Manual of Discipline.

1QSa and 1QSb: attachments to the Manual of Discipline.

1QH: the Thanksgiving Hymns.

1QM: the War Scroll.

1QApoc: the Genesis Apocryphon.

CDC: the Damascus Rule (the Zadokite Fragment).

4QFlor: the Blessing of Jacob.

4QTest: a collection of 'proof-texts'.

Various commentaries on Biblical books have been found, and these have a small p before the abbreviation of the biblical book.[3] Thus

---

[1] For connections between Gen. Apoc. and other Midrashim, see G. Sarfatti, 'Notes on the Genesis Apocryphon'.

[2] Though the review itself contains mistakes or misprints.

[3] p represents the Hebrew *pesher*.

1QpHab is the commentary on Habakkuk found in Cave 1, 4QpNah is the commentary on Nahum found in Cave 4. The equivalent Hebrew abbreviations are given here, because the references in Habermann's concordance are in Hebrew:

מבא: the War Scroll.

מבד: the Damascus Rule.

מהו: the Thanksgiving Hymns.

מה : the Manual of Discipline.

פה: the Commentary on Habakkuk.

3

NON-RABBINIC LITERATURE

It would be a mistake to assume that after the fall of Jerusalem the rabbinic interpretation[1] of Judaism immediately or even rapidly excluded all others. There is evidence that the rabbis of Yavneh[2] tried, not only in their own immediate circle but also beyond it, to ensure that there would be no disintegration of Judaism after the catastrophe. But it does not follow that they were able to impose their views on all Jews throughout the world, and it is clear that other interpretations of Judaism continued. E. R. Goodenough has argued vigorously and at length that many Jews lived completely outside the orbit of Pharisaic/ Rabbinic Judaism, not only in the diaspora but also in Palestine itself.[3] Thus he commented on the work of G. F. Moore:[4]

Moore says: 'About the relations of the Palestinian schools to the Greek-speaking part of the Jewish world comparatively little is known', and with this, if we might change the 'comparatively little' to 'nothing important whatever', we could heartily agree. Moore goes on to point out that there is no way to ascertain the relation of earlier Alexandrian halacha[5] to contemporary Palestinian teaching, and concludes that 'on the whole . . . it seems probable that Alexandrian scholars of his (Philo's) day did not feel themselves bound by the authority of their Palestinian colleagues'. He should have admitted that the combined effort of many scholars has unearthed no evidence that the situation was different in Rome or Ephesus, or that Greek-speaking Jews were 'bound' by rabbinic traditions for centuries to come.

[1] Rabbinic Judaism was an extension and development of Pharisaic tradition and practice, and in time it became the prevailing 'interpretation' of Judaism and thus eventually 'orthodoxy'; this interpretation was then read back into the earlier periods as though Pharisaic/Rabbinic Judaism had always been 'orthodoxy'—whereas in fact the earlier situation was far more open; see further pp. 40–2.

[2] During the first Jewish Revolt, and more particularly after it, some of the rabbis withdrew to Yavneh (Jamnia), and there they began the reconstruction of Judaism without the Temple. For a summary of some of the main effects of Yavneh, see J. Neusner, *A Life of Rabban Yoḥanan ben Zakkai*; and W. D. Davies, *The Sermon on the Mount*.

[3] Goodenough, *Jewish Symbols in the Greco-Roman Period, passim*.

[4] *Judaism in the First Centuries of the Christian Era.*   [5] See pp. 43f.

That is, we must consider the rabbis as a group of Jewish scholars who aspired to much power in regulating the lives of Jews, and eventually got it, but who for centuries even in Palestine fought a hard battle for popular prestige and support. We know that the rabbis in Palestine were held in high esteem by Jews to the east in Babylonia, where the seat of rabbinic Judaism soon had to move, and where, when this was done, popular education under Rabbinic direction at last can be seen definitely to have created 'normative' Judaism, i.e. a way of life generally regarded by the Jews (in Babylonia) as standard. But nothing indicates that Jews in the Roman world, while they knew of the rabbis, occasionally contributed to their support, and respected them, ever came under their influence to any appreciable extent. I do not say that this in itself implies that the Jews in Rome or Ephesus were therefore all Philonic Jews . . . All we have learned thus far is that there is no evidence to show that the Jews of the imperial diaspora were led by rabbinic thinkers, or were 'normative' or 'halakic'[1] Jews.[2]

Goodenough was undoubtedly right to emphasise that rabbinic literature must not be regarded as the total content of Jewish thought. However, the gap he found between hellenised Judaism and Pharisaic/ Rabbinic Judaism is in some respects too wide and rigid. Basically, it implies that the two types of Judaism can be understood sufficiently for them to be defined, but in fact they represent such diverse phenomena, particularly in the early days, that this is virtually impossible. Hellenistic Judaism was not a coherent body of thought but a method of interpretation. That it *produced* coherent thought, as in the case of Philo, is certainly true, but the term 'hellenistic Judaism' should not, therefore, be confined to Alexandrian Judaism. The term can be applied to any form of Judaism which accepted, however partially, Hellenistic ideas and images as a legitimate method of interpretation— that is to say, as a legitimate weapon in the quest for a definition of what Judaism ought to become.[3] This was possible in any area of Judaism, Palestine as much as Alexandria, as Goodenough has rightly pointed out. But 'hellenism' was also possible within Pharisaic/Rabbinic Judaism itself (and *vice versa*), and it is that which makes the picture so confused.

Goodenough's purpose was to concentrate on non-rabbinic Judaism and on the archaeological evidence illuminating it.[4] As a result he

---

[1] See pp. 43 f.

[2] Goodenough, *Jewish Symbols*, I, 17; for a further summary of his views, see p. II n. I.

[3] See p. 8.   [4] See *Jewish Symbols*, I, 33.

failed to assess adequately the extent to which rabbinic Judaism changed its character as it evolved, particularly the extent to which it was itself 'hellenised'. Such an assessment is, of course, difficult to make since later generations did their best to suppress what they felt to be unworthy or unorthodox in earlier times. Perhaps the clearest example of this is in the case of mystical and magical Judaism. The later rabbis thought that mystical experience was dangerous, perhaps because it was too 'uncontrolled' and so outside the more straightforward and orderly study of Torah. But they were unable to eliminate mysticism altogether. Thus an attempt was made to prohibit the reading in synagogue of the visionary chapters of Ezekiel, which formed a basis for mystical contemplation and experience,[1] but the attempt failed. M.Meg. iv. 10 records: 'They may not use the chapter of the Chariot as a reading from the Prophets.'[2] But the passage significantly continues, 'But R. Judah allows it'; and his opinion prevailed.[3] The prohibition also occurs in M.Ḥag. ii. 1, but again it is qualified: 'The Chariot may not be interpreted[4] before one on his own unless he is one of the Wise[5] that has understanding out of his own knowledge.'

In rabbinic Judaism an attempt was made to bring mysticism under control, but the rabbis were unable to deny that some of the early rabbis had made *merkabah* mysticism a part of their religious experience. Those 'early rabbis' included even Joḥanan b. Zakkai,[6] the great leader in the reconstruction of Judaism after the fall of Jerusalem. Mysticism continued in Judaism throughout the rabbinic period,

---

[1] The visions were based on the early chapters of Ezekiel, especially chs. i and x, sometimes referred to as the 'chariot' (*merkabah*) chapters; for that reason the mysticism is usually known as *merkabah* mysticism, or *ma'aseh merkabah* (the 'work of the chariot').   [2] I.e. as *haftarah*—see p. 73.

[3] For an example of Ezek. i being used as *haftarah* see B.Meg. 31 a—but note that the opinion is not unanimous.

[4] √ *darash*.

[5] *Ḥakam*. In this way the Mishnah was able to account for the fact that some early rabbis (who are often referred to collectively as *ḥakamin*, the Wise) were known to have participated in *merkabah* mysticism.

[6] For a summary see J. Neusner, *A Life of Rabban Yoḥanan ben Zakkai*, pp. 97 f. The accounts of this early *merkabah* mysticism have important connections with the visions and conversion of Paul. There seems little doubt, from a close analysis of the material, that Saul had participated in *merkabah* mysticism as a part of his Jewish religious experience: see my forthcoming study of the visions of Joḥanan and of Paul.

despite the suspicion with which it was regarded by many of the rabbis, and as a result it left its mark on works which are predominantly rabbinic (like P.R.E.),[1] and also on works which represent a more eclectic Judaism (like III Enoch).[2] It also produced works in its own right, of which a typical and frequently referred to example is Sefer Yeṣirah (for the text see the bibliography under L. Goldschmidt, I. Kalisch and P. Mordell). A good summary of mysticism in Judaism has been made by G. Scholem, *Major Trends in Jewish Mysticism* and *Jewish Gnosticism, Merkabah Mysticism, and Talmudic Tradition.*

It was equally impossible to eradicate the more popular, 'magical', Judaism, which relied on spells, charms, incantations and other magical devices in an attempt to make the universe a little less hostile or perplexing.[3] Little of this appears in rabbinic literature, but amulets and charms have been recovered by archaeologists, and a few texts have survived. M. Margolioth recently reconstructed a second-century work, The Book of Secrets, from fragments in various libraries, and a report of his work gives an indication of the contents of a magical text: 'It is shocking, the Talmudic scholar said, to discover that in the second century there were Hebrews who gambled on horses, worshipped Aphrodite, prayed to Greek gods, coveted other men's wives, dodged bill collectors and concocted ways to become invisible.'[4] It is easy to see why the rabbis frowned on 'popular' Judaism, and did their best to make their own interpretation universal. But the fact remains that other interpretations of Judaism existed and flourished, particularly in the early days. It was the great achievement of Goodenough to draw together material which enabled this to be seen more clearly, and it must certainly be remembered, particularly in dealing with Judaism in the N.T. period, that the Pharisaic/rabbinic expression of Judaism was only a part of a far more complex whole.[5]

---

[1] See p. 85.

[2] III Enoch is a work of the very greatest importance. It is made up of different elements, in which *merkabah* mysticism, angelology and speculations about Metatron (see the notes on Gen. v. 24) are prominent. For text, translation and notes see H. Odeberg, *III Enoch.*

[3] It is worth remembering that the Theodosian Code shows how difficult it was for Christianity to eliminate similar pagan practices and beliefs.

[4] *The Times,* 30 Dec. 1964; for a more sober account of spells in relation to evil and demons, see C. H. Gordon, 'Leviathan, Symbol of Evil'.

[5] Glimpses of Jewish life can be recovered from the papyri. See the bibliography under V. Tcherikover.

4

CLASSICAL RABBINIC
LITERATURE

Halakah and Haggadah, Midrash and Mishnah

These basic words can be very broadly defined as follows: *halakah* and *haggadah* describe the content of rabbinic literature, *midrash* and *mishnah* describe the method and form of that literature. Putting it as simply as possible, *halakah* is regulative material (showing how written Torah should be applied in life), *haggadah* is illustrative material (illustrating what scripture means); *midrash* describes the way in which both sorts of material were collected together by being attached to the text of scripture, *mishnah* describes the way in which the material was collected together in its own right, without necessarily being attached to a text of scripture. Those general definitions can now be explained in greater detail.

It has been pointed out already that the foundations of Judaism were laid in Torah and in scripture in general. The vitality of Judaism has always depended on the effectiveness with which Torah can be made relevant, applicable and inspiring to any generation of people at a later time. The Pharisees emerged in the second century B.C. as a group (or better, 'groups', since there was no internal unanimity) determined to work out the full implications of Torah for every succeeding generation, and to maintain the total relevance of Torah to life. To them this meant unceasing study of Torah, searching constantly for its interpretation, particularly when it seemed to have lost its relevance in ever-changing situations. That did not mean altering or abandoning Torah; it meant believing that Torah was the revelation of God for all time, and that the solution to any problem lay within the text of Torah itself.[1] Obviously, situations repeatedly arose which could not

---

[1] This is the basic function of what came to be known as *pilpul*, lit. 'argument' or 'sound reasoning', the discovery of meaning, the reconciliation of conflicting texts.

possibly have been foreseen in the time of Moses, and the problem was to apply the past revelation in the present. The classic and basic methods of achieving relevance were *gezeroth* and *taqqanoth*. A *gezerah* was an enactment for a particular local or limited purpose, a temporary measure often annulled when the need for it disappeared. A *taqqanah* was a modification or reinterpretation.[1] But beyond those particular methods of defining relevance, a much wider and more general work of study and interpretation grew up, extending in time to cover not only actual situations as they arose, but also almost any situation that could be conceived. The interpretations were never arbitrary. They took into account the work of previous scholars (hence the importance of tradition in Pharisaic Judaism), and gradually in the Pharisaic period rules of exegesis and interpretation began to emerge.[2] Thus in Pharisaic Judaism a large body of traditional teaching and interpretation began to build up, which came to be known as oral Torah, or *torah shebe'al peh*. In time oral Torah came to exercise as much authority as written Torah; both, for example, were held to be the direct revelation of God on Mt Sinai.[3] Other groups in Judaism were also concerned to apply

---

[1] S. Zeitlin has written a series of articles on early *taqqanoth*: for references see 'The Takkanot of Rabban Johanan ben Zakkai'.

[2] See Appendix II.

[3] A good expression of this is given in Shem.R. xlvii. 7: 'How do we know that he (Moses on Mt Sinai) did not fall asleep or even feel sleepy? It is like a king who loved his treasurer (*tesauweran*, probably from *thesaurus*) and said to him: "Measure out for yourself golden dinars." In his joy he had no desire to eat or drink. He felt sleepy, but he said, "If I sleep, I will lose them (i.e. I will not be able to measure out so many)." So also Moses, measuring out Torah, forgot to eat and drink. He felt sleepy, but he said, "If I sleep I will lose (much), because God will only speak to me for forty days". The Holy One, blessed be he, said: "You are distressed, yet I swear to you that you will not lose any. On the first tables were only the ten commandments, but since you have been distressed, I will give you *halakoth*, *midrashim*, and *haggadoth*, as it is written, *Write thou these words* (Exod. xxxiv. 27) . . . " What the Holy One, blessed be he, meant was, "*write thou* Torah, Prophets and the Writings (the three divisions of the Hebrew canon), and they will be in writing, but *halakoth*, *midrash* and *haggadoth* and the *talmud* will be learned (lit. 'will be by mouth', '*al peh*)".' The same belief is frequently expressed. Sifre on Deut. xxxiii. 10, for example, interprets that verse, *They shall teach Jacob thy judgements, and Israel thy law*, as meaning that Torah was revealed, as a whole, but that Moses wrote only a part of it down, so that Torah existed from the first in two parts. That is why Torah is often referred to as a double-edged sword. Shir.R. on i. 2 (5) interprets Ps. cxlix. 6, *Let the high praises of God be in their mouth, and a two-edged sword in their hand*, in that way: 'As a

written Torah to life, but none of them developed an oral tradition of interpretation to anything like the same extent. The Sadducees, for example, were certainly determined to maintain Torah and to apply it scrupulously in the Temple, and there is evidence that when necessary they issued decisions on disputed points similar to *gezeroth*.[1] However, they regarded the accumulating oral tradition of the Pharisees as a threat to Torah itself, and this feeling became increasingly strong as oral Torah gained weight and authority among the Pharisees. Josephus saw this as one of the main differences between them: '. . . the Pharisees had passed on to the people certain regulations handed down by former generations and not recorded in the Law of Moses, for which reason they are rejected by the Sadducaean group, who hold that only those regulations should be considered valid which were written down (in scripture), and that those which had been handed down by the fathers need not be observed'.[2] Many of the famous disputes between the Sadducees and the Pharisees are simply symptoms of this basic disagreement about the methods and scope of exegesis.[3] But after the fall of Jerusalem and the destruction of the Temple it was the Pharisees who were able to survive and to rebuild Judaism, because almost by definition their faith was relevant in any situation; for years they had been studying Torah in such a way that it did not depend on a particular place. It could survive without the Temple. Pharisaism flowed directly into Rabbinic Judaism, and the rabbis (the scholars and teachers) were the direct successors of the Pharisees.

sword cuts on both sides, so Torah gives life in this world and the next . . . R. Judah said, "Torah was proclaimed first by one voice, then by many". R. Nehemiah said, "Two Torahs were given, one written and the other oral". See also Ps. Jon. on Gen. iii. 24, and B.Ber. 5a, quoted on p. 7 above. It must be remembered that this process of tracing back items of oral Torah is by no means entirely artificial, even though it came to be developed into an all-embracing theory. From the moment that Torah was accepted as binding, the work of interpretation, of applying Torah to diverse situations in life, was necessary. Thus the Pharisees inherited both a process and items of interpretation which were in existence long before the Pharisees emerged as a distinct group in Judaism.

[1] Thus a gloss on Meg. Taan. iv. 1 (on Meg. Taan. see p. 90) states that 'there was written and deposited (in the Temple) a book of decisions (*sefer gezeroth*) for the Sadducees'. The destruction of this book was celebrated by the Pharisees/Rabbis, hence the reference in Meg. Taan.

[2] *Ant.* xiii. 297.

[3] Some of the disputes are summarised in *J.E.*, art. 'Sadducees'. They are analysed in greater detail by L. Finkelstein, *The Pharisees*, but from the point of view of a sociological theory that seems at times over-complicated.

The basic purpose of Pharisaic and Rabbinic exegesis was to discover the meaning of the text of scripture. There were then two further tasks of particular importance: first, to show how the original revelation of Torah was to be applied in the constantly changing situations of life (as stated above), and secondly, to inspire and to encourage people to accept and follow those decisions as being the proper 'way before God'. These two objectives correspond roughly to the two main paths of exegesis, *halakah* and *haggadah* (or *'aggadah*, from the Aramaic): *halakah* defines the implications of Torah and how it should be applied; *haggadah* illustrates Torah, and encourages people to accept it as binding on themselves.[1]

Halakah is a technical word from the root *halak*, 'he walked', and it is the word used to refer to authoritative rabbinic decisions about disputed or uncertain rules of conduct, both for the individual and for the community. *Halakah* is the rule by which a man walks in the path of Torah; it is the interpretation of written Torah to show how it should be applied to life. Hence the word is also used as the name of those parts of rabbinic literature containing regulative material.

The plural *halakoth* means 'rules' or 'decisions', and it is also applied to collections of such decisions.

The purpose of *halakah* was to draw out and clarify the implications of written Torah. *Halakah* could be established in several different ways, of which the most usual were:

(i) Because it could be proved from scripture by the accepted rules of exegesis.[2]

(ii) Because it was traditional or customary.[3]

[1] One of the most important functions of *haggadah* was to fill in the 'gaps' of the narrative material, just as it was one of the functions of *halakah* to fill in the 'gaps' of the regulative material. Biblical narratives are usually told with great economy, and they are often introduced abruptly, without detailed reference to the context. In particular, *haggadah* supplied the 'psychological gaps', the motives, feelings and thoughts of characters involved. This was done, not arbitrarily, but with reference to all that was known about the character, and to the Bible at large.

[2] For the standardisation of exegetical rules, see Appendix II.

[3] That this was a way of establishing *halakah* can be seen from the fact that it appears in the Mishnah. See, for example, M.B.M. vii. 1: 'If a man hired labourers and bade them to work early or to work late, he has no right to compel them to do so where the custom is not to work early or not to work late; where the custom is to give them their food he should give it to them, and where the custom is to provide them with sweet stuff he should provide

(iii) Because it could be traced back to a recognised authority in the past, which is why so much rabbinic literature consists of quotations from earlier rabbis.

(iv) Because it was accepted by the majority. The principle is based on Exod. xxiii. 2,[1] translated as 'follow after the majority'. It was primarily used in actual legal cases, where the majority decision of the judges had to be accepted.[2] But occasionally it appears in a more general sense, as in the story in B.B.M. 59*b* where R. Eliezer tried to establish a *halakah* on a disputed matter of cleanness or uncleanness but the other rabbis refused to accept his arguments. He then brought various miracles to his support, but they remained unimpressed: 'He said, "If the *halakah* agrees with me, let this stream prove it". At once the stream began to flow backwards. They said "A stream of water is no proof at all" . . . At last (after other miracles) he said to them: "If the *halakah* agrees with me, let it be proved from heaven." At once a *bath qol*[3] proclaimed: "Why do you argue with R. Eliezer? In all matters

it. Everything should follow local use . . .' For further details see *J.E.*, 'Custom'. Note also the principle, when in Rome do as the Romans do; see the notes on p. 211. But it is important to remember that 'custom' did not always become *halakah* automatically.   [1] See, for example, B.San. 3*b*, B.Ḥull. 11*a*.

[2] Much *halakah*, of course, originated in actual legal proceedings, where the practical need to establish *halakoth* was urgent. See also p. 55.

[3] Lit. 'daughter of a voice', the divine voice from heaven. Inspiration was traditionally ascribed to *ruaḥ haQodesh*, the 'holy spirit', but later Judaism believed that the cessation of prophecy was a sign that the Holy Spirit had been withdrawn from Israel. ('Our rabbis have taught, "When Haggai, Zechariah and Malachi died, the Holy Spirit departed from Israel, but they still retained the *bath qol*". Once they were sitting in an upper room of Gurya's house in Jericho when a *bath qol* was given them from heaven which said, "There is one among you who deserves to have the *Shekina* (the divine presence; in the same story in T.Sot. xiii. 3, it is 'Holy Spirit') descend upon him, but this generation is unworthy of it". At once they all looked at Hillel the elder. When he died they mourned over him saying, "Alas, the just man, alas, the humble man, the disciple of Ezra". ' B.Sot. 48*b*; see also T.Sot. xiii. 2 and B.Yom. 9*b*, and cf. Matt. iii. 17, Mark i. 11, Luke iii. 22, John xii. 28.) In some ways the *bath qol* can be regarded as a lesser level of inspiration, but often it simply implies a belief that God remains in communication with men, but without the same obvious immediacy as in prophecy. The *bath qol*, the 'echo of his voice', was an attempt to reconcile an increasing sense of God's majesty and 'otherness' with a continuing belief in his concern for the affairs of men. Eventually the *bath qol* tended to replace the Holy Spirit, but the process by which this happened was gradual, and it always remained possible to speak of the Holy Spirit in connection with scripture, as the Targums bear witness. There are many passages in the Palestinian

the *halakah* agrees with him." But R. Joshua stood up and said, *It is not in heaven . . .*[1] What did he mean? R. Jeremiah said: "He meant that Torah had already been given on Mt Sinai, therefore we take no notice of a *bath qol*, since it was long ago written in Torah, *Follow after the majority*[2]." ' R. Eliezer was in a minority of one and therefore his *halakah*, or ruling, could not be accepted; cf. Pes.R. xxi. 5.

It follows from the above that although teaching of *halakah* was closely related to scripture, it could be recorded independently of it.[3] So we find that the collecting and building up of *halakah* developed along two lines, those of *midrash* and *mishnah*, the former closely connected with scripture, the latter less so. *Midrash* (from the root *darash*, 'search out' or 'look for') is the word used for 'biblical exposition'. The word *midrash* is applied to various aspects of biblical study of which the three most usual are:

(i) The actual work of studying the scripture, as in *beth haMidrash*, the house or school of study.[4]

Talmud speaking of the Holy Spirit which in the Babylonian Talmud have been changed to the *bath qol*. The constant shift of nomenclature makes it difficult to say what Jewish ideas of the Holy Spirit were at any particular time. It is easier to think of the ways in general in which God was believed to manifest himself in the world and make contact with the lives of men, of which three are particularly frequent, the Holy Spirit, the *Shekina* and the *bath qol*.

Generally speaking, the confusion and hesitation in the terminology seems to have arisen as follows: the majority of Jews in the period immediately preceding the fall of Jerusalem tended to confine the activities of the Holy Spirit to prophecy and inspiration (particularly, perhaps, the inspiration of scripture). The Holy Spirit, therefore, appears (frequently) in the Targums in those two activities. But various sectarians, including, for example, the early Christians and those who produced the sectarian documents found at Qumran, widened the scope of the Holy Spirit and related the work of the Holy Spirit directly and immediately to the life of their own community. This is particularly clear in the Christian application of Joel ii. 28–32 in Acts ii. 17–21. The sectarian use of 'the Holy Spirit' explains why the Pharisees/Rabbis increasingly restricted the functions of *ruah haQodesh*, and why they tended to substitute other terminology.   [1] Deut. xxx. 12.   [2] Exod. xxiii. 2.

[3] That is to say, *halakoth* depend on scripture, since they are decisions about how written Torah should be applied. But *halakoth* could be taught and recorded quite separately from scripture, because they were important in their own right.

[4] These 'houses of study' perhaps go back as far as the time of Ben Sira: *Turn unto me, ye unlearned, And lodge in my house of instruction* (Ecclus. li. 23). They are certainly well established in the Mishnah: 'Why are certain among the scriptures not read? Lest they make the House of Study of none effect (by distracting from the study of Torah).' (M.Shab. xvi. 1; see also M.Ber. iv. 2, M.Beẓ. iii. 5, M.Aboth v. 14, M.Yad. iv. 3, 4.)

(ii) The consequence of biblical study, a particular piece of exposition or interpretation.

(iii) Literary works of biblical exposition, which are known (in the plural) as Midrashim.

Midrash, therefore, is a term which applies to the exegesis and interpretation of scripture *in general*. *Midrash* becomes a *vehicle* of *halakah* when the exegesis of scripture produces a regulative decision or ruling. This frequently happens in exegesis of the Pentateuch, particularly of those parts which contain commandments or laws, since at least a part of the meaning will be the way in which those laws or commandments ought to be applied in life. It is possible to describe *midrash* as a vehicle of *halakah* because a *midrash* (an interpretation) can be halakic, and Midrashim (works of exegesis) can contain *halakah*. Eventually Midrashim were produced which are almost entirely halakic, for example Sifra and Sifre,[1] and they are known as halakic Midrashim.[2] They teach *halakah* in connection with the passage from the Pentateuch on which the *halakah* is based or from which it can be derived; thus Sifra on Lev. xix. 1 f. reads: '*And the Lord spake unto Moses, saying, Speak unto all the congregation of the children of Israel, and say unto them, Ye shall be holy: for I the Lord your God am holy.*' Why was this section of Torah to be said before all the congregation? Because most of the important commandments of Torah are to be found in it.' The teaching is attached to the text of scripture, which is quoted.

The second way in which *halakah* was collected and preserved was in Mishnah. The word *mishnah* is derived from *shanah*, 'he repeated', hence 'repetition' or 'learning by repetition'. From that it came to be applied to what is learnt, either to a particular oral Law, in which case it is almost equal to *halakah*, or else to the whole tradition of oral Law taken together. Hence it is the name applied to the recognised authoritative collection of *halakoth*, the Mishnah. As might be expected, the collections of oral Law became vast. Written Torah is often extremely brief and general, and the attempt to make it cover every conceivable situation led to an enormous number of *halakoth*. M.Ḥag. i. 8 says: 'The *halakoth* about the Sabbath Festal-offerings and Sacrilege are as

[1] See pp. 69–72.
[2] Technically they should be referred to as Midrash Torah in which *halakah* occurs.

mountains hanging by a hair, for (teaching of) scripture (thereon) is scanty but the *halakoth* (decisions about how they should be observed) many.' For a long time oral Law was specifically oral and had to be learned by heart, but eventually, by about the second century A.D. and perhaps earlier, various attempts were made to organise and codify *halakoth*, and these attempts culminated in the present Mishnah.

The Mishnah, therefore, is a collection of *halakoth* assembled one after another, which only rarely quotes texts of scripture. Whereas Midrash is concerned with the exegesis of scripture in general (and may therefore include *halakoth*), Mishnah is almost exclusively concerned with the preservation and transmission of *halakoth* and includes little else. Mishnah and Midrash were alternative ways of preserving *halakoth* and there seems to have been an occasional dispute about which was the better method. B.Qid. 49a asks: 'What is Mishnah? R. Meir said, "*Halakoth*" (i.e. decisions collected together and not attached to a text of scripture). R. Judah said "Midrash" (i.e. decisions related to the text from which they were derived).' The form of the Mishnah shows that although *halakah* was derived from scripture it could be stated and taught quite independently of it: the Mishnah very rarely quotes the scriptural passages on which a *halakah* depends or from which it was derived; it more often quotes the rabbi with whom the decision originated. Thus in contrast to the halakic Midrashim, which quote the texts of scripture on which the *halakoth* depend, Mishnah records *halakah* in its own right, as the body of tradition to be 'repeated' and thus learned.[1] The inevitable outcome of this was that oral Torah came to be regarded almost as highly as written Torah, and eventually, as was said above, it was believed that both were revealed to Moses on Mount Sinai.[2]

[1] Texts of scripture are, of course, quoted in the Mishnah, and there are traces of Midrash Torah—that is to say, some sections of the Mishnah seem to have originated as commentaries on scripture; thus M.M.Sh. v. 10–14 on Deut. xxvi. 13–15; M.Yeb. xii. 6 on Deut. xii. 6; M.Sot. viii. 1–6 on Deut. xx. 2–9; ix. 1–6 on Deut. xxi. 1 ff.; M.San. ii. 4–5 on Deut. xvii. 15–19. But in general the Mishnah quotes *halakoth* without specific reference to the texts from which they were derived, or with which they might have been supported.

[2] On the distinction between Midrash and Mishnah in preserving *halakah* see J. Z. Lauterbach, *Rabbinic Essays*, 'Midrash and Mishnah' (which first appeared in *J.Q.R.* 1915), pp. 163–256: 'Midrash . . . represents the *Halakah* as an interpretation and exposition of the Torah . . . The other form, the Mishnah, represents the *Halakah* as an independent work, giving its dicta as

Halakah, then, gathers up rabbinic decisions about the ways in which written Torah should be applied in life. It remained equally important to inspire and encourage individuals to accept and follow those decisions. That was largely the function of *haggadah*.

Haggadah (from *higgid* (*nagad*) 'announce, tell') means 'what scripture tells' in addition to its obvious meaning. Theoretically, therefore, the word could be applied to all exegesis of scripture, including halakic (and indeed the term *haggadah* originally did include *halakah*),[1] but almost invariably it is the word used to describe non-halakic interpretation. Haggadic interpretation often stays close to the text, searching out every possible meaning of it, but it also includes a great deal of more independent material, parables, proverbs, legends, miracle-stories, historical anecdotes, stories from the lives of the rabbis—anything, in fact, which would be likely to instruct or encourage the seeker after God.[2] It follows that *haggadah* not only interprets scripture but also illustrates it, adding details and stories which clarify the meaning of scripture and its application in the lives of others. It will be clear that Ps. Jon. on Genesis usually records haggadic interpretation, but many rabbinic works, particularly the Talmuds, combine both *halakah* and *haggadah* together.

The Transmission of Oral Torah

As was said briefly in the last section, the amount of material, both halakic and haggadic, increased rapidly. The work of interpretation was unceasing, and the interpretations of previous generations were

such without any scriptural proof, and teaching them independently of and not connected with the words of the written law' (pp. 163 f.). See also D. Hoffmann, *Die erste Mishna und die Controversen der Tannaim.*

[1] For a summary of this point see R. Loewe, 'The "Plain" Meaning of Scripture . . .', p. 150: 'Although rabbinic evidence is predominantly later than Philo, the rabbinic scheme of two fundamental categories, *halakah* and *'aggada*, is both broad enough and of sufficiently marked dominance to justify us in carrying it back with some confidence to Philonic times . . . '*Aggada*, *haggadah*, or at the very least its participial counterpart *maggid*, originally meant as a dialectic term nothing more than *exegesis*, and indeed included halakhic as well as aggadic exegesis.'

[2] For a brief description of the nature and contents of *haggadah*, see the summary of J. H. Hertz, quoted on p. 65. L. Zunz put it briefly when he said that the purpose of *haggadah* was to 'bring heaven closer to men and men closer to heaven' (*Die Gottesdienstlichen Vorträge . . .*, 2nd edn. p. 362).

carefully preserved and handed on. The material, despite its ever-increasing quantity, was transmitted by word of mouth and by memorisation, not by written documents. There were many reasons for this: books were not easy to produce or circulate; memorisation was, in any case, the basis of education in the Hellenistic world; the danger to books was very great, since libraries could easily be destroyed in war; and, perhaps even more important, a tradition transmitted orally could not be alienated by non-Jews, as the scriptures (from the Jewish point of view) were alienated by the Christians.[1]

Memorising the tradition formed the basis of education. The elementary school was known as the *bet sefer*, where knowledge of written Torah was acquired. The advanced school was *bet haMidrash*, where knowledge of traditional interpretation began. A basic rule was, 'A man must speak in the words of[2] his master'.[3] In Aboth ii. 8 Rn. Johanan praised R. Eliezer: 'R. Eliezer ben Hyrcanus is a caulked cistern which does not lose a drop.' The basic method was repetition, even if the pupil did not understand what he was repeating: 'A man should go on reciting even though he forgets, and even though he does not understand what he is saying.'[4] Those who successfully learned the tradition were known as *shonim* or *tannaim*, 'repeaters' or 'transmitters' of the tradition.[5] B.Qid. 49b summarised a necessary standard: 'If a man says to a betrothed woman, "I am a *tanna*", he must have learned Torah, Sifra, Sifre and Tosefta.'[6] The *tanna* is described

---

[1] The oral tradition was the 'mystery', the secret heart of Judaism. See the passage from Pes. R. quoted on pp. 12 f., and cf. also Bem. R. xiv. 10, Tanh.B. i. 58, Pes. R. 7b.

[2] Lit. 'in the tongue of'.

[3] See, for example, M.Eduy. i. 3, B.Shab. 15a, B.Bek. 5a, B.Ber. 47a, B.Erub. 53a.   [4] B.A.Z. 19a.

[5] The word '*tannaim*' is slightly confusing, because it is also applied to the first generations of rabbis as a collective name, and that is its most common use. The rabbis before (roughly) 220 are known as the Tannaim, but after that date, when the Mishnah had been published, the rabbis are known as the Amoraim (because after that date they become commentators on the Mishnah). This means, as S. K. Mirsky has pointed out, that the word *tannaim* has two senses, the historical and the functional. In the historical sense it is applied to those scholars who lived before the publication of the Mishnah and to that period in general; in the functional sense it is applied to the skill and to the action of reciting oral material, and to the professional 'reciter'. In some cases a *tanna* in the latter sense also became a *tanna* in the former, but there remained a distinct group of professional 'reciters'.

[6] On these see pp. 61, 69–72.

with great aptness in B. Meg. 28*b*: 'There was once a man who used to repeat *halakoth*, Sifra, Sifre and Tosefta. When he died they came to R. Naḥman and said, "Master, will you give the funeral address?" He said, ". . . Alas! a basket full of books has been lost". ' The purpose of the *tanna* was to be exactly that, a living library, a basket full of books.

It is important to remember that although memorisation of the tradition was vital, it was not an end in itself. It was simply the foundation on which the continuing work of interpretation was based. The *tanna*, having learned the tradition, provided it as a basis for fuller interpretation, either to himself or to others.[1] The learning of Mishnah was not considered meritorious in itself. It was regarded as a preliminary which made more advanced work possible,[2] and it was also for purposes in life of greater importance—'to learn in order to teach, and to learn in order to practise' (Aboth vi. 6).

The task of learning the tradition was not easy. The amount of material involved was enormous, and it was increasing all the time. Various methods were devised to help the student, some of which may be summarised here:

(i) The material was not repeated in an ordinary tone of voice; it was intoned or chanted. B.Meg. 32*a* records: 'R. Shefetiah said in Rn. Johanan's name: "If a man reads scripture without melody or repeats Mishnah without a chant, it is of him that scripture says, *Moreover also I gave them statutes that were not good*, . . .[3] "'[4]

(ii) Material was grouped in ways that would make it easier to memorise. Thus material of similar content would be learned together; or it might be material of different content but having some feature in common (material, for example, coming from the same authority, or introduced by the same formula). Again, *halakoth* having little or nothing in common with each other might be attached to a text of scripture; the text would then act as a kind of trigger to release the *halakoth*. According to T.San. xi. 5, Eliezer ben Hyrcanus attached 300 *halakoth* to Exod. xxiii. 17.

[1] Thus the successful *tanna* was not necessarily an exegete as well (as is implied in the fact that the *tanna* did not necessarily understand what he had learned), but of course many men combined both functions, and this is why the first generations of rabbis can be referred to as the Tannaim.

[2] See, for example, B.Taan. 7*b*–8*a*, B.Meg. 26*b*, B.Sot. 22*a*, B.B.M. 33*a*, B.B.B. 145*b*, B.San. 100*b*.

[3] Ezek. xx. 25.　　　　　　　　　　[4] Cf. also B.San. 99*b*.

(iii) Various mnemonic techniques were devised, known later as *simanim* or 'signs'. These might be either by initial letters or numerically. Thus, for example, M.Men. xi. 4 says: 'The two loaves (for the Wave-offering) were seven (handbreadths) long and four wide and four fingers thick. The Shewbread (loaves) were ten (handbreadths) long and five wide and their horns were seven fingers thick. R. Judah said, "To prevent you making a mistake, zadad yahaz".'[1]

(iv) The material was compressed as much as possible, not by eliminating parts of it, but by constantly reducing it to its shortest possible form. An ideal way of teaching was *derek qezarah*, the shortest way possible.[2] A particular aspect of that principle was the constant search for *kelal*, a kind of total statement which would embrace more detailed particulars. The most famous example is Hillel's summary of Torah in the negative form of the Golden Rule: ' "Whatever you would not have people do to you, do not do to them." That is the whole Torah, the rest is commentary upon it.'[3] There are many other examples: according to Sifra on Lev. xix. 18, R. Aqiba called that verse, 'the great *kelal* in Torah'; R. Simeon b. Azzai said that the great *kelal* was Gen. v. 1, man created in the image of God. But more frequently a *kelal* is used in the Mishnah to summarise a series of *halakoth*.[4] That would obviously be a great help in memorising material, since a *kelal*, like a text of scripture, would act as a trigger to release more detailed elements.

(v) A more obvious assistance to study was discipline, though that was only applied when necessary. The underlying feeling was that Torah was worth studying for its own sake, but sometimes encouragement was needed. Thus according to B.B.B. 21a, 'Rab said to R. Samuel b. Shilath: "Do not take pupils before they are six years old. After that age you can take them and stuff them with Torah like an ox . . . When you punish a pupil, strike him only with the latchet of a shoe." ' Verbal encouragement was preferred, though it often contained the threat of ultimate sanctions: in Aboth iii. 9, R. Meir is recorded as saying: 'Everyone who forgets a single word

---

[1] The numerical values of the letters are 7, 4, 4, 10, 5, 7.
[2] B.Pes. 3b, B.Ḥull 63b.
[3] B.Shab. 31a.
[4] See, for example, M.Peah i. 4, M.Sheb. vii. 1 and 2, M.Maas. i. 1, M.Shab. vii. 1.

from his *mishnah*, scripture reckons it to him as though he had lost his soul.'[1]

(vi) The use of written notes. Despite the absolute insistence that the oral tradition must be passed on by word of mouth and never in writing,[2] mention is occasionally made of written notes, and they were evidently designed to help in revision.[3] But the ideal still remained a living 'basket of books'.

In these ways the oral tradition was passed on from one generation to another. The sheer quantity of the material to be learned demanded some sort of artificiality, as in (ii), (iii), and (iv) above. Yet it is precisely those methods of grouping diverse material together which make rabbinic literature so difficult at first sight for the general reader. The works of rabbinic literature represent points at which the oral tradition (or parts of the oral tradition) have been committed to writing, and inevitably, therefore, they reflect the way in which the material was organised for the purposes of memorisation. That is why in rabbinic works it is often difficult to follow the sequence of thought, particularly in translation, and why they give the impression of being anthologies of the sayings of the rabbis, one after another, without particular reference to the date at which any of them lived.[4] The problem of dating individual items of material in rabbinic works is notoriously difficult: any work, even the latest, may be drawing on material from the oral tradition, which in origin may go back to a period before the fall of Jerusalem. It is not enough simply to go by the name of the

---

[1] This was evidently thought to be too severe, because the Mishnah continues: 'Could this be the case if his study (lit. "his *mishnah*") was too difficult for him? In fact the teaching goes on, *And lest they depart from thy heart all the days of thy life* (Deut. iv. 9, continuing the quotation on which the original dictum was based). Thus he does not harm his soul unless he deliberately puts the words away from his heart.'

[2] 'You shall not transmit written sayings orally: you shall not transmit oral sayings in writing.' B.Gitt. 60b.

[3] See J.Maas. ii. 4, J.Kil. i. 1, B.Shab. 6b, 89a, 96b, 156a, B.B.M. 92a. B.Men. 70a, B.Ḥull 60b.

[4] It must also be remembered that material continued to be memorised and transmitted which had in fact been superseded. Thus E. Wiesenberg has put it briefly: 'The *Halakah* is intrinsically opposed to being systematised ... There is hardly any doubt that this nature of the *Halakah* is mainly due to its gradual growth in the course of centuries. Later formulations render earlier formulations antiquated or entirely superfluous. Yet, by reason of the veneration of tradition, which is characteristic of the Halakist, the earlier formulations are retained.' ('Observations on Method ...', p. 35.)

rabbi who is cited as the authority for the particular item in question, even if he can be identified (which is not always the case): he may be the first to have made the interpretation, or he may simply be a link in the train of transmission, the beginnings of which have been lost; again, the interpretation may have changed during the course of its transmission, or it may not. As with the Targums, much work needs to be done on the history of the transmission of individual items. The golden rule in using rabbinic evidence is not to rely on a single mention but wherever possible to see how that item appears in other rabbinic sources. That creates a further problem for the reader who does not know the relevant languages, since comparatively few rabbinic works have been translated into English, a defect which ought to be remedied as soon as possible. What needs to be remembered is that the date of a particular item does not depend on the date of the work in which it is found.[1]

There is no doubt that works like the Mishnah or the Talmuds seem very confused and difficult to follow at first sight, but if it is borne in mind that they reflect the ways in which the material of the oral tradition was organised for the purposes of memorisation, then some at least of the confusion will dissolve, and the great riches contained in these works will become more accessible.

Rabbinic Literature[2]

I. MISHNAH, TOSEFTA AND THE TALMUDS. The general nature of the Mishnah has emerged in the preceding sections. It is a written recension of the oral tradition, consisting almost entirely of *halakoth*.[3] In view of the emphatic insistence that oral Torah should be transmitted by memory and not in writing, it may seem strange that a written Mishnah should have emerged at all, but in fact, even when a written Mishnah was compiled and was accepted as the authoritative basis of further study (see further, p. 64), it did not eliminate the rule of memorisation, nor was it intended to do so. Even when the present Mishnah was

---

[1] Most dating is done by the 'generation' in which a rabbi lived. Thus a rabbi will be referred to as, 'first generation of the Tannaim' or 'second generation of the Amoraim'. Obviously, these references tend to express relationship rather than exact dating, and it is only rarely that precise dates can be given. For a table of different systems, see Appendix VI.

[2] This section gives an account of the main works only.

[3] The main exception to that is the tractate Pirqe Aboth; see the introduction to Aboth de Rabbi Nathan, p. 87.

officially known and recognised, it continued to be learned by heart. Efforts to organise Mishnaic material, culminating in written Mishnah, seem to have been a kind of 'stocktaking', an attempt to bring the rapidly increasing oral traditions into some sort of order and control. The phrase 'the oral tradition' has been used frequently already, but it must be remembered that it was composed of diverse and varied elements. What the oral tradition comprised was not necessarily the same for one rabbi as it was for another, particularly if one of them lived in Palestine and the other lived in Babylon. Geographical separation was not the only reason for differences. There were differences between rabbis in close contact with each other, since the interpretation of scripture would not necessarily produce uniform results. Furthermore, there were important disputes over the methods legitimate and appropriate for the exegesis of scripture. The most famous of these rivalries is that between R. Aqiba and R. Ishmael (and between their respective 'schools' after them). Broadly speaking, the difference between them was that R. Aqiba was prepared to allow new and elaborate exegetical methods in order to extract even further meaning from the text of scripture, whereas R. Ishmael resisted such innovations, and kept to the traditional methods as they had been developed up to his time.

The causes for this dispute lie far back in the period before the fall of Jerusalem, and it is worth summarising the way in which it developed, since it helps to fill in some of the background of rabbinic Judaism. From the time of Ezra onwards, the work of interpreting scripture lay in the hands of the *Soferim* (usually translated 'Scribes', but perhaps more accurately 'those concerned with books and writing'). They were responsible not only for the correct writing of the text but also for its interpretation, although their interpretations tended to be limited and conservative; their basic principle was that the text of scripture is 'sufficient unto itself'. A good picture of the early scribe is given in Ecclus. xxxviii. 24 ff. They kept as close to the text of scripture as they could, only altering it or interpreting it when it was absolutely necessary. They also gave advice on how Torah should be applied to life, and those decisions, known as *dibre soferim* (the words of the Scribes), were recognised as authoritative, particularly in Courts of Law. Later on, the rabbis quoted *dibre soferim* as fundamental authorities in halakic disputes or uncertainties. But as time went by the study of scripture spread beyond the professional group of the

Scribes, and ordinary people began to study the text and meaning of scripture as well. At the same time (the second century B.C.) the Law Courts began to find that relying on the Scribes to define the Law was a slow process, and they started to interpret the Law in their own right. In both those ways, the Pharisees rose to prominence and replaced the Scribes in their function of interpreting Law and establishing *halakah*. The Pharisees, usually referred to in this period as the *Ḥakamim* ('the Wise' or 'the Sages'), took over from the Scribes the task of establishing *halakah*, and the Scribes, much reduced in status, were increasingly limited to the profession of writing, and to ensuring the correct transmission of the text of scripture. So effectively did the Pharisees replace the Scribes that they began to be called '*soferim*' themselves in their function of making authoritative decisions (as in T.Teb.Yom. ii. 14). All this helps to explain why *halakoth* in Mishnah were collected and taught without quotation of the text and exegesis on which they depend. The way in which responsibility for *halakoth* shifted from the Scribes to the Pharisees meant that although *halakoth* were always based on scripture, the actual scriptural proof did not need to be quoted on every occasion. *Halakah* was something in its own right. The great achievement of R. Aqiba was that he succeeded in relinking *halakoth* with scripture, but to do that he had to have much greater subtlety in exegesis (since the ways in which *halakoth* might once have been linked to scripture were either forgotten or obscure; *halakoth* had given birth to more *halakoth*, and the chain was almost impossible to unravel). R. Ishmael saw the need to link *halakoth* to scripture, but he resisted the artificiality of new and exotic methods of exegesis, which would certainly have simplified the task, but only by inventing previously unknown 'rules' of exegesis. Hence with R. Ishmael's name there is associated a conservative 'canon' of exegetical rules, the 13 Rules of R. Ishmael (see Appendix II). R. Aqiba's view prevailed and the new ways of interpreting scripture came to be accepted, thus opening the way to even more extensive interpretations. But the exegesis produced by R. Ishmael and his school did not entirely disappear. It has survived in various rabbinic works, particularly in the Mekilta.[1]

---

[1] See p. 70. On the extremely complicated problem of the relationship of the Scribes to the Pharisees, see E. E. Urbach, 'The Derasha as a Basis of the Halakah and the Problem of the Soferim'. On Aqiba and Ishmael see S. K. Mirsky, 'The Schools...', in *Essays Presented to I. Brodie* (ed. H. J. Zimmels), London, 1967, pp. 291–9.

There was thus no artificial or monolithic unity among the rabbis. There were important differences and disputes between them. Nevertheless, the distinctions should not be pressed too far. There was also considerable and deliberate interchange between the rabbis,[1] and the written Mishnahs (*mishnayoth*) probably emerged to help that process of control and consolidation.

The history of the process by which the Mishnah reached its present form is complex, and the details are far from being established.[2] The name traditionally associated with the formation of the Mishnah is that of R. Judah haNasi,[3] known also as Rabbi as a tribute to his greatness.[4] He was born, according to tradition, in A.D. 135, the year in which his great predecessor, R. Aqiba, was put to death by the

[1] In the case of the contacts between Palestine and Babylonia see J. Neusner, *History . . .*, vol. I.

[2] For an example of the complexity of the work involved, see P. R. Weiss, *Mishnah Horayoth*; A. Goldberg, *The Mishnah Treatise Oholoth*; and the works of B. de Vries (see the bibliography).

[3] The title haNasi means 'the prince'. It is a title with a complicated history. Post-exilic uses are derived from Ezek. xl–xlviii, a 'blueprint' for the Temple after the exile. In those chapters the king, who had held such a vital position in the pre-exilic state, was replaced by *haNasi*; *haNasi* was to be a religious leader in a theocratic community, and the title was thus a religious, not a secular one. When the Hasmonaeans took over the high-priesthood, it seemed as though authority in religious matters was passing back into secular (i.e. religiously unqualified) hands. Therefore the *Bet Din*, the Sanhedrin, emerged to exercise religious authority. The head of the Sanhedrin would most naturally have been known as *Rosh Bet Din*, head of the *Bet Din*, just as the deputy head was actually called *Ab Bet Din*, father of the *Bet Din*. But the name given to the head of the Sanhedrin was in fact haNasi, and that is because he was seen as the direct successor of the functionary in Ezekiel. Aboth gives a 'succession list' from Moses onward, and for the period in question lists two men in each generation (for five generations in succession). Those are the five *zugoth* or 'pairs', and traditionally (M.Ḥag. ii. 2) they were *haNasi* and *Ab Bet Din* in their time. Gamaliel I, living in the first half of the first century A.D., began to concentrate all authority in himself and he was known by a new title, *Rabban*, our master. After the fall of Jerusalem, the title Rabbi (in Babylon Rab) was given to all qualified scholars, and the title *haNasi* became an honorific. (This does not mean that the title rabbi did not exist earlier, but that it could not have had this technical sense.) See S. Zeitlin, 'The Titles High Priest and the Nasi of the Sandhedrin'. The term *nasi* also occurs in other contexts (as, for example, in the title *nesi Israel* on coins from the period of the Bar-Kokeba revolt), but this is not surprising, since the term is basically a biblical one and could, therefore, be used differently by different people.

[4] He is also referred to as Rabbenu haQadosh, our holy teacher.

Romans for his part in the Bar-Kokeba revolt.[1] Although the Mishnah itself makes no direct reference to its own composition or to Rabbi's part in it, its redactor and compiler was traditionally recognised to be Rabbi. But at the same time there is little doubt that previous attempts had been made to organise the Mishnah, and that Rabbi made use of them. This is argued principally on three grounds: (i) references to earlier Mishnahs; (ii) the probability that some tractates, or parts of tractates, existed already, and were incorporated by Rabbi *en bloc*; (iii) the nature of Mishnaic material.

(i) The Mishnah includes references to earlier mishnahs. On a particular ruling M.San. iii. 4 records: 'R. Jose said, "That was the mishnah of R. Aqiba, but the first mishnah included . . .".'[2] What is uncertain is whether 'mishnah' refers to an organised collection or to the oral tradition as such. There undoubtedly seems to be a certain formality in the way in which R. Aqiba's teaching was recognised. T.Zab. i. 5 says: 'When R. Aqiba set in order *halakoth* for his pupils . . .'; R. Johanan ben Nappaha, who died in A.D. 279, said: 'Any anonymous teaching in Mishnah comes from R. Meir, in Tosefta from R. Nehemiah, in Sifra from R. Judah, in Sifre from R. Simeon, and all of them derive from R. Aqiba'; J.Shek. v says: 'R. Aqiba established *midrash*, *halakoth* and *haggadoth*.' It seems probable, therefore, that R. Aqiba and his pupil R. Meir both made attempts to organise and co-ordinate material in the oral tradition, and no doubt other teachers did the same before them.[3] What is completely uncertain is when these organisations of material began to be written down. It is quite possible that the first compilations (including that of Rabbi) were made on an oral basis, and only subsequently written down. But as was said above, commitment to writing did not eliminate the need for learning by heart, and there is no reason why the greater part of the present Mishnah should not have been written down in the time of Rabbi.

(ii) The probability that Rabbi incorporated whole blocks of material

[1] Ber. R. lviii. 2. On R. Aqiba's part in the formation of the Mishnah, see (i) on this page.

[2] Cf. T.M. Sh. ii. 1. Other references to 'the first mishnah' include M. Ket. v. 3, M.Naz. vi. 1, M.Gitt. v. 6, M.Eduy. vii. 2.

[3] B.Men. 18*a* refers to Eliezer b. Hyrcanus, and B.Yeb. 49*b* to R. Eliezer b. Jacob, both of the generation of R. Aqiba. It must also be remembered that there were at this time rival schools of exegesis, which would have had an effect on the organisation of oral tradition; see the introduction to the Mekilta, p. 69.

(not necessarily, but possibly, in written form) is seen in the fact that individual tractates were apparently known before his time. At the end of the tractate Kelim a comment on the tractate has been attached as a summary: 'R. Jose said: "You are blessed, Kelim, because you began with uncleanness and ended with cleanness." '[1] That implies that R. Jose knew Kelim in a form which at least began and ended as it does now; and R. Jose was a contemporary of R. Meir. B.Hor. 13b records an occasion when R. Meir and R. Nathan tried to humiliate R. Simeon b. Gamaliel[2] by making him expound the tractate Uqzin, with which he was not familiar. He learned the tractate overnight and was able to expound it. Several tractates are attributed to early authorities: part of Middoth[3] is attributed in B.Yoma 16a to R. Eliezer b. Jacob, who was alive while the Temple was still standing; Tamid[4] and Yoma[5] are attributed in B.Yoma 14b to Simeon of Mizpah, who was a contemporary of Gamaliel I; Qinnim is associated with R. Joshua b. Hananiah.[6] It is of interest that B.Ned. 41a records a story which says that Rabbi learned thirteen 'ways of *halakoth*' (*appey hilkatha*), though it is difficult to know exactly what the words *appey hilkatha* imply: 'Rabbi studied his teaching in thirteen different ways, and he then taught R. Hiyya seven of them. It happened that Rabbi fell ill (and forgot what he had learned), so R. Hiyya reminded him of the seven, but the other six were lost. But there was a certain fuller who had overheard Rabbi when he was learning them, so R. Hiyya went to him and learned them from him, and then went and repeated them to Rabbi. When Rabbi met the fuller, he said, "You have made both R. Hiyya and myself".'

(iii) Careful analysis of material in the Mishnah reveals something of the process by which the Mishnah reached its present form. B. de Vries, in a series of articles comparing material in different rabbinic sources,[7] has tried to show that Rabbi worked from an older collection, whose order he changed and rearranged as he incorporated other

---

[1] M.Kelim xxx. 4. Kelim i. 1 lists various things that convey uncleanness, and Kelim xxx. 4 ends, 'A glass funnel continues always clean'.

[2] Gamaliel II.

[3] Lit. 'measurements'; the tractate is a description of the Temple.

[4] On the daily offerings. It is often held to be the oldest tractate in the Mishnah.

[5] On the Day of Atonement.

[6] B.Zeb. 67b, 68a.

[7] See the bibliography.

source material. Traces of the order and language of an earlier collection can still be seen in the Tosefta.[1] He suggested that stylistic considerations (as, for example, the avoidance of tautology) prompted Rabbi to make many of the changes.

In view of these traces of formally organised material predating the present recension of the Mishnah, it has been held that the first attempts to form a 'Mishnah' may well have been a part of the activities of the rabbis at Yavneh. In that case the first moves towards the formation of the present Mishnah would have been a part of the effort to consolidate Judaism after the fall of Jerusalem. This would mean that much mishnaic material would go back to a period before that event. L. A. Rosenthal[2] in fact argued that the earliest Mishnah was a summary of arguments against the Sadducees. References to the so-called 'first Mishnah' (see p. 57) are almost always on cultic or ceremonial matters, or on questions to do with public life. It is by no means out of the question that the earliest collections of mishnaic material were made before the fall of Jerusalem. It is impossible to be precise because of the difficulty of deciding at exactly what point a highly coherent oral tradition has actually been committed to writing. What seems probable is that this had begun to happen before the time of R. Judah.

If, then, it is true that Rabbi's recension was part of a process in the compilation of Mishnah, is it possible to see what his own particular intentions were? Broadly speaking, two answers have been given to that question: first, that he was trying to produce an official and accepted 'canon' of *halakoth*; or second, that he was trying to make a collection of *halakoth*, getting in as much as he could find from different sources and from rival schools of exegesis.[3] There is no doubt

---

[1] See pp. 61–4.   [2] *Über den Zusammenhang...*, §§32–56.

[3] This is, for example, the view of H. Albeck in *Mabo laMishnah*, though he argued that R. Judah's method was not simply random. He followed various principles in assembling the material—in particular, by topic and by association—but otherwise he embodied the material as he found it. The fact that he followed different principles would account for the doublets and inconsistencies in the Mishnah as we now have it. Albeck held further that R. Judah's concern to record faithfully what he found accounts for the uneven character of the Mishnah. The attempt to explain and interpret the material, and to reconcile the inconsistencies, would then have been a quite separate activity, a part of his teaching or lectures (*talmud*) to his students. Thus R. Judah was not only the compiler of Mishnaic material; he was also the foundation of Talmud (commentary on the Mishnah). Against this B. de Vries argued: 'Why should R. Judah the Prince have abandoned his predecessors' method and have

that the Amoraim[1] thought that Rabbi had intended to make a definitive 'canon' of *halakoth*, but, as A. Goldberg has pointed out, that is because they accepted the Mishnah as canonical![2] It does not prove anything about Rabbi's own original intentions. Goldberg took the view that Rabbi was not simply anthologising, but that he collected and grouped the material for instructional purposes. He illustrated his argument from four important principles underlying the organisation of the material: comprehensiveness in giving varying views;[3] simplicity;[4] the anonymous mishnah is carefully selected;[5] topics are selected first, and the material is then grouped around it.[6]

It seems clear, therefore, that the Mishnah was already in the process of formation before the time of Rabbi, but that he gave the process a decisive shape and form.[7] It would be wrong to say that he gave it a *final* form, because it is clear that the Mishnah continued to change and develop after his time. That is particularly clear at the end of the tractates where opinions are occasionally recorded of rabbis who lived later than Rabbi.[8] Yet in fact the Mishnah soon achieved a recognised form and position, and it became the basis and foundation of subsequent study. That study eventually issued in the Talmuds which were built and shaped around the Mishnah, and which, in a sense, are commentaries upon it.

The material in the Mishnah is grouped in six main Orders, known as *sedarim*. The *sedarim* are Zeraim ('Seeds'), Moed ('Set Feasts'), Nashim ('Women'), Neziqin ('Damages'), Qodashim ('Holy Things'),

refrained from tampering with either form or content of existent *Halakoth*? . . . If it can be demonstrated that the *Tannaim* in general did, indeed, give juridical rulings, make alterations, and establish and correct the text of *mishnahs* known to them, there are no grounds for maintaining that R. Judah did not follow suit, even though he was collecting his material from various sources.' (Review of *Mabo laMishnah*, pp. 179–80.)

[1] The later rabbis; see p. 49 n. 5.
[2] 'Purpose and Method in R. Judah haNasi's Compilation of the Mishnah.'
[3] E.g. M.Sukk. v. 4–5; M.Ohal. ii. 1–2, 5–6, iii. 1.
[4] E.g. M.Ohal. ii, where the simpler view is given first.
[5] That is important, because in the Mishnah the anonymous mishnah is authoritative, as in the saying, 'Halakah agrees with the anonymous mishnah' (B.Shab. 46a, B.Yeb. 42b). See further W. Bacher, *Rabbanan, die Gelehrten der Tradition*.
[6] E.g. M.Shab. xvi.
[7] On passages which show signs of deliberate organisation and planning see the summary in E. Wiesenberg, 'Observations on Method . . .', p. 34.
[8] See for example M.Sot. ix. 15.

Tohoroth ('Cleannesses'). The *sedarim* are then subdivided into tractates, *massektoth*. References to the Mishnah are to the name of the tractate and to the divisions within it. Thus M.Ber. i. 1 indicates the tractate in the Mishnah, Berakoth, the opening chapter and verse. A list of the tractates is given in Appendix v, in alphabetical order and also with the Order in which they occur in the Mishnah.

The Mishnah has been translated into English by H. Danby.[1] P. Blackman, *Mishnayoth* (1951–63), combines both text and translation. A translation of the Mishnah is included in the Soncino translation of the Babylonian Talmud (see p. 68).

The Tosefta is a work closely resembling the Mishnah. It, too, is a work collecting *halakoth* (although it also includes much more haggadic material than the Mishnah), and it is organised in almost exactly the same way, in *sedarim* (orders) and *massektoth* (tractates). The six *sedarim* have the same names and occur in the same order, but the *massektoth* vary slightly (see below). The resemblance between the Mishnah and the Tosefta is at first sight so close that it explains the name 'Tosefta'. The word *tosefta*[2] means 'addition' or 'supplement', and it implies that the Tosefta was taken to be a supplement to the Mishnah; and that is exactly how the Tosefta was traditionally regarded.

According to tradition,[3] the author was R. Ḥiyya, a pupil of Rabbi. Sherira said that the only uncertainty about the authorship was whether R. Ḥiyya made the compilation while Rabbi was still alive, or whether he made it after Rabbi's death. But in fact the view that the Tosefta is a supplement to the Mishnah does not stand up well to detailed examination, and the actual relationship between the two remains one of the most vexing problems of rabbinic scholarship. The problem can be put quite simply: the Tosefta undoubtedly resembles the Mishnah in the ways outlined above, but at the same time it differs from it in many important respects. For example, many of the *halakoth* recorded in the Tosefta are opposed to those recorded in the Mishnah; others come from an early period, certainly before the fall of Jerusalem, and yet they were not recorded by Rabbi; sometimes *halakoth* are recorded in both, but the variations in form and style are not consistent; many *halakoth* in the Tosefta are also to be found, not in the Mishnah, but

---

[1] *The Mishnah.*   [2] Or *tosephta*.
[3] Sherira Gaon, *Epistle*, p. 34 (Levin), p. 13 (Neubauer).

as *baraitoth* in the Talmuds;[1] sometimes *halakah* in the Tosefta agrees with the way it appears in the Talmuds as *baraita*, sometimes it does not. Even more striking is the fact that the Tosefta does not contain as many tractates as the Mishnah. Aboth, Tamid, Middoth and Qinnim do not occur. These distinctions show why it is difficult to find any consistent pattern underlying the selection of material for the Tosefta which will adequately satisfy the complexity of its relationship to the Mishnah and to the Talmuds.

Because of the great difficulties involved, it is not surprising that many different theories have been put forward. Z. Frankel laid the foundations of modern study by suggesting that the Tosefta was put together from two independent collections of *baraitoth*, one coming from R. Ḥiyya, the other from R. Hoshaiah. Additions were then made to it from *baraitoth* preserved in the Talmuds.[2] Other scholars went even further away from the traditional ascription to R. Ḥiyya, and suggested that the Tosefta was edited after the completion of the Talmuds and drew on several sources including the Talmuds.[3] Then M. S. Zuckermandel, who edited the Erfurt MS of the Tosefta, introduced a new theory, that the Tosefta was the original Mishnah of Rabbi. The present Mishnah was a version of Rabbi's compilation changed and altered by the Babylonian Amoraim. The Tosefta, in his view, lies closer to the original Palestinian Mishnah than the Mishnah. That suggestion won some support at the time,[4] but closer examination of the Tosefta has made it seem less and less probable. The difficulty of finding a solution that would explain all the anomalies consistently led A. Spanier[5] and A. Guttmann[6] to suggest that the Tosefta was in fact a random composition, put together from manuscript pages which were not in their proper order. But in 1935 B. Cohen published a

---

[1] The word *baraita* (lit. 'outside', i.e. extraneous material) is used to describe Tannaitic (i.e. early) material which was not included in the Mishnah. *Baraitoth* are preserved in the Tosefta, the Tannaitic midrashim (Mekilta, Sifra and Sifre, see introduction *ad loc.*) and the Talmuds. In the Talmuds *baraita* material is much more scattered.

[2] *Darkey haMishnah*, pp. 304–8.

[3] So, for example, J. H. Dunner, *M.G.W.J.* (1870) (see also bibliography); J. H. Weiss, *Dor Dor weDorshaw*, II.

[4] See, for example, H. Malter, 'A Talmudic Problem and Proposed Solutions'.

[5] *Die Toseftaperiode in der tannaitischen Literatur.*

[6] *Das redaktionelle und sachliche Verhältnis zwischen Mischna und Tosefta.*

careful comparison of the treatment of the tractate Shabbath in the Mishnah and the Tosefta.[1] He concluded that the Tosefta frequently recorded *halakoth* in a form earlier than that of the Mishnah, even though, in his view, the Tosefta was compiled *later* than the Mishnah:

The order of the statements in the Tosefta goes back to older and different collections and in numerous cases actually represents the better and more original sequence. This would not presuppose that the Tosefta went thru [*sic*] a series of redactions at a time previous to our Mishnah. The first redaction of the Tosefta could have taken place after the completion of R. Judah's Mishnah, and the older arrangement of the Tosefta is due to the peculiar method of combining various sources used by the ancients in the compilation of tradition. That the compilers of the Tosefta intended to elucidate and supplement our Mishnah is obvious from the fact that many of its comments can be understood only in connection with the Mishnah.[2]

More recently, B. de Vries has taken this line of approach much further by extending the comparison to other tractates.[3] As a result he has concluded that the plan of the Tosefta in individual tractates did not depend on the Mishnah. The Tosefta is earlier than the Mishnah in form and layout, and it preserves an older form of the text. In a particular study of the other side of the problem, the relationship between the Tosefta and the Talmuds, de Vries concluded that the Amoraim knew and used a collection of *baraitoth* which they regarded as supplementing and explaining the Mishnah. That collection was not identical with the present Tosefta, since the sequences and the order of particular items differ. Exactly how that collection developed into the present Tosefta cannot, with any certainty, be traced.[4]

The text of the Tosefta, based on the Erfurt MS, was published by M. S. Zuckermandel. A better edition, based on the Vienna codex and supplying a much wider range of variants, has been published by S. Liebermann.[5] There is no complete translation of the Tosefta into English, though this is much to be desired.[6] References to the Tosefta usually resemble those to the Mishnah: they start with T, followed

---

[1] *Mishnah and Tosefta: a Comparative Study.*   [2] *Op. cit.* p. 51.

[3] See above, p. 58; for details, see the bibliography.

[4] B. de Vries, 'The Problem of the Relationships of the Two Talmuds to the Tosefta'.   [5] See the bibliography.

[6] Two tractates (Berakoth and Sanhedrin) were translated in the S.P.C.K. series, *Translations of Early Documents*, III, *Rabbinic Texts*; see the bibliography under Danby and Lukyn Williams. There is a German text and translation in six parts edited by G. Kittel and K. H. Rengstorf, in process of appearing.

by the name of the tractate in abbreviated form (see Appendix v for the abbreviations), and then give the subdivision by chapter and verse. Thus a full reference reads, T.Ber. i. 1.

It would be far beyond the scope of this book to give an introduction to the Talmuds. S. Schechter once described the Talmud as 'a work too varied, too disconnected, and too divergent in its elements, to be concisely defined at all, or to be even approximately described within the limits of an English sentence'. All that can be attempted here is a general description.

After the Mishnah was completed and recognised as the most basic and authoritative collection, work did not cease. The refining and extension of *halakoth*, and the production of inspiring and illuminating *haggadoth*, continued. But work was increasingly based on the Mishnah: the Mishnah itself (after scripture) became the object of study, and the purpose of the Amoraim was to elucidate and clarify its text and meaning. The work went on in many different centres in both Palestine and Babylonia. In Palestine the chief centre of study was Tiberias, until it was eliminated in about A.D. 425, and other important centres were Caesarea and Sepphoris. In Babylonia the chief centres were Sura and Nehardea; after Nehardea was destroyed (A.D. 259), Pumbeditha rose to prominence. Other important centres were Huẓal and Nisibis.

In those various academies the work was produced which eventually went into the two Talmuds, the Palestinian and the Babylonian. They were formed during the course of the fifth century (the Palestinian earlier than the Babylonian), but work continued on the Babylonian Talmud after that time. Thus the Talmuds are the product of roughly two or three hundred years' work, although they also include material from the period before the formation of Mishnah.[1] The language of both Talmuds is primarily Aramaic (with noticeable Hebrew sections) but the dialect in each case is different.

The two Talmuds differ greatly in content, but they resemble each other in form. Both collections of material are based on the Mishnah. The Mishnah is quoted verse by verse, and to each verse comments or illustrative material are then attached. The commentary is known as the *gemara*. The basic purpose of the material assembled in the *gemara* was to expound the verse of the Mishnah to which it was attached, but, as so

---

[1] The so-called *baraita* material, referred to on p. 62.

often happens in rabbinic work, further material was also attached to the *gemara* itself, simply because something within the *gemara* (a word, for example, or an idea, or a rabbi's name) seemed to provide a link and, in consequence, an appropriate context for the introduction of the further material. The contents of the *gemara* vary enormously. Usually the Palestinian *gemara* tends to be simpler than the Babylonian *gemara*, and its exegesis of scripture is not so ingenious. A good summary of the general characteristics of the *gemara* has been made by J. H. Hertz:

The Gemara, which word came to denote 'teaching', explains the terms and subject-matter of the Mishnah; seeks to elucidate difficulties and harmonise discrepant statements; to refer anonymous decisions to their proper authors in the Mishnah, or in the parallel compilations of Tannaitic teachings contemporary with the Mishnah in which the same subject is treated; and to determine to what extent they are in agreement. Finally, it reports in full the controversies that took place in the Palestinian or Babylonian Academies concerning these subjects. But the Gemara is more than a mere commentary. In it are sedulously gathered, without any reference to their connection with the Mishnah, whatever utterances had for centuries dropped from the lips of the Masters; whatever Tradition preserved concerning them or their actions; whatever bears directly, or even distantly, upon the great subjects of religion, life, and conduct. In addition, therefore, to legal discussions and enactments on every aspect of Jewish duty, whether it be ceremonial, civic, or moral, it contains homiletical exegesis of scripture; moral maxims, popular proverbs, prayers, parables, fables, tales; accounts of manners and customs, Jewish and non-Jewish; facts and fancies of science by the learned; Jewish and heathen folklore, and all the wisdom and unwisdom of the unlearned. This vast and complex material occurs throughout the Gemara, as the name of an author, a casual quotation from scripture, or some other accident in thought or style started a new association in ideas.[1]

Although the two Talmuds were assembled on the same principle, their contents are different. They also differ in the number of tractates

[1] Foreword to *The Babylonian Talmud, Nezikin* 1 (Soncino Press, 1935), pp. xvii f. The comprehensiveness of the Talmuds was also summarised well by S. Grayzel, *A History of the Jews*, p. 230: 'The ultimate aim of education was not merely to acquire information, but what was more important, to establish good habits of life. They studied the laws which regulated man's relations to God, and also those which guided man's relations to his fellow man. Philanthropy and business, wages and the rules of common politeness, morality and ethics were as much part of their religious studies as were synagogue regulations and the rules of penitence for sin committed. The attitudes towards one another were as much a subject for discussion as the observance of the Sabbath. There was no difference in their attitude towards Law, Ethics and Morals; all were part of Religion.'

from the Mishnah to which they attach *gemara*. Neither Talmud provided a commentary on all the tractates. The Palestinian Talmud has *gemara* on all the tractates in the first three Orders; in the fourth order (Neziqin) it has *gemara* on all the tractates except Eduyyoth and Aboth; it has no *gemara* on the tractates in the remaining two Orders except for three chapters in Niddah. Even where the Palestinian Talmud provides *gemara*, it is very uneven, and the work as a whole does not form a unity. It bears some signs of being a rescue operation, designed to record material that might otherwise have been lost. That would be understandable, since Judaism in Palestine was under much greater pressure from Christianity than Judaism in Babylonia. On the other hand, traces have been found (for example in the Cairo Geniza) of *gemara* on other parts of the Mishnah, which suggests that the Palestinian Talmud was originally more extensive. Its present attenuated form may have been caused directly, as well as indirectly, by Christian pressure. Another possible reason for the unevenness of the Palestinian Talmud is the fact that it did not rival the Babylonian Talmud as authoritative for most Jews. The Babylonian Talmud became *the* Talmud in the greater part of Judaism, and the Palestinian Talmud was not the subject of further study in the same way or to the same degree.

The Babylonian Talmud has *gemara* on fewer tractates than the Palestinian, but despite that it is a great deal longer. In the first Order (Zeraim) it has *gemara* on the first tractate (Berakoth) only; in the second Order it has no *gemara* on Sheqalim; the third is complete; in the fourth it has none on Eduyyoth and Aboth; in the fifth it has none on Middoth or Qinnim (and only the first three chapters of Tamid have *gemara*); in the sixth only Niddah has *gemara*. It must, of course, be remembered that much of the comment on tractates that did not receive *gemara* was in fact included in the *gemara* on other tractates.

Just as the Mishnah became, after its codification, the object of further study, so the Babylonian Talmud became the basis of subsequent work. The first generations of rabbis who worked on the Talmud are known as the Saboraim (in, roughly, the sixth century), and the generations following them are known as the Geonim. Only gradually was any final uniformity attained. The middle ages produced the great Talmud commentators, without whom the Talmud would be almost impossible to understand. Of these one of the most outstanding was Rashi, whose comments are sometimes quoted in this book.[1]

References to the Babylonian Talmud are similar to those to the Mishnah and the Tosefta. They start with the initial B[2] and follow with the name of the tractate in abbreviated form.[3] But the place in the tractate is indicated, not by chapter and verse, as in the Tosefta and the Mishnah, but by page or folio number, since the Babylonian Talmud (following Bomberg's edition) is always printed uniformly, with the same material on every page. References are given to the front of a page (a) and to the back (b), thus: 2a, 2b, 3a, 3b, . . .[4] So a full reference would read: B.Ber. 2a. That means: Tractate Berakoth in the Talmud Babli, the front side of the second page. The text of the Talmud is printed with the Mishnah followed by the *gemara* in the centre of the page. Surrounding it, printed in smaller print and different type, are some of the great commentaries on the Talmud. All the material is thus grouped together on one page.

The Palestinian Talmud is indicated by the initial letter J or Y or sometimes P.[5] The name of the tractate follows in an abbreviated form, but the place in the tractate is indicated in different ways. Sometimes the reference is given to the folio, front or back, exactly as in the Babylonian Talmud. But more frequently it is given by 'chapter and verse', as in the Tosefta or the Mishnah. Unfortunately the division

[1] Rashi was born about 1030 and lived in France. He is mentioned here because he also wrote commentaries on scripture, and extracts from these, particularly from his commentary on Genesis, are occasionally quoted in this book. Although Rashi is late, he has been quoted because his summaries of rabbinic interpretations of a particular verse are often clear and precise (and he is thus able to save space in showing how a particular interpretation arose), and also because he is recognised as perhaps the greatest commentator in Judaism. On Rashi see J. Z. Lauterbach, 'Rashi the Talmud Commentator'; E. Shereshevsky, 'The Significance of Rashi's Commentary on the Pentateuch'; *The Rashi Anniversary Volume*, ed. H. L. Ginsberg (1941). A convenient text and translation of Rashi on the Pentateuch will be found in M. Rosenbaum and A. M. Silbermann, *Pentateuch* . . . .

[2] Babli or Babylonian.

[3] For the abbreviations, see Appendix v.

[4] There is never a folio 1.

[5] J and Y stand for Jerushalmi (Jerusalem); j in English transliteration represents Hebrew y. The name 'Jerushalmi' is misleading, since Tiberias was the centre of Palestinian study, not Jerusalem, and for that reason some prefer to indicate the Palestinian Talmud with the initial P.

into chapters and verses is not entirely uniform, and some of the verses are in any case very long. This means that a reference can be difficult to track down.

An English translation of the Babylonian Talmud has been published by the Soncino Press. There is no English translation of the Palestinian Talmud, another defect that needs urgently to be remedied. There is a French translation by Moïse Schwab, but it needs to be used with caution.

There are a number of shorter works, associated with the Babylonian Talmud, known as the additional and minor tractates. Many editions of the Babylonian Talmud include at the end of the Fourth Order (Neziqin) eight additional tractates (or seven, if the two versions of Kalla are counted as one). They appear to be late in composition but, like most rabbinic works, some of them contain important early material. The tractates are:

(i) Aboth de Rabbi Nathan: see the introduction on pp. 87 f.

(ii) Soferim (scribes).[1]

(iii) Ebel Rabbathi (mourning); it is also known euphemistically as *Semaḥot*, 'joys'.

(iv) Kalla (bride); also the longer Kalla Rabbathi, the first two chapters of which are a *gemara*-type commentary on Kalla.

(v) Derek Ereẓ: 'moral conduct'.

(vi) Derek Ereẓ Zuta: the epithet *zuta* means 'small', and was added later to distinguish it from (v).

(vii) Pereq haShalom (the Chapter of Peace).

In addition to these tractates, there are seven minor tractates which are not always included in editions of the Babylonian Talmud. These are:

(i) Sefer Torah (the writing of Torah).

(ii) Mezuzah: on the writing of *mezuzoth*.[2]

(iii) Tephillin (phylacteries).[3]

---

[1] On Masseket Soferim see the bibliography under H. Bardtke.

[2] A *mezuzah* is a small scroll on which are written the words of Deut. vi. 4–9, xi. 13–21. It is put in a holder and fixed to the right-hand doorpost of a house.

[3] These were tied on to the arm and head in accordance with Deut. vi. 8, xi. 18. It is important not to confuse this word with another word *tephillah*, which means 'prayer' in general, and in particular it refers to *the* prayer, the Prayer of Benedictions, to be said thrice a day (four times on sabbath and

(iv) Ẓiẓith (fringes; Num. xv. 37 ff., Deut. xxii. 22).

(v) Abadim (slaves).

(vi) Kuthim (Samaritans).

(vii) Gerim (proselytes).

These tractates were not originally included in the Soncino transla-tion of the Babylonian Talmud, but they have since been published (see the bibliography under A. Cohen). They are not regarded as equal to other parts of the Talmud. For the text, see the bibliography under M. Higger; for an introduction to each tractate, see the Soncino translation.

2. TANNAITIC MIDRASHIM. The general character of Midrash has been outlined above.[1] It is exegesis of scripture which attaches the exe-gesis to the text which it is expounding or from which it has been derived (as opposed to Mishnah, where the material is recorded inde-pendently of scripture). Obviously the content of the exegesis will vary from one midrashic work to another. The word *midrash* is primarily a description of function and method, not of content.[2]

The Tannaitic Midrashim are Mekilta, Sifra and Sifre, commen-taries on parts of Exodus, Leviticus, Numbers and Deuteronomy. As the name implies, they contain material from the Tannaitic period[3] or earlier. The commentaries are largely (but not entirely) made up of *halakoth*, and for that reason the Tannaitic Midrashim are also known as halakic midrashim.[4] The Tannaitic Midrashim are of particular interest because they contain material from rival schools of exegesis, particularly those of R. Aqiba and R. Ishmael.[5] The method used is to quote a text of scripture and then attach commentary to it.

festivals, five times on the Day of Atonement). The Tephillah (in the particular sense) is also known as the Shemoneh Esreh (lit. the Eighteen), parts of which go back long before the fall of Jerusalem. On the Shemoneh Esreh, see S. Zeit-lin, 'The Tefillah, the Shemoneh Esreh'.

[1] Pp. 45 f.

[2] Similarly, words like Mishnah, Talmud, Gemara should not primarily describe content but method and purpose. On this important point see E. E. Hallevy, 'What is Haggadah?' (introduction to *Bereshith Rabbah*, p. 12).

[3] See p. 49.

[4] As explained above (p. 46), the title is erroneous. Technically they should be known as midrash torah which contains *halakoth*, i.e. exegesis of Torah, containing *halakoth*.

[5] See p. 54.

The Mekilta[1] is a midrash on certain chapters of Exodus.[2] It is one of the earliest midrashim to have survived, and although it has undergone subsequent revision and expansion it belongs basically to the Tannaitic period. Some of its material does not occur elsewhere.

The Amoraim knew of a midrash on Exodus but not, apparently, as a separate work. It was thought of as part of a larger midrash on Exodus, Numbers, Leviticus and Deuteronomy, which was called by them Sifre debe Rab, or more usually Sifre.[3] At an early date the midrash on Leviticus was detached and was known as Sifra (debe Rab), *the* Book. The Midrash on the other three continued to be known as Sifre.[4] Much later the name Sifre was confined to the midrash on Numbers and Deuteronomy.

It is difficult to know how far the present Mekilta corresponds to the midrash on Exodus included by the Amoraim in their Sifre. It cannot be regarded as identical since it is the product of more than one redaction and revision. But there seems no reason why the early midrash should not have formed the basis of the work as it now is.

The book is also known as Mekilta deRabbi Ishmael, because of the frequency with which the teaching of R. Ishmael and his followers is recorded.[5] It is possible that his exposition formed the original basis of the work, but it now contains teaching of other Rabbis, even that of his great rival R. Aqiba. This was recognised by R. Johanan[6] (though it would only apply if Sifre in his time included the nucleus of the midrash on Exodus):

'R. Johanan said: "Any anonymous statement in Mishna comes from R. Meir, in Tosefta from R. Nehemiah, in Sifra from R. Judah, in

---

[1] The word Mekilta has been taken loosely to mean 'a collection' of inter-pretations, etc. (see e.g. Jastrow, 782*b*), but more technically it is connected with the basic meaning of the root *kwl*, 'measure'. It is then connected with *middoth*, which also means 'measures', but more technically 'the rules of exegesis' (as in Appendix II); thus the name Mekilta was given to this midrash, because it follows the *middoth* of exegesis (see *J.E. ad loc.*).

[2] xii. 1–xxiii. 19, xxxi. 12–17, xxxv. 1–3. The chapters chosen are those which contain most of the legal material in Exodus, which indicates that the basic intention of the book was to be halakic. But in fact a great deal of *haggadah* is included.   [3] 'Books.'

[4] Sometimes in full, *Shear* (the remaining) Sifre debe Rab.

[5] On R. Ishmael and his rivalry with R. Aqiba, see p. 54. Some of the rabbis quoted in the Mekilta, for example R. Josiah and R. Jonathan, were so closely identified with R. Ishmael that they do not even occur in the Mishnah at all.   [6] Third century A.D.

Sifre from R. Simeon, and all are taught according to the opinions of R. Aqiba.'[1]

If R. Ishmael's exposition did form the nucleus, then some of the teachings other than his must have been attached to it early on, at a date, in fact, very close to that of the original composition. There is a text and English translation of the Mekilta by J. Z. Lauterbach, published by the Jewish Publication Society of America. References to the Mekilta vary, chiefly because the different editions of the Mekilta break up the text in different ways.[2] The most usual system is to refer to the names given to the divisions of Exodus in the Hebrew Bible and to Tractates;[3] otherwise the reference may be given to the particular chapter and verse on which the Mekilta is commenting, as Mek. on Exod. xii. 1.

There is also a Mekilta deRabbi Simeon b. Johai on Exodus. For the text of this, see the bibliography under J. N. Epstein, and see also D. Hoffmann, *Mechilta deRabbi Simeon b. Johai*; 'Zur Einleitung in Mechilta deRabbi Simeon b. Johai'.

Sifra[4] is a commentary on Leviticus, containing very little *haggadah*. According to R. Johanan's view[5] the basic authority in the compilation of Sifra was R. Judah (bar Ilai). It belongs to the school of R. Aqiba, rather than that of R. Ishmael, even though it begins with an exposition of R. Ishmael's Rules (see p. 55). There is no complete translation of Sifra into English. References to Sifra vary greatly, and it is simplest to refer to the passage from Leviticus on which Sifra is commenting; otherwise references are frequently made to the page number of Weiss' edition (Vienna, 1862).

Sifre is the name given to the commentaries on Numbers and Deuteronomy. Sifre on Numbers begins with chapter v, which is where the legal material in Numbers starts. As with the Mekilta, the choice of those chapters betrays the intention of the work to be halakic, but it also includes *haggadah*. Later Jewish writers in the middle ages quoted from another Tannaitic midrash on Numbers. The work is only known through their quotations, but it is important because it contains

---

[1] B.San. 86*a*.
[2] The texts most usually referred to are those of M. Friedmann and Lauterbach, and less frequently those of Horowitz and Weiss.
[3] For the names of these, see p. 359.
[4] The name Sifra is explained in the introduction to the Mekilta.
[5] Quoted above, p. 70.

Mishnaic passages which differ from the form they take in Rabbi's Mishnah, and because it drew on rabbis otherwise little known. It is referred to by the name Sifre Zuta[1] on Numbers. Parts of Sifre on Numbers were translated by P. P. Levertoff; there is a translation into German by K. G. Kuhn.[2]

Sifre on Deuteronomy is also confined to the legal material, chs. xii–xxvi; there is also commentary on parts of the earlier chapters,[3] but it appears to be derived separately from the school of R. Ishmael. Fragments of Tannaitic midrashim on Deuteronomy were recovered by D. Hoffmann from the Midrash haGadol,[4] and he published them separately in *Midrash Tannaim* . . . References to Sifre are either to the biblical chapter and verse on which Sifre is commenting, or else by sections. Both kinds of reference are used in this book, because in that way more precise indications can be given. The usual edition is that of M. Friedmann, but see also H. S. Horowitz. For German translations of the Tannaitic midrashim see the bibliography under K. H. Rengstorf.

3. HOMILETIC MIDRASHIM. This name refers to a number of works which have made a collection of synagogue sermons. It was pointed out earlier[5] that the original function of the Synagogue was to promote the study and exposition of scripture. What that meant fundamentally was the public recitation of Torah, which came to be governed by precise rules,[6] and also by set lectionaries, the text of Torah being divided into sections for the purpose. The sections are called *sedarim*,[7] and the reading from Torah is sometimes referred to as the *seder*-reading. Various different lectionaries existed: the old Palestinian lectionary was divided into 154 *sedarim* which took three years to complete, hence it is known as the triennial lectionary. Traces remain of a lectionary which divided Torah into 175 *sedarim* which took $3\frac{1}{2}$ years to complete, hence

---

[1] I.e. the 'small' Sifre.
[2] For the text of Sifre on Numbers and Sifre Zuta see the bibliography under H. S. Horowitz.
[3] i. 1–30, iii. 23–9, vi. 4–9, xi. 10–32.
[4] Midrash haGadol is a late work, but because it is basically an anthology it contains some early material. For a brief account of Midrash haGadol see S. Fisch, 'The Midrash Haggadol . . .'. For texts see the bibliography under S. Fisch, N. Z. Hasidah, M. Margolioth, and E. N. Rabinowitz.
[5] Pp. 9–12.
[6] See p. 12.
[7] Singular *seder*.

it is known as the septennial lectionary.[1] The Babylonian lectionary (which has continued down to the present day) divided the text into 48–54 *sedarim* to be completed every year.[2] Special lessons were also appointed for festivals and the Special Sabbaths.[3] Although the lectionaries allocated the *sedarim* with some care, there was still considerable variety within them: that is to say, there was not absolute agreement where a particular *seder* began or ended, so that there is always a slight 'shift' in the *sedarim*, particularly in the old Palestinian lectionary.[4]

At an early date[5] the reading from Torah was supplemented by a second reading from the Prophets known as the *haftarah*.[6] The *haftaroth* were also very carefully chosen; a *haftarah* had to have some link with the *seder*-reading, either through similarity of content or, more particularly, because of the same word or words occurring in both passages.[7] The *haftarah* was basically ten verses in length, but the verses did not have to be consecutive. Skipping was allowed, and the final verse or verses were supposed to end on a happy or optimistic note. There is even greater variety and shift in the *haftaroth* than there is in the *sedarim*.

[1] So Masseket Soferim (the Tractate on Scribes, see p. 68) xvi. 10: 'The rabbis appointed 175 *sedarim* for the sabbaths which they intended to be as obligatory as Tamid.'

[2] It may be helpful, in connection with the second part of this book, to give the present-day *sedarim* in Genesis, since references often make use of them. The form in which they are usually abbreviated is shown by putting the rest of the title in parentheses. The title is determined by the first, or the first significant, word in the *seder*. (For *sedarim* in Exodus see p. 359.)

Gen. i–vi Ber(eshith).	Gen. xxv. 19–xxviii. 9 Told(oth).
vii–xi Noah.	xxviii. 10–xxxii. 3 Vayeẓe.
xii–xvii Lek leka.	xxxii. 4–xxxvi Vayish(laḥ).
xviii–xxii Vay(era). (The V may,	xxvii–xl Vayesh(eb).
of course, appear as a W, as	xli–xliv. 17 Miq(qeẓ).
also in the other titles.)	xliv. 18–xlvii. 27 Vayyig(ash).
xxiii–xxv. 18 Ḥay(yey Sarah).	xlvii. 28–end Vayeḥi.

[3] For the four Special Sabbaths see p. 75 n. 8.

[4] For some of the problems connected with the lectionaries, see J. Mann, *The Bible as Read and Preached* . . . ; for a recent discussion, see J. Heinemann, 'The Triennial Cycle and the Calendar'.

[5] The exact date is not known, but it was almost certainly before the fall of Jerusalem; for a summary of the arguments, see my article 'Speeches in Acts . . .', p. 99 n. 1.

[6] Plural *haftaroth*.

[7] On the requirements demanded of the *haftaroth*, see J. Mann, *op. cit.*

In those two ways scripture was set forth in synagogue; it was made meaningful, first by the targum, which expressed the meaning of the passages read in a language that could be understood by all present; and second, by the homily or sermon. It is these homilies which the Homiletic Midrashim have collected.

The homilies that have survived fall into roughly two groups, the proem and the yelammedenu homilies.[1] The proem homily is so called because it starts from a proem (introductory) text; the text was chosen from a part of scripture outside the *seder* and the *haftarah* of the day, and formed a bridge between them. The yelammedenu homily is so called because it derives from a request for instruction, *yelammedenu rabbenu* ('let our teacher instruct us'). The question raised was usually halakic, and it takes the place of a proem text. The homilies were constructed on very precise lines[2] in which the basic method was *haruzin*. The word *haruzin* means 'stringing beads together', or in other words stringing texts of scripture together, leading from the proem text (or halakic question) to the *seder*-reading. Homilies usually end by quoting a text from the *seder* of the day. On to the 'necklace of texts' was attached exegetical material, both halakic and haggadic, in profusion. Throughout the homily the *haftarah* for the day was implied but scarcely ever quoted. It was, as Mann put it, 'in the preacher's mind throughout'.[3] Thus the homilies usually wove together the lectionary readings for the day, using as a basic thread texts from all parts of scripture.

The three earliest collections of homilies are Pesiqta, Pesiqta Rabbati and Tanhuma.[4]

The name Pesiqta is derived from a word meaning 'cut', hence 'division'. It recognises the fact that each homily recorded in it is an

---

[1] There are some homilies which do not fall into the very brief description given here, but the majority are in these categories.

[2] For a summary of some of the rules governing the construction of homilies, see my article 'Speeches in Acts . . .'.

[3] Mann, *op. cit.* pp. 11 f. It was the great achievement of Mann to show the close connection between the homilies preserved in the homiletic midrashim and the old Palestinian lectionary. Although he did not live to complete his work, it is an essential preliminary to all further study. For a critical summary of the ways in which Mann's work has been assessed, see I. Sonne's preface to the (posthumous) vol. II of *The Bible as Read . . .*, pp. xxi–xxviii.

[4] A later collection of homilies relevant to Genesis is *Aggadath Bereshith*, (compiled in about the tenth century), ed. by S. Buber.

independent unit. Pesiqta is usually known as Pesiqta deRab Kahana[1] since one of the homilies begins 'R. Abba bar Kahana pathaḥ . . .'[2] It is a work of Palestinian origin: it quotes Palestinian rabbis and it contains Palestinian Aramaic. The existence of Pes.K. was predicted by L. Zunz before any manuscripts of it had been found. He based his prediction on allusions and quotations in other Jewish works, particularly Aruch. S. Buber published a text of Pes.K. based on four manuscripts. In 1892 M. Friedmann described two other manuscripts,[3] and in 1962 B. Mandelbaum published in two volumes a new edition of Pes.K. which included a new manuscript and several Cairo Geniza fragments.

The homilies collected in Pes.K. are on the festivals and Special Sabbaths. They fall into five groups:[4] Rosh haShanah[5] to the Day of Atonement; Sukkoth[6] and related festivals; Ḥannukah[7] and the four Special Sabbaths;[8] Passover to Shabuoth; the sabbath after the seventeenth of Tammuz to the sabbath before (or after) Rosh haShanah. Mandelbaum concluded: 'Thus, it would appear, the original order of the Pesikta followed the cycle of the Jewish calendar, beginning with Rosh Hashanah, as Zunz surmised, and in accordance with the order in the newly discovered manuscript ₁א.'[9]

Translations and references in this book have been made from Mandelbaum's edition. The references are to the homilies by number (there are twenty-eight in all) and to the subdivision within them. References in older books will usually have been made to S. Buber's

---

[1] Abbreviated P.R.K. or more frequently Pes.K.

[2] Lit. 'R. Abba bar Kahana opened (his discourse) . . .' It is a common formula at the beginning of a homily.

[3] *Beth Talmud*, v.

[4] Mandelbaum, introduction, vol. I, p. 14 (English introduction, vol. II, p. xiv).

[5] New Year.

[6] The Feast of Tents (Tabernacles), or (according to its celebration) Booths.

[7] The Feast of Rededication (commemorating the rededication of the Temple after the Maccabean revolt).

[8] The four Special Sabbaths are: (1) *Shekalim*; Exod. xxx. 11–16 was read on (or on the sabbath preceding) Adar I as a reminder that the tax was due. (2) *Zakhor*; Deut. xxv. 17–19 was read on the sabbath before Purim. (3) *Parah*; Num. xix. 1–22 was read on the sabbath preceding *haḤodesh*. (4) *haḤodesh*; Exod. xii. 1–20 was read on (or on the sabbath preceding) Nisan I as a reminder of the approaching Passover.

[9] Introduction, II, p. xvi; cf. Hebrew introduction, pp. 15 f., where the same conclusion is given in shorter form.

edition (Lyck, 1868), and in that case they are either given in the same way, or else by the folio number, front and back, as with the Babylonian Talmud. Mandelbaum's edition includes an introduction in Hebrew. There is also an English introduction in vol. II (pp. v–xxi), but the two introductions are not identical. There are notes and variant readings, and some additional notes by S. Liebermann (pp. 473–7).

Pesiqta Rabbati means 'the great Pesiqta', given that name in order to distinguish it from Pes.K. It contains homilies on the festivals and Special Sabbaths, but, in contrast to Pesiqta, over half of them are yelammedenu homilies, beginning with the formula 'R. Tanḥuma *pathaḥ* . . .' R. Tanḥuma, who lived at some time around the beginning of the fifth century A.D., was particularly associated with the work of collecting homilies; and in fact there are more homilies in the name of R. Tanḥuma than of any other rabbi. Pesiqta Rabbati is abbreviated Pes.R., and the edition used is that of M. Friedmann. References are usually given to folios (front and back), as with the Babylonian Talmud.

Tanḥuma is so called because several of the homilies are in R. Tanḥuma's name. It may also imply that he was instrumental in forming the nucleus of this collection. The work used sometimes to be referred to as Yelammedenu, because of the number of yelammedenu homilies which it contains; but for reasons given below the name is confusing, and the work is now almost invariably referred to as Tanḥuma. It is a collection of homilies on the whole Pentateuch, and it was probably intended originally to have one homily for each *seder*. But Tanḥuma changed greatly during the course of its history, particularly through substitution: it was easy to take out one homily and insert another wherever it seemed preferable. This means that by the time Yalqut was assembled it was able to draw on two separate collections,[1] one of which

---

[1] The word *yalqut* means 'assembled, collected' (lit. 'that in which something is collected', e.g. a bag) and it is the name given to later anthologies of rabbinic material. Some of these are extremely important because they draw on works otherwise lost, and they give variant versions of material which has survived elsewhere. The most substantial anthology is Yalqut Shime'oni, usually referred to simply as Yalqut. It collected material on the whole of the Old Testament. Other important anthologies and late works including earlier material are Yalqut haMakiri (which quotes Tanḥuma/Yelammedenu in forms not otherwise known; for the text see the bibliography under S. Buber), Midrash haGadol (see p. 72) and Lekaḥ Tob (see the bibliography under

it called Tanḥuma, the other Yelammedenu. The considerable shift in the homilies means that modern editions also vary among themselves. The editions most commonly used are those of Stettin (1864), Warsaw (1875), Lublin (1879), and of S. Buber, Wilna (1885).[1] References to Buber's edition are usually made clear by the addition of his name in brackets, either in full or by use of the intial B (thus, Tanḥ.B., followed by the reference). References to Tanḥ. may be made either to the page or folio number, or by stating the actual part of scripture to which the homily is attached, as Tanḥ. on Gen. i. 1; or again, the scripture reference may be given according to the divisions (sedarim) in the Hebrew Bible, as Tanḥ. Ber. i. 1; more frequently the final part of the reference is made to the subdivision within the Hebrew seder: Tanḥ. Lek 6.[2] References in this book to Buber's edition are given by volume and page number,[3] to other editions by seder division and subsection.

The Pesiqtas and Tanḥuma have not been translated into English, though a translation of Pesiqta Rabbathi by W. G. Braude is being produced in the Yale Judaica Series.

4. THE MIDRASH RABBAH. The word rabbah means 'great', and the Midrash Rabbah is thus the Great Midrash. It is a complete commentary on the Pentateuch and on the five Megilloth, Song of Songs, Ruth, Lamentations, Ecclesiastes and Esther. The Midrash Rabbah is not a unity. Some of the commentaries are much earlier than others and indeed some of the later works use the earlier ones as sources. The title 'rabbah' was originally given to the commentary on Genesis, but when commentaries on other books were attached to it, the title was

S. Buber, and for further references see H. L. Strack, Introduction, p. 349). The work of recovering individual Midrashim continues. A collection frequently referred to is A. Jellinek, Bet haMidrasch (6 vols. 1853–77). See also the bibliography under J. D. Eisenstein.

[1] Buber's edition was published in 4 volumes, vol. 1 being the introduction. Two important MSS must also be noticed, Sassoon 597 and the Vatican MS Cassuto 34.

[2] For the titles given to the sedarim in Genesis, see p. 73 n. 2.

[3] In references to Buber's edition the first volume (introduction) is ignored. The references are complicated by the fact that vol. III includes Tanḥ. on Lev., Num. and Deut., and Buber began renumbering the pages at the beginning of each book. Tanḥ.B. on Num. is indicated by iv, Tanḥ.B. on Deut. is indicated by v; but both iv and v are to be found in vol. III.

extended to cover the complete collection. References to the Midrash Rabbah are easy to distinguish: they give the name of the individual book (in abbreviated form) followed by a capital R: Gen.R. It is more usual now to give the Hebrew name of the book. The titles and English equivalents are:

Ber(eshith)	Genesis	Shir (haShir)	Song of Songs[1]
Shem(oth)	Exodus	Ruth	Ruth
Vay(yiqra)	Leviticus	Ekah[2]	Lamentations
Bem(idbar)	Numbers	Qoh(eleth)	Ecclesiastes
Deb(arim)	Deuteronomy	Est(her)	Esther

The references to subdivisions within each commentary vary, and they will be explained in the introduction to the individual books.

The Midrash Rabbah on the Pentateuch has recently been edited by E. E. Hallevy (8 vols. Israel, 1956–63), and quotations in this book have been translated from that text. Four volumes (I, III, V, VIII) include important essays on *haggadah* (in Hebrew). There is a translation of the whole Midrash Rabbah into English, based on a different text, published by the Soncino Press (10 vols. 1939). Mention must also be made of Theodor's edition of Ber.R., not least because of its notes and its references to parallel passages.

Ber.R. is an 'anthologising' work, and it combines both types of *midrashim* already described, the Tannaitic and the homiletic. Basically it is a verse-by-verse commentary, but it is divided into sections (*parashiyyoth*, sing. *parashah*) and references are given to these sections and to the subdivisions within them.[3] Almost every *parashah* begins with a proem homily on a text taken from the point reached in Genesis; it seems likely that the proem homilies were introduced to an already existing midrash on Genesis.[4] There are other signs of variety in the

---

[1] It is frequently referred to as Cant(icles) R., or (in Jewish works) as Ḥaz(itha) R., since the first proem text is Prov. xxii. 29, which begins: *ḥazitha 'ish mahir . . . .*

[2] Technically it should have a soft breathing, 'Ekah, but it is usually omitted.

[3] Ber.R. is divided into roughly 100 *parashiyyoth*, though the number varies between 97 and 101 in different MSS and editions. This means that references to the final *parashiyyoth* are not always easy to track down. References in this book follow E. E. Hallevy.

[4] Twenty-eight homilies on Genesis are collected in *Aggadath Bereshith*, following the triennial lectionary. The material is similar to that of Tanḥuma (Buber's edn.). For the text, see Jellinek, *Bet haMidrasch*, IV, and S. Buber

compilation. The commentary on Vayyigash[1] ceases to be a verse-by-verse commentary and resembles much more a homiletic midrash. Some of the later *parashiyyoth*, particularly those covering Vayehi,[2] contain material akin to that in Tanhuma, and they may have been supplied from that work.

Ber.R. is thus a diverse compilation, but basically it appears to be a Palestinian work of the fifth century (though drawing, of course, on earlier material). The Amoraim it quotes are predominantly Palestinian; the Babylonian Amoraim quoted are from the early generations only. It is mostly written in late Hebrew, but some sections are in Galilean Aramaic, the dialect that is found in the Palestinian Talmud.[3] It also shares material with the Palestinian Talmud.

Ber.R. was traditionally ascribed to R. Hoshaiah, a Palestinian Amora of the first generation, who was known as R. Hoshaiah Rabba (hence perhaps the title Rabbah given to the whole work, though J. Theodor (*Bereschit Rabba . . .*, on i. 1) disputed the connection). In fact, the traditional ascription of Ber.R. to R. Hoshaiah may simply have arisen because the first proem homily is in his name.

Shem.R. falls into two distinct parts. The midrash on Exod. i–xi (*parashiyyoth* 1–14) is a verse-by-verse commentary (perhaps intended to be a continuation of Ber.R.), but the second part (from Exod. xii to the end) is a homiletic midrash, sharing much material with the Pesiqtas and Tanhuma. The division may reflect the division within Exodus itself, which starts with narrative and ends with legal material; that division would have been underlined by the fact that Mekilta was itself selective, concentrating on the legal chapters.

Shem.R. used to be regarded as one of the latest parts of the Midrash Rabbah. L. Zunz put the date of its composition in the eleventh or twelfth century A.D.,[4] on the grounds that it contains late expressions, that it copies short sections of the Babylonian Talmud, and that it was apparently unknown to the early commentators (for example, Rashi) and to the compiler of the Midrash haGadol. That view was contested

(bibliography). A further collection of homilies on Gen. xi–Exod. xv will be found in Sekel Tob (for the text see the bibliography under S. Buber).

[1] See p. 73 n. 2.
[2] See p. 73 n. 2.
[3] See H. Odeberg, *The Aramaic Portions of Bereshit Rabba*. Note that in E. E. Hallevy's edition the Aramaic sections have been translated into Hebrew.
[4] Zunz, *Die gottesdienstlichen Vorträge . . .*, pp. 268 f.

by S. Liebermann,[1] who argued that expressions from the Babylonian Talmud might have been interpolated, as they are at the beginning of the Palestinian Talmud. It must be remembered that copyists were very much influenced by the Babylonian Talmud, particularly as it began to acquire far more general authority than the Palestinian. Furthermore, passages which were thought to have been quoted by Shem.R. from the Babylonian Talmud can be explained better as having been quoted by both from earlier sources independently of each other. Liebermann also pointed out that some works had a limited geographical circulation, which may explain why the early commentators did not know of it.

Hallevy agreed with Liebermann in rejecting a late date. He offered six arguments: (i) The Aramaic elements, though slight, in stories, proverbs and individual words point to a Palestinian background. (ii) The presence of Greek words. (iii) Palestinian Amoraim predominate, exactly as in Ber.R., and only first-generation Babylonian Amoraim are quoted. (iv) There are affinities with the Palestinian Talmud. (v) Technical words from the Palestinian tradition do not receive a Babylonian explanation. (vi) There is scarcely a hint of the geonic period, or of the Islamic invasion (apart from hostility to Ishmael), or of later history in general.

For those reasons, Hallevy suggested a date at the beginning of the seventh century, drawing on earlier midrashic elements.

The Wilna text of Shem.R. contains many abbreviations. For example, Shem.R. xxxix on Exod. xxx. 12 begins: 'R. Tanḥuma bar Abba opened his discourse with *Thy navel is like a round goblet.*[2] Continue with the proem homilies on the Special Sabbaths.' This technique of referring to earlier works without actually quoting them in full used to be regarded as a sign of a late date; but of course it does not follow that the original text was in that form. It may simply be that in the course of transmission copyists noticed overlapping material and saved themselves the trouble of writing it out in full. Hallevy's edition fills in the abbreviations from MSS and editions; the points where he has added material are clearly indicated.

Vay.R. is one of the earliest parts of the Midrash Rabbah. Like Ber.R. it quotes Palestinian Amoraim, with only a few Babylonian

[1] In his introduction to Deb.R.
[2] Song of Songs vii. 2, the proem text.

Amoraim mentioned, and it relies on the Palestinian Talmud. L. Zunz dated its composition in the seventh century, but since it draws on Mishnah, Tosefta and the Palestinian Talmud and not on specifically Babylonian works, it is unlikely to be later than the beginning of the fifth century. It also resembles Ber.R. in the way in which it draws on much the same circle of authorities, and in the way in which it mixes Hebrew and Aramaic; but it is unlike Ber.R. in so far as it is not a verse-by-verse commentary; it is a homiletic midrash, and its homilies are distinctive in form.

Hallevy's edition is based on that of M. Margolioth, with abbreviations and omissions filled in.

Bem.R. is the latest part of the Midrash Rabbah, at least in its final composition. It is also quite unlike the other commentaries in the Midrash Rabbah in several ways. Hallevy listed five differences in particular:[1] (i) It combines verse-by-verse commentary, as in Ber.R., with homiletic commentary, as in Vay.R. (ii) It is the only part of the Midrash Rabbah of which it can certainly be said that it uses the Babylonian Talmud. (iii) It is the only one to use certain sources, for example Sifre Zuta,[2] Seder Eliyahu Rabbah[3] and Midrash Tadshe.[4] (iv) It is the only one to include material from the halakic midrashim, particularly Sifre on Num. and Sifre Zuta. (v) It is the only one to include haggadic material which Rashi also quotes in his commentaries as coming from R. Moses haDarshan.[5] This means that in its present form Bem.R. can scarcely have been compiled before the eleventh or twelfth century A.D. That is not to say that it does not include earlier material; in fact, it certainly does, since parts of it rely heavily on Tanhuma. Furthermore, although a redactor at one stage preferred the Babylonian Talmud to the Palestinian, he did not rely on it exclusively, as later generations did.

Bem.R. falls into two quite distinct parts. It consists of 23 *parashiyyoth*,[6] and of those, 14 are devoted to the first two *sedarim* only (Num. i–vii). The last 9[7] are in the form of the homiletic midrashim, and the homilies were drawn from Tanhuma. Some of the *parashiyyoth*

[1] Hallevy, introduction, p. 29.
[2] See p. 72.
[3] See p. 90.
[4] A short midrash based on Gen. i. 11 (hence the name), printed in Jellinek, *Bet haMidrasch*, III. See also the bibliography under A. Epstein.
[5] Lit. 'interpreter', i.e. the Preacher.
[6] 22 in the MSS.
[7] 8 in the MSS.

open with the formula *yelammedenu rabbenu*, as in Tanḥuma,[1] and in two of them[2] the formula is introduced during the course of the *parashah*. But the tendency is to convert the homilies into proem homilies for the *sedarim* of the sabbath lectionary. What is of interest is that in the first part of Bem.R. (which also drew on Tanḥuma), the formula is not to be found, even though some of the material which it quotes is introduced with that formula in Tanḥuma. This suggests that the compilers of the first and second parts of Bem.R. were different.[3]

Hallevy's edition follows the Wilna edition with important corrections based on the MSS. There is very little Aramaic in Bem.R. but, as in the other Midrashim, Hallevy has translated it into Hebrew.

Deb.R. exists in two different MS traditions, which S. Liebermann argued[4] came from the two main Jewish communities of the middle ages, the Sephardi in Spain and the Ashkenazi in France. It is a compilation of homilies, yelammedenu in type, based on the *sedarim*. The homilies are unlike those in Tanḥuma in some respects: instead of opening with the formula *yelammedenu rabbenu*, they open by posing a halakic question; they simply state, 'Halakah', and then ask the question. In form, as well, they are different in that they divide the material into two parts; that which comes from the Tannaim (referred to as the Wise[5] or as 'our teachers'), and that which comes from the Amoraim. Nevertheless, Deb.R. is related to Tanḥuma, and some writers in the thirteenth and later centuries, quoting from Deb.R., actually called it Tanḥuma. Deb.R. is recognisably similar to Tanḥuma in language and style (particularly in the ways in which it closes homilies; see M. Margolioth, introduction to Vay.R., p. xiv), and since the present Tanḥuma on Deuteronomy and Deb.R. differ so much in content, it seems safe to assume that Deb.R. was in origin one of the oldest editions of Tanḥuma. When it was detached to become a separate work, new material was supplied to Tanḥuma for Deuteronomy. There are certainly signs of early material in Deb.R. although its final compilation in its present form is late, probably at some time in the tenth century. It does not, for example, take so much care as earlier works in preserving accurately the names of authorities and sources.

---

[1] xv, xvi, xvii, xxi, xxiii. This formula does not appear in the Soncino translation, but see Hallevy *ad loc.* and his introduction to Bem.R. p. 13.

[2] xx and xxii.   [3] See Hallevy, introduction, p. 13.

[4] *Midrash Debarim Rabbah.*   [5] *Ḥakamim.*

The commentaries on the five Megilloth in the Midrash Rabbah[1] also vary greatly in date, and that is largely to be explained by the different use made of the individual books in the synagogue liturgy.

Shir.R. is a relatively late compilation, drawing heavily on earlier works. It is a verse-by-verse commentary, but it quotes large sections (and occasionally complete homilies) from the Homiletic Midrashim, particularly Pes.K. The main sources were the Palestinian Talmud, Ber.R. and perhaps Vay.R., and some of its interpretations are also found in Sifre and Mekilta. A date between 600 and 750 is suggested by the fact that it still prefers readings from the Palestinian Talmud to those from the Babylonian, and its Aramaic is close to that of the Palestinian Talmud.

Two important collections of homilies on Song of Songs survive and make an interesting comparison with Shir.R.: Agadath Shir haShirim,[2] and Midrash Shir haShirim.[3] References to Shir.R. are given, first by identifying the chapter and verse in Song of Songs, and then by giving the subdivision within the commentary: thus Shir.R. i. 1. 1 means the first section of Shir.R. on Song of Songs ch. 1 verse 1. For an introduction to Shir.R. see S. T. Lachs, 'Prolegomena to Canticles Rabba', and 'The Proems of Canticles Rabba'.

Ruth R. is also a composite work, drawing particularly on the Palestinian Talmud, Ber.R., Vay.R. and Pes.K., but it also contains independent material. It contains, for example, an account of the famous apostate, Elisha b. Abuyah, which differs considerably from the account in B. Ḥag. 15a. Ruth R. falls into two parts. The first section is a collection of six proem homilies, followed by a long exegetical section (§7) whose purpose is to show that passages in scripture beginning '*Vayyehi bimey* . . .' denote trouble.[4] After that, Ruth R. becomes a verse-by-verse commentary divided into eight *parashiyyoth* (sections). References, therefore, are given either to the proem number, or to *parashiyyoth* and subdivisions.

---

[1] A separate Midrash Zuta (i.e. the small Midrash) on Megilloth was published by S. Buber in 1894; the commentaries are not a unity and were drawn from different sources.

[2] Ed. S. Schechter (1896); it also appears in Midrash Zuta above.

[3] Ed. L. Grünhut (1897).

[4] *And it came to pass, in the days of* . . . The interpretation was reached by redividing the first word and reading, *Way yehi*, 'there will be woe'. The passages discussed are (in order of appearance): Gen. xiv. 1, Isa. vii. 1, Jer. i. 3, Esther i. 1, Ruth ii. 1.

Ekah R. is an early Palestinian midrash, put together probably during the fourth century. Lamentations was recited in synagogue on the 9th Ab, the day which commemorated the destruction of Jerusalem. Thus homilies on Lamentations were preached from an early date, and it is not surprising that a large part of Ekah R. is a collection of homilies (34 in number, or in some editions, 36). The second half is a verse-by-verse commentary, so that references are given either to the proem number, or to the text of Lamentations followed by the sub-division of the material in Ekah R. For the text see the bibliography under S. Buber.

Qoh.R. is a verse-by-verse commentary, but it drew much material from homiletic midrashim, particuarly Pes.K. It had a preference for the Palestinian Talmud, but it also drew on the Babylonian Talmud, and at one point (v. 8. 2) apparently refers to some of the additional tractates.[1] It is worth noting that Mas. Soferim xiv. 3 listed four of the five Megilloth, but omitted Qoh. Qoh. was read in synagogue at the feast of Tents (Booths), but that seems to have been a late practice. It would not, therefore, be surprising to find that the compilation of Qoh.R. was late, perhaps in the seventh century. References are given to the chapter and verse of Qoh. followed by the subdivisions in the Midrash.

Est.R. was an important work, since the purpose of Esther itself was to support and encourage Jews in times of persecution. Esther was read at the feast of Purim, and a tractate in the Mishnah (Megillah) is devoted to the rules governing its reading. The authorities quoted are mostly Palestinian Amoraim of the fourth century, and it drew on the Palestinian Talmud, which points to a date of compilation some time in the late fourth or early fifth century (when pressure on the Jews in Palestine was becoming increasingly intense). Est.R. opens with a collection of proem homilies (or fragments of homilies) on Esther i. 1. It then becomes a verse-by-verse commentary divided into 10 *parashiyyoth* (in some editions 6). The commentary is fuller on the early chapters of Esther, and it has no commentary on anything after Esther viii. 15. References are given to the 10 *parashiyyoth* and to the subdivisions within them.[2]

---

[1] It is always possible, however, that this may be the result of a campaign on behalf of these tractates and not conclusive as regards date.

[2] On Esther see also Aggadath Esther, ed. by S. Buber (1897) (a late compilation).

5. NARRATIVE MIDRASHIM.[1] The early stages of narrative midrashim have already been mentioned. They are the works which retell the biblical narrative in their own words, introducing stories and comments freely which do not appear in the biblical text at all. Good early examples are Jubilees and Pseudo-Philo. It remained a popular way of expounding the meaning of scripture, and as time went by these works began to incorporate more and more rabbinic material in their exegesis. The outstanding example is Pirqe deRabbi Eliezer.

P.R.E. is a free account of various incidents from the Bible which are told partly in the biblical order but partly in groups of related subjects; for example, there are sections on the value of repentance, on the resurrection of the dead, and on the Two Ways. In its present form it is a late work (perhaps as late as the eighth or ninth century), and it is also a composite work. The early chapters are much concerned with some of the classic subjects of rabbinic mysticism, the work of creation,[2] the divine chariot,[3] the secret of redemption,[4] and above all (in the case of P.R.E.) the secret of the calendar;[5] 6–8 are devoted to complicated calculations and may well have been incorporated from a separate work. The later chapters are constructed roughly around a record of the ten descents of God to the earth,[6] but many other stories have been added. The book in its edited form is incomplete, since it deals with only eight descents.

P.R.E. is important, because the forms in which it presents its legends and interpretations of the Bible are often close to those of Ps. Jon. Like Ps. Jon. it is an important witness to a developed stage of exegesis of which the origins are frequently very early indeed.

There is an English translation, with introduction and notes, by G. Friedländer. For the text see the bibliography under M. Higger.

There are several other works in this category. Sefer haYashar is a retelling of the biblical narrative from Adam to the time of the Judges. It was a popular work, but it appears to be even later than P.R.E. Nevertheless, it gives several alternative interpretations, and for that reason it is occasionally quoted or referred to in this book. It was translated by M. M. Noah (1840).

[1] Also referred to as historical Midrashim.
[2] *Ma'aseh bereshith.*
[3] *Ma'aseh merkabah,* based on the visions in Ezek. i and x, a prominent part of Jewish mysticism; in P.R.E. there is scarcely any elaboration of it.
[4] *Sod ge'ullah.*   [5] *Sod ha'ibbur.*   [6] See P.R.E. 14, beginning.

Two other works may, in their original form, go back to an earlier date, the Chronicle of Moses and the Chronicle of Jeraḥmeel. What is certain is that since these works are anthologies they include very early material.[1] Yashar is a more connected and organised narrative than Chron. Jer., the compiler of the latter being quite unperturbed by contradictions in the different Midrashim which he quoted. Indeed at one point he specifically wrote: 'As this[2] is simply to be taken as a legend, we do not care to reconcile it with the other, which makes Abraham live in the time of Nimrod the Wicked.'[3]

In the case of Chron. Jer. one of the main motives for the compilation was simply to preserve what might otherwise have been lost. Thus the compiler wrote at the beginning of his work:

my spirit bore me aloft and filled me with enthusiasm in the days of my youth, when I was easy-going and keen-witted. For I saw many books scattered and dispersed here and there. I then resolved to collect them, and write them in one book. I then made a collection of the words of the wise and their aphorisms, and wrote them down in a book for the use of those who love parable and history, and for wise men generally who are not otherwise occupied, in order that they may reflect upon these things, so that they may see, understand, and know the truth concerning a few of the events which have taken place under the sun, and of a few of the troubles and afflictions which our ancestors endured in their exile, and what vicissitudes they underwent when the tempest swept over them, so that they may not be forgotten by their seed.

Like other Narrative Midrashim, Chron. Jer. took the biblical narrative as its thread, but then attached to it an enormous variety of material. Some of it is drawn more from popular folk-lore than from biblical exegesis as, for example, in its quotation of the 'Seven Ages of Man':

And why does it[4] cry? Because of the world it has left behind. For at that moment seven new worlds are awaiting it. In the first world it is like a king after whose welfare all people ask; all desire to see it and embrace it, and kiss it, because it is in the first year. In the second year it is like a swine which wallows in mire; a child does the same until it reaches two years. In the third world it is like a kid that skips and gambols about on the meadows. Thus, a child skips about here and there until it is five years of age. In the fourth world it is like a horse which strides along haughtily. In the same way does a child walk along proud of his youth until he is

---

[1] Chron. Jer., for example, included narratives from the biblical Apocrypha.
[2] A preceding narrative about Nimrod.
[3] Chron. Jer. xxxiii. 1.
[4] A newborn baby.

eighteen years old. In the fifth world he is like an ass upon whose shoulders burdens are placed. In the same manner burdens are heaped upon man's shoulders; he is given a wife by whom he begets children. He must wander to and fro in order to obtain food for them until he is about forty years old. In the sixth stage he is like a dog, insolent, wandering about in all places for food: stealing and robbing in one place and enjoying it in another. In the seventh stage he is like an ape, whose appearance is changed in every respect. All the household curse him and desire his death. Even the young children make fun of him, and even the smallest bird wakes him from his sleep.[1]

In general, Chron. Jer. contains material of great interest and entertainment. It has been translated by M. Gaster in the Oriental Translation Fund New Series, and quotations in this book are taken from that translation.

6. OTHER WORKS. Various works do not fit easily into the categories already surveyed. A brief account of them follows:

Aboth deRabbi Nathan

A.R.N. is usually described as a tosefta, or supplement, to the tractate in the Mishnah, Pirqe Aboth, 'The Chapters of the Fathers'.[2] Pirqe Aboth is quite different from the other tractates in the Mishnah; whereas they are mostly concerned with halakah, Pirqe Aboth covers a much wider field. It is more haggadic in content, and it is mostly in the form of sayings of individual rabbis. It contains several summaries of biblical exegesis and often groups things together numerically.[3]

Pirqe Aboth drew the bulk of its material from the early period of rabbinic Judaism, from authorities or rabbis between the years 200 B.C. and A.D. 200. A.R.N. is of the same character as Pirqe Aboth and for the

---

[1] Chron. Jer. ix. 9. See also Qoh.R. i. 2. 1 for a slightly shorter version.

[2] Often referred to as 'The Sayings of the Fathers'. For a brief introduction see J. A. Guttmann, 'Tractate Abot . . .'.

[3] For example P.A. v: 'By ten sayings the world was created . . . there were ten generations from Adam to Noah . . . with ten trials our father Abraham was tested . . . there are seven marks of the foolish man and seven marks of the wise . . . There are four kinds of men: the one that says, "What is mine is mine and what is yours is yours"; that is the usual kind, though some say that is the kind of Sodom (i.e. selfish; see the Targum and notes on Gen. xiii. 13); the one that says, "What is mine is yours and what is yours is mine", that is the unintelligent kind; the one that says, "What is mine is yours and what is yours is yours", that is the saintly kind; and the one that says, "What is yours is mine and what is mine is my own", that is the evil kind.' The same kind of numerical summaries are also found in the Targums. See, for example, Ps. Jon. on Gen. xxviii. 10, 'Five miracles were performed for Jacob . . .'.

most part is based on it. Usually it quotes a part of Pirqe Aboth and then adds further illustrations or interpretations. Sometimes these in turn suggest entirely new topics and A.R.N. goes off in pursuit of them; in this it is typical of many rabbinic works. There is no attempt to draw up a systematic treatise.

A.R.N. appears in two different forms. One is usually known as A.R.N. A, and is often printed as an additional tractate in the Talmud.[1] The other is known as A.R.N. B, and was edited by S. Schechter.[2] There are differences between the two, and it is disputed whether they represent two different versions of an original A.R.N., or whether they are independent of each other.[3] It used to be held that A.R.N. as we have it now is a late work, probably from some time in the seventh or eighth century A.D. or a little later. But the present form certainly rests on a much earlier composition: the authorities quoted are all Tannaitic,[4] it is based on a form of Pirqe Aboth which differs from the present form of that tractate,[5] and almost everything about it, its language and its substance, belongs to the Tannaitic period. The composition of A.R.N. may therefore best be ascribed to a date some time in the third century. It remains possible that it contains elements dating from at least as early as the first century.[6]

If it is possible to identify the rabbi Nathan of the title the most likely candidate is a Babylonian rabbi of that name who lived roughly at the same time as R. Judah haNasi, redactor of the Mishnah. It has been suggested that R. Nathan made his own redaction of Pirqe Aboth, which became the basis of the present work. But the identification is uncertain. The work was highly regarded in later Judaism, and quotations were frequently made from it.

There is a complete English translation, with a fuller introduction, by J. Goldin in the Yale Judaica series; a more detailed introduction is provided by the work of L. Finkelstein referred to in n. 6; it is also translated in the Soncino translation of the minor tractates (see p. 68).

---

[1] See p. 68.

[2] *Aboth de Rabbi Nathan* (Vienna, 1887; New York, 1945).

[3] For a summary of some of these differences see the introduction to *The Fathers according to Rabbi Nathan*, by J. Goldin, pp. xxi–xxii.

[4] I.e. not later than the early years of the third century A.D.

[5] For a summary of the differences see Goldin, *op. cit.* pp. xix–xx.

[6] See the analysis of the individual elements by L. Finkelstein in his introduction to A.R.N., *Mabo leMassektot* . . . .

Midrash on Samuel

Midr. Sam., sometimes referred to as Aggadath Shemuel, is a compilation of midrashim relevant to the text of Samuel. It is thus not a commentary on the complete text, but on those parts only for which midrashim could be found. It draws on early works from the Palestinian tradition, and only Palestinian Amoraim are mentioned. The usual editions are those of Stettin (1860) and S. Buber (1893).

Midrash Tehillim (Midrash on Psalms)

Midr. Teh. has a history even more confused and uncertain than most other rabbinic works. As early as the second century A.D. there seem to have been some collected works of interpretation on the Psalms. Ber.R. xxxiii. 3 records: 'Our teacher[1] was once praising R. Ḥiyya the Elder to R. Ishmael b. R. Jose, who said: "A great man! a holy man! I once saw R. Ḥiyya at the baths but he did not acknowledge me" ... R. Judah (later) asked him: "Why did you not acknowledge him?" R. Ḥiyya said, "Because I was reflecting on a haggadah of the Psalms." R. Judah's response was to attach two of his disciples to him. They had to go with him to the steam room in case he should stay there too long to the detriment of his health.'[2] But the compilation of Midr. Teh. in its present form is much later than that. It is generally agreed that the Midrash on Psalms cxix–cl was added to the Midrash on the earlier psalms after that earlier part of the Midrash had reached its final form.[3] Dates have been suggested for the final composition of the earlier part of the Midrash ranging from the seventh century to the ninth or even later.[4] But it seems better to think in terms of a process of gradual extension and accretion. The individual elements, therefore, in this Midrash need to be considered carefully in their own right. The Midrash has been translated into English and supplied with a brief introduction by W. G. Braude.[5] For the text see the bibliography under S. Buber.

[1] R. Judah haNasi.
[2] J.Kil. ix. 3 and J.Ket. xii. 3 both say that it was a haggadah of the whole book of Psalms, but that may be an exaggeration.
[3] MSS stop at Ps. cxviii.
[4] For a summary of some of the arguments involved see the introduction by W. G. Braude to his translation of Midrash Tehillim in the Yale Judaica Series, pp. xxv–xxxii.　　　　　　　　　　　　　　　　[5] Ibid.

Midrash on Proverbs

Midr. Prov. was compiled at a late date, probably some time in the tenth century. It contains some haggadic material of interest, particularly its description of martyrdoms. The usual edition is that of S. Buber (Wilna, 1893).

Megillath Ta'anith

Meg. Taan., 'the Scroll of Fasts', is a record of days which were prohibited as fast days. The general reason for a prohibition was that a happy or joyful event had at some time taken place on that day. It follows that Meg. Taan. is potentially an important chronological source,[1] but it needs to be used with caution. A text was edited by A. Neubauer, *Mediaeval Jewish Chronicles*, II (1895), but see also H. Lichtenstein, *Megillath Taanith*, pp. 318–51; G. Dalman, *Aramaische Dialektproben*. A translation of the main body of the text (but not of the often important glosses) will be found in A. Edersheim, *The Life and Times of Jesus the Messiah*, II, 698–700.

Seder 'Olam

Seder 'Olam is another chronological work, listing and dating biblical and post-biblical events down to the revolt of Bar-Kokeba. It was later supplemented by Seder 'Olam Zuta which carried the dating down to the death of R. Hazub (c. A.D. 800). Traditionally, the work was ascribed to R. Jose ben Halafta[2] who died c. A.D. 160, but it seems more likely that it was compiled in the early Amoraic period. For the text, see the bibliography under B. Ratner.

Tanna debe Eliyyahu

This work, also known as Seder Eliyyahu Rabba, is a collection of largely haggadic material taught to Rab Anan[3] by the prophet Elijah. The story is told in B.Ket. 106a. For a long time T.d.E. has been regarded as a late work, but it is increasingly recognised that some of its midrashic material is at least as early as the third century. On T.d.E. see M. Friedmann, *Seder Eliahu rabba . . .*; and M. Kadushin, *The Theology of Seder Eliahu*.

---

[1] See, for example, S. Zeitlin, 'Megillath Taanith as a Source . . .'. Meg. Taan. was also utilised by W. R. Farmer, *Maccabees, Zealots and Josephus*.

[2] B.Nidd. 46b.   [3] A pupil of Rab.

7. RELATED WORKS. Rabbinic exegesis and interpretation did not remain within a narrow circle of Judaism. Not only did it draw on extraneous material, but it was also known outside its own circles. Christian writers at various points took an interest in Jewish interpretation, and made use of it in their own works.[1] There were also several groups which stood half-way between Christianity and Judaism, and their writings often throw interesting light on rabbinic exegesis. In particular, they show how it developed on a divergent path. Some of these works are quoted in this book to give examples of what happened to Jewish interpretations outside Judaism. Of particular importance from this point of view are the works in a group known as 'The Cave of Treasures'. These works are in the form of narrative midrashim, retelling parts of scripture. They usually included the story of creation at least, and continued the narrative to various different points, depending on the interests of the individual work. The main works in the group are Pseudo-Athanasius, *The Cave of Treasures*, the Syriac *Cave of Treasures*,[2] the Arabic *Kitab alMajal*,[3] *Adam and Eve*, *The Testament of Adam*, and *The Book of the Bee*. Although these works are related to each other, the relationship is extremely complicated and they have become independent works in many respects. Some of them are strongly anti-Jewish, but at the same time there is no doubt at all that much of their material was Jewish in origin. It is possible that they are all divergent forms of a Jewish original. They are quoted occasionally in this book, because they show how traditions which appear in Ps. Jon. also appear outside Judaism.

For the same reason a few quotations are made from a Christian Syriac commentary on Genesis. The commentary, a compendium of early Syrian exegesis,[4] is contained in one of the Mingana manuscripts.[5] The first half of it has been edited and translated by Abraham Levene,[6] and it reveals clearly the extent to which Jewish exegesis was known and shared by a non-Jewish community. Levene illustrated this in such detail that there is no need here to do more than draw attention to the fact. Levene also pointed out the main reason why it came about.

---

[1] Obvious examples are Justin and Jerome.
[2] Translated by E. A. Wallis Budge. Quotations in this book are from his translation. [3] The Book of the Rolls.
[4] Mostly Nestorian Christians. [5] Mingana 553.
[6] *The Early Syrian Fathers on Genesis*; the quotations in this book are from Levene's translation.

The very close proximity of the Christian seminaries at Nisibis, Edessa, and Keneshrin to the Jewish seminaries at Nisibis, Pumbeditha, Sura, Nehardea, and Mahuza; the common language (the dialect of Edessa) spoken by Christians and Jews alike; the fact that the first Christians were Jewish converts, and that Jews and Christians looked to the O.T. as the repository of prophecies referring to themselves, were factors which . . . must have been of the deepest significance.[1]

Levene drew particular attention to the use of 'the basic principle of Rabbinic typology, "Ma'aseh 'abot siman labanim" (the lives of the Patriarchs prefigured the lives of their descendants)',[2] though in the case of Christian exegesis the 'Old' Testament was not complete and final in itself but prefigured particularly Christ.

For a full introduction to the work, see the book by Abraham Levene.

The Versions

It will be seen that references are frequently made to translations of the Bible into other languages. The purpose, again, has been to show to what extent an interpretation recorded in the Targums was also made the basis of interpretation in one or more of the other versions. Here LXX is of particular importance, since it goes back to an early date. For a brief introduction to the Versions see O. Eissfeldt, *The Old Testament* . . .; B. J. Roberts, *The Old Testament Text and Versions*; and F. S. Kenyon, *Our Bible and the Ancient Manuscripts*.

[1] Levene, p. 315.　　　　[2] Levene, p. 316.

PS. JONATHAN ON
SELECTED CHAPTERS OF
GENESIS

Explanatory Note

The purpose of the second part of this book is to give substantial illustration of targum-method and material. It consists of a translation of Ps. Jonathan on the following chapters or passages in Genesis: i–ix; x. 8–14; xi. 1–9, 27 f.; xiii. 10–13; xiv. 13–15, 18–20; xv. 1–6; xvi. 1–6; xviii. 1–25; xix. 24; xx. 13; xxi. 1–2, 33; xxii; xxvi. 5; xxxvii; xxxix–l.

The translation of Ps. Jonathan of each chapter or section is followed, for the purpose of comparison, by a translation of selections from other Targums on the same passages. (So far as the Fragmentary Targum is concerned, it should be noted that the Fragmentary Targum does not exist for every verse in Genesis; but wherever a verse, or part of a verse, occurs in Ginsburger's edition, reference has been made to it, even if it has not been translated. In this way, the reader will know whether a particular verse occurs in Ginsburger's edition of the Fragmentary Targum or not. Similarly, a complete index of the passages edited by P. Kahle from the Cairo Geniza will be found in Appendix VII.)

The selections from other Targums are then followed by notes, in which the background of the targum interpretations is explained. These notes consist largely of further translations of rabbinic or other works, and they are thus intended to give even greater illustration of the methods and techniques of Jewish and rabbinic exegesis.

It will be seen that the translation of the Targums appears in two different kinds of type, italicised and roman. The italicised type represents the places where the Targum is close to the Hebrew text, and it is in fact a quotation of the Revised Version. The roman type represents the places where the Targum interpretation differs from the Hebrew text. By using two different types, it is hoped that the interpretation will stand out more clearly and obviously. It should, however, be remembered that in any translation from one language to another every single word is, in a sense, an interpretation; consequently, the division into plain and italicised type should be taken only as a guide to draw attention to the larger and more obvious interpretations.

The abbreviations which have been used for the Targums in this book are listed on p. 28.

GENESIS I

1 At^a the beginning^b *God created the heaven and the earth.*

2 *And the earth was waste and void,*^c desolate without the sons of men,^d and empty of animals. *And darkness was upon the face of the deep: and the spirit of* mercies^e from before God blew *upon the face of the waters.*

3 *And God said, 'Let there be light* to lighten the world'. *And* immediately *there was light.*

4 *And God saw the light, that it was good: and God divided the light from the darkness.*

5 *And God called the light Day,* and he made it so that the dwellers on the earth might labour^f during it; *and the darkness he called Night,* and he made it so that the creatures might have rest during it. *And there was evening and there was morning, one day.*

6 *And God said, 'Let there be a firmament*^g *in the midst of the waters, and let it divide the waters* above *from the waters* below'.

7 *And God made the firmament,* its thickness being three fingers between the limits of the heavens and the waters of the ocean. *And he divided the waters which were under the firmament from the waters which were above* in the vault^h of *the firmament: and it was so.*

8 *And God called the firmament Heaven. And there was evening and there was morning, a second day.*

9 *And God said, 'Let the* lower *waters* which are left over *under the heaven* be for a single place, *and let* the earth be dried up that *the dry land* may be visible'. *And it was so.*

a Or 'from'.

b *Min awala*; cf. Targ. Job xx. 4.

c Both Ps. Jon. and F.T. (see below *ad loc.*) kept close to the Hebrew *tohu wabohu*, but the phrase they used should perhaps be translated more specifically 'confused and in disorder'; see Ber.R. ii. 2, quoted in the notes on p. 102.

d *Bene nash.*

e See Ps. Jon. on Gen. viii. 1.

f Or 'worship'.

g R.V. mg. *expanse*; Ps. Jon. has here the same word as the Hebrew.

h Or perhaps more accurately, 'in the storehouse of the firmament': see B.Taan. 8*b*: 'A tanna taught: "In heaven there is a storechamber from which rain comes forth."'

10 *And God called the dry land Earth; and* the assembly[a] *of the waters called he Seas: and God saw that it was good.*

11 *And God said, 'Let the earth* increase putting forth the herb whose seed produces seed, and the tree, fruit *bearing fruit after its kind, wherein is the seed thereof, upon the earth'. And it was so.*

12 *And the earth brought forth* the herb whose seed produces seed (*after its kind*), *and tree bearing fruit, wherein is the seed thereof, after its kind:* and God saw that it was good.

13 *And there was evening and there was morning, a third day.*

14 *And God said, 'Let there be lights in the firmament of the heaven to divide the day from the night; and let them be for signs and for seasons*[b] of festivals and for numbering by them the reckoning of days, and for sanctifying by them the new moon days and the new year days, the intercalations of the months and the intercalations of the years, the solstices of the sun and the appearance of the new moon, and the solar cycles:

15 *and let them be for lights in the firmament of the heaven to give light upon the earth'. And it was so.*

16 *And God made the two great lights,* and they were equal in glory[c] for 21 years less 672 parts of an hour.[d] Then the moon reported against the sun a false report, and was diminished. And he designated the sun to be *the greater light to rule the day, and* the moon to be *the lesser light,*[e] and *the stars.*

17 *And God set them* in their courses *in the firmament of the heaven to give light upon the earth,*

18 *and to rule over*[f] *the day and over the night, and to divide the light* of day *from the darkness* of night: *and God saw that it was good.*

19 *And there was evening and there was morning, a fourth day.*

20 *And God said, 'Let* the miry lakes[g] *of the waters* swarm forth swarms of living creatures,[h] and the bird which flies, and makes its nest on the earth, and let the way of its flight be through the air of the *firmament of heaven'.*

[a] Lit. 'the house of assembly', the title of the synagogue (see p. 9).
[b] As T.O.
[c] I Enoch lxxii. 37 regarded the sun and moon as having been originally equal in size.
[d] See S. Poznanski, 'The Calendar', in *E.R.E.*, and *J.E.* art. 'Calendar'.
[e] Mg. 'to rule the night'.　　　　　　　[f] Mg.; text, 'minister over'.
[g] Or perhaps simply 'mire'.　　　　　　[h] See R.V. mg.

21 *And God created the great* tannins,[a] the leviathan and its mate[b] which were made for the day of consolation, *and every living creature* which swarms, *which the* clear *waters brought forth abundantly, after their kinds,* the kinds which are clean and the kinds which are not clean, and every bird flying with wings *after its kind,* the kinds which are clean and the kinds which are not clean: *and God saw that it was good.*

22 *And God blessed them, saying, 'Be fruitful, and multiply, and fill the waters in the seas, and let fowl multiply in the earth.'*

23 *And there was evening and there was morning, a fifth day.*

24 *And God said, 'Let the* clay of *earth bring forth the living creature after its kind,* the kinds which are clean and the kinds which are not clean, *cattle, and creeping thing, and the beast of the earth after its kind'. And it was so.*

25 *And God made the* living creature[c] *of the earth after its kind,* the kinds which are clean and the kinds which are not clean, *and the cattle after their kind, and every thing that creepeth upon the ground after its kind,* the kinds which are clean and the kinds which are not clean: *and God saw that it was good.*

26 *And God said* to the angels who minister before him and who were created on the second day of the creation of the world, '*Let us make* man[d] *in our image, after our likeness:*[e] *and let them have dominion over the fish of the sea, and over the fowl of the air* of heaven, *and over the cattle, and over all the earth, and over every creeping thing that creepeth upon the earth.'*

27 *And God created man in his own* likeness, *in the image of God created he him* with 248 members and 365 sinews,[f] and he laid skin over them, and filled it with flesh and blood: *male and female* in their body *created he them.*

---

a The word *tannin* is related to the Gk. θύννος. Its original meaning may be connected with the word *tana*, meaning 'repeat' (as later in Tannaim; see p. 49). It might have been applied to sea-monsters, because they appeared to rise repeatedly (i.e. in repeated coils) above the surface of the sea, but the explanation is conjectural.

b The same phrase was used for Adam's wife in F.T. on Gen. ii. 18 (Gins. p. 5).

c The word is different from that in verse 24.

d *Adam.*

e *Deyokan:* Jastrow: 'A reverential transformation of *'ikon'* = Gk. εἰκών; but Levy takes it as from two Gk. words, δύο and εἰκών.

f Lit. 'threads', perhaps 'nerves' or 'arteries'.

28 *And God blessed them, and God said unto them, 'Be fruitful, and multiply, and* fill the earth with sons and daughters, *and subdue it; and have dominion over the fish of the sea, and over the fowl of the* heaven, *and over every living thing that moveth upon the earth.'*

29 *And God said, 'Behold I have given you every herb yielding seed, which is upon the face of all the earth, and every tree* unfruitful for the purposes of building and for burning; (and every tree) *in the which is the fruit of a tree yielding seed; to you it shall be for meat:*

30 *and to every* living creature *of the earth, and to every fowl* of the heaven, *and to every thing that creepeth upon the earth, wherein there is life, (I have given) every green herb for meat.' And it was so.*

31 *And God saw every thing that he had made, and, behold, it was very*[a] *good. And there was evening and there was morning, the sixth day.*

Selections from other Targums on Genesis i

N.B. the whole of Gen. i occurs in F.T. (Gins. pp. 3 f.), even though it is not all translated here.

1-2 F.T. (Gins. p. 3, cf. also pp. 74, 91): In[b] wisdom the Lord *created*, and he perfected[c] *the heaven and the earth.* (2) *And the earth was waste and void,* desolate without the sons of men, and without any cultivation[d] at all. *And darkness was* spreading *upon the face of the deep: and the spirit* of mercies from before the Lord blew *upon the face of the waters.*

T.O.: In the earliest times[e] the Lord *created the heaven and the earth.* (2) *And the earth was* desolate[f] and empty.[g] *And darkness was upon the face of the deep: and* a wind[h] from before the Lord blew *upon the face of the waters.*

3 F.T. (Gins. p. 3): *And* the word[i] of the Lord *said, 'Let there be light'. And there was light* in[j] his word.[k]

a Lit. 'singularly'.   b Or 'by means of'.
c The same word is used in T.O. on Gen. i. 1, Ps. Jon. on Gen. xxii. 13.
d Or 'service', perhaps in the sense of 'worship' as a deliberate play on words.
e *Beqadmin.*
f *Ṣadya*: the other Targums and Pesh. transliterated both words (so far as they could) and then interpreted them, but T.O. translated them, as did Aq. in a similar way; cf. LXX and Vulg. The words used by T.O. for 'desolate and empty' are the same as those used by the other Targums for their interpretation.   g *Reqanya.*   h Or 'spirit'.
i *Memar.*   j Or 'by means of'.   k *Memar.*

4 F.T. (Gins. p. 3): *And* there was revealed before the Lord the light *that it was good:* [a] *and* the word of the Lord *divided the light from the darkness.*

5 F.T. (Gins. p. 3; see also p. 74): *And* the word of the Lord *called the light Day, and the darkness he called Night. And there was evening and there was morning,* and it was the order of the work of creation,[b] the first day.

6-9 occur in F.T. (Gins. p. 3; see also p. 74).

10 F.T. (Gins. p. 3): *And* the word of the Lord *called the dry land Earth; and* the assembly[c] *of the waters called he Seas: and* it was revealed before the Lord *that it was good* and sound.

-13 occur in F.T. (Gins. p. 3).

14 F.T. (Gins. pp. 3 f.): *And* the word of the Lord *said, 'Let there be lights in the firmament of the heaven to divide the day from the night, and let them be for* marks and *for signs (and for seasons), and for* sanctifying by them the new moon and new year days.'

T.O.: *And* the Lord *said, 'Let there be lights . . ., and let them be* for numbering by them *days and years.'*

15 occurs in F.T. (Gins. p. 4).

16 F.T. (Gins. p. 4): *And* the word of the Lord created *the two great lights;* the great light to minister in the day, and the small light to minister in the night, and the order of *stars.*

7-25 occur in F.T. (Gins. p. 4).

26 F.T. (Gins. p. 4): *And* the word of the Lord *said, 'Let us* create the son of man[d] in the resemblance[e] corresponding to us, *and let them have dominion, etc.'*

27 F.T. (Gins. p. 4; see also slight variants on pp. 74, 91): *And* the word[f] of the Lord *created man*[g] *in his own* resemblance, in the resemblance from before the Lord *created he* them,[h] *male and* his partner *created he them.*

8-31 occur in F.T. (Gins. p. 4).

---

[a] Cf. Gins. F.T. p. 91.
[b] *Bereshith;* cf. F.T. on Gen. i. 1.
[c] See footnote a, p. 96. The same phrase also occurs here in T.O.
[d] *Bar nash.*
[e] *Demuth;* cf. T.O. *ad loc.*   [f] *Memra.*
[g] *Adam.*   [h] *N.B.* the plural. See p. 117, n. a.

5370

Notes on Genesis i

1 The first word in Genesis provoked much discussion. It was the first of the revealed words of God, and in consequence it was thought, almost inevitably, that it would be of particular significance. The Hebrew word *bereshith*[a] seemed to demand comment in any case, because its form is unusual: in form it looks like a word in the construct state, but in fact there is no noun following it.[b] All three Targums changed the Hebrew word, but in different ways.

The interpretation in F.T. looks the most unusual, but it was based on the fact that the word *reshith* occurs elsewhere in the O.T.[c] One of the passages is Prov. viii. 22, where Wisdom is made to say, *The Lord possessed*[d] *me, the beginning*[e] *of his way*. Wisdom was thus thought to have been called in that verse the *reshith* of God; or in other words, *reshith* was thought to be a name of Wisdom. The name was then applied to Gen. i. 1 to produce the interpretation of F.T.: 'By means of *reshith* (Wisdom) God created . . .'[f]

That interpretation was extremely common,[g] and it was extended still further by identifying Wisdom with Torah. Thus Sifre on Deut. xi. 10 commented: 'Torah, because it was loved more than all things, was created before all things, as it is written, "The Lord possessed me, the beginning of his ways".' See also Ber.R i. 1, Yalqut on Prov. viii. 14 (§941), and compare LXX Prov. viii. 30.

---

a *In the beginning.*
b The 'construct state' is a Hebrew construction by means of which a genitive relationship is expressed. Phrases like 'the house of the man', 'the key of the door', were treated as a unity, and the first word in the phrase was shortened slightly to make it run on more rapidly to the second. A rough analogy would be the way in which the English genitive phrase is inverted to read 'the man's house'. The first word in its changed form is known as being in the construct state. The word *bereshith* has the appearance of being in the construct, but there is no word following it. Theoretically *in the beginning* should have been followed by something like 'of the world'.
c For a summary see W. Eichrodt, 'In the Beginning', in *Israel's Prophetic Heritage* (London, 1962), pp. 1–10.
d Or 'created'.
e *Reshith*; R.V. *in the beginning*, but there is no preposition in the Hebrew.
f In contrast, in Gen. i. 5 F.T. has *bereshith*, illustrating the way in which *bereshith* becomes a noun in its own right, representing *ma'aseh bereshith*.
g See, for example, Tanh.B. i. 11: 'You find that by (or "in") wisdom the Holy One, blessed be he, created the heaven and the earth.'

The phrase used by T.O. can also mean 'in ancient times', and it was used by T.O. in that sense in Gen. iii. 15: '*I will put enmity between thee and the woman, and between* your sons and her sons. He will remember what you did to him long ago, and you will watch out for him to the end.'[a] Similarly the phrase used in Ps. Jon. can mean simply, 'an early season', and it was used by the Targum to translate Hos. ix. 10: *I saw your fathers as the first-ripe in the fig tree at her first season.* But it could also mean 'from the beginning', and it was used to translate Job xx. 4: *Knowest thou not this of old time, since man was placed upon earth, . . .?* Thus Ps. Jon. and T.O. avoided the problems involved in *bereshith* by finding a new form of words.

A good summary of some of the difficulties was made by Rashi:

This phrase can only be interpreted in the way that our rabbis interpreted it: 'God created for the sake of his Torah', which is called 'the beginning of his way', 'and for the sake of Israel', who is called 'the beginning of his increase'.[b] But if you wish to explain it in its plain sense,[c] explain it in this way: 'At the beginning of the creation of heaven and earth, when the earth was waste and void, and there was darkness, God said, *Let there be light.*'[d] The phrase was not intended to point out the order of creation by saying that heaven and earth were created first. If that had been intended it would have said, 'As a beginning he created . . .'[e] But *reshith* never occurs except in the construct state . . .[f] Thus here you must translate it as though it read, *bereshith bero*[g] . . . But if you insist that the purpose of the phrase was to say that heaven and earth were created first, then its interpretation is, 'at the beginning of everything he created these'. If that is so you should be surprised at yourself, because in fact the waters came first, as it is written, . . . *and the spirit of God moved on the face of the waters.*[h] But since the passage has not made clear when the creation of the waters was, you must infer that the waters came before the earth . . . .

'Waste and void':

The words were also taken to mean 'dismayed[i] and bewildered', as explained by a parable in Ber.R. ii. 2:

[a] The limitations of *miqqedem* as a translation are discussed in Tanḥ.B. i. 2.
[b] Jer. ii. 3, where R.V. translates *reshith* as 'firstfruits'; cf. Ass. Mos. i. 12, II Bar. xiv. 18 f.
[c] *Peshuto.*
[d] Ibn Ezra slightly varied the 'plain sense' of Rashi: 'In the beginning, when God created heaven and earth, the earth was waste and void . . .'
[e] *Barishonah bara.*
[f] Rashi offers as examples Jer. xxvi. 1, Gen. x. 10, Deut. xviii. 4.
[g] 'At the beginning of his creating . . .'
[h] Gen. i. 2.　　　　　　　　　　　　　　[i] Or 'astonished'.

R. Abbahu said: 'It is like a king[a] who bought two slaves at the same sale at the same price. One he ordered to be maintained, but the other he ordered to labour for his food. The latter was dismayed and bewildered,[b] and he said: "We were both bought for the same price, but he is maintained, while I have to labour for my food." In the same way the earth was dismayed and bewildered, saying, "The heavenly beings and the earthly beings were created at the same time, but the heavenly beings are sustained by the glory of the Shekina, while the earthly beings must labour if they are to eat." '[c]

Rashi commented on the two words: 'The word *tohu* means "astonished and surprised", because a man would have been astonished and surprised at the emptiness . . . *Bohu* means emptiness and desolation.' 3 The addition in Ps. Jon. was perhaps supplied from Gen. i. 15, but the actual wording there is different. It is possible, therefore, that it is a reference to the dispute whether light was created before the world, or the world before light. From Gen. i. 1 it was argued that the world came first, but from Ps. civ. 2[d] it was argued that light came first. The argument was summarised in Shem.R. 1. 1:[e]

R. Nehemiah and R. Judah disagreed. R. Judah said: 'The Holy One, blessed be he, created the light first, and after that he created the world. It is like a king who wanted to build a palace, and the place was completely dark. What did he do? He lit lights and torches in order to know where to start the foundations. In the same way, light was created first.' But R. Nehemiah said: 'The world was created first. It is like a king who built a palace, and then made it splendid with lights.'

There was a similar dispute about whether the heavens were created before the earth (which is the order of Gen. i. 1), or the earth before the heavens (which is the order of Gen. ii. 4). It was one of the disputes between Hillel (who held that the earth was created first) and Shammai (who held the opposite).[f] Both disputes occur as two of the ten ques-

[a] Parables about kings are extremely common in rabbinic literature. See I. Ziegler, *Die Königsgleichisse des Midrasch.*
[b] *Toheh uboheh.*
[c] Cf. the variant in Yalqut on Gen. §4, where the earth laments because it is subject to death.
[d] 'Who coverest thyself with light as with a garment; who stretchest out the heavens like a curtain.'
[e] See also Ber.R. iii. 1.
[f] Hillel and Shammai were one of the five *zugoth* (see Introduction, p. 56), and they are probably the best known of the 'pairs'. Their disputes were frequently recorded. In general, Hillel took the more lenient line in interpreting Torah, though not invariably so. In B.Shab. 77*a* reference is made to

tions put by Alexander the Great to the elders of Israel.[a] See also Mek. Pisḥa I (where the conflict between the two verses was taken to mean that both were created simultaneously, which is the view recorded also in P.R.E. 19), J.Ḥag. ii. 1, B.Ḥag. 12a.[b] Chron. Jer. i. 8 has :'On the second day he created the firmament, the angels, the heat of the living bodies, and the heat of Gehinnom. But were not the heavens created on the first day? . . . What then is this heaven which was created on the second day? R. Eliezer says: "That firmament which is above the heads of the four holy creatures." '

5 On Ps. Jon. compare B.Erub. 65a: 'Rab Judah said: "Night was created for sleep only." But R. Simeon b. Laqish said: "The moonlight was created to encourage study." '

F.T. took up the curious phrase in Gen. i. 5, 'one day'; it might have been expected that the Hebrew would have 'the first day', since the sequence goes on (in verses 8 ff.), 'second', 'third', 'fourth' . . . The unusual Hebrew 'one day' caused considerable comment: see, for example, Josephus, *Ant*. i. 29, Philo, *de Opif. Mund*. ix. 35, B.Naz. 7a.

6 The 'expanse of the sky' was thought to be a thin sheet or crust. Thus Josephus wrote: 'After this, on the second day, he set the heaven above the universe, when he was pleased to sever this from the rest and to assign it a place apart, congealing ice about it and without rendering it moist and rainy to give the benefit of the dews in a manner congenial to the earth.'[c]

Ber.R. iv. 3 expressed the same idea with greater elaboration: 'R. Phinehas said in R. Hoshaiah's name: "As there is hollow space between the earth and the firmament, so there is between the firmament

six disputes in which the school of Hillel was more severe than that of Shammai; see also B.Erub. 13b. On this particular point, see Tanḥ.B. i. 11 f., J.Ḥag. ii. 1. For a list of differences as recorded in the Mishnah and early Midrashim, see Strack, *Introduction*, pp. 302f.

[a] B.Tam. 31b–32a.
[b] The dispute is summarised in Ber.R. i. 15, where again it is phrased in parables of a king building his palace.
[c] *Ant*. i. 31. Cf. also Syr. Comm. (Levene, p. 73): 'Scripture calls it *firmament*, because from the substance of water was it consolidated and firmly established . . . *In the midst of the waters*: Scripture says *waters* in order that we may know that as much water did he raise above it as he left beneath it (firmament); . . . just as below the firmament it vaporised on account of the luminaries, so above the firmament, it became frozen and was preserved in its state of compression . . .' For a slightly different application of the idea, see Chron. Jer. i. 6.

and the upper waters: *Let there be a firmament in the midst of the waters, that is, between them.*" '

Rain was then thought to be the upper waters slowly oozing through the heat of the firmament without any of the drops mingling with each other as they fell. Hence Ber.R. continues:[a]

> The firmament resembles a lake, and above the lake is an arched vault. From the heat of the lake the vault oozes out drops of water, which fall into the salt waters, yet do not mix with them.[b] R. Jonah said: 'Do not think it incredible, because the river Jordan passes through lake Tiberias but does not mix with it.' This is certainly miraculous, because when a man sifts wheat or chaff through a sieve, the grains only drop the depth of two or three fingers and they mix; but these raindrops have been falling many years without mixing.

Ber.R. xiii. 10 observed the equal importance of clouds in distilling water gathered up from the earth[c] (argued on the basis of Deut. xi. 11 and II Sam. xxii. 12): 'Why are the clouds called *shehaqim*?[d] Resh Laqish said: "Because they break up the water into drops." R. Abba b. Kahana said: "They do it like the digestive system of animals." '

The dews were thought to be stored up in 'the treasuries of heaven'; see, for example, Ps. Jon. on Gen. xxvii. 27 and xlix. 25.

7 See the notes on i. 6 above, and compare Ber.R. iv. 5:

> The thickness of the 'expanse' equals that of the earth: it is written, *It is he that sitteth upon the circle[e] of the earth . . .,*[f] and it is written, *And he walketh in the circuit[e] of heaven.*[g] *Ḥug*, in both, shows that both are the same. R. Aḥa said in the name of R. Ḥanina: 'It is like a thin metal plate.' R. Joshua b. R. Nehemiah said: 'It is two or three fingers thick.'

See also T.Ḥag. ii. 6, J.Ḥag. ii. 1, B.Ḥag. 15 a, Ber.R. ii. 4.

9 See the notes on i. 6 above.

14 For an example of the importance attached to these calculations see M.R.H., and compare Syr. Comm. (Levene, p. 74), Pes.K. v. 1, Chron. Jer. iv.

a iv. 5; cf. Midr. Teh. on Ps. xviii. 12 for a variant version.
b Hence the distinction between sea-water and drinking-water.
c So Ps. Jon. on Gen. ii. 6, *q.v.* Midr. Teh. on Ps. xviii. 12 recorded the opinion of Resh Laqish in a briefer form: 'Because they grind against each other.'
d In II Sam. xxii. 12, Job xxxviii. 37.
e *Ḥug*.
f Isa. xl. 22.   g Job xxii. 14.

16 The purpose here was to explain why the moon was smaller in size and brilliancy than the sun. A discrepancy was noticed and explored in the verse in Genesis:

R. Simeon b. Pazzi noted a contradiction: the verse begins, *And God made the two great lights*, and it goes on, *the greater light* and *the lesser light*. The moon said to the Holy One, blessed be he: 'Lord of the Universe, can two kings wear a single crown?' He said, 'Go and make yourself smaller.' He said, 'Lord of the Universe, must I make myself smaller because I said what was right?' He said, 'Go and rule by day and by night.' The moon said, 'What use is a lamp in daylight?' . . . He said, 'Go, and the righteous will be named after you.' Thus we find, Jacob the small,[a] Samuel the small[b] and David the small'[c] . . .[d]

Similarly Ber.R. vi. 3: 'R. Judan in R. Tanhum b. R. Hiyya's name, and R. Phinehas in the name of R. Simon said: "After calling them both 'great' he reduces one in stature by 'the great light' and 'the small light'. It is because the one invades the other's domain."'[e]

A similar story was told in P.R.E. 6 (see also Chron. Jer. iii. 1):

'They became rivals: one said, "I am larger than you", the other said, "I am larger than you". What did the Holy One, blessed be he, do to make peace between them? He made the one larger and the other smaller . . .'

A different reason for the diminishment of the moon was given in III Bar. ix. 5–7:

'Then I (Baruch) said: "Why does the moon sometimes increase and sometimes decrease?" He said, "Listen, Baruch: . . . At the transgression of the first man, the moon was close to Sammael[f] when he used the serpent as a disguise.[g] But far from hiding itself, the moon increased, so that God in his anger punished it and shortened its days.'

The difference between the sun and moon is also the subject of comment in B.Sheb. 9a, Tanh.B. ii. 47, Pes.K. v. 1, Pes.R. 78a, Ps. Jon. on Num. xxviii. 15.

20 A problem was created by the fact that fish and birds are mentioned in this same verse: were birds created out of water? Ps. Jon. added the word 'mire' to resolve the difficulty. For the same solution see B.Hull. 27b.

---

[a] Amos vii. 2.
[c] I Sam. xvii. 14.
[e] The moon can sometimes be seen by day.
[f] See the Targum and notes on Gen. iii. 6.

[b] A tannaitic teacher.
[d] B.Hull. 60b.
[g] Or 'garment'.

21 B.B.B. 74*b*, 75*a* identifies the tannins as Leviathan and its mate, and explains the allusion above:

R. Johanan said: 'The verse refers to Leviathan the swift[a] serpent and to Leviathan the crooked[b] serpent',[c] for it is written: *In that day the Lord with his sore . . . sword shall punish . . .*[d] . . .Rab Judah said in the name of Rab: 'Everything that the Holy One, blessed be he, created in the world he created male and female. So he created Leviathan the gliding serpent and Leviathan the winding serpent (as) the male and the female; but if they had mated they would have destroyed the world. So what did the Holy One, blessed be he, do? He castrated the male and killed the female preserving it with salt for the righteous in the world to come, as it is written, *And he shall slay the dragon that is in the sea*[e] . . . Rabba said in the name of R. Johanan: 'The Holy One, blessed be he, will make a feast in the time to come for the righteous out of the flesh of Leviathan, . . . and the Holy One, blessed be he, will make a feast in the time to come for the righteous out of the skin of Leviathan . . .'

See also Ber.R. vii. 4, xi. 9, Pes.K. p. 455 (additional section for Sukkoth), Chron. Jer. v–vi. 1.

26 The introduction of the angels explains the plural reference in the Hebrew, 'Let us make', thus emphatically preserving the unity of God. Christian exegesis often saw in references of this kind an indication of the Trinity: for example, Augustine said of this verse: 'If the Father had created man without the Son, it would not have been written: *Let us make man . . .*'[f]

The Christian argument based on this verse was common, and it came to be almost a standard case. It is expressed briefly and precisely in the following example:

'He who commands must be commanding someone else; and that person, we have to believe, is none other than the only begotten Son of God, God (himself), to whom in fact he said, *Let us make man . . .*'[g]

The argument appeared early. Justin worked through it in some detail, in his *Dialogue* with Trypho, the Jew:[h]

But that you may not pervert the meaning of these words, by urging what your teachers tell you, that God either said, 'Let us make', to himself, as we

---

[a] R.V. marg. *gliding.*   [b] R.V. marg. *winding.*
[c] Isa. xxvii. 1.   [d] Isa. xxvii. 1.
[e] Isa. xxvii. 1.   [f] *De Trin.* i. 14.
[g] Conc. Ant. *Ep. Paul.* 2. Cf. Cave of Treasures (Budge, p. 51): 'Now by this word, "Us", he makes known concerning the glorious persons (of the Trinity).'
[h] *Dial.* 62 (trans. G. J. Davie); cf. Ep. Barn. v. 5, vi. 12.

often do when on the point of setting about something, or to the elements, that is, the earth, and those other substances of which we think that man is composed; I will recount the words of Moses himself, from which we may be assured indisputably, that he spoke to one different in number from himself, and who was possessed of reason: they are as follows: *And God said, Behold Adam is become as one of us, to know good and evil.*[a] But the words, *one of us,* show a number of persons to be mutually present, that is two at least; for I cannot think that to be true which is taught by what is considered by yourselves to be a heresy, or that its propagators are able to prove, that he spoke to angels, and that the human body is the work of angels.[b]

The Jews consistently rejected the Christian argument,[c] and the actual debate was recorded in Deb.R. ii. 13:

For what great nation is there, that hath a god so nigh unto them . . .?[d] Some heretics[e] asked R. Simlai: 'How many powers[f] created the universe?' He said to them, 'Let us look together at (the account of) the six days of creation.' They said, 'Then is it written, *In the beginning God*[g] *created*? In fact it is, *In the beginning God*[h] *created*. He said to them 'Then is it written, "they created"? In fact it is *he created*'[i] . . . When they came to the account of the sixth day, they said triumphantly, 'But here it is written, *Let us make man in our image.*' He replied, 'Then is it written, "And *they* created man in *their* image"? In fact what it says is, *And God created man in his image.*' They said to him, 'But here it is written, *For what great nation is there, that hath gods*[j] *near to it?*' He replied, 'Then does it go on, "As the Lord our God is whensoever we call upon *them*"? In fact it is, *Whensoever we call upon him.*'

The same dispute was recorded in a slightly different form in Ber.R. viii. 9. Compare also J.Ber. ix. 2 (1), Midr. Teh. on Ps. viii. 2, where the angels resist the creation of man until he proves his wisdom by naming the animals.[k] According to the rabbis, LXX translated the verse as, '*I* shall make man in image and likeness'. It was one of the 18 recognised variants in LXX. For a list of them, see Appendix III.

The unity of God was further emphasised in Ps. Jon. by stressing that the angels themselves belong to the created order. The same is

<hr/>

a Gen. iii. 22.
b Justin probably had in mind the delegation of creation in Gnostic systems, which were as much opposed by Judaism as they were by Christianity.
c For a summary, see Rashi on Gen. i. 26.
d Deut. iv. 7.   e *Minim.*
f *Reshuyoth*; see the notes on Gen. i. 1.
g *Eloha*, sing.   h *Elohim*, plur.
i I.e. the verb is sing. not plur.   j *Elohim.*
k Cf. also T.Sot. vi. 5. The belief that angels contested the creation of man is extremely common.

implied in Ber.R. ii. 2, quoted in the notes on Gen. i. 1, and an actual 'conversation' with the angels was supplied in B.San. 38*b*:

Rab Judah said in the name of Rab: 'When the Holy One, blessed be he, wished to create man, he created a host of ministering angels, and he said: "Do you agree to our making man in our image?" They said, "Lord of the universe, *What is man, that thou art mindful of him? And the son of man that thou visitest him?*"[a] At that he stretched out his little finger towards them and consumed them with fire. The same happened with a second number. The third host (of angels) said: "Lord of the universe, what use was it that those before us spoke to you? The whole world is yours, so whatever you wish to do there, do it." '[b]

Later in the same section (38*b*) a saying is attributed to R. Johanan: 'The Holy One, blessed be he, does nothing without consulting the company of the heavens, as it is written, *The sentence is by the decree of the watchers, and the demand by the word of the holy ones.*'[c]

The creation of the angels on the second day was disputed. The dispute is alluded to in Ber.R. i. 3:

'When were the angels created? R. Johanan said, "On the second day, as it is written, *Who layeth the beams of his chambers in the waters*, and after that, *Who maketh winds his messenger*".[d] R. Ḥanina said, "On the fifth day, as it is written, *And let fowl fly above the earth*,[e] and also, ... *with twain he did fly.*" '[f, g]

According to Jub. ii. 2–3, II Baruch xxi. 6, Kit. alMaj. 91*a*, Cave of Treasures (Budge, p. 44), their creation was on the first day. According to II Enoch xxix. 1 ff., Tanḥ. Ḥay. 3 it was the second day. See also Tanḥ.B. i. 1, 12, Shem.R. xv. 22, Yalqut on Gen. §5.

The analysis of man into 248 limbs was common. Thus A.R.N. 16 [27] recorded the view:

When a man excites himself and goes to act immorally, the whole oᶠ his body obeys him, because the evil *yeẓer*[h] rules over his 248 limbs. When he goes to

[a] Ps. viii. 4 (5).
[b] See p. 102 above, and compare Chron. Jer. vi. 3–5.
[c] Dan. iv. 17 (14). See also B.San. 38*b* quoted in the notes on Gen. xi. 7.
[d] Ps. civ. 3 (4) R.V. marg. *his angels winds*.
[e] Gen. i. 20.
[f] Isa. vi. 2; if angels can fly, they must be counted as birds, and birds were created on the fifth day.
[g] Ber.R. i. 3.   [h] See p. 115.

do something good, his limbs are heavy, because the evil *yeẓer* rules over his 248 limbs, and the good *yeẓer* is like a prisoner in captivity, as it is written, *For out of prison he came forth to be king*.[a]

A curious application of this analysis to the change of Abram's name was made in B.Ned. 32*b*:

'R. Ammi b. Abba said, "Abram is written, then Abraham[b] because at first God gave him control over 243 limbs, and then later over 248, the extra ones being the two eyes, the two ears and the sexual organ".'

The interpretation was deduced from the difference between the numerical values of Abram and Abraham.[c] Hence it was suggested that as a reward for circumcision he was given control over the members which lead most easily into sin.

[a] Eccles. iv. 14. [b] Gen. xvii. 5.
[c] $a = 1, b = 2, r = 200, m = 40$; the added $h = 5$.

GENESIS II

1 *And* the creatures of *the heaven and the earth were finished, and all the host of them.*

2 *And on the seventh day God finished his work which he had made,* and the ten things which he created between the suns; *and he rested on the seventh day from all his work which he had made.*

3 *And God blessed the seventh day* more than all the days of the week,[a] *and hallowed it: because that in it he rested from all his work which God had created* and was still to do.[b]

4 *These are the generations of the heaven and of the earth when they were created, in the day that the Lord God made earth and heaven.*

5 *And no plant of the field was yet in the earth, and no herb of the field had yet* germinated:[c] *for the Lord God had not caused it to rain upon the earth, and there was not a man to till the ground.*

6 The cloud of majesty came down from the throne of majesty and filled itself with water from the ocean, and then rose up from the earth and gave rain to water *the whole face of the ground.*

7 *And the Lord God* created man with two inclinations.[d] And he took *dust* from the place of the Temple and from the four winds[e] of the world, and he mixed them from all the waters of the world and he created him ruddy, black and white.[f] *And he breathed into his nostrils*

---

[a] The particular forms of blessing are elaborated in Ber.R. xi.

[b] The change is probably in accordance with the view of R. Hoshaiah (as reported by R. Pineḥas) that although the work of creation was finished, God still had the work of sustaining the universe in controlling the wicked and rewarding the righteous. See Ber.R. xi. 10.

[c] So also T.O.

[d] From *yeẓer*; the phrase could mean 'with two aspects'; see further the commentary on p. 117.

[e] Or 'quarters'; see B.Soṭ. 5a.

[f] P.R.E. 11 adds a fourth colour, yellow. Josephus gives a simpler version: 'Now this man was called Adam, which in Hebrew signifies "red" because he was made from red earth kneaded together; for such is the colour of the true virgin soil' (*Ant.* i. 34). The four colours would probably refer to the different races of men, the three colours to his composition of blood, entrails and bone. Cf. B.Nid. 31a, and see also II Enoch xxx. 13, Sib. Or. iii. 25. In Chron. Jer. vi. 7 the four colours are specifically applied to the varied composition of a man.

the breath of life: and the living breath was in the body of Adam for a spirit able to speak, for the enlightening of the eyes, and for the hearing of the ears.

8 *And* there *had been planted* by the word[a] of *the Lord God a garden* from Eden for the righteous before the creation of the world, and he made to dwell *there the man whom he had formed.*

9 *And out of the ground made the Lord God to grow every tree that is pleasant to the sight, and good for food; the tree of life also in the midst of the garden* whose height was a journey of five hundred years, *and the tree* of which those who eat its fruit know the distinction between *good and evil.*

10 *And a river went out of Eden to water the garden; and from thence it was parted, and became four heads* of rivers.

11 *The name of the first is Pishon: that is it which compasseth the whole land of* Hindiki, *where there is gold.*

12 *And the gold of that land is* proved: *there is bdellium*[b] *and the* precious stones of beryl.[c]

13 *And the name of the second river is Gihon: the same is it that compasseth the whole land of Cush.*

14 *And the name of the third river is* Diglath:[d] *that is it which goeth toward* the east of[e] *Assyria. And the fourth river is* Pherath.[f]

15 *And the Lord God took* Adam from the mountain of worship where he had been created and caused him to dwell in *the garden of Eden to* work in the Law and to keep its commandments.

16 (*And the Lord God commanded the man, saying, 'Of every tree of the garden thou mayest freely eat):*

17 *but of the tree of* which those who eat its fruit are wise to distinguish *good and evil, thou shalt not eat of it: for in the day that thou eatest thereof* you will condemn yourself[g] *to death'.*

18 *And the Lord God said, 'It is not* right[h] *that* Adam *should* sleep *alone; I will make him* a wife[i] *that she may be an help before him'.*

---

[a] *Memra.*	[b] *Bedilḥa*; cf. T.O. and M.T.
[c] See R.V. marg.	
[d] So also T.O., Pesh. and Arab. Vers. = (R.V. marg.) Tigris.	
[e] See R.V. marg. The alternative renderings which are possible in Heb. have been eliminated in Ps. Jon., as also in T.O. Cf. my article 'Haggadah in the Targum Onqelos', pp. 54 ff.	
[f] So M.T.	[g] Lit., 'be guilty of'.
[h] So also T.O.	[i] Or 'woman'.

19 *And out of the ground the Lord God formed every beast of the field, and every fowl of the air; and brought them unto* Adam *to see what he would call them: and whatsoever* Adam *called every living creature, that was the name thereof.*

20 *And* Adam *gave names to all cattle, and to* all[a] *the fowl of the air, and to every beast of the field; but for* Adam *there was not* up to this point *found an help* before him.

21 *And the Lord God caused a deep sleep to fall upon* Adam, *and he slept; and he took one of his ribs*—it was the thirteenth rib on the right side[b] —*and he closed up* its place with flesh:

22 *and the rib, which the Lord God had taken from* Adam, *builded he into*[c] *a woman, and brought her unto* Adam.

23 *And* Adam *said,* 'This time and never again woman will be created from man just as this one has been created from me, *bone of my bones, and flesh of my flesh;* this is rightly to *be called Woman, because she was taken out of Man.*'

24 *Therefore shall a man leave* and part from the house of the bed of *his father and his mother, and shall cleave unto his wife: and* both of them[d] *shall be one flesh.*

25 *And they were both* wise, Adam *and his wife,* but they did not remain in their glory.[e]

Selections from other Targums on Genesis ii

1 F.T. (Gins. p. 5) has the verse.

2 F.T. (Gins. pp. 5, 91) And *on the seventh day* the word[f] of the Lord was filled with desire[g] for *his work which he had made: and he rested on the seventh day from all his work which he had made.*

3 F.T. (Gins. p. 5) has the verse.

5 F.T. (Gins. p. 92) has the verse.

9 F.T. (Gins. pp. 5, 74) has most of the verse, but not the interpretation in Ps. Jon.

[a] So LXX and Pesh. but not M.T.
[b] Cf. Jub. iii. 5 f., where the rib is not specified, but the event takes place on the thirteenth day of creation.
[c] R.V. marg.
[d] So also LXX, Pesh., Sam. Pent. and Arab. Vers., but not M.T.
[e] Cf. Ps. xlix. 12 (13): *Adam did not abide in glory* (the same root as the Targum here).
[f] *Memra.*   [g] *Weḥamid*: so also T.O., Complutensis.

15 F.T. (Gins. p. 5): *And* the word[a] of *the Lord took* Adam *and put him into the garden of Eden,* to work in the Law and to keep its commandments.

18 F.T. (Gins. pp. 5, 74) has part of the verse.

19 F.T. (Gins. p. 74) has three words.

22 F.T. (Gins. p. 5) has one word.

24 F.T. (Gins. pp. 5, 74) has part of the verse.

25 F.T. (Gins. pp. 5, 92) has part of the verse.

Notes on Genesis ii

2 (F.T.) The Hebrew text says, *on the seventh day God finished his work,* but that could be taken to mean that he finished the work he had been doing during the course of that day. The effect of that might have been to undermine the theoretical basis of the sabbath. The LXX avoided the possibility by completely changing the translation. LXX has: 'And God completed his works which he had made, on the sixth day, and he rested from his works . . . on the seventh day.'[b] Jubilees[c] avoided the difficulty in the same way: 'He created heaven and earth and everything that he created in six days, and God made the seventh day holy, for all his works.'

M.T. read *wayekal* (R.V. 'finished'), and the Targum took this as being from *kalah,* 'desire' or 'long for', as in II Sam. xiii. 39, 'And the soul of king David longed (*wattekal*) to go forth unto Absalom'.

(Ps. Jon.) The phrase 'between the suns' means 'between sunset and sunrise', or more precisely here, 'in the evening'. The phrase is common as in Ps. Jon. on Gen. xxii. 13 and Exod. xii. 5.[d] Here the phrase means 'the ten things which God created on the eve of the (first) Sabbath'. The tradition was widespread; for example, Mek. Vayas. 6 says:

This (manna) was one of the ten things that were created on the eve of the Sabbath[e] at twilight: they are the rainbow, the manna, the rod (of Moses), the

---

a *Memar.*

b So also the Sam. Pent., Pesh. and the Syriac Comm. The LXX here is one of the recognised variants: see Appendix iii.

c ii. 25.

d So also T.O. *ad loc.*

e The phrase is again 'between the suns'.

writing, the *shamir*,[a] the tables of stone,[b] the opening up of the earth to swallow the wicked,[c] the mouth of the ass of Balaam the wicked, the tomb of Moses and the cave in which Moses and Elijah stood.[d] And there are those who say: the garments of the first man[e] and the rod of Aaron . . . There are seven things hidden from men: the day of death, the day of consolation,[f] the depths of judgement. No man knows by what he can profit, no man knows what is in the heart of his neighbour, no man knows when the kingdom of the house of David will be restored to its former place, nor when this evil kingdom will be overthrown.

B.Pes. 54*a* has a slightly different list:

Ten things were created on the eve of the Sabbath at twilight. They are: the well,[g] the manna, the rainbow,[h] the writing and the writing instruments, the tables, the tomb of Moses, the cave in which Moses and Elijah stood, the opening of the ass's mouth, and the opening up of the earth to swallow the wicked. R. Nehemiah said in the name of his father: 'Also fire, and the mule.' R. Josiah said in the name of his father: 'Also the ram[i] and the *shamir*.' R. Judah said, 'Tongs as well'; for he said 'You need tongs to make tongs, so who made the first tongs?'

[a] Exod. xx. 25 (22) forbids the use of iron in the building of an altar (perhaps a primitive aversion, because iron can be made into instruments of death and destruction): *If thou make me an altar of stone, thou shalt not build it of hewn stones: for if thou lift up thy tool upon it, thou hast polluted it.* Cf. also I Kings vi. 7. M.Mid. iii. 4 makes the point even clearer: 'Iron disqualifies by touch alone . . . Iron was created to shorten man's days, but the altar was created to prolong man's days.' Cf. also Tanḥ. Yitro 17. How, then, could stone be split to build the Temple? By the use of a fabulous worm called *shamir* which, when it was laid on the stones, cut into them. 'Solomon said to the rabbis: "How shall I manage (to build a temple without iron tools)?" They said, "There is the *shamir* which Moses brought for the stone of the ephod".' (B.Gitt. 68*a*. For an extravagant version of the legend, see Midr. Teh. on Ps. lxxviii. 45, and see also J.Sot ix. 13.) There is a possible reference to this feeling about iron in the Qu'rān lvii. 25. 'And we sent down iron. In it is great *bas* and usefulness to man, that God may know who will help him.' *Bas* means 'strength', in which case it would simply define in what way iron is useful; on the other hand, it can also mean 'evil', 'misfortune' (although in this sense the form is more often *bus*), and in that case it would correspond to the feelings suggested in the rabbinic exegesis. In favour of the latter meaning, it would provide the alternatives by which God would discover who was his helper and who was not.

[b] Of the Law.   [c] Num. xvi. 30.   [d] Exod. xxxiii. 22, I Kings xix. 9.
[e] See the notes on Gen. iii. 21.   [f] See Ps. Jon. on Gen. i. 21.
[g] Possibly referring to Num. xxi. 16–18; cf. Ps. Jon. on Num. xxii. 28; or the reference may be to the well of Jacob. P.R.E. 30 identified it with the well found by Hagar in Gen. xxi. 19.   [h] Gen. ix. 13 f.
[i] The ram which Abraham sacrificed instead of Isaac; see Ps. Jon. on Gen. xxii. 13.

Later on B.Pes. 54*a–b* repeated the list but added two other alter-native suggestions: the evil spirits and the garments of Adam.[a] Ps. Jon. on Num. xxii. 28 gives a list of ten, which varies from the others by including the clouds of glory and demons. Compare also Chron. Jer. i. 3.

The motive behind these ideas (of some things having been created before their time, or even before the creation of the world)[b] was partly to stress their importance, but also to emphasise that all things, even the most adverse, were within the foreknowledge of God, and hence were always in his control. On Gen. iv. 16 Ps. Jon. adds to the list the land of Cain's exile, to show that even Cain's offence did not take God by surprise,[c] and on Gen. xxvii. 25 it suggests that the wine given to Isaac by Jacob was also in this category. See also Aboth v. 6 (giving variants), Sifre on Deut. §355, Midr. Tann. 219.

5 The purpose here was to explain the contradiction between Gen. i. 12, 26 (where grass and herbs are created before man) and Gen. ii. 5–7, *And no plant of the field was yet in the earth . . . And the Lord God formed man . . .* The contradiction was resolved in B.Ḥull. 60*b*:

The plants started to grow but stopped just before breaking through the soil. Then Adam came and prayed for rain for them, and as soon as the rain fell they began to shoot up. Thus you may learn that the Holy One, blessed be he, longs for the prayer of the righteous. R. Naḥman b. Papa had a garden in which he sowed his seeds, but they did not grow. As soon as he prayed, the rain fell and they began to grow.

There is an indirect reference to the difficulty in Syr. Comm.:[d] 'Scripture specifies herbs as "grasses", i.e. those that grow out of the earth, whether they have been sown by man or have grown themselves.' Against this both Philo, *de Opif. Mund.* xii. 40–xiii. 44 and Josephus, *Ant.* i. 31 emphasise that the seeds sprang up immediately.

6 See the comments on Gen. i. 6.

7 The word *yeẓer*, translated here 'inclinations', is a general word mean-ing 'formation' or 'aspect', but it usually has a technical connotation, and it is probably in the technical sense that Ps. Jon. used it.

The idea of the 'two inclinations' is fundamental in Jewish thought. It gives expression to men's ambivalence between good and evil, the inclination to good (*yeẓer haTob*), and the inclination to evil (*yeẓer haRa'*). By saying that God created man with these two inclinations the

---

a As in Mekilta above.   b See the notes on Gen. ii. 8.
c See the notes *ad loc.*   d Levene, p. 73.

Jews asserted that all things, both good and evil, are in the control of God, since they are a part of his creation. The same view is expressed frequently elsewhere—for example:

The words of Torah are like a life-giving medicine. It is like a king who grievously wounded his son. He put a bandage on the cut, and said, 'My son, while the bandage is in place you can eat and drink and wash yourself without harm. But if you take it off, the wound will fester.' In the same way God said to the Israelites, 'I created the *yeẓer haRa'* within you, but I also created Torah as a remedy. While you make Torah your concern, the *yeẓer haRa'* will not overcome you. But if you do not make it your concern, then you will fall into the power of the *yeẓer haRa'*, and it will be directed fully against you.'[a]

See also Test. Ash. i.

The same interpretation is found in II Enoch xxx. 13 ff.:

And I appointed him a name, from the four component parts, from east, from west, from south, from north (the initial letters in Greek form Adam), and I appointed for him four special stars and I called his name Adam, and showed him the two ways, the light and the darkness, and I told him: 'This is good, and that bad', that I should learn whether he has love towards me, or hatred, that it be clear which in his race love me.

The exegesis of Ps. Jon. rests on a small detail in the Hebrew text. The verb *yaẓar*[b] is used in Gen. ii. 7 of man and in ii. 19 of animals, but in verse 7 it is written *wayyiẓer*, and in verse 19 it is written *wayiẓer*. The double *y* in verse 7 suggested that there is something different in the creation of man. The double *y* was taken to imply some form of double creation, and various different suggestions were made. Ber.R. xiv. 2–5, for example, lists several alternatives: Adam and Eve, heavenly creatures and earthly creatures, discernment of good and evil, man as he is in this world and as he is in the world to come. J.Yeb. iv. 2 derived from it two formations of the embryo, seven and nine days after conception. B.Ber. 61a says:

R. Naḥman b. R. Ḥisda said: 'What is meant by the verse, *And the Lord God formed man . . .?* The double *y* shows that God created two inclinations, the

---

[a] Sifre on Deut. xi. 18. The parable is evoked by a play on words: the Hebrew text says, *Therefore shall ye lay up (wesamtem) these my words in your heart...*; a change of vowel and a division of the word (*wesam tam*) makes it, 'And a perfect remedy these words shall be . . .' (cf. B.Qid. 30b). But the idea in general is common; see, for example, B.B.B. 16a. For further illustrations of the 'two inclinations', see *A Rabbinic Anthology*, ch. xi and the index under 'evil inclination'; see also the notes on Gen. ii. 25 and cf. iv. 7.

[b] R.V. *formed*.

one good, the other evil.' R. Naḥman b. Isaac differed: 'If that is so, animals, of whom it is not written *wayyiẓer*, should have no inclination to evil, but in fact they hurt, bite and kick . . .' R. Jeremiah b. Eleazar said: 'God created two aspects in the first man, as it is written *Thou has beset me behind and before* . . .'[a]

The idea that Adam was created 'from the place of the Temple' was common. An example showing supplementary exegesis occurs in Ber.R. xiv. 8:[b]

'R. Berekiah and R. Ḥelbo in the name of Samuel the elder said: "He was created from the place of his atonement, as it is written, *An altar of earth*[c] *thou shalt make unto me* . . ."'[d]

See also Gen. ii. 15 and xxii. 2.

The rest of the verse is an attempt to account for the varied composition and appearance of men, and at the same time to stress their solidarity and unity. M.San. iv. 5 makes the point clear:

'Only one man on his own was created, to promote peace among men. No one could say to another, "My father was superior to yours".'

'From the four quarters': P.R.E. 11 commented: 'Why was it from the four quarters? The Holy One, blessed be he, said: "If a man travels from the east to the west, or from the west to the east, and the time comes for him to die, the earth where he is will not be able to say, The dust of your body does not belong to me. Go back to the place from which you were created."'[e] Compare also Tanḥ. Peq. 3, B.San. 38 *a–b*, Philo, *de Opif. Mund.* li. 146, *de Dec.* viii. 31, *de Somn.* i. 3. There is a particularly important passage in A.R.N. 31, where man is analysed as a microcosm. For a more elaborate legend, see Chron. Jer. vi. 6.

8 'Seven things were created before the world was created: Torah, repentance, the garden of Eden, Gehenna, the throne of Glory, the

---

[a] Ps. cxxxix. 5. This last opinion is explained in Vay.R. xix. 1: 'R. Levi said "When man was created he was created with two fronts and he divided him in two, so that two bodies were made, one for the man, the other for the woman".' It is probably meant to imply that Adam was bisexual, as in Ber.R. viii. 1. The LXX, according to the Rabbis (see Appendix III), translated Gen. v. 2 'Male and female created he *him*'. See the Targum and notes *ad loc*.

[b] Cf. the simpler statement in Midr. Teh. on Ps. xcii. 1 (the heading). See also J.Naz. vii. 2.

[c] *'adamah*.

[d] Exod. xx. 24 (21).

[e] The same is also in Chron. Jer. vi. 9.

Temple and the name of the Messiah.'[a] These were argued on the basis of Prov. viii. 22, Ps. xc. 2 f., Gen. ii. 8, Isa. xxx. 33,[b] Jer. xvii. 12,[c] Ps. lxxii. 17. These are the absolute necessities if life is to proceed at all, hence their creation has to anticipate that of the world. See also the Targum and notes on Gen. ii. 2 and iv. 16. Midr. Teh. on Ps. lxxii. 17 has a similar list, but includes Israel instead of the throne of Glory; on Ps. xc. 3 it gives the list as in B.Pes. See also Chron. Jer. i. 2.

The pre-creation of the garden of Eden was argued from this verse by taking *miqqedem*, not as 'eastward' (as in R.V.), but as 'from of old';[d] Ps. Jon. here made this quite specific. Ber.R. xv. 3 disputed the interpretation of Ps. Jon., but also understood *miqqedem* in the same sense: 'R. Samuel b. Nahmani said: You may take it to mean "before the creation of the world", but that is not the meaning. It means "before Adam", because Adam was created on the sixth day, but the garden of Eden on the third.'

9 'R. Judah b. R. Ilai said: "The tree of life covered a journey of five hundred years, and all the original waters branched out in streams from beneath it." '[e] This is part of a general tendency to increase the size of things in the primeval world. Adam, for example, filled the universe:

R. Berekiah and R. Helbo and R. Samuel b. Nahman said: 'When the Holy One, blessed be he, created the first man, he created him from one side of the universe to the other. How do we know from east to west? Because it is written, *Thou hast formed me from west and from east.*[f] How do we know from north to south? Because it is written, . . . *God created man upon the earth, and from the one end of heaven unto the other . . .*[g,h]

The stature of Adam was one of the things lost by Adam in his fall, as Bem.R. xiii. 12 makes clear: 'These things were taken from Adam: his shining appearance, his (immortal) life, his stature, the fruit of the

[a] B.Pes. 54a, B.Ned. 39b; cf. also Yalqut on Jer. §298 and T. d. E. 31.
[b] Tophet is understood as Gehenna.
[c] For both the throne and the Temple, but B.Ned. 39b adds Ps. xciii. 2 for the throne.
[d] So also T.O. quoted in the notes on Gen. i. 1; cf. the statement of the alternatives in Syr. Comm. (Levene, pp. 76 and 147). Aq., Pesh. and Vulg. took it as 'from of old', LXX as 'in the east'. The same variations 'east of' and 'before' occur in ii. 14.
[e] Ber.R. xv. 6.
[f] Ps. cxxxix. 5. R.V. *behind and before*, but *'ahor* and *qedem* also mean 'west' and 'east'   [g] Deut. iv. 32.
[h] Vay.R. xiv. 1 and xviii. 2; see also P.R.E. 11, B.R.H. 11a, B.B.B. 75a, Ber.R. viii. 1, xxi. 3, xxiv. 2, Tanh.B. iii. 37.

earth,[a] the fruit of the tree and the (full) lights (of sun and moon) . . .
His stature, as it is written, *And the man and his wife hid themselves . . .,*[b]
which means, he was reduced in stature to one hundred cubits[c] . . .'[d]

J.Naz. vii. 2 indicates that his life span was reduced as well:

'It is written: *Yet shall his days be an hundred and twenty years.* But
in fact Adam lived almost a thousand years; so why does it say 120?
Because at the end of 120 years in the grave, the mortal flesh of Adam
was reduced by decomposition to dust.'

The tendency to exaggerate numbers in the primeval age is already
present in Genesis, a time of giants and longevity.

15 The problem involved in this verse was recognised by Philo: 'Why does
(God) place the man in Paradise for two things, to work and guard it,
when Paradise was not in need of work, for it was complete in all things
as having been planted by God, and was not in need of a guardian,
for who was there to be harmed?' (*Quaes. Gen.* i. 14.)

Philo answered the question straightforwardly, saying that ploughing
and irrigating the ground were necessary, and that some defence was
needed against wild animals. The answer of Ps. Jon. was common (see
below), and it is probable that T.O. was aware of it, since it used the
same word, *pelaḥ,* to translate 'to dress it'. *Pelaḥ* has a double sense, to
work and to worship.

On the creation of Adam being connected with the place of the
Temple, see the notes on Gen. ii. 6 and compare J.Naz. vii. 2:

'R. Judah b. Pazzi said: The Holy One, blessed be he, took dust
of the earth from the place where the altar of the Temple was later to
stand, and with it he created the first man, and he said: "Since man has
been created by means of this earth which is going to be consecrated,
he will find in it a strong support . . ."'

On the connection of this verse with the keeping of the Law, see
Ber.R. xvi. 5 and 6, II Enoch xxxi. 1, Sifre on Deut. §41, Midr. Tann. 22,
and Yalqut on Gen. §22:

If you say there was work to be done in the Garden of Eden, ploughing and
breaking the ground, did not the trees in fact grow of their own accord? And

---

[a] Without his having to toil for it.   [b] Gen. iii. 8.
[c] Previously he had filled the universe, now he was able to hide among the
trees, hence his stature must have been reduced; cf. Pes.K. i. 1: 'R. Aibu
said: "At that time the first man Adam was reduced in stature, and was
made 100 cubits high."'
[d] See also Ber.R. xii. 6, xix. 8, Pes.R. 68*b*, Chron. Jer. vi. 12.

if you say there was work to be done there watering it, did not a river go forth from Eden to water the Garden? In fact, 'to dress it and to keep it' means to engage in the study of Torah and to keep its commandments.

17 The purpose here was to reconcile the contradiction between Gen. ii. 17 (where God says to Adam that if he eats of the fruit of the tree, 'thou shalt surely die') and Gen. vi. 5 (which says that Adam lived 930 years). Ps. Jon. suggested that the decree was not meant to be immediately applicable. With this compare Pes.K. xiv. 4, and see also Jub. iv. 30, Justin, *Dial.* 81.

18 Both Targums avoided the word 'good'. Gen. i. 31 has already said, *God saw everything he had made, and, behold, it was very good.* It would be contradictory to allow God to say at this point, 'It is not good . . .' Pesh. also recognised the difficulty, and translated it as 'it is not fitting'.[a]

23 Ps. Jon. attempted to explain the phrase in Genesis 'this now'. Various other explanations were offered. Rashi, for example, wrote:[b] 'This teaches that Adam went to all the beasts and animals, but was not satisfied with any of them.' He derived the comment from B.Yeb. 63a.

Ber.R. xviii. 4 says: 'R. Judah Berabbi said: "When God created her first he saw her full discharge and blood, so he took her from him, and created her a second time, as it is written, 'This time she is bone of my bones'."' On the contrast between Adam and Eve, see also J.Shab. ii. 6.

25 Rashi's comment[c] indicates some of the meaning behind this change: 'They had no knowledge of the customs of modesty distinguishing between good and evil, because although enough understanding had been given to him (Adam) to give names (to the animals) the inclination to evil[d] was not given to him until he ate from the tree . . .'

Syr. Comm. (Levene, p. 77) has: 'It is implied that they were unaware of the shyness consequent on their nakedness, as innocent children are.'

Ps. Jon. avoided the word 'naked' by taking *'arummim* as the plural of *'arum*, 'wise' or 'crafty'.

---

[a] On a possible haggadic element at the end of this verse (whether woman was to be a help or a hindrance to man) see A. E. Silverstone, *Aquila and Onkelos*, pp. 92 f.

[b] *Ad loc.*   [c] *Ad loc.*

[d] See the notes on Gen. ii. 7.

GENESIS III

1 *Now the serpent was* wiser for evil *than any beast of the field which the Lord God had made. And he said unto the woman,* 'Is it in truth that the Lord *God hath said, Ye shall not eat of any tree of the garden?'*

2 *And the woman said unto the serpent,* '*Of the* other *fruit of the trees of the garden we may eat:*

3 *but of the fruit of the tree which is in the midst of the garden,* the Lord *God hath said, Ye shall not eat of it, neither shall ye touch it, lest ye die.'*

4 *And the serpent* acting as an informer[a] to its creator *said unto the woman:* 'You will not die at all for every craftsman hates his fellow-craftsman.[b]

5 It is revealed before the Lord that *in the day* on which you eat of it, *your eyes shall be* enlightened, *and ye shall be as* the mighty angels[c] who are wise (enough) to distinguish between *good and evil.'*

6 *And the woman saw* Sammael, the angel of death, and she was afraid, and she knew *that the tree was good for food, and that* it was a remedy for the enlightenment of *the eyes, and that the tree was to be desired to make one wise, she took of the fruit thereof, and did eat; and she gave also unto her husband with her, and he did eat.*

7 *And the eyes of them both were opened, and they knew that they were naked,* stripped of the clothing of onyx[d] in which they had been created, and they saw their shame; *and they sewed fig leaves together, and made themselves aprons.*

8 *And they heard the voice of* the word of *the Lord God walking in the garden in the* resting-time[e] *of the day. And* Adam *and his wife hid themselves from the presence of the Lord God amongst the trees of the garden.*

9 *And the Lord God called unto* Adam *and said unto him:* 'Is not all the world which I have created open before me, the darkness the same as the light? So how can you think in your heart to hide yourself from before me? Can I not see the place in which you are hiding? And where are the commandments which I commanded you?'

[a] *Delator.*   [b] Lit. 'son of . . .'.
[c] T.O., 'like the mighty ones'.
[d] I.e. translucent as a fingernail: see further the notes on Gen. iii. 21.
[e] Or 'decline'.

10 *And he said, 'I heard* the voice of your word[a] *in the garden, and I was afraid, because I was naked,* and the laws which you commanded me I have transgressed, *and I hid myself* for shame.'

11 *And he said, 'Who told thee that thou wast naked,* except *thou hast eaten of* the fruit of *the tree, whereof I commanded thee that thou shouldest not eat?'*

12 *And* Adam *said, 'The woman whom thou gavest to be with me, she gave me of* the fruit of *the tree, and I did eat.'*

13 *And the Lord God said unto the woman, 'What is this thou hast done?'* *And the woman said, 'The serpent beguiled me* with his cleverness and deceived me with his wickedness, *and I did eat.'*

14 *And the Lord God* brought the three of them to judgement, and he *said unto the serpent, 'Because thou hast done this, cursed art thou above all cattle, and above every beast of the field; upon thy belly shalt thou go,* and your feet will be cut off, and your skin you will cast off once in every seven years, and the poison of death will be in your mouth, *and dust shalt thou eat all the days of thy life:*

15 *and I will put enmity between thee and the woman, and between* the seed of your offspring and the seed of her offspring; and it shall be that when the offspring of the woman keep the commandments of the Law, they will aim right (at you) and they will smite you on the *head*; but when they abandon the commandments of the Law, you will aim right (at them), and you will wound them in the *heel*. However, for them there will be a remedy, but for you there will be none, and in the future they will make peace with[b] the heel in the days of the king, Messiah.'[c]

16 *Unto the woman he said, 'I will greatly multiply thy sorrow* by the blood of your virginity *and thy conception; in sorrow thou shalt bring forth children; and thy desire shall be to thy husband, and he shall rule over thee* for good and for ill.'[d]

17 *And unto Adam he said, 'Because thou hast hearkened unto the* word *of thy wife, and hast eaten of* the fruit of *the tree, of which I commanded thee, saying, Thou shalt not eat of it; cursed is the ground* because it did not show forth your guilt; *in toil shalt thou eat of it all the days of thy life;*

---

[a] *Memar.*

[b] Or 'a cure for'.

[c] This verse and its possible relevance to the New Testament has been discussed by M. McNamara, *The New Testament and the Palestinian Targum . . .,* pp. 217–22.

[d] Lit. 'for righteousness and for sin'; the same phrase occurs in Ps. Jon. on Gen. iv. 7, *q.v.*

₁₈ *thorns also and thistles shall it bring forth* and increase on account of you; *and thou shalt eat the herb* which is on the face *of the field.*' Adam answered and said: 'I pray by the mercies which are before you, O Lord, that we may not be reckoned as cattle to eat grass in the open field.[a] Let us stand up and labour with the labour of the hands, and eat food from the food of the earth, and in this way let there be a distinction before you between the children of men and the cattle.'

₁₉[b] '*In the sweat of* the palm of your hands *shalt thou eat* food *till thou return unto the* dust from which you were created. *For dust thou art, and unto dust shalt thou return,* and from the dust you will arise in the future to render reckoning and account for all that you have done, on the day of the great judgement.'

₂₀ *And* Adam *called his wife's name Eve, because she was the mother of all* the sons of men.

₂₁ *And the Lord God made for Adam and for his wife* glorious garments from the skin cast off by the serpent on the skin of their flesh, instead of their onyx[c] which had been cast away; and he *clothed them.*

₂₂ *And the Lord God said* to the angels who minister before him, '*Behold,* Adam is unique[d] in the world as I am in the heavens above; and in the future there will arise from him men who know how to distinguish between *good and evil.* If he had kept the commandments which I commanded him he would have lived and flourished as the tree of life for ever; but in fact he has not kept what I commanded him, so we are going to decree against him and forbid him the garden of Eden before he stretches out his hand and takes for himself from the fruit of the tree of life. For if he eats from it he will *live* and flourish *for ever.*'

₂₃ So *the Lord God* took him out of *the garden of Eden,* and he went and dwelt on mount Moriah, *to till the ground from whence he was* created.

₂₄ So *he drove* Adam *out and he* set the glory of his Shekina to *the east of the garden of Eden* between the two Cherubim. Before God created the world he created the Law,[e] he prepared the garden of Eden for the righteous that they might eat and be satisfied with the fruit of the tree, because they would have observed in their lives the instruction of the Law (in this world) and would have maintained the commandments;

---

[a] Lit. 'on the face of the field'.
[b] Note that the verse begins without indicating that it is now God who is speaking; this suggests that the speech of Adam was interjected.
[c] See verse 7.   [d] So also T.O.
[e] See the Targum and notes on Gen. ii. 8.

and he prepared Gehinnom for the wicked[a] which is like the sharp sword devouring with two edges, and he prepared within flashing sparks of fire and burning coals for the judgement of the wicked who rebelled in their lives against the instruction of the Law. Better is the Law for the one who attends to it than the fruits of the tree of life—the Law which the word [*memra*] of the Lord has prepared in order that it may be kept, so that man may live and walk by the paths of the way of the life of the world to come.

Selections from other Targums on Genesis iii

1 T.O.: 'Is it in truth that the Lord *God hath said* . . .?'

5 T.O.: 'It is revealed before the Lord *that in the day ye eat thereof* . . .'

6 T.O.: . . . *and that it was* a cure *to the eyes* . . .

7 F.T. (Gins. pp. 5, 74, 92) has a few words.

8 F.T. (Gins. p. 5): *And they heard the voice of* the word of *the Lord walking in the garden in the* height *of the day: and* Adam *and his wife hid themselves from the presence of the* word of the *Lord amongst the trees of the garden.*

T.O.: *And they heard the voice of* the word of *the Lord God* . . . *in the* resting-time *of the day.* . .

9 F.T. (Gins. p. 5; see also p. 74): *And* the word of *the Lord called unto* Adam *and said unto him:* 'Is not all the world which I have created open before me? The darkness the same as the light is open before me. So how can you think that the place where you are hiding is not open before me? And where are the commandments which I commanded you?'

10 F.T. (Gins. p. 5): '*I heard* the voice of your speaking[b] walking *in the garden.* . .'

T.O.: '*I heard* the voice of your word[c] *in the garden* . . .'

14 F.T. (Gins. p. 92) has part of the verse.

15[d] F.T. (Gins. p. 5; see also pp. 74, 92) has a long and similar expansion.

16 F.T. (Gins. p. 92) has one word.

17 F.T. (Gins. p. 5) has the verse, following the Hebrew closely and not adding the interpretation of Ps. Jon.

18 F.T. (Gins. pp. 5 f.; see also pp. 74, 92) has the added prayer of Adam in a similar form.

---

[a] So also Yalqut on Gen. §34, and cf. Lactantius, *Instit.* xii. 13.

[b] *Dibbur.* [c] *Memar.*

[d] For T.O. on this verse, see the notes on Gen. i. 1.

19 F.T. (Gins. p. 6): '*In the sweat of thy face shalt thou eat* food until the time of your *return unto the ground*, because from it you were created. *For dust thou art, and unto dust shalt thou return*, and from the dust you will arise to render reckoning and account for what you have done.'

20 F.T. (Gins. p. 6) has the verse, following the Hebrew.

21 F.T. (Gins. p. 6): *And* the word of *the Lord God* created *for Adam and his wife* glorious garments from the skin of their flesh, *and clothed them.* T.O.: *And the Lord God made for Adam and for his wife* glorious garments on the skin of their flesh, *and clothed them.*

22 F.T. (Gins. p. 6; see also p. 74) has the verse with a similar expansion; for the interpretation of T.O. see the notes on p. 130.

23 F.T. (Gins. p. 6; see also p. 92): And the word of the Lord *sent him forth from the garden of Eden to till the ground from whence he was* created.[a]

24 F.T. (Gins. p. 6; see also pp. 74, 92) has a long and similar expansion.

Notes on Genesis iii

4 A variant of this version of the serpent's speech appears in Ber.R. xix. 4:[b]

'R. Joshua Siknini said in the name of R. Levi: "The serpent acting as an informer to its creator, said: God ate of this tree and then created the world, and therefore he orders you not to eat from it, so that you cannot create other worlds; for everyone hates his fellow-craftsman." '

Compare Tanḥ.B. iii. 47, Midr. Teh. on Ps. i. 1 (in a section applying the whole of Ps. i to Adam), Kallah R. iii. 22.

6 Sammael was the great opponent of men and of God. He was the exact opposite of Michael: in Shem.R. xviii. 5 they are likened to prosecuting and defending counsel; in Deb.R. xi. 10 they both wait hopefully for the soul of Moses. A full account of Sammael's agency in the fall of man is given in P.R.E. 13 and 21. In that account the angels fear the authority of man on earth (he is able to give names to the animals and they are not); therefore they say: 'If we do not devise against this man some way in which he may sin against his creator, we shall not be able to stand against him.' At this, Sammael took the initiative, and finding

[a] So also T.O.
[b] And also in Midr. Teh. on Ps. i. 9.

the serpent (which at that time looked something like a camel[a]) he rode on it to attack Adam and Eve. In P.R.E. 21 Sammael comes riding on the serpent to Eve and she conceives Cain: for that version see Ps. Jon. on Gen. iv. 1.

The legend was recorded more fully in Kit. alMaj. 94*b*–95*a*, which reads in part:

Satan retained his envy of Adam and Eve because of the favour which the Lord conferred on them. And he contrived to enter into the serpent, which was the most beautiful of animals, and its form was according to the form of a camel... And the reason why Iblis the cursed hid in the serpent was his ugliness... And if Eve had seen him without his being hidden in the serpent when she spoke with him, she would have fled from him.

The version in The Cave of Treasures[b] is slightly different:

And when Satan saw that Adam and Eve were happy and joyful in Paradise, that Rebel was smitten sorely with jealousy, and he became filled with wrath. And he went and took up his abode in the serpent, and he raised him up, and made him to fly through the air... Now, why did Satan enter the body of the serpent and hide himself therein? Because he knew that his appearance was foul...

In III Enoch Sammael was made the representative of Rome: he is the prince of the accusers and the prince of Rome (xiv. 2, xxvi. 12).

For the connection between Sammael and the serpent see also Asc. Is. i. 8, III Bar. iv. 8, ix. 7, Chron. Jer. xxii. 2.

Eve was associated with the coming of death as early as Ecclus. xxv. 24:

'From a woman was the beginning of sin;
And because of her we all die.'

7 Kit. alMaj. 95*b* (but not The Cave of Treasures) recorded the same tradition:[c] 'When he, and the woman as well, ate the deadly fruit, they were stripped of their glorious clothing and their glory was taken from them, and they were deprived of the light which had been their clothing.' Compare Syr. Comm. (Levene, p. 77): 'It is probable that they were clothed in a kind of glory from the first.'

---

[a] Cf. Ber.R. xix. 1 where it is made clear that the serpent before the fall could have been a strong and therefore reliable messenger and carrier of burdens: 'R. Hoshaiah the elder said: "It stood up straight like a reed and had feet..."' (see also the notes on Gen. iii. 14). R. Simeon b. Eleazar said: "It was like a camel. The world lost greatly, because if the fall had not happened, it would have been possible to use it as a carrier and it would have gone (safely) to and fro."' So also A.R.N. 1 in greater detail.

[b] Budge, p. 63.   [c] See also P.R.E. 14.

On Adam being deprived of his glory see the notes on Gen. ii. 9. Compare also the form of these legends in Jerome, *Ep.* xxii. 19.

8 The Hebrew phrase translated literally is 'in the wind (*ruaḥ*) of the day', but the sense of that phrase was not apparent. LXX has, 'in the evening', Pesh. 'towards the end of day', Vulg. 'ad auram post meridiem' (cf. Sam. Pent.), Arabic Vers. 'during the course of'.

9 The Targums made this addition to avoid an apparent limitation in God's knowledge. Rashi also commented: 'He knew where Adam was, but he had to draw him into speech, so that he would not be overwhelmed in his reply (as he might be) if God punished him all of a sudden.' Josephus[a] also avoided saying that God had to look for Adam, but he did in fact suggest that Adam's shamefaced behaviour took God by surprise: 'But, when God entered the garden Adam, who ere then was wont to resort to his company, conscious of his crime withdrew; and God, met by action so strange, asked for what reason he who once took delight in his company now shunned and avoided it.' Note also Justin, *Dial.* 99: '. . . It was not from want of understanding in God that he asked Adam where he was, and Cain where Abel was; but to convince each what kind of a person he was.'

14 Ps. Jon.'s expansion of the text was based on observation of the present appearance of snakes, interpreted in terms of punishment. On 'the feet' Ber.R. xx. 5 said specifically: 'Ministering angels descended and cut off its hands and feet.' See also notes on Gen. iii. 6 and for a fuller version P.R.E. 14. Ps. Jon. on Exod. vii. 9 added at the end of the verse: 'All the dwellers in the earth will hear the sound of Egypt's cry when I shatter them, just as all the creatures heard the sound of the serpent's cry when it was stripped of its limbs.' The same interpretation was given by Josephus:

At that epoch all the creatures spoke a common tongue, and the serpent, living in the company of Adam and his wife, grew jealous of the blessings which he supposed were destined for them if they obeyed God's behests. . . He (God) deprived the serpent of speech, indignant at his malignity to Adam; he also put poison beneath his tongue. . .; he further bereft him of feet and made him crawl and wriggle along the ground.[b]

For 'the three' being brought to judgement, see also Ber.R. xx. 2 f., P.R.E. 14.

[a] *Ant.* i. 45.
[b] *Ant.* i. 41 and 50–1. See also T.Sot. iv. 18, B.Sot. 9*b*, Ber.R. xx. 4, 5, Qoh.R. x. 11. 1.

15 'A remedy'; 'R. Levi said: "In the age of the Messiah[a] all will be healed except for the serpent and the Gibeonite: the serpent as it is written: *And dust shall be the serpent's meat*;[b] the Gibeonite, as it is written: *And they that labour in the city, out of all the tribes of Israel, shall till it*[c] (which means that all the tribes of Israel shall make them serve who served before)".'[d]

'Peace': this addition was derived from a play on words. The Hebrew text has *yeshupheka* and *teshuphenu*;[e] Ps. Jon. has *shephiyutha* ('peace').

16 Eve was usually thought to have suffered ten penalties: see A.R.N. 1, B. Erub. 100*b*.

17 P.R.E. 14: 'Granted that Adam sinned, what was the sin of the earth that it should be cursed? It did not denounce the deed, therefore it was cursed.'

18 The same plea for the dignity of man was recorded in B.Pes. 118*a*:

R. Joshua b. Levi said: 'Adam wept bitterly when the Holy One, blessed be he, said, *Thorns also and thistles shall it bring forth to thee*,[f] and he begged him saying, Lord of the universe, shall I and my ass eat out of the same manger? But he was content at once when he was told: *In the sweat of thy face shalt thou eat bread*.'[g]

An even closer connection is made in Ber.R. xx. 10: 'When Adam heard it, his face began to sweat[h] and he said, "Shall I be bound to the manger like an animal?" The Holy One, blessed be he, said: "Your face has sweated, therefore *shalt thou eat bread*." '

19 Compare Aboth iii. 1:

Akabiah b. Mahalaleel said: 'Set your mind to three things and you will not fall under sin: know where you came from, and where you are going to, and who it is you must appear before to give a reckoning and an account. Where did you come from? from a putrid drop. Where are you going to? to a place of dust, of worm and maggot. Who is it you must appear before, to give a reckoning and an account? before the King of the Kings of Kings, the Holy One, blessed be he.'

Note also the Syr. Comm. (Levene, p. 78): 'With regard to *dust shalt thou eat*—it hints at Hades, because he was deprived of heaven.'

[a] *Le'athid.*
[b] Isa. lxv. 25: even in the Messianic age described in Isaiah lxv. 8 ff., dust remains the serpent's food.   [c] Ezek. xlviii. 19.
[d] Ber.R. xx. 5; see also xcv. 1 and Tanḥ.B. iii. 47, Midr. Teh. on Ps. i. 2.
[e] R.V. 'bruise'.   [f] Gen. iii. 18.   [g] Gen. iii. 19.
[h] With anxiety; in A.R.N. 1 it is said that Adam 'trembled' and in that way showed his penitence.

20 'Eve': the same interpretation was recorded in Ber.R. xx. 11, and also in the Syr. Comm. (Levene, p. 78): 'The name Eve means "life", or the mother of life, since she is the mother of all; she brought forth living children.'

21 'Glorious[a] garments from the skin cast off by the serpent': this makes more specific the phrase in Genesis, *coats of skins*. The same identification was made in P.R.E. 20: 'From the skin which the serpent cast off the Holy One, blessed be he, made worthy garments for Adam and his partner.' Midr. Teh. on Ps. xcii. 1 says the same, adding that they were made as a matter of decency.

However, other possibilities were suggested, particularly since there was a different reading in the Hebrew text at this point:

> In R. Meir's text it was found written 'garments of light'.[b] This means that the garments of Adam were like a torch, broad at one end and narrow at the other. Isaac the elder said: 'They were as smooth as a fingernail and beautiful as a precious stone'.... It means those that were closest to the skin. R. Eliezer said, Skin of goats; R. Joshua said, Skin of hares; R. Jose b. Ḥanina said: 'A garment made from skin with its wool.'[c]

Rashi[d] tried to combine some of the alternatives: 'There are writings of *Haggadah*[e] which say they were smooth as a fingernail sticking closely to the skin; but some say: material made from skin, such as the fur of hares ...' In The Cave of Treasures[f] it is the soft bark of trees, as also in the Syr. Comm. (Levene, p. 78).

Bem.R. iv. 8 suggests that the garments became the vestments of the high priest, which were handed down from Adam through the line of the first-born:

> They were worthy garments which the first-born afterwards used. When Adam died he handed them on to Seth, and Seth to Methuselah, and Methuselah when he died to Noah ... and Noah when he died to Shem. But was Shem the first-born? Surely Japheth was the first-born, as it is written, *Shem ... the brother of Japheth the elder?*[g] Why did he hand them on to

---

a Or 'worthy'; cf. Philo (*Quaes. Gen.* i. 53): 'Some may ridicule the text when they consider the cheapness of the apparel of tunics, as being unworthy of the touch of such a Creator.'

b '*or* instead of '*or.*

c Ber.R. xx. 12.

d *Ad loc.*

e See Introduction p. 48.

f Budge, p. 65.

g Gen. x. 21. The translation preserved the Hebrew order from which it is apparent that 'the elder' could in fact apply to either.

Shem? Because Noah saw in advance that the patriarchs would descend from him. . . Shem when he died handed them on to Abraham[a] . . . Abraham when he died handed them on to Isaac, Isaac to Jacob. But was Jacob the first-born? No, but craftily he took it from Esau.[b]

It is a matter of interest that the Targum still allowed that Esau did receive Adam's garment;[c] see also xlviii. 22. According to P.R.E. 24 Ham gave the garments to Nimrod who was thereby able to usurp a part of the authority that properly belonged to God.

Mek. Vayas. 6 and B.Pes. 54 a–b (quoted above on Gen. ii. 2) included the garments of Adam among the things created before the creation of the world.

22 'Adam is unique':[d] the word might mean 'alone', and it was used in that sense by P.R.E. 12 to describe Adam before Eve was created. But here it seems to be a phrase of special distinction, as when used of Abraham and of Israel. See, for example, Targ. Isa. li. 2: 'Bear in mind Abraham your father and Sarah who conceived you; for when Abraham was alone in the world I brought him to my service and blessed him and multiplied him.' In the present instance, Ps. Jon. avoided the more direct statement of Genesis, 'Behold, the man is become as one of us', partly because of its anthropomorphic tendencies, but partly because of its use by Christians as an indication of the Trinity in the Old Testament.[e] It is possible to translate the Hebrew as, 'He is become like the unique One amongst us'. The translation of Ps. Jon. made impossible any suggestion that man is 'like God'.

In Mek. Vayehi 7 two other possible interpretations were recorded:

R. Pappias interpreted it as, 'like one of the ministering angels'. R. Aqiba said to him, 'Not so, Pappias. . . It does not mean, "like one of the ministering angels". It can only mean that God put before man the two ways, the way of life and the way of death, and he chose for himself the way of death.'[f]

---

[a] A discussion follows about the way in which Abraham could be regarded as a first-born; see Gen. xi. 27 and Ber.R. xxxviii. 14.

[b] Gen. xxv. 31.

[c] See Gen. xxvii. 15.

[d] T.O. avoided saying that man is 'like God' by redividing the verse: 'Behold, Adam is unique (i.e. alone); from himself (it is) to know good and evil.' Compare also Chron. Jer. vi. 13.

[e] E.g. Justin, Dial. 129; see also the notes on Gen. i. 26.

[f] On 'the two ways' see the notes on Gen. ii. 6. In Ber.R. xxi. 5 the story ends, ' . . . and he chose one way'. See also Yalqut on Gen. §34.

The Syr. Comm. says, 'With regard to,"Behold, the man has become as one of us", he (God) is deriding him; he says it according to what Adam thought when he was deceived by the accuser.'[a]

23 'Mount Moriah': the mountain on which Abraham prepared to sacrifice Isaac[b] was identified as the site of the Temple.[c] On Adam's creation from the earth on which the altar was later to be built, see the notes on Gen. ii. 7. See also P.R.E. 20, B.Erub. 19a, Midr. Teh. on Ps. xcii. 1.

[a] Levene, p. 79.   [b] Gen. xxii. 2.
[c] See Ps. Jon. on Gen. xxii. 2.

GENESIS IV

1 *And* Adam was aware that *Eve his wife* had *conceived* from Sammael
the angel, and she became pregnant *and bare Cain,* and he was like
those on high, not like those below; and she *said, 'I have* acquired *a man,*
the angel of *the Lord.*'ᵃ

2 *And* she went on to bear from Adam, her husband, his twin sister and
Abel. And Abel was a keeper of sheep, but Cain was a man working in the
earth.

3 *And* it was at the end of the days on the fourteenth of Nisan *that Cain
brought of the fruit of the ground,* the seedᵇ of flax, *an offering* of first
things before *the Lord.*

4 *And Abel, he also brought of the firstlings of his flock and of the fat thereof.
And* it was pleasing before the Lord, and the Lord showed favour *unto
Abel and to his offering:*

5 *but unto Cain and to his offering he* did not show favour. *And Cain was
very wroth, and* the image of his face *fell.*

6 *And the Lord said unto Cain, 'Why art thou wroth? and why is* the image
of your face *fallen?*

7 Is it not the case that if you have done your work *well* your guilt will
be forgiven you? But if you have not done your work *well* in this world
your sin will be kept for the day of the great judgement, and at the doors
of your heart sin lies waiting. And into your hand I have given the
power of the inclination to evil,ᶜ and towards you will be its *desire,*
and you will have authority over it for righteousness or for sin.'

8ᵈ *And Cain* said to Abel his brother: 'Come, and let us both go into the
field.' So it was that when they had both gone out into the field Cain
answered and said to Abel: 'I can see that the world was created in love,
but it is not ordered by the issue of good works, because there is
partiality in judgement; thus it is that your offering was accepted with

---

ᵃ Or 'I have acquired (begotten) as man the angel of the Lord'.
ᵇ Lit. 'offspring'. ᶜ See the notes on Gen. ii. 7.
ᵈ The Hebrew of this verse translated literally says: 'And Cain said to Abel
his brother and it came to pass . . .' Inevitably there was much speculation
about what Cain said (LXX, for example, supplied, 'Let us go into the
field', as also Sam. Pent., Pesh., Vulg.), and the Targums added a longer
discussion (for other Targum versions, see p. 134).

favour, but my offering was not accepted with favour.' Abel answered and said: 'Certainly the world was created in love, and by the issue of good works it is ordered, and there is no partiality in judgement. But because the issue of my works was better than yours, so my offering has been accepted before yours with favour.' Cain answered and said to Abel: 'There is no judgement and no judge and no world hereafter; there is no good reward to be given to the righteous, nor any account to be taken of the wicked.' Abel answered and said: 'Certainly there is judgement and a judge and a world hereafter; there is a good reward to be given to the righteous, and the wicked will be called to account.' And because of these words they fell into a dispute in the open field, and *Cain rose up against Abel his brother*, and drove a stone into his forehead, *and slew him.*

9 *And the Lord said unto Cain, 'Where is Abel thy brother?' And he said, 'I know not: am I my brother's keeper?'*

10 *And he said, 'What hast thou done? The voice* of the bloods of the killing of your brother which were swallowed into the clay cry before *me from the ground.*

11 *And now* because of your killing him *cursed art thou from the ground which hath opened her mouth to receive* the bloods *of thy brother from thy*

12 *hand: when thou tillest the ground it shall not* increase to give *unto thee strength* of her fruits. *A fugitive and a wanderer shalt thou be in the earth.'*

13 *And Cain said* before *the Lord:* 'Severe indeed is my rebellion, more than to be borne, and yet it is possible with you to forgive it.

14 *Behold, thou hast* cast me forth *this day* on[a] *the face of the ground; and from* before you can I ever *be hid?* But since I am *a fugitive and a wanderer in the earth,* any just person who *findeth me shall slay me.'*

15 *And the Lord said unto him, 'Therefore whosoever slayeth Cain* for seven generations it will be exacted from him'. *And the Lord* marked on the face of Cain a letter from the great and glorious name, that *any finding him* should not kill him when they saw it on him.

16 *And Cain went out from* before *the Lord and dwelt in the land* of the wandering[b] of his exile which was made on account of him from old, like the garden of *Eden.*

17 *And Cain knew his wife; and she conceived, and bare Enoch: and he builded a city, and called the name of the city, after the name of his son,* Enoch.

[a] Or 'from'. [b] Cf. R.V. marg.

18 *And unto Enoch was born Irad: and Irad begat Mehujael: and Mehujael begat Methushael: and Methushael begat Lamech.*

19 *And Lamech took unto him two wives: the name of the one was Adah, and the name of the other Zillah.*

20 *And Adah bare Jabal: he was the* lord *of such as dwell in tents and* are masters of *cattle.*

21 *And his brother's name was Jubal: he was the* lord *of all such as* take part in the song with *the harp and pipe.*

22 *And Zillah, she also bare Tubal-cain,* the lord of all workers who know the making of *brass and iron: and the sister of Tubal-cain was Naamah;* she was supreme in laments and songs.[a]

23 *And Lamech said unto his wives:* 'Adah and Zillah, hear my voice: ye wives of Lamech, hearken unto my speech: for I have* not *slain a man* that we should be killed on his account, nor have I injured *a young man* that my offspring should be destroyed on his account.

24 Now *Cain* who had sinned and turned in repentance had seven generations extended to him; so is it not just that *Lamech,* the son of his son, who has not sinned, should be extended for seven and seventy?'

25 *And Adam knew his wife again* at the end of 130 years after the killing of Abel, *and she bare a son, and called his name Seth: for* she said: 'The Lord has given me another *instead of Abel* whom *Cain slew.*'

26 *And to Seth, to him also there was born a son; and he called his name Enosh.* That was the generation in whose days they began to err and make idols for themselves, and *to call* their idols by *the name of* the word of *the Lord.*

Selections from other Targums on Genesis iv

1 F.T. (Gins. p. 92): *And* Adam was aware that *Eve.*

T.O.: *And* Adam *knew Eve his wife; and she conceived and bare Cain, and said, I have gotten a man* from before[b] *the Lord.*

3 T.O.: *And* it was at the end of the days *that Cain brought* . . .

4 T.O.: *And* it was pleasing from before the Lord . . .

C.G.: *And* the word of the Lord accepted with favour Abel and the gifts of his hand.

7 F.T. (Gins. p. 71) has a long addition; see also Gins. pp. 6, 74.

T.O.: 'Is it not the case that if you do your work *well* it will be forgiven you, and if you do not do your work *well* sin will be stored up for the

---

[a] Cf. Ber.R. xxiii. 3.   [b] See further the notes on p. 136.

day of judgement to be accounted for by you (or, "to take vengeance on you"), if you do not repent; but if you do repent, it will be forgiven you?'

C.G.: 'Is it not the case that if you do your works *well* in this world it will be held over and it will be forgiven you in the world to come? And if you do not do your works *well* in this world, your sin will be kept for the day of judgement. Truly at the door of your heart sin lies waiting...'a

8 F.T. (Gins. pp. 6, 72) has a similar dispute; see also Gins. p. 74.

T.O.: the dispute appears in a shorter form in the Lisbon edn., printed in the Tosefta in Sperber's edition, I, 354.

C.G. has the same as Ps. Jon. with slight variations.

9 F.T. (Gins. p. 7): The word of *the Lord said unto Cain* ...

C.G.: The word of *the Lord said* ...

10 F.T. (Gins. p. 7; see also p. 75): '*The voice* of the bloods of the crowds of righteous generations which were to be established in the future from Abel your brother cry out against you before me *from the ground.*'

T.O.: '*The voice* of the bloods of the generation which were to come from your brother cry out ...'

C.G.: '*The voice* of the bloods of the many righteous generations which were to be established in the future from Abel your brother cry out against you before me *from the ground.*'

13 T.O.: *And Cain said* before the Lord: 'Great is my guilt, more than to be forgiven.'

C.G.: *And Cain said* before the Lord: 'Many are my sins, more than to be defended, and they are many before you to be absolved and forgiven.'

14 T.O.: '*Behold thou hast* rejected me this day onb *the face of the ground, and from* before you I cannot hide. But since I am *a fugitive and a wanderer in the earth, whosoever findeth me shall slay me.*'

C.G.: '*Behold thou hast* cast me forth this day onc *the face of the ground, and from* before you, Lord, it is not possible for the son of mand to hide. And Cain will be *a fugitive and a wanderer in the earth*, and it will be so that *whosoever findeth* him *shall slay* him.'

15 F.T. (Gins. p. 92) has one word ('sign').

C.G.: *And* the word of *the Lord* swore on oath, saying, '*Whosoever slayeth Cain*, for seven generations it will be attached to him.'

---

a Continues as Ps. Jon. with only slight variants.

b Or 'from'.   c Or 'from'.   d *Bar nash.*

16 F.T. (Gins. p. 7; see also pp. 75, 92): ... exile and wandering,[a] and for as long as Cain had not killed Abel the earth brought forth for him fruits like the fruits of the garden of *Eden*, but when he turned and killed Abel his brother it turned and produced thorns and thistles.

T.O.: ... *in the land of* exile and wandering which was made on account of him from of old[b] in the garden of *Eden*.

C.G.: *And Cain went out from* before *the Lord and dwelt in the land* of exile and wandering to the east of the garden of Eden, and for as long as Cain had not killed Abel the earth brought forth for him fruits like the fruits of the garden of Eden, but when he killed [MS breaks off]

21 F.T. (Gins. p. 92) has two words.

22 Part of the verse occurs in F.T. (Gins. p. 7).

23-4 F.T. (Gins. p. 72) has the verse; see also Gins. pp. 74, 92.

T.O. has the same interpretation, but with variations in the actual language.

26 F.T. (Gins. p. 7) has a similar interpretation.

T.O.: In his days the sons of men gave up[c] praying in *the name of the Lord*.

Notes on Genesis iv

1 The belief that Cain was the child of Sammael, from whom he inherited his evil character, was derived from Gen. v. 3, which says that Adam *begat a son in his own likeness, after his image; and called his name Seth*. This is not said of Cain, the implication being, therefore, that Cain was not Adam's son. Hence arose the statement in Ps. Jon. on Gen. v. 3, that Eve bore Cain, 'who was not like Adam'. See also Yalqut on Gen. §35, B.Yeb. 103*b*, B.A.Z. 22*b*, B.Shab. 146*a*, P.R.E. 21; see also the Targum and notes on Gen. iii. 6*a*. LXX here has 'through the Lord'.

It is possible that T.O. should simply be 'before the Lord', in which case it would mean, 'I have acquired a man (to be) before the Lord (when we have died)'.

With the words in Ps. Jon. compare Noah Frag. (I Enoch cvi. 5), where Lamech is made to say of his son: 'I have begotten a strange son, diverse from and unlike man, and resembling the sons of the God of heaven; and his nature is different and he is not like us ...'

[a] F.T. retained Heb. *Nod*.   [b] Or possibly 'at the east of'.
[c] Two MSS (Sperber D) have 'began'; so also Aq., Pesh. and Vulg. See further the notes on pp. 140 f.

2 The 'twin sister' is an allusion to the extensive discussion about whom Cain and Abel could possibly have married. Ber.R. xxii. 2 put it succinctly: 'R. Joshua b. Qarḥa said: "Two lay down and seven rose up: Cain and his twin sister, Abel and his two twin sisters." ' B. San. 38b says they rose up as four, and A.R.N. 1 quoted both: 'On that day two lay down and four rose up. R. Judah b. Bathyra said: "Two lay down and seven rose up." ' J.Yeb. xi. 1[a] observed that although marrying a sister breaks the Law, these instances were a necessary exception: *And if a man shall take his sister, his father's daughter, or his mother's daughter, and see her nakedness, and she sees his nakedness; it is a shameful thing* . . .[b] 'Does this mean that in marriage only this kind of union is forbidden . . .?' R. Abin said: 'Not so: scripture only makes a point of this prohibition in order to prevent anyone arguing the opposite on the basis that Cain and Abel married their sisters. Also we have here[c] the word *ḥesed*[d] which means usually "gracious favour"; thus in fact it was a special favour allowed to the first men by God to unite in this way in order to people the world, as it is written, "*ḥesed* will build the world".'[e]

Jubilees filled in some of the detail: 'And in the third week in the second jubilee she gave birth to Cain, and in the fourth she gave birth to Abel, and in the fifth she gave birth to her daughter Awan . . . And in the sixth week he begat his daughter Azura.'[f] Josephus put it quite simply: 'Two male children were born to them . . . They also had daughters.'[g] See also Ps. Philo i. 1 (Appendix 1), P.R.E. 21, Cave of Treasures (Budge, p. 61).

3 On the date see the notes on Gen. vii. 11; but contrast here Ber.R. xxii. 4.

The specific offering of Cain was deduced from Lev. xix. 19, Deut. xxii. 11, where garments made of combined materials, particularly wool and linen, were forbidden. Wool was a part of Abel's offering, since it was on the backs of the animals (Gen. iv. 4), so by deduction flax was part of Cain's offering. See also P.R.E. 21, Tanḥ. Ber. 11.

7 This was an attempt to make it quite clear that Cain was responsible for the failure of his offering, and it was extended into a reminder of

[a] Cf. B.Yeb. 62a.
[b] Lev. xx. 17.
[c] Lev. *ad loc.*
[d] R.V. *shameful.*
[e] R.V.: *Mercy shall be built up for ever,* Ps. lxxxix. 2 (M.T. 3); see Yalqut *ad loc.*
[f] Jub. iv. 1, 8.
[g] *Ant.* i. 52.

responsibility in general. Similar lessons were also derived in Ber.R. xxii. 6. Josephus[a] made it equally clear that Cain was responsible for the failure of his sacrifice, although he gave a different reason: instead of being satisfied with what grew naturally, Cain broke open the ground (that is, ploughed it) in the hope of finding more.

The verse was also connected with the evil inclination in A.R.N. 16:[b]

R. Reuben said: 'How can anyone escape the evil inclination when the first drop put by a man into a woman is the evil inclination? It lies at the beginning[c] of the heart, as it is written, ... *sin coucheth at the door* ...' R. Judah haNasi said: 'Let me give you a parable: to what may this be likened? The evil impulse is like two men entering a place of lodging where one of them is arrested as a thief. He was asked, "Is there anyone with you?" He might have said, "No one", but in fact he thought, "If I am going to be executed, let my companion be executed with me." Likewise the evil inclination says: "Since there is no hope for me in the world to come, I will destroy the whole body as well." '

See also Ber. xxii. 6, B.San. 91 *b*, Midr. Teh. on Ps. ix. 6.

8 Compare Ber.R. xxii. 7:

About what did they dispute? They said, 'Come, let us divide the world.' One (Cain) took the land and the other everything that could be moved. Cain said: 'The land you are standing on is mine', but Abel said: 'The clothes you are wearing are mine'; and he said, 'Take them off'. But Cain said, 'Fly (and get off the ground)' ... R. Joshua Siknini said in the name of R. Levi: '... One said, "The Temple must be built in my area", the other said, "It must be built in mine", as it is written: *And it came to pass, when they were in the field* ...'[d] 'Field' refers to 'the temple', because we read: *Therefore shall Zion for your sake be plowed as a field.*[e]

Rashi commented: 'He started an argument with him, striving and contending with him, looking for an opportunity to kill him.' On Gen. i. 1 he commented: ' "*God* created": it does not say " *The Lord* created", because at the first God intended to create the world under the rule of justice: he saw that the world would not survive it, so he put first the rule of mercy ...'[f] Justice in relation to mercy is part of Ps. Jon.'s dispute. The dispute was discussed by Philo in *Quod Det.* i. 1 f.

'A stone': 'With what did he kill him? R. Simeon said: "With a cudgel, because *and a young man for bruising*[g] means it was something

---

[a] *Ant.* i. 52 ff.   [b] So also, but less directly, in Sifre on Deut. xi. 18.
[c] Or 'opening'.   [d] Gen. iv. 8.   [e] Mic. iii. 12.
[f] Cf. also the argument of Abraham, quoted in the notes on Gen. vi. 3.
[g] Gen. iv. 23.

that causes a bruise." The rabbis said: "With a stone, because *for I have slain a man for wounding me*[a] means it was something which causes a wound.[b]"[c]' Jub. iv. 31 f. recorded the following legend on the same basis:

At the close of this Jubilee Cain was killed after him in the same year; for his house fell upon him and he died in the midst of his house, and he was killed by its stones; for with a stone he had killed Abel, and by a stone was he killed in righteous judgement. For this reason it was ordained on the heavenly tablets: 'With the instrument with which a man kills his neighbour with the same shall he be killed; after the manner that he wounded him, in like manner shall they deal with him.'

Compare I Pet. ii. 4–9, and see also P.R.E. 21, Tanh. Ber. 9. C.G. did not specify the weapon.

This verse and its possible relation to various New Testament passages has been discussed by M. McNamara, *The New Testament and the Palestinian Targum* . . ., pp. 156–60.

10 'R. Judan said: "It is not written *the blood of your brother* but *the bloods*[d] *of your brother*, his blood and the blood of his descendants." '[e] The same interpretation is made by A.R.N. 31, which adds: 'From this you may learn that one man's life equals the whole work of creation.'[f] Compare M.San. iv. 5, B.San. 37*b*.

14 Compare Ber.R. xxii. 11, 13:

Cain said: 'You bear[g] the heavens and the earth; can you not bear my sin? My sin is greater than my father's: my father disobeyed a small command and was driven out of the garden of Eden, but this killing is a serious offence: how much greater is my sin . . .' R. Ḥanina said: 'Cain went out[h] rejoicing, as it is written: . . . *he cometh forth to meet thee: and when he seeth thee, he will be glad in his heart.*[i] Adam met him and said: "What happened to you?" He said: "I repented and was reconciled." At that Adam lamented and said: "I did not realise how great was the power of repentance." '[j]

a Gen. iv. 23.
b It could not have been iron or a knife because these were first made by Tubal-cain, Gen. iv. 22.
c Ber.R. xxii. 8.
d *Demey*, plural.   e Ber.R. xxii. 9.
f Supported from Gen. v. 1 and ii. 4.
g The same root as in Ps. Jon. on Gen. iv. 13.   h Gen. iv. 16.
i Exod. iv. 14; the verses are connected by the same Heb. word for 'he went out'.
j The same story was recorded in Midr. Teh. on Ps. c. 1, but it is supported there by Esther v. 9.

Cain's response was also understood as an act of repentance by Josephus: 'God . . . exempted him from the penalty merited by the murder, Cain having offered a sacrifice and therewith supplicated him not to visit him too severely in his wrath.'[a]

See also B.San. 37*b*, Pes.R. 160*a*, Tanḥ. Ber. 9, Midr. Teh. on Ps. c. 1, Vay.R. x. 5, Yalqut on Gen. §38, P.R.E. 21.

15 Rashi recorded the same interpretation:[b] 'He inscribed for him a letter from his name on his forehead.' Seven different suggestions were recorded in Ber.R. xxii. 12, 13. Tanḥ. Ber. 10 suggested an eighth, the sabbath, which was a 'sign' of the bond between Israel and God (Exod. xxxi. 13).

On the seven generations, see Ps. Jon. on Gen. iv. 23–4.

16 See the notes on Gen. ii. 2 and ii. 8. For comments on this verse see my article, 'Haggadah in the Targum Onqelos', pp. 54–6.

23-4 The Targums here represent an attempt to make sense of a difficult Hebrew text. Part of the interpretation appears in Ber.R. xxiii. 4: 'Cain killed, but judgement was suspended for him for seven generations;[c] surely for me it will be suspended for seventy-seven.' See also Tanḥ. Ber. 11, Jerome, *ad Damasum* 125, where a further detail was added that according to Jewish tradition seventy-seven descendants of Lamech died in the flood.

On the repentance of Cain see the notes on iv. 13.

A very common story[d] supplied a completely different reason for Lamech's song by suggesting that he accidentally killed Cain. The version in Kit. alMaj. is as follows:

Lamech was passing by a thicket leaning on his son, being old. And he heard a noise in the thicket, which was the noise of Cain, since it was not possible for him to stay still in one place after he had killed his brother. Now Lamech thought that the noise was from some wild animal, so he picked up a stone from the ground, and threw it towards the noise. And the stone hit Cain between the eyes and killed him.

26 Ps. Philo ii. 10 (Appendix 1) gave a different set of offences.

The underlying problem here was the statement of Exod. vi. 3, *I appeared unto Abraham, unto Isaac, and unto Jacob, as God Almighty, but*

---

[a] *Ant.* i. 58. [b] *Ad loc.*
[c] Contrast Test. Ben. vii. 3: 'Therefore was Cain also delivered over to seven vengeances by God, for in every hundred years the Lord brought one plague upon him.'
[d] See M. R. James, *The Lost Apocrypha of the Old Testament*, pp. 10–11.

by my name יהוה (*The Lord*) *I was not known to them.* But if the Hebrew text of Gen. iv. 26 is right, men began to call on the name of 'the Lord' long before Abraham. How, then, did Abraham not know the name? It was to avoid this problem that the Targums made their radical alteration. Ber.R. xxvi. 4 shows how Ps. Jon. arrived at its interpretation: 'In three places this word[a] is used to mean rebellion: *Then they rebelled by calling upon the name of the Lord;*[b] *When man rebelled in multiplying on the face of the earth;*[c] *He (Nimrod) rebelled when he was a mighty one in the earth.'* [d]

For the same interpretation see Ps. Philo ii. 8 (Appendix I). For a more elaborate legend, see Chron. Jer. xxiii. 6–7, xxiv. 9.

[a] *Huḥal*: R.V. 'began', LXX 'hoped'; the root *ḥll* means in the hiphil 'begin' but in the piel 'profane'.
[b] Gen. iv. 26, understanding the verse as the Targum does.
[c] Gen. vi. 1.   [d] Gen. x. 8.

GENESIS V

1 *This is the book of the* genealogy of the *generations of Adam. In the day that* the Lord *created* Adam, *in the likeness of* the Lord *made he him;*

2 *male* with female parts[a] *created he them; and blessed them* in the name of his word, *and called their name Adam, in the day when they were created.*

3 *And Adam lived an hundred and thirty years, and begat* Seth who resembled his likeness and his appearance. For before that time, Eve had borne Cain who was not from him (Adam) and did not resemble him, and Abel was killed at the hands of Cain, and Cain was cast out, and his descendants were not recorded in the book of the genealogy of Adam. And after that there was born one who resembled him, and he *called his name Seth.*

(4-21 These verses, recording the line of descent from Adam to Enoch, appear in Ps. Jon. as in the Hebrew text, and are therefore not reproduced here.)

22 *And Enoch* served[b] before the Lord in uprightness *after he begat Methuselah three hundred years, and begat sons and daughters:*

23 *and all the days of Enoch* with the dwellers on earth *were three hundred sixty and five years:*

24 *and Enoch* served[b] before the Lord in uprightness, and, behold, *he was not* with the dwellers on earth, for he was withdrawn and went up to the firmament by the word before the Lord, and his name was called Metatron the great scribe.

(25-8 These verses, continuing the line of descent from Methuselah to Lamech, follow the Hebrew.)

29 *And he called his name Noah, saying, 'This same shall comfort us for our work* which is not successful, *and for the toil of our hands from the ground which the Lord hath cursed* because of the offences of the sons of men.'

(30-2 These verses, tracing the line of descent to the birth of Shem, Ham and Japheth, follow the Hebrew.)

---

[a] But see the notes for an alternative translation.

[b] Or 'worshipped'.

Selections from other Targums on Genesis v

2 F.T. (Gins. p. 7): A man and his pair.

T.O.: A man with female parts[a] *created he them* . . .

5 F.T. (Gins. p. 74) has one word, 'before him'.

22 T.O.: *And Enoch walked* in the fear of the Lord *after he begat Methuse-lah* . . .

24 F.T. (Gins. p. 7; see also p. 75): *And Enoch* served[b] before the Lord in uprightness, and, behold, *he was not*, and we do not know what he was in his end because he was taken away from before the Lord.

T.O.: see the notes on p. 147.

Notes on Genesis v

2 This is one of the recognised LXX variants,[c] referred to already in the notes on Gen. ii. 7. The LXX was taken to say, 'Male and female created he *him*' (singular), which implied that in the original creation of Adam male and female were combined, and were only separated later.[d] In Ber.R. viii. 1 Adam is described as *anderoginos*, the Greek ἀνδρόγυνος, hermaphrodite. Mek. Pisḥa 14 recorded the variant with the words *zakar uneqabauw*, and both Ps. Jon. and T.O. translated this verse with those words; on the other hand they both retain the plural suffix ('them'), and it is possible that the full force of *naqab* has been lost, and that it may simply mean 'male and female'. This is supported by the fact that exactly the same phrase was used by both Targums in Gen. vi. 19; cf. also vii. 2, 3, 9, etc.

3 See the Targum and notes on Gen. iv. 1.

22 Both Targums avoided a possibly anthropomorphic expression, but in slightly different ways. See also the notes on v. 24 below. LXX and Pesh. have, 'And Enoch pleased God', both here and in verse 24. Pesh. has the same of Noah in Gen. vi. 9, and of Abraham in xvii. 1 (where Ps. Jon. and Onq. have 'serve' or 'worship').

24 The interpretation of Ps. Jon. gives a high status to Enoch, but the interpretation was disputed in Judaism. Hesitations about Enoch arose for three principal reasons: first, the meaning of the phrase in the

---

[a] But see the notes for an alternative translation.
[b] Or 'worshipped'.
[c] See Appendix III.   [d] Gen. ii. 22.

Hebrew text, *and he was not*, was uncertain; Ps. Jon. followed a long tradition of exegesis in which the phrase was taken to mean that Enoch did not die; but others took it to mean exactly the opposite, that he *did* die. Secondly, the interpretation that Enoch was specially favoured by being removed from the earth without dying gave rise to extravagant and often unorthodox speculations about him. The most obvious example of that tendency is the extensive apocryphal literature produced in his name. There were some who felt it necessary to limit those speculations as much as possible. Thirdly, Christian exegesis also made much of Enoch, and that again was a strong reason why Jewish exegesis came to treat Enoch cautiously. Exactly the same happened in the case of Melchizedek.[a]

The popularity of Enoch goes back a long way. Literature, containing many legends about him, was being produced in his name from about the second or first century B.C., and he appears as a well-established and highly regarded figure in the New Testament,[b] the Genesis Apocryphon[c] and Jubilees.[d] His perfection was also noted in Ecclus. xliv. 16 and xlix. 14–16, and in Wisdom iv. 10.

There seems to have been little hesitation about Enoch in early times. Josephus, for example, wrote quite simply: 'Enoch lived 365 years and then returned to the divinity, whence it comes that there is no record in the chronicles of his death.'[e] There were some who argued that Enoch had been wicked for a part of his life and had then repented, but that suggestion was based on the LXX translation of Gen. v. 21 and 24, which says: 'Enoch was pleasing to God after begetting Methuselah 200[f] years.' Hence Philo commented:

On becoming a man and father, in his very procreation, he made a beginning of probity, being said to have been pleasing to God. For although he did not altogether remain in piety, none the less that period of time was reckoned to him as belonging to the order of the praiseworthy, for he was pleasing (to God) so many years . . . For not very long after the forgiving of Cain it introduces the fact that Enoch repented, informing us that forgiveness is wont to produce repentance.[g]

---

[a] See the Targum and notes on Gen. xiv. 18.
[b] Jude verses 14 ff. quotes from I Enoch i. 9.
[c] Col. ii.
[d] For the estimate of Enoch in Jubilees, see the notes on Metatron below.
[e] *Ant.* i. 85.   [f] Heb. 300.
[g] *Quaes. Gen.* i. 82; see also i. 83–4, and Ps. Philo i. 16 (Appendix i).

But he was quite clear that the end of Enoch was of no ordinary kind:

What is the meaning of the words, *And he was not, for God had translated him?*
First of all, the end of worthy and holy men is not death but translation and
approaching another place. Second, something very marvellous took place.
For he seemed to be rapt away and become invisible. For then he was not
found. And this is shown by the fact that when he was sought, he was invisible, not merely rapt from their eyes. For the translation to another place is
nothing else than another position; but he is said (to have moved) from a
sensible and visible place to an incorporeal and intelligible form. This gift the
proto-prophet[a] also obtained, for no one knew his burial-place. And still
another, Elijah,[b] followed him on high from earth to heaven at the appearance
of the divine countenance, or, it would be more proper and correct to say, he
ascended.[c]

In some circles legends about Enoch became more and more fantas-
tic,[d] and it is not surprising that there was an increasing mistrust of
these speculations in Rabbinic Judaism. At the same time, the Christian
use of Enoch made him even more suspect. The Christian use of Enoch
was often entirely innocent, without any polemic intentions at all,
simply taking it for granted that Enoch had not died in the ordinary
way.[e] Much, therefore, of their discussion was an attempt to unravel
the implications of this. For example, Gregory of Nazianzus wrote:[f]
'Enoch was translated, but it is not yet clear whether it was because he
already comprehended the divine nature or in order that he might
comprehend it.' Similarly, when Augustine considered Enoch in *De
Pecc. Mer. et Rem.*,[g] his main concern was to decide in what form or
state Enoch and Elijah existed after their translation:

If God supplied clothes and shoes for the Israelites which were not worn out
over the course of many years,[h] why should it seem surprising if he supplies
to the man who obeys him the same power, so that although he has a body
both mortal and belonging to the created order, he has in it a certain quality
by which . . . when God wills it he may pass from mortality to immortality

---

[a] I.e. Moses.   [b] II Kings ii. 11.

[c] *Quaes. Gen.* i. 86; cf. the account of the ascension, Acts i. 9–11.

[d] See, for example, the legends in The Cave of Treasures and Kit. alMaj.

[e] A typical comment would be that of Cyprian (*De Mort.* 13): 'Since Enoch
was found pleasing in the sight of God, he was deemed worthy to be removed
from the contamination of the world.' Cf. the comment in Syr. Comm.
(Levene, p. 80). It must be remembered that Christians might be as uneasy
about the speculative use of Enoch as Jews.

[f] *Orat.* xxviii. 18 (*Theol. Orat.* 11).   [g] i. 3.

[h] Deut. xxix. 5; cf. the discussion in Midr. Teh. on Ps. xxiii. 2.

without passing through death? I suggest that this kind of condition . . . was allowed to those who were translated hence without dying; for neither Enoch nor Elijah wasted away through old age . . . However, I do not think that they have already been changed into that spiritual state of body which is promised in the resurrection.

The Jews had little need to be disturbed by arguments like these, but the Christians also had a polemic use for Enoch: they regarded him as one of those who were righteous before Torah was given on Mt Sinai, and from that they argued that Torah, however helpful for a time, was not entirely necessary; it was possible to be righteous without it.[a] Irenaeus gave a typical expression of the argument in *Adv. Haer.*[b] when he was discussing the place of the Law in general, and of circumcision and the Sabbath in particular:

The proof that men are not justified by these, but that these were given as signs to the people, lies in the fact that Abraham himself, while he was still uncircumcised and not keeping the sabbath, *believed God, and it was reckoned unto him for righteousness; and he was called the friend of God.*[c] Furthermore, Lot while still uncircumcised was taken out of Sodom, being delivered by God. So also Noah, although he was uncircumcised, pleased God . . . And Enoch as well, although he was uncircumcised, was pleasing to God, and despite the fact that he was a man he acted like an envoy to the angels, and was translated and is kept to this hour as a witness of the justice of God's judgement; for while the angels having sinned fell down to earth in judgement, a man having won approval was translated into salvation. To this must be added all those many others who were righteous before the time of Abraham, as well as the patriarchs who lived before Moses, and were justified without the things under discussion and without the Law of Moses.

For another expression of the same argument, see Justin, *Dial.* 19, quoted in the notes on Gen. xiv. 18.

The Jews met these arguments in the case of Enoch in two ways: in the first place, they transferred to other Jewish figures many of the functions previously attributed to Enoch; and in the second place, they directly attacked the argument that Enoch's perfection was proved by his translation to heaven without dying, and they did so by saying that he was *not* perfect and that he *did* die. The actual debates were recorded in Ber.R. xxv. 1.

---

[a] Enoch was also used to illustrate the Ascension: see, for example, Act. Pil. xvi. 6.

[b] iv. 16. 2. [c] Jas. ii. 23.

R. Ḥama b. R. Hoshaiah said: 'It[a] means that he was not written in the roll of the just but in the roll of the wicked.' R. Aibu said: 'Enoch was two-faced,[b] sometimes acting justly, sometimes wickedly.' Therefore the Holy One, blessed be he, said: 'I will take him away at a time when he is acting justly.'[c] Some sceptics[d] said to R. Abbahu: 'We do not find that Enoch died.' R. Abbahu asked, 'Why not?' They said: 'The word *take* is used here and it is also used of Elijah.'[e] He replied: 'If you rely on the word *take*, then in Ezekiel it is written, . . . *behold, I take away from thee the desire of thine eyes.*[f] R. Tanḥuma said, 'He answered them well'.[g]

The popularity of Enoch is witnessed by the fact that Ps. Jon. retained a high estimate of Enoch, despite hesitations elsewhere in Judaism.[h] T.O., on the other hand, took the opposite point of view, and said specifically, 'And he was not, because the Lord caused him to die'. Yet even here the uncertainty about Enoch becomes apparent, since some MSS[i] add the word 'not', 'because the Lord did *not* cause him to die'. The 'agnosticism' of F.T. summarises, perfectly, Jewish hesitations about Enoch.

'Metatron': Metratron was an angel who came to play an increasingly important part in Jewish angelology. He became the great defender of Israel's interests and was identified with 'the prince of this world'. He was thought by some, for example, to intercede for Israel:

When the Holy One, blessed be he, commanded Israel to erect the Tabernacle he commanded the ministering angels to do likewise. When they erected the one below, the other was erected on high. The one on high was that of the servant whose name is Metatron: in it he offers up the souls of the righteous to make atonement for Israel in the time of their exile.[j]

[a] The phrase, 'and he was not'.   [b] *Ḥanaph.*
[c] I.e. he understood the phrase as meaning simply, 'he died'.
[d] *Appiqorsin*, i.e. Epicurean, used as a general term for 'heretic'.
[e] II Kings ii. 1.
[f] Ezek. xxiv. 16: the reference is to the death of his wife.
[g] Cf. also the summary of Rashi, 'He was just, but his understanding inclined to turn and be evil . . .'
[h] Though of course favourable estimates appear: see, for example, Pes.K. xxiii. 10 (a section making various lists of 'seven' people who were loved by God), or Chron. Jer. xxiv. 2, ' . . . Enoch the righteous whom God took to himself and trained for the day which is entirely sabbath' (see also xxvi. 20).
[i] Sperber U, y[b], d[1].
[j] Bem.R. xii. 12. The efficacy of intercession was disputed (see my article, 'Intercession in the Qur'ān . . .'). Bem.R. is a late source, and Metatron's intercession was not always so effective. According to Tanḥ. Vaeth. 6 Moses asked Metatron to intercede with God to avert his death. Metatron replied: 'It is to no avail, for I have heard what is said behind the veil, that your prayer will not be answered.'

It is clear that he even usurped some of the functions and position which had previously belonged to Michael. For example, Ps. Jon. on Exod. xxiv. 1 reads: 'And Michael, the prince of wisdom, said to Moses . . ., *Come up before the Lord* . . .' But B.San. 38*b* (discussing Exod. xxiv. 1, because apparently it was used by Christians as an argument for the Trinity in the Old Testament)[a] says:

A heretic[b] once said to R. Iddi: 'It is written: *And he said unto Moses, Come up unto the Lord* . . .[c] But it should have been written, "Come up unto *me*. . .".' R. Iddi said: 'It was Metatron (who spoke): his name is like that of his Lord, as it is written, . . . *for my name is in him*.[d]' The heretic said: 'In that case we should worship him.' R. Iddi replied: 'No, because the same verse says, *Provoke him not*,[e] that is, do not exchange[f] me for him.'

Rashi commenting on the same verse explained why the name of Metatron was estimated so highly: 'Our rabbis said that the *him* referred to is Metatron whose name is like the name of his Lord: Metatron has the same numerical value as Shaddai.'[g]

As a result actions were believed to have been delegated to Metatron by God: B.A.Z. 3*b* asks: 'Who instructed children before (the destruction of the temple)? You may, if you wish, say Metatron, or you may say that God did this as well as all the rest.' Metatron could also be invoked to explain difficult passages:

R. Samuel b. Naḥmani said in the name of R. Jonathan: 'This verse was spoken by the prince of the world: *I have been young, and now am old*.[h] Who else could it have been? You cannot say it was the Holy One, blessed be he, because old age does not apply to him. Was it David? He did not grow so old. Therefore it must have been the prince of the world.'

The high promotion of Metatron may have been useful, but it contained great dangers, particularly since it hovered on the edge of dualism. B.Ḥag. 15*a* regarded this as having been the offence of a well-known apostate, Elisha b. Abuyah, referred to after his apostasy as *Aḥer*, 'another'; his name, in other words, was not to be mentioned: 'Aḥer

[a] See the notes on Gen. i. 26.   [b] *Min.*
[c] Exod. xxiv. 1.
[d] Exod. xxiii. 21. See III Enoch xii. 5 quoted below, p. 150.
[e] *'Al-tammer.*
[f] He understood *tammer* as being from the root *mur*, 'exchange'.
[g] 'Almighty', a frequent name of God in the Old Testament, for example Gen. xvii. 1, Exod. vi. 3. The numerical value of the letters in each is 314.
[h] Ps. xxxvii. 25.

saw that Metatron had been allowed to sit down and record the merits of Israel, so he said: "It is taught traditionally that there is no standing or sitting in heaven . . . Perhaps there are two divinities." ' However, it is quite possible that B.Ḥag. *inserted* this as one of Elisha's offences in order to provide a warning against the tendency to promote Metatron too far: there is no record of such an offence in the account of Elisha b. Abuyah in J.Ḥag. ii. 1:

It is said of him (Elisha b. Abuyah) that he brought about the death of every pupil that he saw engaged in the study of the Law. In addition, he went to places of study and when he saw any young people sitting before the rabbi he told them they had nothing to do there: they would be far better off as a builder or a locksmith or a soldier or a tailor. When the young people had heard him express himself thus, they left the rabbi to take up work with their hands.

The passage goes on to suggest that Elisha informed against the Jews in a time of persecution, probably that of Hadrian.

The passage quoted from B.Ḥag 15 *a* is important for another reason: it indicates the link by which Enoch and Metatron were identified. Both were regarded as the scribe who recorded the merits or demerits of Israel.[a] Jub. iv. 23 says of Enoch: 'Enoch was taken from amongst the children of men, and we conducted him into the Garden of Eden[b] in majesty and honour, and behold there he writes down the condemnation and judgement of the world, and all the wickedness of the children of men.'

Jub. x. 17 adds: 'For Enoch's office was ordained for a testimony to the generations of the world, so that he should recount all the deeds of generation unto generation, till the day of judgement.' Similarly, I Enoch xii. 3–5 has:

And I Enoch was blessing the Lord of majesty and the King of the ages, and lo! the Watchers called me—Enoch the scribe—and said to me: 'Enoch, scribe of righteousness, go, declare to the Watchers of the heaven who have left the high heaven, the holy eternal place, and have defiled themselves with women, and have done as the children of earth do, and have taken to themselves wives: "You have wrought great destruction on the earth . . ." '

[a] In Asc. Is. ix. 21 this function was ascribed to Michael. See the discussion on Exod. xxiv. 1 above. Enoch was described as a scribe because he was believed to have been 'the author of many writings' (Chron. Jer. xxvi. 20).
[b] Cf. Kit. alMaj. 107 *a*: 'God took him back to the land of life, and made him live in Paradise in the land where there is no death.'

The identification of Enoch and Metatron reached its height in III Enoch, where Enoch/Metatron is even called 'the lesser Yahweh',[a] a clear indication why speculations about Enoch were treated with suspicion in more orthodox circles. For more detailed discussion of Enoch/Metatron, see H. Odeberg's edition of III Enoch, pp. 79–146. See also M. Black, 'The Origin of the Name Metatron', *V.T.* 1 (1951), 217–19.

[a] *Yahweh haQatan*, III Enoch xii. 5: 'And he called me "the lesser Yahweh" in the presence of all his heavenly household; as it is written, *For my name is in him* (Exod. xxiii. 21).' See also xlviii. 7 (C), xlviii. 1 (D).

GENESIS VI

1 *And it came to pass when* the sons of *men began to multiply on the face of the ground, and* beautiful *daughters were born unto them,*

2 *that the sons of* the great ones *saw* that *the daughters of men* were beautiful, with eyes painted[a] and hair curled, walking in nakedness of flesh, and they conceived lustful thoughts; *and they took them wives of all that they chose.*

3 *And the Lord said* by his word: 'None of the evil generations to arise in the future will be judged by the order of judgements applied to the generation of the flood, which is to be destroyed and eliminated from the world. Have I not put my holy *spirit* in them, that they may do good works? But see, their works are evil! I have given them an extension of *an hundred and twenty years,* in the hope that they would work repentance, and they have not done so.[b]

4 Shamhazai and Azael fell from heaven and were on the earth *in those days, and also after that, when the sons of* the great ones *came in unto the daughters of men, and they bare children to them: the same are* called men of the world, *the men of renown.*[c]

5 *And the Lord saw that the wickedness of man was great in the earth, and that every imagination*[d] *of the thoughts of his heart was only evil continually.*

6 *And it repented the Lord* in his word *that he had made man on the earth,* and he debated the matter concerning them in his word [*memra*].

7 *And the Lord said, 'I will destroy man whom I have created from the face of the ground; both man, and beast, and creeping thing, and fowl of the air; for it repenteth me* in my word *that I have made them.*

8 *But Noah,* who was righteous, *found grace* before *the Lord.*

9 *These are the* genealogies of the family *of Noah. Noah was* an innocent[e] man, *perfect* in good works *in his generations: Noah walked* in the fear of the Lord.

---

a So also P.R.E. 22.
b Or perhaps (reading *r* for *d*), 'and not transgression'; see Jastrow on Targ. on Prov. x. 23 (*Dictionary*, p. 1038a).
c See also Sifre on Num. §86, Sifre Z. 194, Justin, *Dial.* 79 (by implication).
d I.e. the evil *yeẓer.*   e *Zakkai.*

10 *And Noah begat three sons, Shem, Ham, and Japheth.*

11 *And the earth was corrupt* because of the inhabitants who wandered from the path of uprightness before the Lord, *and the earth was filled with violence.*

12 *And* the Lord *saw the earth, and, behold, it was corrupt; for all flesh* without exception *had corrupted his way upon the earth.*

13 *And* the Lord *said unto Noah, ' The end of all flesh is come before me; for the earth is filled with violence through* their evil works; *and behold, I will destroy them with the earth.*

14-15 *Make thee an ark of* cedar wood; construct one hundred and fifty cabins for the ark on the left side[a] with thirty-six in its breadth, and ten rooms in the centre, to store provisions in them, and five for water on the right and five on the left; and smear it *within and without with pitch.*

16 Go to Pishon and take from there a precious stone, and put it in the ark to give you *light.* With the measure of *a cubit shalt thou finish it from above:*[b] *and the door of the ark shalt thou set in the side thereof; with lower, second, and third* compartments[c] *shalt thou make it.*

17 *And I, behold, I do bring the flood of waters upon the earth, to destroy all flesh, wherein is the breath of life, from under heaven; every thing that is in the earth shall* be withdrawn.

18 *But I will establish my covenant with thee; and thou shalt come into the ark, thou, and thy sons, and thy wife, and thy sons' wives with thee.*

19 *And of every living thing of all flesh, two of every sort shalt thou bring into the ark, to keep them alive with thee; they shall be male and female.*

20 *Of the fowl after their kind, and of the cattle after their kind, of every creeping thing of the ground after its kind, two of every sort shall come unto thee* by the hand of an angel, who will take them and bring them in to you *to keep them alive.*

21 *And take thou unto thee of all food that is eaten, and gather it to thee; and it shall be for food for thee, and for them.'*

22 *Thus did Noah; according to all that God commanded him, so did he.*

Selections from other Targums on Genesis vi

2 T.O.: *that the sons of* the great ones *saw . . .*

3 F.T. (Gins. p. 7; see also p. 75) has a similar interpretation. T.O.: see the notes on p. 155.

---

[a] Or perhaps 'in its length'.   [b] R.V. marg.   [c] T.O. has the same word.

₆ F.T. (Gins. pp. 75, 92) has part of the verse.

T.O.: *And it repented the Lord* in his word *that he had made man on the earth*, and he said[a] that he would break their strength as he pleased.

₈ F.T. (Gins. p. 7): *But Noah, because he was righteous in his generation, found grace* and favour[b] *before the Lord.*

₉ T.O.: *Noah was* an innocent[c] man, *perfect in his generations: Noah walked* in the fear of the Lord.

₁₁ F.T. (Gins. p. 75) has one word.

₁₄ F.T. (Gins. pp. 8, 92): of cedar wood.

T.O.: see the notes on p. 159.

Notes on Genesis vi

₂ The phrase *bene elohim* might have been understood in too crude or literal a sense as 'God's sons'. To avoid this the Targums changed the noun, and Ps. Jon. added further descriptions. At the time when Ps. Philo was written it was still possible to write 'sons of God' (iii. 1, Appendix 1), but the alteration became standard and expected.[d] In Ber.R. xxvi. 5 it occurs in extreme terms: 'R. Simeon b. Johai called them "the sons of the great", and he cursed all who called them "the sons of God".' The same section (xxvi) also imputed lust and immorality to 'the daughters of men' (no doubt to make more specific *the wickedness of man* mentioned in Gen. vi. 5): 'R. Berekiah said: "A woman would go out into the open, see a young man, and becoming passionate for him, would go and lie with him and give birth to a young man like him." '[e]

Gen. Apoc. (Col. ii) recorded that Lamech was suspicious about the birth of Noah, and accused his wife: 'Then I thought to myself that the conception was from the watchers and the holy ones . . . and from the giants . . . and I was deeply troubled because of the child. So I went quickly to Bath-enosh (my) wife and said, ". . . Tell me (truthfully) and not falsely . . ."' See also Noah Frag. (I Enoch cvi).

[a] Sperber A and L add, 'in his word'.
[b] *Ḥesed*; T.O. has 'mercies'.
[c] *Zakkai*.
[d] Pesh., for example, transliterated *elohim* letter by letter, and thus avoided its usual word for 'God'; the same is true of Gen. vi. 4.
[e] Ber.R. xxvi. 7. In Chron. Jer. xxiv. 10 the *bene Elohim* were identified as the seed of Seth, the daughters of men as the seed of Cain.

The summary in P.R.E. 22 extended the accusation of immorality: 'R. Meir said: "The descendants of Cain, both men and women, walked about naked like animals, and debased themselves with every kind of immorality publicly, a man with his mother or his daughter or his brother's wife or his neighbour's wife, following the evil inclination which is in the imagination of their heart[a] ..."' Even greater detail was given in The Cave of Treasures (Budge, pp. 86 ff.) and Adam and Eve ii. 20. See also Tanh.B. i. 16, 23, 24, Tanh. Ber. 12, Vay.R. xxiii. 9, Justin, *Apol.* i. 55, ii. 5, Tertullian, *Apol.* 22.

3 The first part of this comment was derived from the promise in Gen. ix. 15 (... *the waters shall no more become a flood to destroy all flesh*) referred to in Isa. liv. 9 (... *for as I have sworn that the waters of Noah should no more go over the earth* ...). It led to the famous story about Abraham, told in Vay.R. x. 1:

When Abraham was praying for mercy for the men of Sodom, he said: 'Lord of the universe, you swore that you would never again bring a flood upon the world as it is written: ... *I have sworn that the waters of Noah should no more go over the earth.* Is it only water that you will not bring? Are you going to bring a deluge of fire? Are you evading your oath with cunning? This is the verse: *That be far from thee to do after this manner ... Shall not the Judge of all the earth do right?*'[b] Abraham was saying, 'If you want (strict) justice you cannot have a world: if you want a world you cannot have (strict) justice. You are trying to hold a rope by both its ends: you want a world and you want justice. But if you will not be at all indulgent, your world will not be able to survive.'[c]

Isa. liv. 9 was also applied in Ber.R. xxxiv. 6 in a comment on Gen. viii. 16 (*Go forth from the ark* ...): 'Noah was unwilling to go out, saying, "Shall I go out to beget children to be cursed?" So the Holy One, blessed be he, swore to him that he would not bring another flood upon the world, as it is written, ... *for as I have sworn* ...'

The transformation of this verse into one concerned with 'judgement' came about because of the verb in the Hebrew text, *yadon.* The word *din* came increasingly to refer to legal decisions and judgements. Hence the interpretation in Ps. Jon. here and (as another example) in Ber.R. xxvi. 6: 'R. Judah b. Bathyra interpreted it (this verse): "I will never again judge man with this judgement."'

[a] See Gen. vi. 5.
[b] Gen. xviii. 25.
[c] The same story is told in Ber.R. xxxix. 6.

In Jubilees the verse gave rise to a considerable 'excursus' on judgement:

God destroyed all from their places, and there was not left one of them whom He judged not according to all their wickedness. And he made for all his works a new and righteous nature, so that they should not sin in their whole nature for ever, but should be all righteous each in his kind alway. And the judgement of all is ordained and written on the heavenly tablets in righteousness—even (the judgement of) all who depart from the path which is ordained for them to walk in; and if they walk not therein, judgement is written down for every creature and for every kind. And there is nothing in heaven or on earth, or in light or in darkness, or in Sheol, or in the depth, or in the place of darkness (which is not judged);[a] and all their judgements are ordained and written and engraved. In regard to all he will judge, the great according to his greatness, the small according to his smallness, and each according to his way. And he is not one who will regard the person (of any), nor is he one who will receive gifts, if he says that he will execute judgement on each: if one gave everything that is on the earth, he will not regard the gifts or the person (of any), nor accept anything at his hands, for he is a righteous judge. And of the children of Israel it has been written and ordained: If they turn to him in righteousness, he will forgive all their transgressions and pardon all their sins. It is written and ordained that he will show mercy to all who turn from all their guilt once each year.[b]

In Ps. Philo also the verse was translated, 'My spirit will not judge . . .,'[c] and a part of the comment in J.San. x. 3 is: 'R. Simeon said, "My spirit will not judge him, because I will not put my spirit in them, when I give the righteous their reward." '

However, it is quite clear that the verse caused considerable uncertainty: LXX reads: 'My spirit will not rest in . . .', which is also the way in which Jub. v. 8 understood it, despite its long paragraph on judgement. T.O. seems to have reduced the verb to the demonstrative adjective *haDen*. It reads: 'This evil generation will not stand before me for ever.' But it is possible that it is following Pesh., reading *yador*, 'endure'. Rashi's comment also indicates the extent to which the verse suggested different interpretations: 'My spirit will not be dissatisfied nor will it strive with myself because of man. "For ever", for a long time: for my spirit has been contending[d] within me, whether to destroy or whether to show mercy. This contending shall not be for ever . . .

[a] Cf. Rom. viii. 38–9.
[b] Jub. v. 11–18. Charles regarded the last two sentences as additions.
[c] iii. 2, Appendix 1.　　　　　　　　　　[d] *Nadon*.

There are many *midrash* explanations of *lo yadon*, but this is the one which is its obvious sense.'

For some of these alternative explanations, see further Ber.R. xxvi. 6 and B.San. 108*a*; see also Tanḥ.B. i. 26 f.

The second half of the verse also represents a common interpretation of the phrase *yet* (or 'therefore') *shall his days be an hundred and twenty years*.[a] By this it was understood that God had given men an opportunity for repentance before destroying them in the flood. This is particularly clear in T.O. *ad loc.*: 'I will give them an extension of time, 120 years, to see if they will repent.' Similarly Rashi[b] has: 'For 120 years I will hold back my anger, but if they will not repent, I will bring a flood upon them.' See also the notes on Gen. vii. 10, 'Methuselah'.

An equally common tradition was that Noah delayed while building the ark in order to give people a chance to repent. P.R.E. 23 says that he took 52 years, Yashar[c] that he took 5 years. The reading in P.R.E. may depend on the fact that the dates in Genesis do not fit with each other. A summary of a similar problem is given in B.San. 69*b*:

'And Noah was five hundred years old: and Noah begat Shem, Ham and Japheth.'[d] Hence Shem was a year older than Ham and Ham a year older than Japheth. Now it is written: *And Noah was six hundred years old when the flood of waters was upon the earth*,[e] and it is written: *Shem was an hundred years old, and begat Arphachshad two years after the flood.*[f] But was he 100 years old? Surely he must have been 102? Therefore you have to say that they[g] are listed in order of wisdom (and not of age).

That God allowed a period of repentance was also argued on the basis of Gen. vii. 4 and 10;[h] compare also Aboth v. 2: 'There were ten generations from Adam to Noah, to make clear how far extended is long-suffering with God, because all those generations went on provoking him until he brought the waters of the flood upon them.' Mek. on Exod. xv. 6 says: 'You are gracious and mighty in power because you gave an extension to the generation of the flood to work repentance, but they would not do so...'[i] Ps. Jon. on Gen. xix. 24 states that a

---

[a] Gen. vi. 3*b*. See, for example, Mek. Shir. 5.
[b] *Ad loc.*
[c] v. 34 (A.N.C.L. xviii, p. 344).
[d] Gen. v. 32.
[e] Gen. vii. 6.
[f] Gen. xi. 10.
[g] Shem, Ham and Japheth.
[h] See the notes *ad loc.*
[i] Shir. 5.

similar opportunity for repentance was given to the people of Sodom and Gomorrah.

Josephus knew of the plea for repentance, and wrote, 'Noah, indignant at their conduct and viewing their counsels with displeasure, urged them to come to a better frame of mind and amend their ways'.[a] Cf. II Pet. ii. 5, and see J. P. Lewis, *A Study*..., pp. 92–100.

4   The interpretation of Ps. Jon. was based on taking Nephilim from the root *naphal*, 'he fell'. The 'fallen angels' were then identified. The origins of Shamhazai and Azael are obscure and they rarely occur in early sources. In B.Nid. 61 *a*[b] there is no indication that Shamhazai was a fallen angel at all. However, I Enoch gives a parallel to the Targum version:

And it came to pass when the children of men had multiplied that in those days were born unto them beautiful and comely daughters. And the angels, the children of the heaven, saw and lusted after them, and said to one another: 'Come, let us choose us wives from among the children of men and beget us children.' And Semjaza, who was their leader, said unto them: 'I fear ye will not indeed agree to do this deed, and I alone shall have to pay the penalty of a great sin.' And they all answered him and said: 'Let us all swear an oath, and all bind ourselves by mutual imprecations not to abandon this plan but to do this thing' . . . And they were in all two hundred . . . And these are the names of their leaders: Samiaza, their leader . . . and Asael[c.d]

The legend that the angels were involved in the fall of men was widespread and early. Jubilees, for example, says:

And it came to pass when the children of men began to multiply on the face of the earth and daughters were born unto them, that the angels of God saw them on a certain year of this jubilee, and they were beautiful to look upon; and they took themselves wives of all whom they chose, and they bare unto them sons and they were giants. And lawlessness increased on the earth . . .[e]

Similarly Josephus wrote: 'For many angels of God now consorted with women and begat sons who were overbearing and disdainful of

[a] *Ant.* i. 74.
[b] 'Sihon and Og were brothers, for one taught: Sihon and Og were the sons of Ahijah the son of Shamhazai.'
[c] Asael is one of 18 'leaders of ten' listed by name. A longer version of their fall is given in Yalqut on Gen. §44.
[d] I Enoch vi. 1–8. See also Test. Naph. iv. 5. The complete legend was recorded in Midrash Abkir (quoted in Yalqut on Gen. §44), and in Chron. Jer. xxv. In B.Yom. 67b the names are Uza and Azael (in teaching from the school of R. Ishmael), and in Kall.R. iii. 9 they are Azza and Azzael.
[e] Jub. v. 1–2; see also iv. 22 and vii. 21.

every virtue, such confidence had they in their strength; in fact the deeds that tradition[a] ascribes to them resemble the audacious exploits told by the Greeks of the giants.'[b] The LXX has, both at the beginning and the end of the verse, οἱ γίγαντες. It is probable that Ps. Jon., by not speaking here of angels, was trying to rescue their reputation.

That is certainly true of the Kit. alMaj., which says specifically: 'There are certainly some who think that the Book records and says that the angels came down to earth and mingled with the children of men, that those who came down and mingled with the children of men were angels . . . But whoever imagines that has erred: mingling, that is intimacy, is not in the nature of spiritual beings . . .[c]

6 These changes are a sign of uneasiness about predicating grief of God. To do so might imply that God had made a mistake. The point was made precisely in Ber.R. xxvii. 4:

A non-Jew[d] once asked R. Joshua b. Qarḥah, 'Is it not your belief that the Holy One, blessed be he, foresees the future[e]?' He said, 'Certainly'. 'But is it not written, *And it grieved him at his heart?*' R. Joshua said: 'Have you ever had a son[f] born to you?' He said, 'Yes'. He said 'So what did you do?' 'I rejoiced and caused everyone to do the same.' 'But in fact did you not know that at some time he would have to die?' He said: 'Be glad when it is appropriate, be sad when it is appropriate.' R. Joshua said: 'It is exactly like that with the Holy One, blessed be he . . .'

Tanḥ.B. i. 30 avoided the difficulty in a different way:

R. Abbahu said: 'God did not grieve except over the heart of man, like someone who has made something bad and knows that he has not made a fine thing. And he says, What have I done? In the same way the Holy One, blessed be he, may his name be blessed, said, "It is I who put the bad leaven in the dough, for the inclination of the heart of man is evil from his youth." So where it says, "It grieved him at his heart", it means "man's heart".'

In Ps. Clem. *Hom.* iii. 43. 2 the verse was rejected as self-contradictory; cf. iii. 38. 4.

Rashi shows how the Targums reached their interpretation: 'Man came to his heart as being one who should be called to account, that is, he came to him to be grieved.' Maimonides went further and translated *yithaẓeb* as 'he rebelled', on the basis of Ps. lvi. 5 (6), which he trans-

---

[a] παραδίδονται.   [b] *Ant.* i. 73.

[c] Kit. alMaj. 108*b*; so also The Cave of Treasures (Budge, pp. 102 f.); cf. Philo, *Quaes. Gen.* i. 92.

[d] *Goy.*   [e] *Nolad.*   [f] *Nolad.*

lated as 'Every day my word they rebel against'. The verse then meant: 'And it repented the Lord that he had made man on the earth, for he was a rebel to (or "against") his will.'

LXX had already recognised the difficulty, and translated 'he laid to his heart', that is, he reflected deeply.

9 The phrase 'walked with God' invited comparison with Enoch (Gen. v. 22). LXX, Pesh. and Arab. Vers. have, 'Noah was pleasing to God'. Vulg. and Sam. Pent. remained literal.

14-15 '. . . of cedar wood':[a] T.O. also reads, 'Make for yourself an ark of cedar wood'.[b] Similarly Ber.R. xxxi. 8:

Make thee an ark . . .[c] R. Issi said: 'The phrase *Make thee* is used in four places, in three of which it is explained and in one it is not. These are: *Make thee an ark of gopher wood*; R. Nathan said: "That means with beams of cedar." *Make thee knives of flint*,[d] that means flint knives. *Make thee two trumpets of silver*[e] means what it says. But the meaning of *Make thee a fiery serpent*[f] is not apparent.'

Syr. Comm. indicates the uncertainty: 'With regard to 'gopher wood' . . . The Greek version has 'square timber'[g] that it should not break up in the water. Gopher is very stout wood. Some say that it is acacia wood. Mar Abba and Gabrial of Katar say that teak is gopher.[h]' Josephus (*Ant.* i. 78) followed the LXX in understanding *gopher* as being a description of strength: 'This ark had stout sides and roof so as not to be overwhelmed from any quarter and to defy the violence of the waters.' Ps. Philo[i] has cedar.

'150 cabins': It was common to deduce the number of cells or cabins from these verses, but the actual number was disputed:

R. Judah and R. Nehemiah disagree. R. Judah said: 'It contained 330 cabins, each one 10 cubits square, with 2 passages each 4 cubits wide . . . and there were 2 cubits at the sides.' R. Nehemiah said: 'It contained 900 cabins, each one 6 cubits square, with 3 passages 4 cubits wide, and 2 cubits at the sides.'[j]

16 'A precious stone': 'R. Johanan said: "The Holy One, blessed be he, gave instructions to Noah: Put in the Ark precious stones and jewels to give you light as bright as noon." '[k] There is a play on words here:

---

a *Qadrinon.*   b *Qadros.*   c Gen. vi. 14.
d Jos. v. 2.   e Num. x. 2.   f Num. xxi. 8.
g τετραγώνων; compare also Pesh.
h As also J.Ket. vii. 11 and B.B.B. 8*b*; see also J.R.H. iii. 10 (9).
i iii. 4, Appendix 1.   j Ber.R. xxxi. 11.
k B.San. 108*b*.

ẓohar in Gen. vi. 16[a] suggested *ẓohoraim*, 'noon-time' (as in Aboth iii. 10 (11): "R. Dosa b. Harkinas said: 'Sleep in the morning, wine at mid-day, the talk of children, and sitting in the company of the ignorant[b] put a man out of the world';[c] they are all distractions from the study of Torah).

Ber.R. xxxi. 11 shows that the interpretation was disputed:

R. Ḥunia and R. Phineḥas, R. Ḥanin and R. Hoshaiah could not explain *ẓohar*. R. Abba b. Kahana and R. Levi did explain it. R. Abba b. Kahana said: 'It means a window in the roof'; R. Levi said, 'A precious stone.'[d] R. Phineḥas in R. Levi's name: 'During the whole 12 months that Noah was in the Ark he had no need of the light of the sun by day, nor of the light of the moon by night, since he had a precious stone[d] which he hung up. When it was dim he knew that it was day, and when it was bright he knew that it was night.'[e]

J.Pes. i. 1 gave the same interpretation but added by way of explanation: 'It is said that during the flood the planets were not in operation, so no one knew when it was day or when it was night.'

T.O. avoided the problem by translating *ẓohar* as *nehor* (Pesh. and Aq., 'a noontide light'). See also J.Pes. i. 1.

'Pishon': This is one of the four divisions of the river issuing from the garden of Eden in Gen. ii. 10–14. Of Pishon it says: 'That is it which compasseth the whole land of Havilah, where there is gold; and the gold of that land is good: there is bdellium and the onyx[f] stone.'

20 Compare P.R.E. 23: 'The angels appointed over each kind went down and brought them with their food to Noah in the ark.' The belief that the animals went into the ark of their own accord was common: see, for example, Tanḥ. Noah 12, B.Zeb. 116a, Augustine, *de Civ. Dei* xv. 27, and perhaps Philo, *de Vit. Mos.* ii. 61. C.G. does not have the addition in Ps. Jon.

---

[a] R.V. *a light* or *roof*.
[c] This world and the world to come.
[e] So also Yalqut on Gen. §53.
[f] Or 'beryl'.

[b] Lit. '*amme haAreẓ*.
[d] *Margalit*.

GENESIS VII

1 *And the Lord said unto Noah, 'Come thou and all* the men of *thy house into the ark; for thee have I seen* innocent *before me in this generation.*

2 *Of every clean beast thou shalt take to thee seven and seven, the male and female; and of the beasts that are not clean two, the male and female;*

3 *of the fowl also of the air, seven and seven, male and female: to keep seed alive upon the face of all the earth.*

4 For, behold, I will give you[a] an extension of *seven days.* If they repent it will be forgiven them, but if they will not repent, after a time of seven days *I will cause it to rain upon the earth forty days and forty nights; and* all the bodies of men and animals (*that I have made*) *will I destroy from off the face of the ground.'*

5 *And Noah did according unto all that the Lord commanded him.*

6 *And Noah was six hundred years old when the flood of waters was upon the earth.*

7 *And Noah went in, and his sons, and his wife, and his sons' wives with him, into the ark,* from before *the waters of the flood.*

8 *Of clean beasts, and of beasts that are not clean, and of fowls, and of every thing that creepeth upon the ground,*

9 *there went in two and two unto Noah into the ark, male and female, as God commanded Noah.*

10 *And it came to pass,* that at the time of *seven days* after the end of the mourning for Methuselah the Lord looked, and, behold, the sons of men had not repented. And *the waters of the flood* came down boiling from the heavens *upon the earth.*

11 *In the six hundredth year of Noah's life, in the second month,* the month of Marḥeshvan (for until then they had counted the months from Tishri only, which was the beginning of the year when the world had been completed), *on the seventeenth day of the month, on the same day were all the fountains of the great deep broken up.*[b] And the sons of the giants[c] put their sons there,[d] and they stopped them up, and after that *the windows of heaven were opened.*

---

a Ginsburger, 'them'.   b Cf. Ps. Philo iii. 5 (Appendix 1) and Jub. v. 24 f.
c So T.O. for Nephilim in Gen. vi. 4.
d See also Tanḥ.B. i. 35 f., Tanḥ. Noah 7.

12 *And the rain was upon the earth forty days and forty nights.*

13 *In the selfsame day entered Noah, and Shem, and Ham, and Japheth, the sons of Noah, and Noah's wife, and the three wives of his sons with him,*[a] *into the ark;*

14 *they, and every beast after its kind, and all the cattle after their kind, and every creeping thing that creepeth upon the earth after its kind, and every fowl after its kind, every bird of every sort.*

15 *And they went in unto Noah into the ark, two and two of all flesh wherein is the breath of life.*

16 *And they that went in, went in male and female of all flesh, as God commanded him: and* the word of *the Lord* covered over the door of the ark before his face.[b]

17 *And the flood was forty days upon the earth; and the waters increased, and bare up the ark, and it was lift up above the earth.*

18 *And the waters prevailed, and increased greatly upon the earth; and the ark went* floating[c] *upon the face of the waters.*

(19-22 These verses follow the Hebrew.)

23 *And* all the bodies of men and cattle which were *upon the face of the ground* were *destroyed, both man, and cattle, and creeping thing, and fowl* which flies in the air *of the heaven; and they were destroyed from the earth: and Noah only was left, and they that were with him in the ark.*

24 *And the waters prevailed upon the earth an hundred and fifty days.*

Selections from other Targums on Genesis vii

10 F.T. (Gins. p. 8; see also pp. 75, 92): *And it came to pass,* that at the end of seven days of mourning for Methuselah, *the waters of the* deluge *were upon the earth.*

C.G. has the passage, but without this interpretation.

14 F.T. (Gins. p. 92) has two words.

16 F.T. (Gins. p. 8): *And* the word of *the Lord* was merciful upon him. T.O.: . . . *and the Lord* covered them.[d]

---

[a] So also LXX.　　　　　　[b] The last phrase is also in Pesh.

[c] Lit. 'swimming', perhaps implying it made slow progress: see Ber.R. xxxii. 9.

[d] *Wagen Y 'alohi.* One MS group (Sperber G) adds 'by his word'. *Agen* (af. *gin*) was often used for 'cover' in the sense of 'protect' as, for example, in Ps. Jon. on Deut. xxxii. 10, in the line, 'He compassed him about, he cared for him'. It is certainly not as strong as Heb. *sagar*—a word which was in the Targum vocabulary; the ithpeel was used, for example, by T.O. on Num. xii. 14 to translate, 'let her be shut up without the camp'.

Notes on Genesis vii

4 'An extension': see the notes on Gen. vi. 3 and vii. 10. C.G. has the verse, but without this interpretation.

'Bodies': the addition here and in verse 23 (*q.v.*) is important for ideas of resurrection.

10 'Methuselah': B.San. 108*b* expands the mention of Methuselah:

What was the nature of these seven days? Rab said: 'They were the days of mourning for Methuselah. This teaches that mourning for the righteous postpones retribution.' Another explanation: after the seven days during which the Holy One, blessed be he, reversed the natural order, with the sun rising in the west and setting in the east.[a] Another explanation: the Holy One, blessed be he, gave them a long time[b] and then a short time. Another explanation: after the seven days during which he allowed a foretaste of the world to come, that they might be aware how great was the good of which they were depriving themselves.[c]

That is also one interpretation in Ber.R. xxxii. 7: 'This[d] teaches that the Holy One, blessed be he, gave them a respite during the seven days of mourning for Methuselah the righteous, so that they might repent . . . R. Joshua b. Levi said: "The Holy One, blessed be he, mourned for seven days for his world, before he brought the flood." '[e] The view that the days were given for repentance was known to Philo (*Quaes. Gen.* ii. 13). See also T.Sot. x. 3–5.

'Boiling': the tradition that the waters of the flood were boiling is a common one, and is derived from Gen. viii. 1, since the word *shakak* means basically 'sink down' or 'abate'. Hence it can mean 'to grow cool'. Thus J. San. x. 5 recorded: 'R. Johanan said: "Each drop of water that God caused to fall on the generation of the flood had been heated first by the fire, then dropped on the earth, as it is written: *What time they wax warm, they vanish.*[f]" ' This interpretation was then linked to the offence which caused the flood, understood as being one

[a] I.e. as a warning to bring people to their senses, and to repentance.
[b] The 120 years' grace referred to in Gen. vi. 3, *q.v.*
[c] A.R.N. 32 also gave these four interpretations.
[d] Gen. vii. 10.
[e] The second interpretation was based on Gen. vi. 6 and II Sam. xix. 3. Cf. also Ber.R. iii. 6, Midr. Teh. on Ps. xxvi. 9 (end), where the suggestion that its meaning is that God gave a seven-day respite is attributed to R. Hoshaiah. See also Tanh.B. ii. 21: 'The Holy One, blessed be he, kept seven days of mourning before he brought the flood, because he was grieved.'
[f] Job. vi. 17.

of sexual immorality.[a] Hence in B.San. 108*a* we read: 'R. Ḥisda said: "They sinned with hot passion, so by hot water they were punished;[b] it is written here, *And the water cooled*[c] and elsewhere it is written: *Then was the king's wrath cooled*[d] *down*." '[e]

A slightly different version is found in B.R.H. 12*a*: 'R. Ḥisda said: "They sinned with hot fluid, so with hot fluid they were punished. They sinned with hot fluid, that is in transgression;[f] with hot fluid they were punished, as it is written, *And the waters cooled*, and elsewhere it is written, *Then was the king's wrath cooled down*." ' See also the notes on Gen. xiv. 13.

For an entirely different version see P.R.E. 22, quoted below. It is possible that a form of this legend underlies I Peter iii. 17–iv. 19. See also Yalqut on Isa. lxiv. 1, B.Zeb. 113*b*, Vay.R. vii. 6, Midr. Teh. on Ps. xi. 5, Tanḥ.B. iii. 13, Tanḥ. Zaw 2.

11 'Marḥeshvan': attempts were often made to specify the dates and months in which particular events occurred. One work[g] was written for that precise purpose, and Jubilees was constructed around its own calendrical theory, hence the title given to it. But when it came to specifying actual months, it was very difficult to reach agreement. The problems were considerable. In the first place, the narratives of Genesis (and of other books) are compiled from different sources, sometimes conflicting with each other. In the second place, the calendars used by the Jews changed during the course of their history. In the third place, there was for some time a fundamental dispute about whether a lunar or a solar calendar should be followed.

An echo of that last dispute occurs in Ber.R. xxxiii. 7 in a comment on Gen. viii. 14 (*And in the second month, on the seven and twentieth day of the month, was the earth dry*): 'Should not scripture have said, "On the sixteenth day"?[h] Why does it in fact say *on the seven and twentieth day*? Because of the eleven days by which the solar year exceeds the lunar year.' The book of Jubilees demonstrates that this was a real

[a] See the notes on Gen. vi. 2.
[b] Mek. Shir. 2 works out the principle that men are punished with that by which they sin; see also p. 139.
[c] Gen. viii. 1.   [d] R.V. *pacified*.
[e] Esther vii. 10.   [f] Sexual immorality.
[g] Seder 'Olam.
[h] Because the flood lasted a year, and Gen. vii. 10 states that it began on the seventeenth day.

issue, because it conducts a strong polemic in favour of the solar calendar: it transforms Gen. viii. 14 into: 'On the *seventeenth* day in the second month the earth was dry. And on the *twenty-seventh* thereof he opened the ark, and sent forth from it beasts, and cattle, and birds, and every moving thing.'[a] Elsewhere it campaigns vigorously for the solar calendar:

And all the days of the commandment will be two and fifty weeks of days, and (these will make) the entire year complete. Thus it is engraven and ordained on the heavenly tablets. And there is no neglecting (this commandment) for a single year or from year to year. And command thou the children of Israel that they observe the years according to this reckoning—three hundred and sixty-four days, and (these) will constitute a complete year, and they will not disturb its time from its days and from its feasts. . . For there will be those who will assuredly make observations of the moon—how (it) disturbs the seasons and comes in from year to year ten days too soon . . . they will go wrong as to the months and sabbaths and feasts and jubilees. . .[b]

The acuteness of this dispute, before the lunar calendar prevailed, has been vividly demonstrated by some of the Dead Sea Scrolls, from which it is apparent that those who produced the sectarian documents followed a solar calendar, whereas the authorities at Jerusalem followed a predominantly lunar one. Inevitably, therefore, the festivals and sabbaths of each party failed to coincide.

The difficulties of supplying recognisable and agreed identifications are well exemplified in Josephus at this point:[c]

This catastrophe happened in the six hundredth year of Noah's rulership, in what was once the second month, called by the Madeconians Dius and by the Hebrews Marsuan, according to the arrangement of the calendar which they followed in Egypt. Moses, however, appointed Nisan, that is to say Xanthicus, as the first month for the festivals, because it was in this month that he brought the Hebrews out of Egypt; he also reckoned this month as the commencement of the year for everything relating to divine worship, but for selling and buying and other ordinary affairs he preserved the ancient order.

By the time the Mishnah was compiled[d] there were four 'new years':

There are four new years: on the first of Nisan is the new year for kings and for festivals; on the first of Elul is the new year for tithing cattle, though

[a] Jub. v. 31 and 32.
[b] Jub. vi. 30–8. See also I Enoch lxxiv. 10, lxxv. 2. Parts of Jubilees have been found among the Dead Sea Scrolls.
[c] *Ant.* i. 80–1.   [d] See p. 56.

R. Eleazar and R. Simeon put it on the first of Tishri; on the first of Tishri is the new year for years, for the years of release and jubilee . . .; on the first of Shebat is the new year for tithing trees . . .[a]

Ps. Jon. frequently specified dates and months,[b] but no attempt has been made in these notes to illustrate the possible or suggested alternatives on each occasion; for an example of the complexity of the attempts to reconcile conflicting narratives, see Rashi's comment quoted on Gen. viii. 4–5, and for one other example, see the notes on Gen. viii. 22. On the chronology of the Flood see Seder 'Olam 4.

'. . . and they stopped them up . . .': this legend was derived from the fact that Genesis first mentions the springs then the windows of heaven. P.R.E. 22 gave it in greater detail:

They said: 'If God brings the waters of the flood from above, we are of such great stature that they will only come up to our necks. And if he brings the waters from below, the soles of our feet are large enough to close up all the depths.' What did they do? They put the soles of their feet down and closed up all the depths. What did the Holy One, blessed be he, do? He heated the waters of the deep and they rose up and scalded their feet blistering off the skin, as it is written, *What time they wax warm, they vanish; when it is hot, they are consumed out of their place.*[c] Read here, not 'when it is hot',[d] but 'in his hot waters'.[e]

See also B.San. 108*b* and the references in Tanḥ. quoted on p. 161 n. d above.

16 The Cave of Treasures avoided the possible anthropomorphism of Genesis by saying: 'Now the ark was closed and sealed, and the angel of the Lord stood over one side of it that he might act as the pilot thereof.'[f]

[a] M.R.H. i. 1; for the meaning of the items mentioned see B.R.H. *ad loc.* B.R.H. 10*b*–11*a* recorded another equally fundamental dispute about the month in which the world was created. B.R.H. recorded it at length, but it is summarised in Ber.R. xxii. 4: 'R. Eliezer and R. Joshua differ: R. Eliezer said, "The world was created in Tishri" (a suggestion supported by the fact that "in Tishri", *betishri*, is an anagram of "in the beginning", *bereshit*). But R. Joshua said, "It was created in Nisan."' This dispute inevitably affected subsequent datings. For some of the underlying complexity of the issues involved, see the summary in E. Frank, *Talmudic and Rabbinical Chronology* (1956), ch. 3.

[b] See, for example, Ps. Jon. on Gen. iv. 3, viii. 4, 5, 13, 14, 22.

[c] Job. vi. 17.   [d] *Behumo.*

[e] *Behamimin.*   [f] Budge, p. 113.

GENESIS VIII

1 *And* the Lord in his word *remembered Noah, and every living thing, and all the cattle that were with him in the ark: and* the Lord caused the *wind* of mercies[a] *to pass over the earth, and the waters* were calmed;[b]

2 *the fountains also of the deep and the windows of heaven were stopped, and the rain* was forbidden to descend *from heaven;*

3 *and the waters returned from off the earth continually* falling back: *and after the end of an hundred and fifty days the waters decreased.*

4 *And the ark rested in the seventh month,* which is the month Nisan, *on the seventeenth day of the month, upon the mountains of* Qardon. The name of one mountain is Qardonia, and the name of the other mountain is Armenia, and there the city of Armenia was built in the land of the east.

5 *And the waters decreased continually until the tenth month,* the month Tammuz; in Tammuz, *on the first day of the month, were the tops of the mountains seen.*

6-10 These verses follow the Hebrew, except that in verse 8 the dove is specified as being a (tame) dove of the house.)

11 *And the dove came in to him at eventide; and, lo, in her mouth an olive leaf pluckt off* which she had taken from the mount of Olives: *so Noah knew that the waters were abated from off the earth.*

12 *And he stayed yet other seven days; and sent forth the dove; and she returned not again unto him any more.*

13 *And it came to pass in the six hundred and first year,* in Tishri, in the first of the month, at the beginning of the year,[c] *the waters were dried up from off the earth: and Noah removed the covering of the ark, and looked, and, behold, the face of the ground was dried.*

14 *And in* the month Marḥeshvan, *on the seven and twentieth day of the month, was the earth dry.*

15 *And the Lord spake with Noah, saying,*

16-19 These verses follow the Hebrew.)

20 *And Noah builded the altar before the Lord,* the altar which Adam had built at the time when he was cast out of the garden of Eden and had

---

a *Ruaḥ raḥmin*; see Ps. Jon. on Gen. i. 2.
b Or possibly, 'were dried up', from the root sense, 'to sink down'.
c Cf. Pesh.

made an offering on it; and Cain and Abel made their offerings on it. But when the waters of the flood came down it was destroyed. So Noah rebuilt it, and *took of every clean beast, and of every clean fowl,* and sacrificed four on that altar.

21 *And the Lord* accepted his offering with favour; *and the Lord said in his* word:[a] '*I will not again curse* the earth because of the sins of the children of men, *for that the imagination*[b] *of man's heart is evil from his youth; neither will I again smite any more every thing living, as I have done.*

22 Throughout all the days of *the earth* there shall not fail sowing in the season of Tishri, harvest in the season of Nisan, cold in the season of Tebeth, warmth in the season of Tammuz, *summer and winter,* days and nights.'

Selections from other Targums on Genesis viii

1 F.T. (Gins. pp. 8, 75, 93) has the verse.

C.G.: *And* the Lord in his good mercies *remembered Noah . . .* and the *wind* of mercies from the word of the Lord passed *over the earth, and the waters* calmed.

4 C.G.: . . . *upon the mountains of* Qardo.

T.O.: see the notes below, on verse 4.

11 F.T. (Gins. p. 93) has two words.

20-2 F.T. (Gins. pp. 8, 75, 93) has part of these verses.

Notes on Genesis viii

4 'Qardon': The same identification was made by T.O. and Pesh. (Qardu) and by Ber.R. xxxiii. 4. However, Josephus[c] makes it clear that several names were suggested:

This flood and the ark are mentioned by all who have written histories of the barbarians. Among these is Berosus the Chaldaean,[d] who in his description of the events of the flood writes somewhere as follows: 'It is said, moreover, that a portion of the vessel still survives in Armenia on the mountain of the Cordyaeans, and that persons carry off pieces of the bitumen, which they use as talismans.' These matters are also mentioned by Hieronymus the Egyptian, author of the ancient history of Phoenicia, by Mnaseas and by many others. Nicolas of Damascus in his ninety-sixth book relates the story as follows: 'There is above the country of Minyas in Armenia a great

---

[a] So also T.O.; for T.O. on verse 21 see also the notes on p. 171.
[b] The evil *yeẓer.*   [c] *Ant.* i. 93–5.
[d] See C. Müller, *Frag. Hist. Graec.* ii. 501.

mountain called Baris, where, as the story goes, many refugees found safety at the time of the flood, and one man, transported upon an ark, grounded upon the summit, and relics of the timber were for long preserved; this might well be the same man of whom Moses, the Jewish legislator, wrote.' But elsewhere Josephus recorded the tradition that the relics of the ark were to be found at Karron.[a]

Examples of different suggestions can easily be multiplied: Jub. vii. 1 has: 'Noah planted vines[b] on the mountain on which the ark had rested, named Lubar, one of the Ararat mountains . . .' Qu'rān xi. 46 (44) has: 'The ark rested on mount Judi . . .' Most of these suggestions refer to the same area, but in terms which would be understood locally.

Some of the problems involved in specifying the months by name were summarised by Rashi on Gen. viii. 5:

In the tenth month . . ., that is Ab, which is the tenth (month) from Marḥeshvan when the rain began. And if you say it is Elul, the tenth (month) from Kislev in which the rain stopped (in the same way that you (Rashi) said[c] that *in the seventh month* is Sivan, which was the seventh month after the rain stopped), in fact it is not possible to say this: you have to allow that *the seventh* cannot be counted except from the stopping (of the rain), since the forty days during which the rain fell and the hundred and fifty during which they lasted did not end until the first day in Sivan. And if you say, it is the seventh from the falling (of the rains), this is not Sivan. The tenth (month) cannot be counted except from the time of the falling (of the rains). For if you say, from the time of their stopping, which is Elul, you would not then find *in the first month, on the first day of the month, the waters dried up from off the earth*;[d] it was at the end of forty days when the tops of the mountains were visible, that he sent out the raven,[e] and he waited for twenty-one days while sending out the dove, that is sixty days from the appearing of the tops of the mountains to the drying up of the face of the earth. And if you say, they were seen in Elul, it would be found that the month of drying up would be Marḥeshvan. But it (Genesis) calls it the first month, and this cannot be anything except Tishri, which is the first from the creation of the world—though according to R. Joshua it is Nisan.[f]

See also Ber.R. xxxiii. 7 and the notes on Gen. vii. 10.

[a] *Ant.* xx. 24–5. The problem here is to identify Karron. J. Macquart resolved the problem by suggesting that Karron is a mistake for Kardou, as in the Targum tradition (*Osteuropäische und ostasiatische Streifzüge*, 1903, p. 289 n. 4, quoted by L. H. Feldmann, Loeb *Josephus*, IX, 1965, 402, *q.v.*).
[b] Gen. ix. 20.
[c] Rashi's comment on Gen. viii. 4 begins: 'Sivan, which is the seventh (month) from Kislev in which the rain stopped . . .'
[d] Gen. viii. 13.   [e] Gen. viii. 6.
[f] See the notes on Gen. vii. 11 under 'Marḥeshvan'.

11 This identification was disputed. The underlying problem was to know how, if the world had been submerged, a tree could be found bearing olive leaves. 'From where did she bring it?... R. Levi said: "She brought it from the mount of Olives, for the land of Israel was not submerged by the flood"[a]... R. Berai said: "The gates of the garden of Eden were opened for her and she brought it from there." '[b] Compare also Vay.R. xxxi. 10: 'R. Abba b. Kahana said "She brought it from the mount of Olives." R. Levi said, "She brought it from the branches of the land of Israel." This agrees with those who say, "The land of Israel was not submerged by the waters of the flood ..."[c] R. Mari said: "The gates of the garden of Eden were opened for her and she brought it from there." '

See also Shir.R. i. 15. 4, iv. 1. 2, B.San. 108 b, B.Zeb. 113 a.

13 f See the notes on Gen. vii. 11.

20 'The altar of Adam': possibly this identification was made by stressing the definite article in the second half of the verse, *And he offered burnt-offerings on 'the' altar*. This appears to be the case in Ber.R. xxxiv. 9: 'R. Eliezer b. Jacob said: This (verse) means "on the great altar in Jerusalem", where Adam first sacrificed, as it is written, *And it shall please the Lord better than an ox, or a bullock that hath horns and hoofs*.[d]' The rather obscure quotation from Ps. lxix is explained by a passage in B.A.Z. 8 a:

On the day when Adam was created, he saw the sun setting and said, 'The world is growing dark all around because I have sinned. The whole universe

---

[a] This was argued from Ezek. xxii. 24. Yalqut on Gen. §57 recorded R. Johanan arguing that the land of Israel was not submerged by the flood; Resh Laqish said that it was. The dispute was also recorded in B.Zeb. 113 a. Yalqut also recorded here that the Samaritans held that Mt Gerizim had not been submerged: 'R. Jonathan went up to Jerusalem to pray ... and as he passed Mt Gerizim a Samaritan saw him and said: "Where are you going?" He said: "To pray in Jerusalem." The Samaritan said: "Would it not be better if you prayed on this blessed mountain and not on that cursed mountain?" R. Jonathan asked: "In what way is it blessed?" He said: "It was not submerged by the waters of the flood." At this the rabbi could not give him an answer. After a while, the driver of his ass said: "Rabbi, if you allow me I will give him an answer." So he said to the Samaritan: "How do you think of the mountain? If you think of it as one of the high mountains, it is written, *All the high mountains ... were covered* (Gen. vii. 19); but if you think of it as a low one, scripture does not mention it and does not reckon it as important." ' The same story is told in Ber.R. xxxii. 10. Ps. Philo (vii. 4, Appendix X) is an early witness to the legend that Palestine was not submerged by the flood. [b] Ber.R. xxxiii. 6.

[c] Again quoting Ezek. xxii. 24. [d] Ps. lxix. 31(32).

will become once more *waste and void.*'ᵃ This must be the death to which heaven has sentenced me.' Therefore he sat up all night fasting and weeping, with Eve near him weeping as well. Then when the dawn broke he said, 'This must be customary for the world'. So he got up and offered a bullock whose horns had grown before its hoofs, as it is said: *And it shall please . . .*ᵇ

See also A.R.N. 1.

The identification of the altars was quite common; see, for example, B.Zeb. 115*a* and P.R.E. 23. See also Ps. Jon. on Gen. xxii. 2, 9.

21 'Accepted his offering': Ps. Jon. avoided saying that God *smelled the sweet savour,* no doubt because it sounded too anthropomorphic. T.O. made the same change: 'And the Lord accepted his offering with approval.'

T.O. also changed *in his heart* to 'in his word',ᶜ and continued: 'I will not ever again curse the ground because of the guilt of man; for the inclination of the heart of man is evil from his youth . . .'

Other early sources, for example Ps. Philo iii. 8 (Appendix I), avoided the anthropomorphic statement; but note that P.R.E. 23 simply explained it: 'The sweet savour went up before the Holy One, blessed be he, . . . and it was pleasing to him, as it is written, *And the Lord smelled the sweet savour.*'

22 'Tishri', etc.: another example of attempts to specify the seasons by months is to be found in Ber.R. xxxiv. 11:

R. Simeon b. Gamaliel said in R. Meir's name, and R. Dosa said the same: 'Half of Tishri, Marheshvan and half of Kislev is seed-time; the last half of Kislev, Tebeth and half of Shebat are winter; the last half of Shebat, Adar and half of Nisan are the cold (season); the last half of Nisan, Iyar and half of Sivan are harvest; the last half of Sivan, Tammuz and half of Ab are summer; the last half of Ab, Elul, and half of Tishri are the hot (season).' But R. Judah began counting from Marheshvan, while R. Simeon began with (the start of) Tishri.

B.B.M. 106*b* recorded the same reckoning, but attributed to R. Judah the opinion here attributed to R. Simeon, and *vice versa*—a fairly simple illustration, perhaps, of the great uncertainties involved in these calculations; see the notes on Gen. vii. 11.

ᵃ Gen. i. 2.　　　　ᵇ Ps. lxix. 31(32).　　　　ᶜ *Memra.*

GENESIS IX

(1-3 These verses follow the Hebrew.)

4 '*But flesh* which is torn from the living animal while the life is in it, or that which is torn from a slaughtered animal before all the breath has gone out, *shall ye not eat.*

5 But the blood *of your lives will I require; at the hand of every beast* which kills a man *will I require* that it be killed because of him;[a] *and at the hand of man, even at the hand of* the person who sheds the blood of his brother, *will I require the life* of the man.

6 *Whoso sheddeth man's blood* with witnesses the judges shall condemn to death; but he who sheds it without witnesses, the Lord of the world will bring punishment on him in the day of the great judgement, because he created man *in the image of* the Lord.[b]

7 *And you, be ye fruitful, and multiply; bring forth abundantly in the earth, and multiply therein.*'

(8-13 These verses follow the Hebrew, except that in verse 12 'God' becomes 'the Lord', and the pronoun 'me', of God, becomes 'my word', as also in verses 15, 16 and 17.)

14 '*And it shall come to pass, when I bring* clouds of glory *over the earth, that the bow shall be seen* during the day so long as the sun has not sunk *in the cloud.*'

(15-18 These verses follow the Hebrew.)

19 *These three were the sons of Noah: and of these* they were spread abroad to dwell in *the whole earth.*

20 *And Noah began to be* a man working on the land, and he found a vine which the river had carried down from the garden of Eden, and he planted it in *a vineyard*, and in a single day it was completely sprouted; and its grapes were ripe, and he pressed them;

21 *and he drank of the wine, and was drunken; and he was uncovered within his tent.*

22 *And Ham, the father of Canaan, saw the nakedness of his father, and told his two brethren without.*

---

[a] Cf. Exod. xxi. 28 and M.Sanh. i. 4.

[b] This verse and its possible application to Matt. v. 21 is discussed by M. McNamara, *The New Testament and the Palestinian Targum*..., pp. 126–31.

23 *And Shem and Japheth took a garment, and laid it upon both their shoulders, and went backward, and covered the nakedness of their father; and their faces were backward, and they saw not their father's nakedness.*

24 *And Noah awoke from his wine, and knew* by being told in a dream *what* Ham his son *had done unto him,* who was so slight in merit, who had contrived that Noah should not beget a fourth son.

25 *And he (Noah) said, 'Cursed be Canaan* who is his fourth son, *a servant* bound in slavery *shall he be unto his brethren'.*

26 *And he said, 'Blessed be the Lord, the God of Shem,* whose work is righteous. Therefore shall *Canaan be his servant.*

27 The Lord will adorn the borders of *Japheth*: his sons will be made proselytes and will dwell in the school *of Shem;* and *Canaan* will be their servant.'

28 *And Noah lived after the flood three hundred and fifty years.*

29 *And all the days of Noah were nine hundred and fifty years: and he died.*

Selections from other Targums on Genesis ix

6 T.O.: '*Whoso sheddeth man's blood* with witnesses, on the sentence of the judges *shall his blood be shed.*'

12 T.O. and C.G. also changed the pronoun 'me' into 'my word'.

15 F.T. (Gins. p. 93) has one word.

20 F.T. (Gins. p. 8) *And Noah began to be* a righteous man.
   C.G.: *And Noah began to be* a righteous man to be a worker on the land, *and he planted* for himself *a vineyard.*

, 23 F.T. (Gins. p. 93) has one word in each verse.

27 T.O.: 'May the Lord extend *Japheth* and make his Shekina to dwell in the dwelling[a] *of Shem.*'

Notes on Genesis ix

4-6 The tendency to make the text conform to the requirements of the Pentateuch and to later legal practice is exemplified at even greater length in Jub. vi. 10–38. See also Ber.R. xxxiv. 13 f., B.San. 57 a–b. Compare Josephus, *Ant.* i. 102 f. C.G. does not have any of the expansion in Ps. Jon., nor does it have the small addition of T.O., but it ends: '*For in the image* from before the Lord . . .'

a Or 'tent'.

20 The question to be faced here was raised very precisely by Philo:

> It is proper to fall into perplexity where he should find a plant after the flood, since all those things which were on the earth had wasted away and perished. But what was said a little earlier seemed to be true,[a] (namely) that the earth was dried up at the spring season . . .; accordingly it was natural that both vines and vine shoots were found that could flourish.[b]

Philo gave a more 'natural' solution than Ps. Jon., but other solutions were possible. For example: 'From where did he get it? R. Kahana said: "He took with him into the ark shoots from vines ready for planting as well as shoots from figs and olives." '[c]

The tradition that the vine was brought down out of Eden is derived from another tradition, that the vine was the tree whose fruit caused the fall of Adam and Eve. In the case of Noah, it was recognised that wine caused his downfall as well, and therefore the two traditions were connected. The story is told precisely in III Bar. iv. 9–13:

> Then I (Baruch) said: 'Show me, I beg, which tree it is that led Adam astray.' The angel said: 'It is the vine which Sammael[d] the angel planted: the Lord God was angry at this and he cursed both him and his tree, and he did not allow Adam to touch it; therefore the devil in envy deceived him through the vine.' (9)[e] And I, Baruch, said: 'If the vine has caused such evil, and is under . . . the curse of God . . . how has it now become so useful?' (10) And the Angel said: 'You are right to ask. When God brought the flood upon the earth . . . the water entered paradise and destroyed every plant, but it swept the shoot of the vine right outside and carried it away. (11) Then when land appeared again out of the water Noah . . . began to plant whatever plants he found; (12) but when he found the shoot of the vine, he took it and asked himself what it was . . . (13) and he said, "Shall I plant it or not? Since Adam was destroyed through it, let me not suffer the wrath of God because of it . . ." But God sent his angel Sarasael, and said to him, "Come, Noah, plant the shoot of the vine; for thus says the Lord: its bitterness shall become sweetness and its curse a blessing, and that which is made

---

[a] *Quaes. Gen.* ii. 47.

[b] *Quaes. Gen.* ii. 67.

[c] Ber.R. xxxvi. 3. Rashi (*ad loc.*) has the same.

[d] On Sammael see the Targum and notes on Gen. iii. 6.

[e] R. H. Charles (*Apocr. and Pseud.* II, 536) regarded verses 9–15 as a Christian interpolation modifying the condemnation of wine on account of its use in the Eucharist. However, the legend of Noah and of the vine coming from Eden is so deeply integrated into the Jewish tradition that the Christian addition may be less than Charles supposed. The question was faced and discussed by Philo in *Quaes. Gen.* ii. 67. See also P.R.E. 23, Sifre on Deut. §323.

from it shall become the blood of God". And as mankind was condemned through it, so through Jesus Christ, Immanuel, they will be called on high and given access to paradise.'a

The opinion that 'the tree in the midst of the garden' was the vine is recorded (usually with alternative suggestions) in many places, but a good example is B.San. 70a–b, because it connects the two passages together:

R. Ḥisda said in the name of R. Uqba (though others say it was Mar Uqba in the name of R. Zakkai): 'The Holy One, blessed be he, said to Noah: "Noah, why did you fail to take a warning from Adam, whose offence was caused by wine?" This follows the opinion that the tree from which Adam ate was the vine, as it has been taught: R. Meir said: 'That tree from which Adam ate was a vine, because only wine brings grief to a man.' R. Judah said: 'It was wheat, because until a baby can eat bread it cannot say "father" or "mother".'b R. Nehemiah said: 'It was the fig tree, because they were told to make amends with that by which they had offended, as it is written: *And they sewed fig leaves together.*'c

The alternatives are given at much greater length in Ber.R. xv. 7. See also B.Ber. 40a, Pes.K. xx. 6, Pes.R. 175a, Vay.R. xii. 1, Bem.R. x. 2, I Enoch xxxii. 4, Tertullian, *Adv. Marc.* ii. 2, Origen on Gen. ix. 20. On the other hand, there was a feeling that the silence in Genesis about the name of the tree was deliberate. Thus, for example, Tanḥ.B, i. 105 says: 'The Holy One, blessed be he, said . . .: "When I created my world I tried not to harm any creature, and so I did not divulge to any person what the tree was from which Adam ate." '

24 This addition answered the obvious question how Noah could have known what had happened to himself if he had been drunk and incapable. The phrase *beishteutha*, 'in a report', was also used by Ps. Jon. in its expansion of Lev. xvi. 6, where it virtually amounts to 'confession': 'Aaron shall offer the bullock of the sin offering . . . and shall make atonement in a report of wordsd for himself and for the men of his house.' Cf. Sifra *ad loc.*

'Slight in merit': the same occurs in Syr. Comm.: 'And Ham, though he was grown up, was called, because of his sin, small.'e

Rashi commented:f 'His youngerg son:h the blemished and des-

---

a III Bar. iv. 9–13a, 15.
b I.e. it has no knowledge until then.   c Gen. iii. 7.
d *Beishteutha milleya.*   e Levene, p. 84.
f *Ad loc.*   g *HaQatan.*   h Gen. ix. 24.

picable one, as it is written: *For behold I have made thee small*[a] *among the nations, and despised among men.*'[b]

The word for 'merit' is *zekutha*, probably with the technical implications of *zekuth*; on *zekuth* see p. 202.

On the actual offence of Ham, see the notes on verse 25.

25 'His fourth son': the stress on 'the fourth son' is explained by the interpretation of verse 24 (. . . *and he* (*Noah*) *knew what his youngest son had done*). The Hebrew text does not say exactly what Ham did to Noah, and various different suggestions were made. B.San. 70*a*, for example, says:

> Rab and Samuel dispute, one saying that he (Ham) castrated him,[c] whilst the other says that he abused him. That he castrated him: since he cursed him by his fourth son, he must have harmed him in connection with a fourth son. That he abused him: there is a likeness between *and he saw* in two places. Here it is written: *And Ham, the father of Canaan, saw the nakedness of his father,*[d] and elsewhere it is written: *And Shechem the son of Hamor* . . . *saw her; (and he took her, and lay with her, and humbled her).*[e] However, on the argument that he castrated him, it is appropriate that he should have cursed him by his fourth son; but on the argument that he abused him, why should he have cursed his fourth son? He should have cursed Ham himself. Both offences were committed.[f]

Ber.R. xxxvi. 7 makes this point even clearer:

> R. Berekiah said: 'Noah was greatly distressed in the ark because he had no young son to attend him, so he said: "When I go out I will beget a young son to attend me." But when Ham did what he did to him, he said, "You have stopped me begetting a young son to attend me, therefore your own son[g] will serve his brothers, as they are servants of mine." R. Huna said in the name of R. Joseph: 'You have stopped me doing a deed in the dark, therefore his seed will be ugly and dark.'[h] R. Huna also said in the name of R. Joseph: 'You have stopped me begetting a fourth son, therefore I will curse your fourth son.'

For an entirely different legend see The Cave of Treasures (Budge, p. 118) and The Bee 20; compare also Syr. Comm. (Levene, pp. 84 f.).

27 'The Lord will adorn . . .': B.Yom. 10*a* interpreted this verse in much the same way as T.O.: 'God has enlarged Japheth, but the

---

[a] *Qatan.*
[b] Jer. xlix. 15.
[c] He thus made it impossible for Noah to have a fourth son.
[d] Gen. ix. 22.
[e] Gen. xxxiv. 2.
[f] See also P.R.E. 23.
[g] Lit. 'that man'.
[h] See also B.San. 108*b*, Tanh.B. i. 42–3, Tanh. Noah 11 f.

Shekina dwells in the dwelling of Shem alone.' The passage then goes on to try to identify Japheth with Persia. Similarly Ber.R. xxxvi. 8 says:

This (verse) alludes to Cyrus who caused the Temple to be rebuilt; all the same, 'He shall dwell in the tents of Shem', the Shekina dwells in the tents of Shem alone. Bar Qappara said, 'Let the words of Torah be spoken in the language of Japheth[a] in the tents of Shem'.[b] R. Judan said, 'Thus we learn that translation[c] is allowed'.[d]

Rashi[e] made the point even more precisely: 'Let him make his Shekina dwell in Israel. The *midrash* of the Wise (Ḥakamim) (explains): although God enlarged Japheth in that Cyrus, a descendant of Japheth, built the second temple,[f] the Shekina did not dwell in it. So where did it dwell? In the first temple[g] which Solomon, a descendant of Shem, built.' Compare B.Yom. 21 *b*: '. . . five things in which the first temple differed from the second: the ark, the cover of the ark and the cherubim, the fire, the Shekina, the spirit (of prophecy?), and the urim and thummim. They were there but not as potent as they had been.' See also B.Yom. 9*b*.

'Shekina' is the word which was used to speak of the divine presence and by which, therefore, it was possible to avoid speaking directly of God being present.[h] The usage is too well known to need illustration, but a particularly famous example occurs in B.Ber. 6*a*:

How do you know that if ten people pray together the Shekina is with them? It is written, *God standeth in the congregation of God*.[i] And how do you know that if three are sitting as judges the Shekina is with them? It is written, *He judgeth among the gods*.[j] And how do you know that if two are sitting and studying Torah the Shekina is with them? It is written: *Then they that feared the Lord spake one with another: and the Lord hearkened and heard*[k] . . .

[a] I.e. Greek.
[b] This opinion is recorded in J.Meg. i. 8 (9), B.Meg. 9*b*, Deb.R. i. 1.
[c] *Targum*.
[d] And that therefore the LXX at least could be recognised. For the discussion on this see B.Meg. 9*a*.
[e] *Ad loc.*   [f] *Bayit*.
[g] *Miqdash*.
[h] See p. 44.
[i] Ps. lxxxii. 1. And on the definition of B.San. 2*b* a 'congregation' consists of at least 10 people.
[j] Ps. lxxxii. 1; see the Hebrew.   [k] Mal. iii. 16.

And how do you know that if one man alone sits and studies Torah the Shekina is with him? It is written: . . . *in every place where I record*[a] *my name I will come unto thee and bless thee.*[b]

'In the school of Shem': literally 'in the studying of Shem'.[c] 'Midrash' refers widely to the great work of study and interpretation of the bible, and the *bet haMidrash* to a school of such study.[d] Shem was regarded as the father of the Hebrew race, hence what is implied in this verse is that the foreigner will come under instruction in Torah (which has been entrusted to the Jewish people by God), and by becoming a proselyte will attach himself to the people of God.

The tents of Shem were commonly understood as being a school of instruction in the law, where the patriarchs received their knowledge of the law before it was revealed to Moses; see, for example, Ps. Jon. on Gen. xxii. 18–19 and xxv. 22 and 27.

On Noah's blessing, see also Tanḥ.B. i. 50, Tanḥ. Noah 15, Pes.R. 160a.

---

[a] R.V. marg.: *Cause my name to be remembered.*
[b] Exod. xx. 24; for the whole passage, cf. Aboth iii. 2.
[c] *Bemidrasha.*
[d] 'R. Levi said: "Anyone who goes out of the synagogue and enters the *bet haMidrash*, or out of the *bet haMidrash* and into the synagogue, will be allowed to enter the presence of the Shekina, as it is written, *They go from strength to strength, every one of them appeareth before God in Zion*" ' (Ps. lxxxiv. 7 (8) (B.M.Q. 29a). On the *bet haMidrash* see also p. 49.

8 *And Cush begat Nimrod: he began to be* mighty in sin and to rebel *before the Lord* in the earth.

9 *He was a mighty* rebel *before the Lord: wherefore it is said:* from the day in which the world was created there has not been any *like Nimrod a mighty hunter* and a rebel *before the Lord.*

10 *And the beginning of his kingdom was Babel* the great and Hadas and Nezibin and Qtesiphon *in the land of* Pontos.

11 *Out of that land* Nimrod *went forth* and ruled in Athur, because he did not wish to enter into the counsel of the generation of the divisions.[a] And he left those four cities, and the Lord settled him elsewhere instead, and he built other towns, Nineveh and the town of Pelatyath and Hadyath,

12 and Telasar[b] which was built between Nineveh and Hadyath, itself a great town.

13 *And Mizraim begat* Nivytai and the Maryutai and the Livyqai and the Pentaskinai

14 and the Nasyutai and the Pentapolitai from whom *went forth the Philistines* and the Qaphodiqai.

Selections from other Targums on Genesis x. 8–14

Parts of verses 10, 11, 12, 13 and 14 occur in F.T. (Gins. pp. 8, 75, 93). T.O.: see the notes below.

Notes on Genesis x. 8–14

8 The evil character of Nimrod is not specifically stated in Genesis, and some sources (for example Syr. Comm.) did not regard him unfavourably. But in general Nimrod was regarded as the great rebel against God. This was perhaps suggested by the description of him in Genesis as 'mighty', but it was made more specific by deriving his name, Nimrod, from *marad*, 'he rebelled'. At the same time, *hehel* in verse 8

---

a *Pelugtha*: see Gen. x. 25.
b See Ps. Jon. on Gen. xiv. 9.

was taken as meaning 'rebel' (R.V. 'began'). The interpretation was recorded in Ber.R. xxiii. 7:

'R. Simon said: "In three places the verb occurs and in all three the meaning is 'rebel': *Then men rebelled in calling upon the name of the Lord;*[a] *And it came to pass when man rebelled in multiplying on the face of the ground . . .;*[b] *He (Nimrod) rebelled when he was a mighty one in the earth.*[c]" '

Nimrod came to be regarded as the great antagonist of Abraham, and the conflict between them summarised the antithesis between polytheistic idolatry and the worship of the one true God of Israel.[d] This characterisation of Nimrod is at least as old as Philo: 'It was Nimrod who began this desertion (from God). For the lawgiver says, "he began to be a giant on the earth", and his name means "desertion".'[e][f] It also appears in Josephus:

They (the people who settled at Shinar) were invited to this insolent contempt of God by Nebrodes, grandson of Ham the son of Noah, an audacious man of doughty vigour . . . He threatened to have his revenge on God if he wished to inundate the earth again; for he would build a tower higher than the water could reach and avenge the destruction of their forefathers.[g]

See also Ps. Philo iv. 7, vi. 14 (Appendix 1), B.Ḥag. 13a, B.Pes. 94b, B.Meg. 11a, Ber.R. xxxvii. 2–4.

It seems probable that T.O. intended the same interpretation of Nimrod. Instead of 'a mighty hunter' it has '*taqiph*'. *Taqiph* can mean simply 'powerful' or 'strong', as in Sifre on Deut. xxxii. 4: ' "The Rock" means "the Strong".' But it can also mean 'hard-hearted' or 'severe', as in B.B.M. 64a: 'What if he (a moneylender) is a hard-hearted man who never gives gifts?' It was used by T.O. to translate Deut. xxviii. 50, *a nation of fierce countenance*.

11 'Athur' (Asshur): the reference is made clear in Ber.R. xxxvii. 4:

Asshur went forth from the plan.[h] When he saw them about to campaign against the Holy One, blessed be he, he left his land. The Holy One, blessed

---

[a] Gen. iv. 26, R.V. *began to call.*   [b] Gen. vi. 1, R.V. *began to multiply.*
[c] Gen. x. 8, R.V. *he began to be.* Another passage is suggested in Ber.R., Gen. xi. 6, but R. Simon rejected it as an additional example, because it is the result of Nimrod's incitation. Cf. F.T. (Gins. p. 8).
[d] For the conflict, see the Targum and notes on Gen. xi. 28, and Ps. Jon. on Gen. xxiv. 1.
[e] αὐτομόλησις.   [f] *de Gig.* xv. 66; cf. also *Quaes. Gen.* ii. 82.
[g] *Ant.* i. 113 f.   [h] To build the tower of Babel.

be he, said to him: 'You have gone forth from four towns: as you live, I will give you four others.' *And he builded Nineveh, and Rehoboth-Ir, and Caleh, and Resen* . . .;[a] Resen is Telesar. And he did not remain steadfast, and when he came to join with them in the destruction of the Temple, the Holy One, blessed be he, said to him, 'Yesterday you were a chicken but today you are the egg'.[b]

See also T.d.E. 114.

[a] Gen. x. 11 f.
[b] I.e. you have gone backwards.

GENESIS XI. 1–9, 27–8

1 *And the whole earth was of one language and of one speech* and of one counsel, speaking the holy language by which the world was created at the beginning.[a]

2 *And it came to pass, as they journeyed from the east*[b] *they found a plain in the land of* Babel; *and they dwelt there.*

3 *And they said one to another, 'Go to, let us make* bricks, and let us put them in the furnace'. *And they had brick for stone, and slime*[c] *had they for mortar.*

4 *And they said, 'Go to, let us build us a city, and a tower whose top* comes up to *heaven, and let us make us* an idol on the top of it and let us put a sword in its hand, and it will make formations for battle before [or 'against'] him, before we are scattered over the face of the earth'.

5 *And the Lord* was revealed to punish them for the making of the city, and *the tower, which the children of men builded.*

6 *And the Lord said, 'Behold, they are one people, and they have all one language; and this is what they* have purposed *to do: and now nothing will be withholden from them, which they purpose to do'.*

7 The Lord said to the seventy angels which stand before him, 'Come now we will go down *and there confound their language, that they may not understand one another's speech'.*

8 And the word[d] of *the Lord* was revealed against the city and the seventy angels with him, corresponding to the seventy nations, each one having its own language and the script of its writing in his hand, and *he scattered them abroad from thence upon the face of all the earth* into seventy languages. And no one knew what his fellow said, and they began to kill each other, *and they left off to build the city.*

9 *Therefore was the name of it called Babel; because the Lord did there confound the language of all* the inhabitants of *the earth: and from thence did the Lord scatter them abroad upon the face of all the earth.*

---

a *Min sheyruya*, not the phrase used by Ps. Jon. in Gen. i. 1.
b R.V. marg.; and for a possible interpretation, see Ber.R. xxxviii. 7.
c I.e. mud.
d In Tanḥ. Noah 18 the possible anthropomorphism is avoided differently.

27 *Now these are the generations of Terah. Terah begat Abram, Nahor, and Haran; and Haran begat Lot.*

28 And it came to pass, when Nimrod cast Abram into the fiery furnace because he would not worship his idol and there was no permission for the fire to burn him, Haran's heart became doubtful, and he said: 'If Nimrod prevails, I will be on his side, but if Abram prevails, I will be on his side.' And when all the people who were there saw that the fire had no power over Abram, they said in their hearts: 'Is not Haran, the brother of Abram, full of divinings and charms, and has he not uttered a spell over the fire to stop it burning his brother?' At once fire fell from the heavens above and consumed him (Haran), *and Haran died in the presence of*[a] *his father Terah*, even as he was burned in the land of his birth in the fiery furnace which the Kasdai[b] had made for Abram his brother.

Other Targums on Genesis xi. 1-9, 27-8

1 F.T. (Gins. p. 94): the holy language.

2 F.T. (Gins. p. 8; see also pp. 75 and 94): *And it came to pass* that their hearts wandered from following after the word of him who spoke and the world was at the beginning.[c] *And they found a plain in the land of* Pontus; *and they dwelt there.*

4 F.T. (Gins. p. 8; see also p. 75) has the verse with a similar interpretation.

5 T.O.: *And the Lord* was revealed to punish the work of the city, and *the tower, which the children of men builded.*

7, 8a F.T. (Gins. p. 94) has the same interpretation.

28 F.T. (Gins. p. 94) has three words.

Notes on Genesis xi. 1-9, 27-8

1 On the holy language in connection with this verse see Test. Naph. viii. 3 ff. (quoted in the notes on Gen. xi. 7, 8), J.Meg. i. 2, Tanḥ.B. i. 55.

4 The connection of the tower of Babel with idolatry is also made in B.San. 109a:

R. Jeremiah b. Eleazar said: 'They divided into three parties. One said, "Let us climb up and live there". The second said, "Let us climb up and

---

a Cf. Pesh., which translated 'in the presence of' as 'while Terah was still alive'.   b Chaldaeans.   c *Min sheyruya*

worship idols ". The third said, "Let us climb up and wage war with God ". Those who said, "Let us . . . dwell there ", *the Lord scattered them.*[a] Those who said, "Let us . . . wage war", were turned into apes, spirits, devils and demons. Those who said, "Let us . . . worship idols", *the Lord did there confound the language of all the earth.*[b] It has been taught that R. Nathan said, 'They were all intent on idolatry: it is written here, *Let us make us a name*, but elsewhere it is written, *Make no mention of the name of other gods.*[c] Just as *name* means idolatry there so it does here as well.'

Midr. Teh. on Ps. i. 1 perserved a different version of this:

The man that walketh not in the counsel of the wicked: Abraham[d] did not walk in the counsel of the generation of the dispersion of the nations of men which said, *Go to, let us build us a guardian,*[e] *and a tower.* . . . They meant by *guardian* a god, as it is written, . . . *behold, a watcher and an holy one came down from heaven.*[f] They then divided into three parties. One said, 'Let us build a tower and live there'. The second said 'Let us wage war with God'. The third said, 'Let us climb up and worship another god'. All of them were smitten. One party was turned into apes, demons and evil spirits. The second party was confounded in its language by the Lord. The third party was scattered by the Lord, as scripture says, *The fear of the wicked, it shall come upon him.*[g]

Compare also Midr. Teh. on Ps. lxxiv. 4–5 and Mek. Kas. 4; in P.R.E. 24 the specific reference to idolatry has been dropped. Similar versions also occur in Chron. Jer. xxx, Yashar ix. 33–54.

5 It will be noticed that Ps. Jon. and T.O. avoided the plain statement of Gen. xi. 5, . . . *the city and the tower, which the children of men builded.* That might be taken to imply that the city as well as the tower was finished, but Gen. xi. 8 says, *And they left off to build the city.* In Ber.R. xxxviii. 8 and Yalqut on Gen. §62 R. Judan resolved the contradiction differently by saying that they had finished the tower but not the city. The Targums avoided the contradiction by adding 'the making of . . .'

7,8 Here, as in Gen. i. 26,[h] the introduction of angels was made to avoid any suggestion of plurality in the Godhead. An example of this suggestion can be found in Syr. Comm. (Levene, p. 86): 'In regard to *Go to,* . . . we have a hint concerning the persons of the Trinity as for instance, "Let

[a] Gen. xi. 8.   [b] Gen. xi. 9.
[c] Exod. xxiii. 13.
[d] For the reference to Abraham see the fuller version of the Test. Naph., quoted in the notes on Gen. xi. 7.
[e] Or 'watcher', R.V. *city.* '*ir*, B.H. 'city', also means in Aramaic 'guardian (angel)' or 'one who watches over'.
[f] Dan. iv. 13.   [g] Prov. x. 24.   [h] See the notes *ad loc.*

us make man in our image". ' The argument is directly refuted in B.San. 38*b*: 'R. Joḥanan said: "Wherever heretics find support in scripture for their unbelief, the refutation is near at hand." ' He then quotes the controversial texts to show that those which have a plural referring to God (Gen. i. 26, xi. 7, Gen. xxxv. 1, Deut. iv. 7, II Sam. vii. 23 and Dan. vii. 9) are always closely associated with a singular reference as well (Gen. i. 27, xi. 5, xxxv. 3, Deut. iv. 7, II Sam. vii. 23, Dan. vii. 9). For these disputes see the notes on Gen. i. 26. The verse is an LXX variant (Appendix III).

The idea that each nation had its own angel is found as early as Dan. x. 13, 20, 21, and xii. 1:

'But the prince of the kingdom of Persia withstood me . . . and now will I return to fight with the prince of Persia, . . . lo, the prince of Greece shall come . . . Michael your prince.'

The number seventy was arrived at by counting up the nations derived from the three sons of Noah in Gen. x.[a] Hence Ps. Jon. on Deut. xxxii. 8[b] reads:

The Most High gave the world as a possession to the nations which came from the sons of Noah. And when he gave different languages and different writing to men in the generation of the dispersion, he cast lots with the seventy angels, the princes of the nations, with whom he was revealed to see the town. At that time he set up the boundaries of the peoples corresponding to the number of seventy people who went down into Egypt.[c] When the holy people fell to the Lord of the universe, Michael cried out, 'A good portion, for the name of the word of the Lord is with him'.[d]

Ecclus. xvii. 17 stated the belief clearly (although the context in which it stands is in some disorder): *For every nation he appointed a ruler, But Israel is the Lord's portion.*

Jubilees also stated the belief:

'There are many nations and many peoples and all are his,[e] and over all hath he placed spirits in authority to lead them astray from him.' Jubilees also makes it clear that God was speaking to the angels: 'And

---

[a] This calculation was supported by various other supplementary calculations, as in Ps. Jon. on Deut. xxxii. 8, quoted immediately above. See also Midr. Teh. on Ps. ix. 6.

[b] *When the Most High gave to the nations their inheritance, When he separated the children of men, He set the bounds of the peoples According to the number of the children of Israel.*

[c] See also Sifre on Deut. xxxii. 8.

[d] I.e. Isra-el. The same appears in P.R.E. 24.

[e] Cf. Sifre §40: 'God provides not only for Israel but for all people.'

the Lord our God said unto us:[a] . . . *Go to, let us go down* . . . And the Lord descended, and we descended with him . . .'[b]

See also LXX on Deut. xxxii. 8; for the descent of the seventy angels, see P.R.E. 24.

The legend is told more fully in Test. Naph. viii. 3–ix. 5:[c]

Do not forget the Lord your God, the God of your fathers, who was chosen by our father Abraham when the nations were divided in the time of Phaleg. For at that time the Lord, blessed be he, came down from his highest heavens, and brought down with him seventy ministering angels, Michael at their head. He commanded them to teach the seventy families which sprang from the loins of Noah seventy languages. Forthwith the angels descended and did according to the command of their creator. But the holy language, the Hebrew language, remained only in the house of Shem and Eber, and in the house of Abraham our father, who is one of their descendants. And on that day Michael took a message from the Lord, and said to the seventy nations, to each nation separately: 'You know the rebellion you undertook, and the treacherous confederacy into which you entered against the Lord of heaven and earth, and now choose today whom you will worship, and who shall be your intercessor in the height of heaven'. Nimrod the wicked[d] answered and said, 'For me there is none greater than he who taught me and my people in one hour the language of Kush'. In like manner also answered Put, and Mizrain, and Tubal, and Javan, Mesech, and Tiras; and every nation chose its own angel, and none of them mentioned the name of the Lord, blessed be he. But when Michael said to Abraham our father, 'Abraham, whom do you choose, and whom will you worship?' Abram answered, 'I choose and select only him who spoke, and the world was created; who formed me in the womb of my mother, body within body; who placed in me spirit and soul; him I choose, and to him I will cleave, I and my seed, all the days of the world'.

Christian writers usually calculated 72 nations and tongues, and III Enoch witnesses the transition between the two, since it mentions both 70 and 72.[e] H. Odeberg[f] suggested that the change in III Enoch may have been made to make the angels conform to their heavenly counterparts, there being 72 divisions of the Zodiac (p. 51): alternatively, since the angels form the heavenly *Bet Din* (council), the number may have been changed to make it correspond to the 'seventy-two elders',

[a] The main part of Jubilees is constructed as a revelation from 'the angel of the presence' to Moses (ii. 1).

[b] Jub. x. 22–3.

[c] Heb. Frag., Charles, *Apocr. and Pseudepigr.* p. 363.

[d] See the Targum and notes on Gen. x. 8–14.

[e] Midr. haGad. i. 182 also has 72.   [f] III Enoch, p. 105.

as in M.Zeb. i. 3, M.Yad. iii. 5, iv. 2. For a similar uncertainty about the Great Sanhedrin, see M.San. i. 6. For many other references see Ginzberg, *Legends*, V, 194.

28 Many stories were told of Abraham in conflict with Nimrod, and in particular of Abraham in the furnace from which he was rescued by God. These are largely derived from the fact that the place-name 'Ur'[a] is the Hebrew word for 'a flame'. Hence Gen. xi. 28 says that Haran died in *the flame of the Chaldees*, and xi. 31 says that they went forth *from the flame of the Chaldees*.[b] The Arabic version also took 'Ur' as 'a furnace', both here and in xv. 7.

The stories of Abraham in conflict with idolatry and of the successful outcome of his engagement with Nimrod were very popular, no doubt because of their obvious relevance to the situations in which the Jewish people continually found themselves. The conflict with idolatry was based on Josh. xxiv. 2: 'Your fathers dwelt of old time beyond the River, even Terah, the father of Abraham, and the father of Nahor; and they served other gods.' On the basis of this Kit. alMaj. makes a typical summary:

In the days of Serug idols[c] were worshipped, and were bowed down to instead of God, and people at that time were scattered in the earth ... They wandered in error[d] and rebelled and divided into parties.[e] Some of them worshipped the sun and the moon, some of them worshipped the sky, some ... images, some ... stars, some ... the earth, some ... animals, some ... trees, some ... the waters and the winds and the like. Satan certainly blinded their hearts and left them in darkness without light ...[f]

For an earlier example see Ps. Philo iv. 16 (Appendix I).

A vast number of similar stories were elaborated; Ber.R. xxxviii. 13, for example, gave the following version (of which a similar form appears in Chron. Jer. xxxiii. 1, xxxiv. 9).

R. Ḥiyya said ...: 'Terah was a man who made idols.[g] It happened once that he went away to a certain place and left Abraham to sell them instead.

---

[a] Gen. xi. 28 and 31. It is worth noting that in both places (and in xv. 7) LXX avoided 'Ur' and translated simply, 'from the land of the Chaldaeans'; perhaps there was already uncertainty whether Ur was a noun or a place-name, and the issue was simply avoided.

[b] In Gen. xv. 7 Ur is translated by *nura*.   [c] *Auwthan.*

[d] *Tagu*; cf. the word for 'idol' in the Targum.

[e] Lit. 'became a sect', *shi'a.*

[f] 118*a*–119*a*; see also The Cave of Treasures (Budge, pp. 138 f.).

[g] *Ẓelamim.*

When a man came up wanting to buy one, Abraham said, "How old are you?" He answered, "Fifty [or 'sixty']". Abraham said, "What then! You are sixty and you want to worship something that is only a day old!" The man went away ashamed. Then a woman came up with a plate of sifted flour and said, "Give this to them as an offering". At that Abraham took a club and smashed the idols,[a] and put the club into the hand of the largest of them. Then his father came back and said: "Who has done this to them?" Abraham said: "What can I hide from you? A woman came up with a plate of flour and asked me to offer it to them. I did so, and one of them said, 'I will eat first', but another said, 'I will eat first'. At that the largest sprang up, took the club and smashed them." Terah said: "Why do you mock me? Do the idols know what happens?" Abraham said: "You should let your ears listen to what your mouth is saying."[b] Terah seized him and handed him over to Nimrod who said: "Let us worship fire." Abraham answered, "We ought to worship water which puts the fire out". "Let us worship water, then." "We ought then to worship the clouds which carry the water." "Then let us worship the clouds." "We ought to worship the winds which scatter the clouds." "Then let us worship the wind." "We ought to worship man,[c] who stands up to[d] the wind." He said, "You are playing with words; I worship nothing but fire, and I am going to throw you into it so that the God you worship can come and save you from it."

'Now Haran was standing there undecided and he said: "If Abram prevails I will say that I am on his side, and if Nimrod prevails I will say that I am on his side." After Abram had gone into the furnace and been saved, they said to Haran: "Whose side are you on?" He said: "Abram's." Seizing him at once they cast him into the fire, where he was burnt up and died in the presence of his father, Terah.'[e]

In Jub. xii. 12 ff.[f] the offence of Haran was made more specific:

Abram arose by night, and he burned all that was in the house (of idols), and no man knew it. And they arose in the night and sought to save their gods from the midst of the fire. And Haran hasted to save them, but the fire flamed over him, and he was burnt in the fire . . .

Abraham in the furnace is also alluded to in Ps. Jon. on Gen. xiv. 1, where Amraphel is identified as 'Nimrod who ordered Abraham to be

[a] *Pesilim.*
[b] I.e. of course they have no knowledge of anything, so why worship them?
[c] *Adam.*
[d] Or 'who carries the wind' in his lungs.
[e] He died because he had hesitated in the first place, and waited for some convincing proof.
[f] See also xii. 1 ff. for a dispute over idols with his father Terah.

cast into the fire'. For a completely different story see Ps. Philo vi (Appendix 1). See also the account in Midr. Teh. on Ps. cxviii. 8, where the details vary slightly. In Apoc. Abr. viii Terah and his whole household were burned with fire from heaven, because they refused to listen to Abraham when he told them to turn from idolatry. Several stories were collected from various sources in Chron. Jer. xxxiii–xxxv. 4.

GENESIS XIII. 10–13

10 *And Lot lifted up his eyes* to[a] degeneracy, *and beheld all the Plain of Jordan, that it was* a place of waters *every where, before the Lord destroyed in his wrath Sodom and Gomorrah.* It was a land excellent in trees *like the garden of the Lord,* and in provision, *like the land of Egypt, as thou goest unto Zoar.*

11 *So Lot chose him all the Plain of Jordan; and Lot journeyed east: and they separated themselves the one from the other.*

12 *Abram dwelled in the land of Canaan, and Lot dwelled in the cities of the Plain, and moved his tent as far as Sodom.*

13 *Now the men of Sodom were* evil in their wealth[b] one with another, and they offended in their bodies in uncovering nakedness, and the shedding of innocent blood, and they practised alien[c] worship, and rebelled *against* the name of *the Lord.*

Other Targums on Genesis xiii. 10–13

13 T.O.: *Now the men of Sodom were* evil in their wealth,[d] and rebelled exceedingly *against* the Lord.

Notes on Genesis xiii. 10–13

10 The separation between Abraham and Lot, mentioned in Gen. xiii. 11, is emphasised in Ps. Jon., and Lot's sojourn in Sodom is anticipated. The root *zanah* ('degeneracy') is usually used of sexual offence: 'R. Jose b. R. Ḥanina said: "The whole of this verse indicates shameful desire: *And Lot lifted up his eyes,* as you read, . . . *his master's wife cast her eyes upon Joseph.*"[e][f] The same view was recorded in B.Naz. 23 *a* in the name of R. Joḥanan.

13 The basic offence of Sodom was that its people distorted every fundamental rule by which relationship is made possible and sustained; according to the biblical narrative, they broke the fundamental rules of hospitality and of sex. Hence the essential nature of the offence

[a] Or 'for'.	[b] *Mammon.*	[c] Or 'strange'.
[d] *Mammon.*	[e] Gen. xxxix. 7.	[f] Ber.R. xli. 7.

was that the natural order was inverted or reversed. Having observed that this was the real nature of the offence, Jewish exegesis then tended to multiply examples of it. Therefore we find in B.San. 109*b*:

There were four judges in Sodom, Shaqrai, Shaqurai, Zayyaphi and Mazle-dina.[a] If, then, a man assaulted a neighbour's wife, they would tell (the husband): 'Give her to him to become pregnant for you.' If a man cut off the ear of a neighbour's ass, they would tell (the owner): 'Give him the ass until the ear grows again.' If a man wounded a neighbour, they would tell (the victim): 'Pay him a fee for bleeding you.' If a man crossed the river by the ferry he had to pay four *zuzim*, but if he walked through the river he had to pay eight. Once a man came and they said, 'Pay us four *zuzim*'. He said: 'But I crossed through the river!' They said: 'Then pay us eight *zuzim* for doing so.' He refused, so they attacked him. He appeared before the judge who ruled: 'Pay them eight *zuzim* for crossing through the river plus a fee for bleeding you.'

It happened once that Eliezer, Abraham's servant,[b] was there and was attacked. He came up before the judge who ruled: 'Pay them a fee for bleeding you.' At once he picked up a stone and hit the judge, who cried out, 'What's happening?' Eliezer said: '*You* now owe *me* a fee: give it to them and my money will stay where it is.' Now they had some beds on which they allowed travellers to sleep. If they were too long they shortened them,[c] and if they were too short they stretched them. Eliezer, Abraham's servant, happened to be there, and they said to him, 'Come and sleep on this bed'. He answered: 'Since the day my mother died I have vowed never to sleep in a bed.'

If a poor man happened to arrive there, everyone gave him a dinar having written his own name on it; but no one gave him any bread. As soon as he died, each man came and took back his own (coin). They entered into an agreement with each other, that if anyone invited an outsider to a feast, that man should be stripped of his garments. It happened that Eliezer was once present when a feast was taking place, but no one gave him any bread. Being hungry, he went and sat down at the end. They said: 'Who invited you?' He said to the man who was sitting nearest to him: 'It was you who invited me.' The man immediately thought, 'If they hear that I invited him they will strip my garments from me', and at once he gathered his garments around him and fled. Eliezer then did the same to everyone present until they had all fled; he then ate up the whole feast.

There was a girl once who gave some bread to a poor man, (hidden) in a pitcher, but when they found out about it, they smeared her with honey and laid her on the parapet of a wall, and the bees came and devoured her.

[a] The names mean: Liar, Terrible Liar, Falsifier and Perverter of Justice.
[b] Gen. xv. 2. [c] Cutting off their feet.

It will be seen that all these stories (and the many others like them)[a] are variations on a single theme: that the basic offence of Sodom was to distort all possibilities of relationship. Indeed, the saying 'He's like a man of Sodom' became proverbial in the same sense as 'he's acting like a dog in a manger'.[b] Ps. Jon. on Gen. xviii. 20 lists the offences of Sodom in much the same way, and Josephus extended the offences likewise:

'Now about this time the Sodomites, overweeningly proud of their numbers and the extent of their wealth, showed themselves insolent to men and impious to the Divinity, insomuch that they no more remembered the benefits that they had received from him, hated foreigners[c] and declined all intercourse with others.'[d]

The Syr. Comm. makes it clear why they were accused of hating strangers: 'It is probable that these Sodomites did not do these things from licentiousness, since they could also do this to one another; but as at one time, they fell away from the fear of God, they became very incensed against men, and especially against strangers, such as would not join them.'

See also T.Sot. iii. 12, Mek. Shir. 2, Sifre on Deut. §43, Midr. haGad. i. 282.

[a] See, for example, the stories collected in P.R.E. 25. Cf. also J.San. x. 3.
[b] See, for example, B.B.B. 59a.
[c] μισόξενοι.
[d] *Ant.* i. 194–5. Cf. also Wisdom xix. 14–15.

GENESIS XIV. 13–15, 18–20

13 *And there came* Og who had been spared[a] from the giants that died in the flood; he had ridden above the ark, with a cover over him, being sustained from the food of Noah. He was not spared because of his merit,[b] but that the inhabitants of the world might realise the mightiness of the Lord and say, 'Did not the giants who were of old rebel against the Lord of the world, and he destroyed them from the earth?' Now when these kings waged war, Og was with them. He said to himself:[c] 'I will go and inform Abram concerning Lot, who has been taken prisoner, that he may come to rescue him from the hands of the kings, and be delivered into their hands. So he came on the eve of the day of Passover, and he found him (Abram) making the unleavened bread. Then he laid it before *Abram the Hebrew: now he dwelt* at the crossroads[d] *of Mamre the Amorite, brother of Eshcol, and brother of Aner; and these were confederate with Abram.*

14 *And when Abram heard that his brother was taken captive* he armed the young men whom he had trained for war, having grown up in his house, but they were unwilling to go with him. So he chose from among them Eliezer, the son of Nimrod,[e] who was equal in might to all of them, *three hundred and eighteen, and pursued as far as Dan.*

15 And the night was *divided* for them in the way: one division was for fighting with the kings and the other division was set aside for smiting the first-born in Egypt. And he arose, *he and his servants, and smote them, and pursued* what remained of them to the place remembered for sin[f] which was to be in Dan, which is north *of Damascus.*

18 *And* the righteous king [i.e., *mlk' zdyq'*] who is Shem the son of Noah, king of Jerusalem, came out to meet Abram, and *brought forth* for him *bread and wine;* and at that time he was ministering before *God Most High.*

---

a T.O. has the same root as Ps. Jon. for 'one that escaped', perhaps implying a knowledge of the tradition.

b *Zekuth.*
c Lit. 'in his heart'.

d Or 'lookout'; see Jastrow.
e Yalqut on Gen. § 109.

f R.V. *Hobah*: Hobah is a word meaning 'sin', hence the interpretation given here. The reference is to Judg. xviii, or perhaps to I Kings xii. 28 ff.

19 *And he blessed him, and said, 'Blessed be Abram* before *God Most High,* who for the sake of the righteous established[a] *heaven and earth:*
20 *and blessed be God Most High, which hath* made your enemies like a shield which receives a blow'. *And he gave him a tenth of all* that he had brought back.

Other Targums on Genesis xiv. 13–15, 18–20

14 F.T. (Gins. pp. 75, 94) has part of the verse.
15 F.T. (Gins. p. 75) has some words.
18 F.T. (Gins. p. 9; see also pp. 75, 94): *And Melchizedek, king of* Jerusalem, who is Shem the great[b] *was priest of* the *Most High.* He *brought forth* food *and wine,* and he was standing and ministering among the great priests before God Most High.[c]
T.O.: *And Melchizedek king of* Jerusalem *brought forth bread and wine and he was* ministering before *God Most High.*

Notes on Genesis xiv. 13–15, 18–20

13 The unnamed 'one' who escaped caused much speculation, since Gen. xiv. 13 does not specifically say who it was.[d] In Ber.R. xlii. 8, he was identified as Og[e] because he came and found Abraham sitting and making the unleavened cakes.[f] This appears to be the point of the reference to unleavened bread in Ps. Jon., even though Ps. Jon. did not use the root *'ogah,* and the play on words is thus missing.[g] A second line of argument leading to the same identification appears in the first part of Ps. Jon. on this verse: Og alone escaped from the flood; it was, therefore, reasonable to take *the one that had escaped* as a way of talking about Og.

---

[a] Or 'created'.
[b] Or 'teacher'; see the notes on Gen. ix. 27.
[c] Gins. conj. original: *And Melchizedek, king of* Jerusalem, who is Shem the great, *brought forth* food *and wine: and he was priest of God Most High.*
[d] Gen. Apoc. XXII, for example, suggested that it was 'one of the shepherds of the flocks which Abram had given to Lot'. P.R.E. 27 suggested Michael, because he was known as Palit ('one who escaped'), the legend being that at the time of the fall of the angels Sammael tried to drag down Michael with the others, but God caught hold of Michael and rescued him. Cf. Jude 9.
[e] *'Og.*   [f] *'Ogoth.*   [g] Ps. Jon. has *gerizan patiran.*

The legend that Og escaped the flood was based on Deut. iii. 11: *For only Og king of Bashan remained of the remnant of the Rephaim.*[a] If all the rest perished in the flood then Og must have survived it. Hence B.Zeb. 113*b* included his survival as one of the problems raised by the fact that the waters of the flood were scalding.[b] 'R. Ḥisda said: "The people of the generation of the flood sinned with hot passion, and with hot water they were punished. Therefore, how could the ark endure, and how could Og, king of Bashan, survive?[c] A miracle occurred and the water near the ark was cooled."' See also Ps. Jon. on Deut. iii. 11.

The same interpretation as that in Ps. Jon. is also referred to briefly in B.Nid. 61*a*. Josephus called the oak of Mamre 'the oak called Ogyges' in *Ant.* i. 186.

At a later period Og was identified with Eliezer, the faithful servant of Abraham.[d] See, for example, P.R.E. 16 and compare Yalqut on Numbers §765. A fuller version of the legend of Og surviving the flood occurs in P.R.E. 23.

For Abraham keeping the law before its time, see the notes on Gen. xxvi. 5.

14 The numerical value of Eliezer[e] is 318;[f] noticing this led to the change in the narrative here. Hence Vay.R. xxviii. 4 says: '(Abraham did not need) sword or shield but only prayer and supplication, as it is written, *And when Abraham heard . . . he led forth . . . three hundred and eighteen.* But Resh Laqish said in the name of Bar Qappara: "This was Eliezer, since Eliezer equals 318."'[g] See also Pes.K. viii. 2, Pes.R. 91*b*, Tanḥ.B. i. 73, Tanḥ. Lek 13, B.Ned. 32*a*, Ber.R. xlii. 2, Bem.R. xviii. 21, Midr. Teh. on Ps. cx. 1, P.R.E. 27.

Eliezer achieved considerable prominence: see, for example, the notes on Gen. xiii. 13 and xv. 2. In Jewish-Christian circles Jesus was identified with Eliezer, because his name also has the value 318. See Ep. Barn. ix. 8, Clement, *Strom.* vi. 11. Jesus was thus the strength of Abraham in this encounter.

---

[a] Giants.
[b] See the notes on Gen. vii. 10.
[c] The pitch should have melted and Og should have been scalded.
[d] See the Targum and notes on Gen. xiv. 14 below.
[e] Gen. xv. 2.
[f] $'a = 1$, $l = 30$, $y = 10$, $'a = 70$, $ṣ = 7$, $r = 200$.
[g] Hence two of them defeated four armies.

For a summary of other interpretations of this verse, see A. Neher 'Rabbinic Adumbrations to Non-Violence', in *Studies in Rationalism* ... (ed. R. Loewe), pp. 182-5.

15 The same translation is implied in Ber.R. xliii. 3, commenting on this verse:

> R. Benjamin b. Jepheth said in the name of R. Johanan: 'The night was divided of itself.' Our rabbis say: 'The creator divided it.' The Holy One, blessed be he, said, 'Abraham worked with me at midnight, so I will work for his descendants at midnight. When was that? In Egypt, as it is written: *And it came to pass at midnight, that the Lord smote all the first-born . . .*'[a]

Compare also P.R.E. 27.

18 The figure of Melchizedek caused considerable uncertainty among the Jews for two principal reasons: in the first place, Melchizedek was taken up and used as a strong argument in Christian apologetic against the Jews; in the second place, Melchizedek gave rise to considerable unorthodox speculation as a result of the enigmatic account of Gen. xiv.[b] The Christian use of Melchizedek in argument against the Jews appears as early as Hebrews,[c] and it became thereafter almost a standard case. In essence it pointed out that Abraham, the father and representative of the Jews, received a blessing from one who is specified as being non-Jewish, and he paid for it. That was taken to prove that there was a non-Jewish priesthood in the dispensation of God superior to that of Aaron. A succinct form of the argument is given by Justin in *Dial.* 19:

> If circumcision had been necessary, as you suppose, God would not have created Adam uncircumcised,[d] nor would he have looked with favour on the sacrifice of Abel which he offered in uncircumcision, nor would Enoch have been pleasing to God in uncircumcision—who 'was not found because God took him'.[e] Lot, uncircumcised, was delivered out of Sodom...Noah is the father of the human race; but with his children while he was uncircumcised he entered into the ark. Melchizedek, the priest of the Most High, was uncircumcised, to whom Abraham, the first to receive circumcision

[a] Exod. xii. 29.
[b] Unorthodox speculations about Melchizedek appear on the Christian side as well. See, for example, the account in Epiphanius (*Haer.* lv. 1 ff.) of various sects calling themselves Melchizedekians. For some of the strange legends woven around Melchizedek see Ps. Athanasius, *The Cave of Treasures*, and the works by Bardy and Simon cited p. 197 n. a.
[c] Heb. vii. 1 ff.
[d] The Jews found this argument unconvincing because of their belief that the patriarchs were born already circumcised.
[e] Gen. v. 24; see the notes *ad loc.*

after the flesh, gave tithes, and Melchizedek blessed him. It was according to his order that God declared through David that he would make him a priest for ever.

The polemic use of Melchizedek by Christians appears frequently, usually with much greater elaboration.[a] The Jewish defences against it were not long in appearing. As with Enoch, they made some attempt to reduce the character of Melchizedek to human size. According to Epiphanius,[b] 'the Jews say . . . that because his mother was a prostitute no record has been made of her, nor is his father known'. Epiphanius rejected that argument on the grounds that other prostitutes *are* named in scripture, as, for example, Rahab[c] or Zimri.[d] He also says: 'The Samaritans reckon him to be Shem, the son of Noah.'[e]

The argument attributed to the Samaritans is exactly that of Ps. Jon., and it was a common defence in the Jewish tradition.[f]

An example of great interest occurs in Midr. Teh. on Ps. xxxvii. 1, where Melchizedek is used as an alternative name for Shem and where many legendary elements are gathered together:

When the Holy One, blessed be he, said *Let not thine heart envy[g] sinners,*[h] he meant, by implication, be a rival of *me*. Without such rivalry the world

---

[a] For a summary of these arguments, see in particular G. Bardy, 'Melchisedech dans la tradition patristique' (*R.B.* xxxv, 1926, 496 ff. and xxxvi, 1927, 25 ff.), and M. Simon, 'Melchisedech dans la polémique entre juifs et chrétiens . . .' (*R.H.P.R.* 1937, pp. 58 ff., reprinted in *Recherches d'Histoire Judéo-Chrétienne*, Mouton, 1962, pp. 101 ff.).

[b] *Haer.* lv. 7. [c] Josh. ii. 1. [d] Num. xxv. 14 f.

[e] *Haer.* lv. 6. Epiphanius rejected that suggestion as well, because of the impossible length of time and ages involved. It is of interest that the Kit. al-Maj., which contains many extravagant legends about Melchizedek, also recognised the force of the objection: 'Some people have supposed that Melchizedek will not die, and they support themselves by the saying of David in the Psalms, *Thou art a priest for ever after the form of Melchizedek.* David does not mean by this saying that he will not die; how could he, since he is flesh? But God honoured him and made him his priest. After all, there is no mention in Torah of a beginning to his days . . . Moses did not make mention of him in his book because he was genealogising (only) the patriarchs. But Shem, the son of Noah, has informed us in the book of testaments that Melchizedek was the son of Malaḥ (a mistake for Shalaḥ, Gen. x. 24), son of Arphaxad, son of Shem, son of Noah. And his mother was Jozadak.' This work and the others related to it (The Cave of Treasures, The Bee, Adam and Eve, etc.) contain many elaborate legends about Melchizedek.

[f] See, for example, B.Ned. 32b, where the identification is completely assumed. B.Ned. also added that Melchizedek was a priest but his descendants were not. [g] I.e. be a rival of. [h] Prov. xxiii. 17.

would not continue, because no one would take a wife or build a house.[a] If Abraham had not sought to rival God he would not have become the possessor of heaven and earth.[b] When did Abraham seek to rival God? When he said to Melchizedek, 'Because of what righteous deed did you come out of the ark alive?' He said, 'Because of the alms which we gave in the ark.' Abraham said, 'How could you do so if there were no poor people there? If no one except Noah and his sons was there to whom did you give alms?' Melchizedek said: 'We gave alms to the cattle, wild animals and birds. We had no sleep because we were setting food before them one after another.' Abraham at once thought, 'If they had failed to give alms to the cattle, wild animals, and birds, they would not have come out of the ark alive. The deed will be even greater if I give alms to the children of men.' Thereupon Abraham established an inn[c] at Beer-sheba, that is to say, he gave food, drink and lodging to all the children of men.

Midr. Teh. on Ps. lxxvi. 3 says specifically:

Melchizedek is the same person as Shem the son of Noah, because in the blessing on Shem and Japheth it says, '. . . Shem will dwell in my tent'[d] . . . This shows that Shem was the servant of God. Then the Targum makes *He was priest of God Most High*[e] into 'he was one who ministered before God', to show that Melchizedek is Shem.[f]

Melchizedek, by being identified with Shem, was brought firmly inside the Jewish fold, and thus no priesthood was admitted outside Judaism. It is worth noting that some uneasiness was felt about Melchizedek even before Christian pressure began. Although Gen. Apoc. (Col. XXII) told the story of Melchizedek with scarcely any elaboration, and Philo did little more than identify him with the Logos on one occasion,[g] Josephus made him an admirer of Abraham who then of his generosity offered Melchizedek a gift. Josephus thus altered the emphasis of the story: 'Now this Melchizedek hospitably entertained Abraham's army, providing abundantly for all their needs, and in the course of the feast he began to extol Abraham and to bless God for having delivered his enemies into his hand. Abraham then offered him the tithe of the spoil, and he accepted the gift.'[h]

[a] Cf. Midr. Teh. on Ps. ix. 1 and Ber.R. ix. 7, which say that 'very good' in Gen. i. 31 refers to the evil *yeṣer*, because without it no one would ever take a wife or beget children, and thus the world could not survive.
[b] Taking that phrase in Gen. xiv. 19 as applying to Abraham.
[c] See the Targum and notes on Gen. xxi. 33.
[d] Its own version of Gen. ix. 27; cf. Ps. Jon. *ad loc.*
[e] Gen. xiv. 18.
[f] For later elaborations of the legend see P.R.E. 8.
[g] *Leg. All.* iii. 82.   [h] *Ant.* i. 181.

It seems clear that Jubilees made some sort of statement about Melchizedek but there is a gap at the crucial place in the text, perhaps deliberately caused.[a] Of even greater interest is the fact that a fragment has turned up in the Dead Sea Scrolls which contains speculation about Melchizedek. Depending on the date of the fragment, this might be the earliest direct evidence of Melchizedek speculation. For the text of this fragment see A. S. van der Woude, 'Melchisedek als himmlische Erlösergestalt . . .', in כה, 1965.

It is worth noting, finally, that the Syr. Comm.[b] contradicted the idea that Melchizedek blessed Abraham. It says that Melchizedek stated that Abraham was *already* blessed:

When he blessed Abraham, he did not say, 'Blessed art thou of the Lord' or 'The Lord bless thee' but he said to him, before those who stood by, *Blessed be* (i.e. 'is') *Abram of God Most High*; as one might say, 'I know already that Abram is blessed and meet to be blessed of God who made heaven and earth, and does not need my blessing'.

19 For the idea that God did certain things for the sake of the righteous see the notes on Gen. xv. 6.

    [a] Jub. xiii. 25.   [b] Levene, pp. 87 f.

1 *After these things*, when the kings had assembled and fallen before Abram, and he had killed four kings, and nine encampments had been brought back, Abram thought to himself[a] and said: 'Woe is me, for perhaps I have already received the reward of my obedience in this world, and I have no portion in the world to come; or perhaps the kinsmen[b] and friends of those who were killed will unite in legions and come against me; or perhaps at that time there was found for me the reward of a little merit, so that they fell before me, but on the second occasion no reward will be found for me, and in me the name of the heavens will be profaned.' At that *the word[c] of the Lord* was with *Abram in a vision, saying, 'Fear not, Abram*, for even if these men should unite in legions and come against you, my word[d] will be *thy shield;* and even if they fall before you in this world the *reward* of your good works will be preserved and made ready before me for the world to come *exceeding great*'.

2 *And Abram said, 'O Lord God*, abundance have you bestowed on me, and abundance is in your possession to give me. But what gain is it to me if *I go* from the world *childless*, and *Eliezer* the administrator[e] of my house, at whose hands signs were wrought for me in Darmasek, expects to be my heir?'

3 *And Abraham said, 'Behold, to me thou hast given no son: and, lo, the* administrator of *my house is mine heir'*.

4 *And, behold*, a word[f] from before *the Lord came unto him, saying, 'This man shall not be thine heir; but* a son whom you will beget *shall be thine heir'*.

5 *And he brought him forth abroad,*[g] *and said, 'Look now toward heaven,*

---

[a] Lit. 'in his heart'.   [b] Lit. 'brothers'.

[c] *Pithgama*. T.O. has, 'the word of the Lord was with Abraham in a prophecy'; Sam. Pent. also has 'prophecy' for 'vision'.

[d] *Memar*; so also T.O.

[e] Lit. 'son of the administration of my house'; so also T.O. and Aq., and cf. Sam. Pent. LXX kept Masek as a name.

[f] *Pithgama*.

[g] Although Ps. Jon. stays close to the Hebrew, it is possible that the words were carefully chosen to *avoid* an extravagant and popular interpretation of this verse; see p. 202 n. a.

and tell the stars, if thou be able to tell them': and he said unto him, 'So shall thy children *be'.*

6 *And he* had faith in the word[a] of *the Lord* and it was reckoned[b] *to him for* merit[c] because he did not argue before him with words.

Other Targums on Genesis xv. 1–6

1 F.T. (Gins. p. 9; see also p. 75) also expanded the verse for the same reason.

2 F.T. (Gins. pp. 10, 76) has the verse.

3 F.T. (Gins. p. 10) has part of the verse.

6 T.O.: *And he believed* in the word of *the Lord* and it was reckoned *to him for* merit.

Notes on Genesis xv. 1–6

1 Ps. Jon. has collected together several suggested reasons why God should suddenly have said to Abraham, *Fear not.* Why was Abraham afraid? Ber.R. xliv. 4 also provided three explanations:

R. Levi explained this in two ways, our rabbis in one. R. Levi said: 'Abraham our father was afraid because he thought, "Perhaps there was a righteous man or one who feared God among those whom I killed". This is like a fodder-merchant who passed by the king's fields and saw some heaps of thorns. So he got down and took them, but the king saw him. He attempted to hide, but the king said, "Why do you hide? I needed labourers to remove them: now you have done it, come and receive your reward..."' R. Levi also said: 'Abraham our father was afraid and said, "Perhaps the sons of the kings that I killed will unite and come against me".' ... Our rabbis said: 'Abraham our father was afraid and said to himself: "I went into the fiery furnace and was saved; I went to war with the kings and was saved. Perhaps I have already received my reward in this world and have nothing for the world to come."'

2 On Eliezer see also the Targum and notes on Gen. xiv. 14. Bem.R. ii. 12 gives the tradition in greater detail:

Abraham spoke before the Holy One, blessed be he: 'Lord of the worlds, what pleasure is there for me in all that you have promised, if I have no children?' As it is written, *And Abram said,* ...[d] For Abram saw in a planet[e]

---

a Lit. 'and there was to him faith in the word (*memra*)'.
b *Ḥashab.*   c *Lizeku.*
d Gen. xv. 2.
e *Mazzal*; other texts, *bemazzlo*, 'in his planet'.

that he was not destined to beget children. What did the Holy One, blessed be he, do at that moment? R. Judah son of R. Simon; R. Ḥanin in the name of R. Joḥanan: 'It teaches that the Holy One, blessed be he, lifted him up to a height above the vault of the sky[a] and said to him, "From that very planet which showed you that you were destined not to beget (children), I will show you that you will do so, as it is written, *And he brought him forth abroad, and said, Look now[b] towards heaven, and tell the stars*".[c]'[d]

For the connection between Eliezer and Damascus, see Ber.R. xliv. 9.

6 The word in the Hebrew for (R.V.) 'righteousness' is *ẓedakah*, and both Targums have translated it by the word *zeku*,[e] which relates it to the technical word *zekuth*. *Zekuth* commonly means 'a plea in defence' or 'a verdict of acquittal', as, for example, in M.San. iv. 1, hence the meanings of 'innocence' or 'blessedness'. But in fact *zekuth* came to be an almost technical word meaning 'merit', or, in other words, that by which acquittal might be ensured.[f] It led on to a doctrine of fundamental importance in Judaism, the so-called 'doctrine of merits'. Basically the doctrine of merits was used to express the belief that all effects have a cause. In the case of good effects the question was constantly asked, because of whose merits did they happen? This appears early on in the classic dispute between Shemaiah and Abtalion[g] about the crossing of the Sea at the beginning of the Exodus: was the Sea parted to reward the faith of the Israelites standing there at the time (as Abtalion argued), or was it to reward the faith of Abraham long before (as Shemaiah argued)? The argument that it was the faith of Abraham being rewarded led to the belief in *zekuth aboth*, the merit of the fathers which was believed to stand by Israel in times of trouble. This was believed to be the case not only in present afflictions but also

---

[a] *Raqi'a*. The tradition that Abraham was taken up into heaven to survey the world is extremely common. It is often based exegetically on the verb *habbet* in Gen. xv. 5, which means 'look down from above'. See Rashi on Gen. xv. 5, Ber.R. xliv. 12, xlviii. 6, II Bar. iv. 4, Test. Abr. x–xiv, Apoc. Abr. ix ff., Ps. Philo xviii. 5 (Appendix 1), Qu'rān vi. 75.

[b] *Habbet-na*; see n. a above.

[c] Gen. xv. 5.

[d] See also Jub. xiv. 1 ff.

[e] Pesh. retained *ẓedek*, as did LXX (by implication δικαιοσύνη). Arab. Vers. is of interest, since the sentence appears in slightly altered form: translated literally it reads: 'And he believed in God, and he wrote (*kataba*) it to him as a good deed.'

[f] See, for example, J.Peah i. 1.

[g] Recorded in Mek. Vayehi. 4, an important passage recording many other suggestions.

in the final judgement, hence the importance of, *inter alia*, Abraham's intercession.[a] The doctrine of merits, by which every man's deeds would be weighed in a strict balance, came to include a doctrine of imputed merits, by which the deeds and faith of just men (particularly of the fathers) would carry over and assist others. This belief in imputed merits was popular but it was also strongly contested. For a full account of the dispute and of the doctrine in general, see Dr A. Marmorstein, *The Doctrine of Merits in Old Rabbinical Literature.*

[a] See the Targum and notes on Gen. xviii. 22–3.

1 *Now Sarai Abram's wife bare him no children: and she had an handmaid,*
an Egyptian, whose name was Hagar, the daughter of Pharaoh, whom
Pharaoh gave to her for a handmaid at the time when he took her for a
wife and was struck by a word from before the Lord.[a]

2 *And Sarai said unto Abram, 'Behold now, the Lord hath restrained me*
from bearing; go in, now, *unto my handmaid,* and I will set her free; it
may be that I shall be builded by her'.[b] *And Abram etc.*

3 *And Sarai Abram's wife took Hagar the Egyptian, her handmaid, after*
Abram had dwelt ten years in the land of Canaan, and set her free and
gave her to Abram her husband to be his wife.

4 *And he went in unto Hagar, and she conceived: and when she saw that she*
had conceived, she despised (the honour of) her mistress *in her eyes.*

5 *And Sarai said unto Abram:* 'All my affliction[c] is from you: trusting
that you would act justly towards me, I left my country and my father's
house, and I came up with you to a strange land. And because I was
not able to bear, I set free my handmaid and *I gave* her to lie in your
bosom; and when she saw that she was with child she held my honour
in contempt before her. But now my affliction is revealed before the
Lord and he will spread his peace *between me and thee,* and from us will
the land be replenished. We shall have no need of the offspring of
Hagar, the daughter of Pharaoh the son of Nimrod, who threw you into
the fiery furnace.'

6 *But Abram said unto Sarai, 'Behold, thy maid is in thy hand; do to her*
that which is good in thine eyes'. And Sarai dealt hardly with her, and she
fled from her face.

Other Targums on Genesis xvi. 1–6

5 F.T. (Gins. pp. 10 f.; see also pp. 76, 95): *And Sarai said unto Abram,*
'My cause[d] and my affliction are in your hand: I forsook my land, and
my childhood, and the house of my father, and I went with you in the
faith of the heavens. I have accompanied you before kings of the earth,

---

[a] The incident is described in Gen. xii. 10 ff.   [b] R.V. marg.
[c] So also Pesh.   [d] *Din.*

before Pharaoh, king of Egypt, and before Abimelech, king of the Philistines,[a] and I have said, "He is my brother", that they should not kill you. And when I saw that I was not able to bear, I took Hagar the Egyptian, *my handmaid*, and *I gave* her to you (to be your wife). *And when she saw that* she was with child, she held my honour in contempt before her. And now let *the Lord* be revealed and *judge between me and thee* and spread peace between me and you, and the earth will be replenished from me and from you, and we will not need the offspring of Hagar the Egyptian, the handmaid, who is of the children of the people who threw you into the fiery furnace.'

T.O.: see the note on p. 206.

Notes on Genesis xvi. 1–6

1 The same 'promotion' of Hagar occurs in Ber.R. xlv. 1, where the motive becomes obvious:

R. Simeon b. Johai said: 'Hagar was Pharaoh's daughter. When Pharaoh saw what happened in his own house because of Sarah,[b] he took his daughter and gave her to Sarah, saying, "It is better for my daughter to be a handmaid in that house than to be a mistress in any other".'

This was argued by taking Hagar as *ha agar*, 'this is the reward'.

5 The two versions make an interesting comparison, because they reveal something of the way in which an 'awkward' passage was broken down and made more acceptable. The treatment of Hagar seemed very harsh, especially when it was remembered that Sarah had taken the initiative[c] so that children might be born to Abraham. The attempt to trace Hagar's descent to Nimrod, the arch-enemy of Abraham, and to Pharaoh, the traditional enemy of Israel, is an attempt to malign Hagar's background. Gen. xvi. 5 (*And when she saw that she had conceived, her mistress was despised in her eyes*) offers its own explanation, and Ber.R. xlv. 4 developed a more detailed story on the basis of it:

Why were the wives of patriarchs barren? . . . R. Azariah said in R. Hanina's name: 'So that they might remain dependent on their husbands although beautiful.' R. Huna said in the name of R. Hiyya b. Abba: 'So that for most of their lives they would be unburdened.' R. Huna, R. Idi and R. Abun said in the name of R. Meir: 'So that their husbands might delight in them, because when a woman bears a child she loses her graceful figure.' For this

---

[a] In fact the incident with Abimelech does not occur until Gen. xx. 1 ff.
[b] It was struck by plagues, Gen. xii. 17.   [c] Gen. xvi. 2.

reason Sarah was like a bride for ninety years before she bore a child. Women used to come to see how she was, and she used to say, 'Go and ask how the exulting one is'. Hagar used to say, 'Sarai, my mistress, is not inwardly what she appears to be outwardly, since she seems to be righteous but is not. How can she be righteous? See how many years she has not conceived, but I conceived in one night.' Sarah said, 'Shall I debate this with her? No, I will debate it with her master.'

Josephus made the expulsion a voluntary withdrawal:[a]

Becoming pregnant, this servant had the insolence to abuse Sarra, assuming queenly airs as though the dominion were to pass to her unborn son. Abraham having thereupon consigned her to Sarra for chastisement, she, unable to endure her humiliations, resolved to fly and entreated God to take pity on her.

Philo regarded the affliction as beneficial:

Not all afflictions are harmful, but there are times when they are even helpful. This is what sick people experience at the hands of physicians, and children at the hands of teachers . . .[b]

T.O. also noticed the difficulty but avoided it in a different way: '*And Sarai said unto Abram*, "I have a cause[c] against you . . ." ' T.O. thus avoided the stronger word and accusation in Ps. Jon., F.T. and Pesh. LXX has, 'I have received injustice from you'; Sam. Pent. and Arab. Vers. have, 'my wrong is (or "be") upon you'.

Gen. xvi. 5 is a 'dotted verse'; for the implications of this see Appendix IV.

[a] *Ant.* i. 188.   [b] *Quaes. Gen.* iii. 25.
[c] *Din*, as in F.T. above.

GENESIS XVIII. 1–25

1 *And* the glory of *the Lord* was revealed over[a] him at the crossroads[b] *of Mamre,* and he was ill from the pain of circumcision *as he sat in the tent door in the heat of the day.*

2 *And he lift up his eyes and looked and, lo, three* angels in the form of *men stood over against him.* They had been sent for three separate tasks, because ministering angels cannot be sent for more than one task each: one had come to tell him that Sarah would bear a son, one had come to rescue Lot, and one had come to destroy Sodom and Gomorrah. *And when he saw them, he ran to meet them from the tent door, and bowed himself to the earth,*

3 *and said,* 'I pray, by the mercies from before you, O Lord, that *if now I have found favour* before you the glory of your Shekina may not now depart *from thy servant* until I have received these travellers'.

4 And Abraham said to those men: '*Let now a little water be fetched, and wash your feet, and rest yourselves under the tree:*

5 *and I will fetch a morsel of bread, and comfort*[c] *ye your heart,* and give thanks to the name of the word of the Lord; *after that ye shall pass on: forasmuch as ye are come* at the time of refreshment and have turned aside *to your servant* to take food.' *And they said,* 'You have spoken well; *so do,* according to your word'.

6 *And Abraham hastened into the tent unto Sarah, and said,* '*Make ready quickly three measures of fine meal, knead it and make cakes*'.

7 *And Abraham ran unto the herd, and fetched a calf tender and* fat, *and gave it unto the servant;*[d] *and he hasted to* prepare cooked dishes.

8 *And he took* fat[e] *butter, and milk, and the calf* from which the servant had prepared cooked dishes, *and set it before them* according to the way of human beings who dwell on earth, and he was serving before them, and they sat (*under the tree*), and it appeared to him as if *they did eat.*

9 *And he*[f] *said unto him,* '*Where is Sarah thy wife?*' *And he said,* '*Behold, in the tent*'.

---

10 *And* one of them *said, 'I will certainly return unto thee* in the coming year when you are well; *and, lo, Sarah thy wife shall have a son'. And Sarah* was listening *in the tent door*, and Ishmael was standing behind her and noted what the angel said.

11 *Now Abraham and Sarah were old*, advanced in days; *it had ceased to be with Sarah after the manner of women.*

12 *And Sarah* puzzled in her heart, *saying, 'After I am waxed old*, shall I conceive, *my lord* Abraham *being old also?'*

13 *And the Lord said unto Abraham, 'Wherefore did Sarah laugh, saying, Shall I of a surety bear a child, which am old?*

14 Is it possible for anything to be hidden from before *the Lord? At the* time of the feast *I will return unto thee* at that time and you will be strong *and Sarah shall have a son.'*

15 *Then Sarah denied, saying,* 'I did not puzzle, but I was *afraid'. And* the angel *said*, 'Fear not, *but* in truth *thou didst laugh'.*

16 *And the* angels who had the form of *men rose up from thence.* The one who brought the news to Sarah went up to the heavens above, and two of them *looked toward*[a] Sodom.

17 *And the Lord said* in his word, 'It is not right for me to *hide from Abraham that which I do*, and while it has still not been done it should be made known to him;

18 *seeing that Abraham shall surely become a great and mighty nation, and all the nations of the earth shall be blessed* through his merit?[b]

19 *For* his faithfulness is revealed before me,[c] *to the end that he may command his children and his household after him, that they may keep the way of the Lord, to do justice and judgement; to the end that the Lord may bring upon Abraham* the good things *which he hath spoken of him.*

20 *And the Lord said* to the ministering angels: *'The cry of Sodom and Gomorrah is great*, who oppress the poor and decree that anyone who gives a crumb of bread to the needy shall be burned with fire, and *their sin is very grievous.*

21 I will be revealed *now*,[d] *and see whether* like *the cry of* the maiden Pelitith which ascends before me these wicked ones have made an end of[e] their offences. And if they have showed active penitence shall they

---

[a] Or perhaps, 'became impatient with'. F.T. (Gins. p. 77) has the same.

[b] *Zekuth.*   [c] T.O. also has 'is revealed before me'.

[d] So also T.O. and F.T.

[e] Or 'completed', in the sense of 'being replete with', rendering Heb. *kalah* as 'completely'; so also Pesh. and F.T.

not be innocent[a] before me? And as if I did not *know* so I will not punish.'

22 *And the* angels who had the form of *men turned from thence, and went toward Sodom: but Abraham* begged mercy for Lot and ministered in prayer *before the Lord.*

23 *And Abraham* prayed *and said* 'Will your wrath *consume* the innocent *with the wicked?*

24 *Peradventure there be fifty* innocent *within the city* who pray before you, ten for every city of all the five cities of Sodom, Amorah, Admah, Zeboim and Zoar. Will your wrath *consume and not spare the place* because of the merit[b] of *the fifty* innocent *that are therein?*

25 A profanation it would be for you *to do after this manner, to slay the* innocent *with the wicked, that so the* innocent *should be as the wicked;* a profanation it would be for you: it cannot be that *the Judge of all the earth* should not do justice.'

Other Targums on Genesis xviii. 1–25

2 F.T. (Gins. p. 11; see also p. 76) has a similar interpretation but with slightly different wording; see also the notes on p. 211.

7 F.T. (Gins. p. 95): *And Abraham ran unto the herd.*

8 F.T. (Gins. p. 95): *And he took butter, and milk.*

10 F.T. (Gins. p. 10, see also pp. 77, 95): Ishmael was standing behind.

12 F.T. (Gins. pp. 77, 95) has part of the verse.

13 F.T. (Gins. pp. 77, 95) has a few words.

16 F.T. (Gins. p. 77): see p. 208 n. a.

17 F.T. (Gins. p. 11; see also p. 77): *And the Lord said* in his word: '*Shall I hide from Abraham* my friend *that which I do?* But because Sodom is among the gifts which I gave him, it is right that I should not do it before I have told him.'

20 F.T. (Gins. p. 77) has a few words.

21 F.T. (Gins. p. 11) interprets the verse in a different form.

22 F.T. (Gins. p. 95) has three words.

23 T.O.: *But Abraham* ministered in prayer before the Lord, *and said* . . .

---

[a] *Zekain.*   [b] *Zekuth.*

Notes on Genesis xviii. 1–25

2 Abraham's reception of the angels became the basis for one of his most famous characteristics, his hospitality: 'By opening a generous door to travellers you have opened a door to proselytes.'[a] It was by this means that chapters 17 and 18 were linked together (as Ps. Jon. here suggested but did not expand):

R. Ḥama b. R. Ḥanina said: 'It was three days after his circumcision, and the Holy One, blessed be he, came to see how he was. He drew out the sun so that the just man should not be disturbed by travellers.[b] Abraham sent Eliezer (to look for some), and when he found none Abraham said, "I do not believe you" . . . He went out, therefore, himself and saw the Holy One, blessed be he, standing at the entrance of the tent.'[c]

Rashi[d] slightly varied the comment, probably to avoid the suggestion that Abraham 'saw' God: 'When God saw that he was distressed because no travellers came, he brought angels to him in the form of men.' In Ber.R. lii. 3 his wish to be hospitable was made the motive for his move to Gerar:[e] 'The land of Sodom was destroyed and there were no travellers, so that Abraham's provisions were abundant. So he said: "Why should hospitality cease from my house?" And he went and pitched his tent in Gerar.'

The hospitality of Abraham is equally clear in Josephus: '. . . Lot invited them (the angels) to be his guests, for he was very kindly to strangers and had learnt the lesson of Abraham's liberality.'[f]

On Abraham's hospitality in general, see also the Targum and notes on Gen. xxi. 33.

The emphasis on three angels (usually identified as Michael, Raphael and Gabriel),[g] each with his own task and no other, was derived from the observation that the number of angels in these two chapters of Genesis changes from three[h] to two[i] to one.[j] Thus Rashi summarised:[k]

'And lo, three men': one to bring the news to Sarah, one to destroy Sodom and one to heal Abraham, because one angel may not perform two com-

---

[a] Ber.R. xlviii. 8.   [b] I.e. he made it too hot for anyone to travel.
[c] B.B.M. 86b; see also Tanḥ. Vay. 2, P.R.E. 29.
[d] *Ad loc.*   [e] Gen. xx. 1.   [f] *Ant.* i. 200.
[g] E.g. Ber.R. xlviii. 9 and B.B.M. 86b.
[h] Gen. xviii. 1.   [i] Gen. xix. 1.
[j] Gen. xix. 24, understood as being effected by an angel. See also Gen. xix. 17.
[k] *Ad loc.*

missions. You know this because throughout the whole section it mentions them in the plural—*and they did*,[a] *and they said unto him*,[b] but of the announcement it is said, *And he said, I will certainly return unto thee . . . :*[c] and of the destruction of Sodom it says, *I cannot do anything*[d] . . . Raphael who healed Abraham went on to rescue Lot . . .[e]

F.T. (Gins. p. 95) added at the end of the verse, 'in the custom of the earth', perhaps to avoid the suspicion of idolatry.

3   See also B.Shab. 127*a*, B.Sheb. 35*b*.

4   See the notes on Gen. xxi. 33.

8   It was felt that angels, or any heavenly beings, could not eat, hence the hint in Ps. Jon. that they did not do so. The 'hint' appears as a specific statement in Ber.R. xlviii. 11: 'They[f] said: "In our case we neither eat nor drink."' Compare Ber.R. xlviii. 14: 'R. Tanḥuma said in the name of R. Eleazar, and R. Abun said in the name of R. Meir: "There is a saying, 'When you enter a town observe its customs'.[g] Above there is no eating or drinking . . . but below there is, so we find, . . . *and they did eat*. Did they do so? In fact, they seemed to do so, removing each dish as it came."'[h] In Jubilees the whole of this part of the narrative was omitted, and both Philo[i] and Josephus[j] talk of the eating as in appearance only. The same change was made in Ps. Jon. on Gen. xix. 3. Compare also Syr. Comm. (Levene, p. 90). It was one of the rare points on which Justin and Trypho reached agreement! (*Dial.* 57.)

o*a* This was an attempt to explain the grammatically difficult phrase *ka'et ḥayyah*[k] which might be taken as, 'as the time that lives'. Rashi[l] gave the same explanation: '*ka'et ḥayyah* means, at this time next year:[m] it was the Passover, and at the next Passover Isaac was born, because we read "at *the* time", not "at a time". It also means, at that time there will be life in you[n] and all of you will be sound and well.'[o]

---

[a] Gen. xviii. 8.   [b] Gen. xviii. 9.   [c] Gen. xviii. 10.

[d] Gen. xix. 22.   [e] Healing and rescue were regarded as the same mission.

[f] The angels.

[g] I.e. 'When in Rome do as the Romans do'.

[h] Cf. Shem.R. xlvii. 5.

[i] *Quaes. Gen.* iv. 9, *de Abr.* xxiii. 118.   [j] *Ant.* i. 197.

[k] R.V. 'when the season cometh'.   [l] *Ad loc.*

[m] For the reasoning behind this, see Rashi's comment on I Sam. xxv. 6.

[n] Plural. Cf. Pesh., 'at this time, when she is living (or "giving life")'. This is probably the correct interpretation, 'according to the usual time of a pregnant woman'.

[o] *Qayyamin*, the same word as in Ps. Jon. and T.O.

10*b* The suggestion that Ishmael overheard what the angel said arose from an ambiguity in the Hebrew text, which can either mean that 'it' (the door, as R.V. takes it) was behind him, or that 'he (unspecified) was behind'. If it was 'he' it could only, of the family, be Ishmael.

12 This is one of the recognised LXX variants (see Appendix III). Opinions varied about whether Sarah doubted the power of God or not.

14 The purpose of this alteration was to remove even the slightest hint that God might be unable to do something. On the feast, see Rashi's comment on Gen. xviii. 10, quoted above, and B.R.H. 10*b*–11*a* which identifies the season at which many decisive events occurred, and suggests Passover for the birth of Isaac.

16 The difference between Gen. xviii. 1 and xix. 1 was thus resolved: see also the notes on Gen. xviii. 1.

17 Abraham was first called *the friend of God* in Isa. xli. 8 and II Chron. xx. 7. The adjective was usually changed to *yadid* on the basis of Jer. xi. 15 (but not in C.D.C. iii. 2 or Mek. Shir. 10), and became an extremely common description of Abraham: see, for example, Jas. ii. 23, Jub. xix. 9, Song of 3 Children 12, Dan. iii. 35 (LXX), Philo, *de Abr.* xix. 89, *de Sobr.* xi. 56, T.Ber. vii. 13, B.Men. 53*a–b*, Sifre on Num. §115, on Deut. §352, Mek. Pisha 18, Ekah R. Hom. xxiv and xxvi, Tanh.B. i. 70. On this verse see Tanh.B. i. 88 f., Ber.R. xlix. 2.

20 See the notes on Gen. xiii. 13.

21 The story of Pelitith is told in full in P.R.E. 25:

Pelitith, the daughter of Lot, was married to one of the rulers of Sodom. She once saw a despised poor man in the street and she grieved for him, as it is written: *Was not my soul grieved for the needy?*[a] What did she do? Every day when she went out to fetch water she put food from her home in her pitcher, and she fed the poor man. The men of Sodom said, 'How does the poor man stay alive?' When they found out about it they brought her out to burn her with fire. She said: 'Lord of the world, establish my right and my cause before the men of Sodom.' At once her cry ascended before the throne of glory, and the Holy One, blessed be he, said, 'I will go down now and see whether they have done altogether according to the cry of the young maiden'.

The story is derived from taking the feminine suffix in verse 21 literally 'according to the cry of her'.[b] The 'her' was then identified. A slightly

---

[a] Job xxx. 25.
[b] R.V. *of it*, i.e. the town; cf. Rashi *ad loc.*, who supported this interpretation against the legend.

different story is told in B.San. 109 *b*, quoted in the notes on Gen. xiii. 13, and see also Yalqut on Gen. §83.

On the chance offered to Sodom for repentance see the Targum and notes on Gen. xix. 24 and Yalqut on Gen. §83: 'R. Abba b. Kahana said: "It shows that the Holy One, blessed be he, opened to them a door of repentance." '

In Ps. Clem. *Hom.* iii. 38. 2 this verse was advanced as an argument against the omniscience of God. See also Philo, *Quaes. Gen.* iv. 24 ('Why does God speak like a man . . .?').

22 The merit and intercession of Abraham were important concepts in the Jewish tradition. They were frequently connected with his plea for Sodom,[a] as in the passage quoted in the notes on Gen. vi. 3. In practical terms his prayers were effective in cases of need:

'Abraham used to pray for barren women and they were remembered; and for the sick and they were healed. R. Ḥuna said: "Abraham had no need to go to the sick, for as soon as the sick person saw him he was healed." R. Ḥanina said: "Ships on the sea were saved by Abraham's merit." '[b]

He was believed to be continuing his intercession for the children of Israel:

R. Isaac said: 'When the Temple was destroyed the Holy One, blessed be he, discovered Abraham standing in the Temple, so he said, *What hath my beloved to do in mine house?*[c] Abraham said: "I have come because of what has happened to my descendants." He said: "Your descendants have sinned and gone into exile." Abraham said: "But perhaps it was in error that they sinned." He said, *She hath wrought lewdness.*[d] Abraham said: "But perhaps it was only a few who sinned." He said, *With many.* "But then might you not have remembered for their benefit the covenant of circumcision?" He said, *The holy flesh is passed from thee.* "But if you had waited, might they not have repented?" He said, *When thou doest evil, then thou rejoicest.* At that Abraham put his hands to his head and wept bitterly, saying, "Heaven forbid, but perhaps there is no hope left for them". Then came a *bath qol*[e] saying, *The Lord called thy name, A green olive tree, fair with goodly fruit.*[f] Just as the olive-tree produces its best at the end of the season, so Israel will reach its height at the end of time.'[g]

[a] See Josephus, *Ant.* i. 199 for an early example.
[b] Ber.R. xxxix. 11; cf. the story of the precious stone hung around Abraham's neck by which sick people were healed, B.B.B. 16 *b*.
[c] Jer. xi. 15. [d] Jer. xi. 15. [e] See pp. 44 f.
[f] Jer. xi. 16. [g] B.Men. 53 *b*.

213

Abraham's intercession was regarded as being equally effective in the final judgement. In Test. Abr. xiv, he prays for a soul whose good and evil deeds exactly balance, and when it is saved, the angel says to him, 'It has been saved through your righteous prayer'. In Ber.R. xliv. 16, R. Azariah says of Abraham: 'When your descendants are corpses without bone or muscle left, your merit[a] will stand by them.'

The last quotation shows how closely belief in the efficacy of intercession was linked with the doctrine of merits.[b] The *zekuth* of Abraham was particularly highly regarded. It was because of his merit, for example, that the world was created.[c] See further the Targum and notes on Gen. xv. 6. (For a summary of the importance of intercession and of the restrictions placed upon it in Judaism see my article, 'Intercession in the Qu'rān . . .')

Verse 22 is one of the *tiqqune soferim*, the emendations of the scribes.[d] There are eighteen *tiqqune soferim*, some of which seem to have been made in order to avoid anthropomorphism, though that explanation does not fully account for all the examples. In this verse, it is possible that the text here originally read, 'But the Lord stood yet before Abraham'. This is the only instance of *tiqqun soferim* in Genesis. See further Ber.R. xlix. 7, Tanḥ. Beshall. 16, Sifre on Num. §84, Yalqut on Exod. §247.

24 Prayer as a characteristic of the righteous is common.[e] Midr. Teh. on Ps. cvi. 44 says:

'R. Eleazar said: "Israel will be saved through five things: through affliction, through the pleading of prayer, through the merit of the fathers, through repentance, through the time of gathering in." '

Compare also Midr. Teh. on Ps. v. 5:

'R. Isaac said: "We are now without prophet or priest or offering or sanctuary or altar to help bring us forgiveness. Since the day the Temple was destroyed we have had only the power of prayer." '

The idea that prayer and other religious duties took the place of

---

[a] *Zekuth.*
[b] See p. 202.
[c] The idea was based on Gen. ii. 4, since the word for 'when they were created' (*bhbram*) is an anagram of Abraham. See also Tanḥ.B. i. 11, 62, Midr. Teh. on Ps. civ. 18, Ber.R. xii. 9.
[d] On the scribes, see pp. 54 f.
[e] It is repeated here in verses 26, 30 and 31.

Temple services and sacrifices when they became impossible is frequent. For example, Tanḥ. Vay. 1 says outright:

The Holy One, blessed be he, said to Israel: 'Be constant in prayer (*tephillah*), because there is nothing better than prayer. Prayer is more than all offerings, as it is written *To what purpose is the multitude of your sacrifices unto me?* . . .[a] Even if a man does not deserve to be answered in his prayers and for loving-kindness to be shown him, yet if he prays repeatedly and begs for favour I will show him loving-kindness as it is written, *All the paths of the Lord are loving-kindness and truth.*[b] I set loving-kindness before truth, that is, righteousness before justice.'[c]

'Righteous': both Ps. Jon. and T.O. translated *zadiqm* by *zakkain*. This may mean that they have not noticed the defective spelling (the usual *y* is absent in the Hebrew word), or else they did not regard it as significant. Ber.R., on the other hand, commented on Abraham's prayer:

'You hope that the judgement of the wicked will be waived for the sake of the righteous; but are they righteous? In fact they were pretending to be righteous, because, as R. Joḥanan says, "Wherever *zadiqm* is used in connection with Sodom it is spelt defectively".'[d]

25 Ps. Jon. (and also T.O. in different words) strengthened the phrase, 'that be far from thee' in order to repudiate any suggestion that God might be able to act unjustly; in this they were probably faithful to the original intention of the idiom, which is most likely to have been derived from *ḥll*, 'desecrate'.

[a] Isa. i. 11.   [b] Ps. xxv. 10.
[c] For further illustrations, see the section on prayer in *The Rabbinic Anthology*, pp. 342–81.
[d] Ber.R. xlix. 9; i.e. the defective spelling indicates that their claim to be righteous was defective as well.

24 And the word of *the Lord* brought down showers of favour *upon Sodom and upon Gomorrah* in order that they might work repentance, but they did not do so, but said: 'Works of evil are not revealed before the Lord.' Behold, therefore, *brimstone and fire* descended upon them from before the word of *the Lord out of heaven.*

Other Targums on Genesis xix. 24

F.T. (Gins. p. 12; see also p. 77): And the word of *the Lord* was bringing down *upon* the people of *Sodom and* of *Gomorrah* showers of favour in order that they might work repentance from their evil works, but they did not do so. But when they saw the showers they said, 'Here is confirmation[a] that evil works are not revealed before him'. And he turned to bring down on them *brimstone and fire* from before the Lord *out of heaven.*

Notes on Genesis xix. 24

That Sodom and Gomorrah were given a clear chance to repent agrees with the view that a similar opportunity was given to the generation of the flood; see the notes on Gen. vi. 3. The close connection between the two can be seen in Rashi's comments on Gen. vii. 12 and xix. 24:
vii. 12: '*And the rain was upon the earth:* but later it says, *And the waters prevailed exceedingly upon the earth* . . .'[b] In fact when he poured it forth (first) he poured it forth with mercy, so that if they turned in repentance it would be a shower of blessing. But when they did not turn, it became a flood.'
xix. 24: '*The Lord rained . . . brimstone and fire.* To begin with it rained,[c] then it was made brimstone and fire.' The two floods which became destructive when men refused to repent are discussed together in Mek. Shir. 5. See also Ber. l. i, Yalqut on Gen. §83, and the notes on Gen. xviii. 21.

[a] *Dilma*, usually a technical word used to introduce an illustration.
[b] Gen. vii. 17.
[c] I.e. water; the Heb. word is used of ordinary rain.

The verse was one of those used by Christians as a witness to the Trinity in the Old Testament. See, for example, Justin, *Dial.* 129: 'When it says, *Then the Lord rained . . . brimstone and fire from the Lord out of heaven*, the inspired word shows that they are two in number, one on earth who, as it says, came down to see the cry of Sodom, the other in heaven who is Lord of the Lord upon earth, being his father and God . . .'[a]

Ps. Jon. made that argument impossible, but T.O. retained the same structure of the verse as the Hebrew. It seems probable, therefore, that the change in Ps. Jon. was made deliberately to meet the Christian argument.

[a] See also *Dial.* 56 and 127.

13 '*And it came to pass, when* the worshippers of idols tried to lead me astray, I went forth *from my father's house,* and *I said unto her* . . .'

Other Targums on Genesis xx. 13

T.O.: '*And it came to pass, when* the people went astray after the works of their own hands the Lord brought me to fear him *from my father's house,* and *I said unto her* . . .'

Notes on Genesis xx. 13

13 Abraham's need to reject idolatry is based on Josh. xxiv. 2, and many stories were elaborated from it. For some of these, see the notes on Gen. xi. 28. There were two problems to be faced in the Hebrew of this verse: first, the verb, *caused me to wander,* is in the plural, although apparently Elohim is the subject. Elohim is a plural form, but since God is by definition One, the verb is usually singular. The problem was made more pressing when Christians pointed to instances of the plural verb with Elohim as suggesting persons in the Godhead (see the notes on Gen. i. 26). Secondly, the verb usually means 'cause to stray' or 'err'. In this verse, therefore, the literal meaning would appear to be, 'God caused me to err'.

According to Ber.R.[a] R. Ḥanin suggested three alternative translations by supplying different words in each:

1. When (the people) went astray (in idolatry and tried to kill Abraham for his refusal to join them) God (saved me) from my father's house.

2. When (the people) tried to lead me astray, God (told me to go) from my father's house.

3. When (the people) went astray, God (raised up two men) from my father's house (to protest against idolatry). The two men were Shem and Eber, ancestors of the Hebrews.

Rashi commented:[b]

'Onqelos interprets[c] it with his own interpretation. There is another

---

[a] lii. 11; cf. also J.Meg. i. 8 (9).
[b] *Ad loc.*   [c] *Tirgem.*

way of taking it which fits well: when the Holy One, blessed be he, caused me to go forth from my father's house to be a wanderer, travelling from place to place, I knew that I would pass through places where wicked people are, so I said to her . . .'

Rashi also noticed the plural verb, and wrote: 'Do not be taken aback at this, because there are many places where words expressing the Divine nature or words expressing authority are treated as plurals.' He then quoted as examples Gen. xxxix. 20, xlii. 30, Exod. xxi. 19, xxii. 14, Deut. v. 23, Josh. xxiv. 19, II Sam. vii. 23.

It is of interest that Sam. Pent. retained the literal sense of the word, and said that God caused Abraham to err in his father's house in order to provoke Abraham's response of faith. The Arabic version used a strong word (√hala'a), 'he deprived me' or 'deposed me'. LXX and Pesh. have simply, 'he led me out'.

GENESIS XXI. 1–2

1 *And the Lord* remembered[a] *Sarah as he had said, and the Lord did unto Sarah* a miracle *as* Abraham *had spoken* in his prayer on behalf of Abimelech.

2 *And Sarah conceived, and bare Abraham a son* like to him in his age, *at the set time of which* the Lord *had spoken to him.*

Notes on Genesis xxi. 1–2

1 Raba said to Rabba b. Mari: 'On what do we base the rabbinic deduction that a man who asks consideration for another when he is in need of the same thing himself is heard as well?' He said, 'It is written, *And the Lord turned the captivity of Job, when he prayed for his friends'.*[b] He said, 'You quote that passage, but I say it is, *And Abraham prayed unto God: and God healed Abimelech, and his wife and his maidservants,*[c] and later goes on, *And the Lord visited Sarah as he had said,*[d] that is, as Abraham had said in the case of Abimelech'.[e]

Tanḥ.B. i. 106 commented: 'The ministering angels said to the Holy One, blessed be he, "Lord of the universe, Abraham heals others but himself needs healing. He has healed Abimelech and his house, and they have borne children, . . . but you do not heal him." The Holy One, blessed be he, said, "He is worthy that I should give him sons".'

The actual prayer of Abraham is given in P.R.E. 26, Midr. haGad. i. 303.

2 Ber.R.[f] also said of the phrase *a son in his old age*: 'This is to show that his son's appearance was like his own.' The purpose was to refute the slander that Isaac could not be their son because they were too advanced in years; they must have found and adopted him. The accusation is made precise in B.B.M 87*a*, which is dealing with the problem raised in verse 7 by the fact that Sarah suckled children (in the plural):

In that case, how many children did Sarah suckle? R. Levi said: 'When Abraham weaned his son Isaac, he made a great feast, and everyone in the

---

[a] So also T.O. and Pesh.; T.O. is very close linguistically to Ps. Jon. in this verse, but without the expansion in the second half of it.
[b] Job xlii. 10. [c] Gen. xx. 17. [d] Gen. xxi. 1.
[e] B.B.Q. 92*a*, based on M.B.Q. viii. 7, T.B.Q. ix. 29.
[f] liii. 6; cf. lxxxiv. 8.

world mocked him, saying, "Look at the old man and the old woman who found a child in the street and now ask us to believe that he is their son! They are even making a great feast to convince us!" So what did Abraham do? He went and invited all the mighty men of that time, and Sarah, our mother, invited their wives. When each of them came with her own child (but without the child's nurse) a miracle happened to Sarah in that her breasts opened like two fountains, so that she suckled them all. But they went on mocking and said, "Even if Sarah could give birth at 90, Abraham could never beget a child at the age of 100". At once the features of Isaac's face changed to become like those of Abraham, and at that they said, *Abraham begat Isaac.*[a] Before Abraham there was no mark of old age; but after this someone wishing to speak to Abraham would start speaking to Isaac, and someone wishing to speak to Isaac would start speaking to Abraham.[b] So Abraham prayed and old age began, as it is written, *And Abraham was old, and well stricken in age.*

For other versions of the same, see Ber.R. liii. 9, Yalqut on Gen. §93, Tanḥ. Told. 1, 3 and 6, Tanḥ.B. i. 107 and 176, B.San. 107b.

[a] Gen. xxv. 19. See Ps. Jon. *ad loc.*: 'Because the appearance of Isaac resembled the appearance of Abraham, in truth the sons of men said, *Abraham begat Isaac...*'

[b] They looked identical.

33 *And he planted* an oasis[a] at the Well of the Seven Lambs, and he prepared in it food and drink for those who passed by and returned, and he used to declare to them there, 'Acknowledge and believe in the name of the word of *the Lord, the Everlasting God'*.

Other Targums on Genesis xxi. 33

F.T. (Gins. p. 12; see also p. 77):

And Abraham *planted* an oasis in Beer-sheba and prepared in it food and drink for the people, and when they had eaten and drunk and had tried to pay him for what they had eaten and drunk, our father Abraham would say to them: 'Pray before your father in heaven; from what is his you have eaten, and from what is his you have drunk.' And they did not move on from there until he had made them proselytes and instructed them in the way everlasting.[b] And Abraham worshipped and prayed there in the name of the word of *the Lord, the Everlasting God.*

Notes on Genesis xxi. 33

The hospitality of Abraham was one of his most famous characteristics; see, for example, the Targum and notes on Gen. xviii. 1. B.Sotah 10a–b indicates that the interpretation of *'eshel*[c] was disputed:

Resh Laqish said: 'It means that he planted an orchard with the best fruits in it.' But R. Judah and R. Nehemiah differed, one saying it was an orchard, one that it was an inn.[d] If it was an orchard it is straightforward, but if it was an inn, why does it say *he planted?* It is in the same sense as, *And he shall plant the tents of his palace*[e] . . . Resh Laqish said: 'Do not read, "and he called" but "and he caused to call"[f] which shows that Abraham caused the name of the Holy One, blessed be he, to be spoken by everyone who passed by. How so? Because the travellers, when they had eaten and drunk, prepared

---

[a] *Pardisa.*

[b] Or perhaps, 'in the way of the world', i.e. 'in right behaviour'.

[c] R.V. *tamarisk tree.*

[d] Perhaps derived from taking the initial letters of *'eshel* as standing for *'akal,* 'he ate', *shatah,* 'he drank', and *lan,* 'he took a night's lodging' (or perhaps *liwwah,* 'he escorted a guest').

[e] Dan. xi. 45.   [f] Hiphil instead of Qal.

to bless him, but he said to them: "Have you eaten of what was mine? You ate from that which belongs to the God of the universe; give thanks and praise and blessing to the one who spoke and the world came into existence."'

In A.R.N. 7 a distinction was drawn between the hospitality of Job and of Abraham, which illustrates well the high estimate of Abraham:

'And let the poor be members of your household':[a] ... When the great disaster overtook Job, he said to the Holy One, blessed be he, 'Lord of the universe, is it not the case that I fed the hungry and gave drink to the thirsty? For it is written, *If I have withheld the poor from their desire, ... Or have eaten my morsel alone, And the fatherless hath not eaten thereof; ...*[b] And is it not the case that I clothed the naked? For it is written, *And if he were not warmed with the fleece of my sheep; ...*[c] But the Holy One, blessed be he, said to Job: 'Job, you have not achieved a half of Abraham's achievement. You sit and wait in your house until travellers come to you.[d] To a man used to eating good[e] bread you give good bread. To a man used to eating meat you give meat. To a man used to drinking wine you give wine. But Abraham was not like that, because he went out looking all around, and when he found any travellers he brought them to his house. To a man not used to eating good bread he gave good bread. To a man not used to eating meat he gave meat. To a man not used to drinking wine he gave wine. In addition he set himself to building great houses by the way, leaving in them food and drink so that travellers could eat and drink and give thanks to heaven ... And whatever a man asked for was found in Abraham's house, as it is written, *And Abraham planted a tamarisk tree*[f] *in Beer-sheba.*'

Another example of this verse being connected with Abraham's hospitality is to be found in Midr. Teh. on Ps. xxxvii. 1; it is quoted in the notes on Gen. xiv. 18. See also Ber.R. liv. 6, B.Ber. 58*b*, Tanḥ. Lek 12. In Tanḥ. the form of blessing which Abraham taught them to say is: 'Blessed is the Lord who is to be blessed for ever, and blessed is he who gives bread and sustenance to all flesh.'

[a] The phrase is from Pirqe Aboth: see the introduction on A.R.N. pp. 87f.
[b] Job xxxi. 16 f.   [c] Job. xxxi. 20.
[d] Contrast Abraham in B.B.M. 86*b*, quoted in the notes on Gen. xviii. 1.
[e] Lit. 'wheat'.
[f] A.R.N. made a play on words: *sha'al* is 'he asked', *'eshel* is R.V. *a tamarisk tree*.

GENESIS XXII

1 *And it came to pass after these things, that* Isaac and Ishmael were disputing. Ishmael said: 'It is right for me to be the heir of my father, since I am his first-born son.' But Isaac said: 'It is right for me to be the heir of my father, since I am the son of Sarah his wife, but you are the son of Hagar, the handmaid of my mother.' Ishmael answered and said: 'I am more righteous than you because I was circumcised when thirteen years old; and if it had been my wish to refuse I would not have handed myself over to be circumcised.' Isaac answered and said: 'Am I not now thirty-seven years old? If the Holy One, blessed be he, demanded all my members I would not hesitate.' Immediately, these words were heard before the Lord of the universe, and immediately, the word of the Lord tested *Abraham, and said unto him, 'Abraham'; and he said, 'Here am I'.*

2 *And he said, 'Take now thy son, thine only son, whom thou lovest, even Isaac, and get thee into the land of* worship;[a] *and offer him there for a burnt offering upon one of the mountains which I will tell thee of'.*

3 *And Abraham rose early in the morning and he saddled his ass, and took two of his young men,* Eliezer and Ishmael, *with him, and Isaac his son; and he clave the wood* of the olive and the fig and the palm which are proper *for the burnt offering, and rose up, and went unto the place of which* the Lord *had told him.*

4 *On the third day Abraham lifted up his eyes, and saw* the cloud of glory smoking on the mountain, and he recognised it *afar off.*

5 *And Abraham said unto his young men, 'Abide ye here with the ass, and I and the lad will go yonder* to find if what I was assured—"so shall thy seed be"[b]—will be established; *and we will worship* the Lord of the universe, *and come again to you'.*

6 *And Abraham took the wood of the burnt offering, and laid it upon Isaac his son; and he took in his hand the fire and the knife; and they went both of them together.*[c]

---

[a] *Pulḥana*; so also T.O. and Arab. Vers.; LXX, 'the high country' (cf. LXX on Gen. xii. 6), Vulg. 'the land of vision' (as also some texts of Sam. Pent.).

[b] Gen. xv. 5.

[c] Lit. 'as one'.

7 *And Isaac spake unto Abraham his father, and said, 'My father': and he said, 'Here am I, my son'. And he said, 'Behold the fire and the wood: but where is the lamb for a burnt offering?'*

8 *And Abraham said:* 'The Lord will choose for himself *the lamb for a* burnt offering my son.' *So they went both of them* with a single heart together.[a]

9 *And they came to the place which God had told him of; and Abraham built the altar there* which Adam had built, which had been destroyed by the waters of the flood and which Noah had rebuilt. It had been destroyed in the generation of the division.[b] And he *laid the wood in order, and bound Isaac his son, and laid him on the altar, upon the wood.*

10 *And Abraham stretched forth his hand, and took the knife to slay his son.* Isaac answered and said to his father: 'Bind me well that I may not struggle at the anguish of my soul, and that a blemish may not be found in your offering, and that I may not be cast into the depth of destruction.' The eyes of Abraham looked at the eyes of Isaac, but the eyes of Isaac looked at the angels on high: Isaac saw them but Abraham did not see them. The angels on high answered, 'Come and see these two unique men in the earth; the one slaughters and the other is slaughtered. The one who slaughters does not hesitate, the one to be slaughtered stretches out his neck.'

11 *And the angel of the Lord called unto him out of heaven, and said* to him, *'Abraham, Abraham': and he said, 'Here am I'.*

12 *And he said, 'Lay not thine hand upon the lad, neither do thou any thing evil unto him: for now* it is revealed before me *that thou fearest the Lord, seeing thou has not withheld thy son, thine only son, from me'.*

13 *And Abraham lifted up his eyes, and looked, and behold,* that one ram which was created in the evening of the completion of the world *caught in the thicket* of a tree *by his horns: and Abraham went and took the ram, and offered him up for a burnt offering in the stead of his son.*

14 *And Abraham* gave thanks and prayed there in *that place,* and said: 'I pray to you, by your mercy, O Lord. It is clear to you that there has not been any hesitation in my heart, and that I sought to perform your decree with joy. So, when the descendants of Isaac, my son, come to the hour of distress, may you remember them, and answer them, and

a Lit. 'as one'.
b Gen. x. 25.

deliver them. So all the generations to come will say, In this mountain Abraham bound Isaac, his son, and there the Shekina *of the Lord* was revealed to him.'

15 *And the angel of the Lord called unto Abraham a second time out of heaven*

16 *and said, 'By* my word[a] *have I sworn, saith the Lord, because thou hast done this thing, and hast not withheld thy son, thine only son:*

17 *that in blessing I will bless thee, and in multiplying I will multiply thy seed as the stars of the heaven, and as the sand which is upon the sea shore; and thy* sons *shall possess the* cities[b] of their *enemies;*

18 *and* because of the merit[c] of your sons *shall all the nations of the earth be blessed; because thou hast obeyed my voice'.*

19 And the angels on high led Isaac and brought him to the school of Shem the great,[d] and he was there three years. And on the same day *Abraham returned unto his young men, and they rose up and went together to Beer-sheba; and Abraham dwelt at Beer-sheba.*

20 *And it came to pass after these things,* after Abraham had bound Isaac, that Satan came and told Sarah that Abraham had slaughtered Isaac; and Sarah rose up and cried out and was choked and died because of the anguish. And Abraham came and rested on the way, and *it was told Abraham, saying, Behold, Milcah, she also hath borne children;* she is granted easement[e] through the merit[f] of her sister to bear sons *unto thy brother Nahor;*

21 *Uz his firstborn, and Buz his brother, and Kemuel* the master of the Aramaean diviners.

(22-4 These verses follow the Hebrew.)

Selections from other Targums on Genesis xxii

1 F.T. (Gins. p. 77) has a few words.

3 F.T. (Gins. p. 96) has three words.

6 F.T. (Gins. p. 96) has one word.

8 F.T. (Gins. p. 13; see also pp. 77, 96): *And Abraham said:* 'From before the Lord will *the lamb for a burnt offering* be chosen[g] my son and if not

---

[a] So also T.O.   [b] So also T.O., LXX and Arab. Vers.
[c] *Zekuth.*   [d] Or 'teacher'; see the notes on Gen. xi. 27.
[e] Particularly used of birth pains: see, e.g., T.Sot. ii. 3.
[f] *Zekuth.*
[g] Or 'has been chosen'; see R. le Déaut, *La Nuit Pascale*, p. 158.

then you are the lamb.' *So they went both of them* with a single heart *together*,ᵃ Abraham to slaughter and Isaac to be slaughtered.

T.O.: 'Before the Lord is revealed *a lamb for the* burnt offering my son.'

10 F.T. (Gins. p. 13; see also pp. 77, 96): *And Abraham stretched forth his hand, and took the knife to slay* Isaac *his son.* Isaac answered and said to Abraham his father: 'My father, bind my hands well that I may not struggle at the time of my anguish and trouble you, and your offering be found unfit, and I be cast into the depth of destruction in the world to come.' The eyes of Abraham were fixed on the eyes of Isaac, but the eyes of Isaac were fixed on the angels on high. Isaac saw them but Abraham did not see them. At that moment there came forth a divine voiceᵇ from heaven which said, 'Come and see these two just men unique in the earth: the one slaughters and the other is slaughtered. The one who slaughters does not spare, the one to be slaughtered stretches out his neck.'

11 F.T. (Gins. p. 13; see also p. 77): *And the angel of the Lord called unto him out of heaven and said, 'Abraham, Abraham': and* Abraham answered in the language (later to be used in) the Temple, and *said, 'Here am I'.*ᶜ

12 F.T. (Gins. p. 96): '*Neither do thou anything unto him.*'

14 F.T. (Gins. p. 13; see also pp. 77 and 96): *And Abraham* worshipped and prayed in the name of the word of the Lord God who sees and is not seen:ᵈ 'It is revealed and known before you that there was no divided purpose in my heart at the time when you said, "Offer Isaac your son before me". At once in the morning I rose early and I obeyed your instructions and followed your decree. And now I pray for mercies from before you, O Lord God, that when the offspring of Isaac my son shall come to the hour of distress you may remember for their good the bindingᵉ of Isaac their father, and absolve and forgive their transgressions, and rescue them from every trouble, that the generations which are yet to follow him may say: In the mountain of the templeᶠ of the Lord, Abraham offered Isaac his son, and in this mountain the glory of the Shekina *of the Lord* was revealed to him.'

T.O.: *And Abraham* worshipped and prayed there in that place. He said before the Lord: "Generations shall worship here. It will therefore

---

ᵃ Lit. 'as one'.
ᵇ *Berath qala*, lit. 'daughter of a voice'; see the Introduction, pp. 44 f.
ᶜ Cf. Isa. vi. 8.   ᵈ The formula is common in Judaism; B.Ḥag. 5 *b*.
ᵉ '*aqedah*.   ᶠ Lit. 'holy house'; see Gen. xxii. 2.

be said, On this day[a] in this mountain Abraham worshipped before *the Lord.*" '

24 F.T. (Gins. pp. 13, 77, 96) has a few words.

Notes on Genesis xxii

1 Ps. Jon. has here suggested a reason for the sacrifice of Isaac and for the testing of Abraham. The same suggestion was recorded in Ber.R. lv. 4, where an alternative reason is also given:

After these things: anxiety[b] was felt. Who was anxious? Abraham, because he said: 'I have been happy and have made others happy,[c] but I have not reserved for the Holy One, blessed be he, any bullocks or rams at all.' God said to him: 'I know that you would not hold back even if you were told to sacrifice your only son to me.'

B.San. 89*b* recorded a shorter version of the suggestion in Ps. Jon., and varied the alternative of Ber.R.:

After these things: What does *after* refer to? R. Joḥanan said in the name of R. Jose b. Zimra: 'After the words of Satan, as it is written, *And the child grew, and was weaned.*[d] Satan said to the Almighty: "Lord of the universe, you granted offspring to this old man at the age of one hundred, but out of all the feast which he prepared he did not reserve for a sacrifice before you a single pigeon or dove. He has only honoured his son." He said, "If I tell him to sacrifice his son before me he will not refuse". At once God tested Abraham . . ."'[e]

The tests, or trials, of Abraham were usually reckoned as ten in number, but there was no precise agreement about what they were. Three typical lists are those of P.R.E., A.R.N. and Midr. Teh. P.R.E. constructed its whole record of Abraham as a narrative of the ten trials. According to P.R.E. 26–31 the trials were:

(i) The attempt of men in the land of his birth to kill him, and his being hidden in a cave for thirteen years.

---

a For the traditions connecting the 'Aqedah with Passover, see R. le Déaut, *La Nuit Pascale*, pp. 143 ff. The main Jewish tradition links it with the New Year, for the second day of which (Tishri 2) it forms the lectionary reading.

b *'Aḥar*, 'after' has suggested *ḥirḥer*, 'he (became) heated' (i.e. with anxiety).

c Gen. xxi. 8. d Gen. xxi. 8.

e See also Jub. xvii. 16–18, where it is 'the prince Mastema' who takes the initiative against Abraham. In Ps. Philo xxxii. 1 it is the angels, not Satan, who are jealous (Appendix 1). In Midr. Teh. on Ps. xviii. 31 the nations ask why God loves Abraham so much and they are told it is because of Abraham's complete faith and obedience. Cf. also Tanḥ.B. i. 11, Tanḥ. Vay. 18.

(ii) His imprisonment for ten years (three years in Kutha and seven in Qardi), and his being cast into the furnace.

(iii) His migration.

(iv) The famine.

(v) Sarah being taken by Pharaoh.

(vi) The campaign of the kings against him.

(vii) His foreseeing in the 'covenant of the pieces' the future subjections of his descendants.

(viii) The circumcision of Abraham and Ishmael.

(ix) Ishmael shooting arrows at Isaac as though in play, and Sarah in consequence demanding his expulsion.

(x) The sacrifice of Isaac.

The list in A.R.N. 32 suggests the following:

'Twice when ordered to arise and go,[a] twice in connection with his sons,[b] twice in connection with his wives,[c] once when he fought with the kings, once in the covenant between the pieces, once in the furnace[d] of the Chaldeans, once at the covenant of the circumcision.'

The list in Mid. Teh.[e] is: the furnace of fire, the command to arise and go, two in connection with Sarah,[f] the casting out of Hagar, the casting out of Ishmael, the campaign against the kings,[g] circumcision, the vision of the four exiles at the covenant between the pieces, and the binding of Isaac.

In Jub. xvii. 17 a rudimentary list of trials appears:

And the Lord knew that Abraham was faithful in all his afflictions; for he had tried him through his country and with famine, and had tried him with the wealth of kings,[h] and had tried him again through his wife, when she was torn (from him), and with circumcision; and had tried him through Ishmael and Hagar, his maid-servant, when he sent them away. And in everything wherein he had tried him, he was found faithful[i] and his soul was not impatient, and he was not slow to act; for he was faithful and a lover of the Lord.

In Jub. xix. 8 the trials are referred to as being ten in number.

[a] Gen. xii. 1, 10.

[b] The sacrifice of Isaac and the casting out of Ishmael (Gen. xxi. 10 ff.).

[c] Sarah being taken by Pharaoh and the casting out of Hagar.

[d] Ur.   [e] On Ps. xviii. 31.

[f] When she was taken by Pharaoh and by Abimelech.

[g] Gen. xiv.

[h] Gen. xiv. 17–24.   [i] Gen. xv. 6.

It was often argued that the trials of Abraham prefigured the trials of his descendants or, as Ber.R. xl. 6 put it succinctly: 'You will find that whatever is written in scripture about Abraham is written also about his descendants.' Tanḥ.B. i. 70 put it slightly differently: 'R. Joshua Siknini said in the name of R. Levi, "The Holy One, blessed be he, gave a sign to Abraham that whatever happened to him would happen to his descendants". '[a] Compare also Yalqut on Gen. §69; the same argument is also to be found in Syr. Comm. (Levene, p. 87). On the importance of this basic method of typology, see the Introduction, p. 92. For an example of it in the case of Abraham, see Mek. on Exod. xiii. 21, which bases its exegesis on Gen. xviii.

2 The identification of Mount Moriah with the site of Solomon's temple was made as early as II Chron. iii. 1: *Then Solomon began to build the house of the Lord at Jerusalem in mount Moriah . . .*, where I Kings vi. 1 has simply, *. . . he began to build the house of the Lord*. By an almost inevitable extension, other events were accumulated on the same spot, so that Kit alMaj., for example, suggests:[b]

When Isaac was twelve years old, Abraham offered him to God as an offering on the hill Banus: it is the place where the Messiah was crucified and which is known as Jaljala (Golgotha). There Adam was created; there Abraham saw the tree bearing the lamb by which Isaac was redeemed[c] from sacrifice; there the body of Adam was placed; there was the altar of Melchizedek; there David looked at the angel of God carrying a sword to destroy Jerusalem.

For a precise statement about the altar see Ps. Jon. on Gen. xxii. 9, and see also xxii. 13 f. and ii. 6. For further references in both Jewish and Christian writings, see Ginzberg, *Legends*, V, 253 (n. 253), but note that the identification already occurs in Josephus, *Ant.* i. 224, 226.

3 The identification of the unspecified *two young men* with Eliezer and Ishmael was frequently made. See, for example, Vay.R. xx. 2 and xxvi. 7.

B.Tam. 29*b* discusses the kinds of wood suitable for burning on the altar fire. Olive wood was usually excluded because it was twisted and knotted and would therefore take time to catch fire, and also because olives (and vines) were essential to the economy. See also Test. Lev. (Charles, Appendix II, pp. 23 f.).

P.R.E. 31 introduced a dialogue between Ishmael and Eliezer at this point.

---

[a] The section continues with examples.
[b] 123 *a–b*; cf. also The Cave of Treasures (Budge, p. 149).   [c] *Fadā*.

₄ This addition was made to answer the question how Abraham knew that it was the right place. See also the Targum on Isa. iv. 5.

₅ This interpretation was based on the word *koh* in Gen. xv. 5 ('so'), and in this verse ('*ad koh*, 'yonder'). He went to discover what *koh* in the promise could mean when his son was about to be taken from him. The same interpretation was recorded in Ber.R. lvi. 2: 'R. Joshua b. Levi said: "We will go and see what the result of *koh* is going to be." '

₈ The absence of punctuation (i.e. clause demarcation) in the Hebrew is of critical importance in this verse. It was taken by the Targums as, 'God will provide himself the lamb for a burnt offering: my son.' Therefore they went forward with a single intention because Isaac as well as Abraham knew that he was going to be slain. Rashi achieved the same sense, but by a slightly different means:

So they went both of them together: Abraham, who was fully aware that he was on his way to slay his son, was going with the same willingness and happiness as Isaac—who had no knowledge of the matter at all. *He will provide for himself the lamb:* that is to say, 'God will look out and choose for himself the lamb', and if there is no lamb, 'for a burnt offering will be my son'. Although Isaac then realised that he was making this journey to be slain, they both of them went on together with a common mind.

The suggestion that Isaac knew what was about to happen is at least as old as Josephus.[a] According to Josephus, as they stood before the altar, Abraham addressed Isaac, and in the course of his speech he said:

'. . . quit thou now this life not by the common road, but sped by thine own father on thy way to God, the Father of all, through the rites of sacrifice . . .' Isaac received these words with joy. He exclaimed that he deserved never to have been born at all, were he to reject the decision of God and of his father . . .; and with that he rushed to the altar and his doom.

The change effected by this interpretation is of extreme importance, because it implies the self-offering of Isaac. This is made even clearer in Ps. Philo, where Isaac responds willingly.[b] The '*Aqedah*, or 'binding', of Isaac for sacrifice came to possess an increasingly significant place in thought about the redemption and salvation of Israel. Before the fall of Jerusalem the offering of Isaac was usually seen as the supreme example of martyrdom, a willingness to put faith and trust in God before everything. There is less emphasis on Isaac having been a *sacrifice*. Thus in IV Macc. vii. 14, xiii. 1–17, xvi. 16–23, xviii. 11 Isaac was held up as an

---

[a] *Ant.* i. 228–32. [b] xviii. 5, xxxii. 1–4, xl. 2 (Appendix 1).

example of martyrdom, almost as a prototype of martyrs, but there is little emphasis on the sacrificial efficacy of his death.[a] The blood of the martyrs is spoken of in a general way in IV Macc. as having merit: it is a ransom and a propitiation (xvii. 21 f.). The offering of Isaac could be included in that (although in fact it is not specifically connected), since the whole of the story in Gen. xxii is in a sacrificial context. Similarly, the account in Jub. xvii. 15 ff. places the 'Aqedah at the time of Passover (perhaps implying typological exegesis, as in the notes on Gen. xxii. 1), but the sacrificial implications are not drawn out. The emphasis is on the testing of Abraham's faithfulness, as it is also in Ecclus. xliv. 20 and I Macc. ii. 52.

After the fall of Jerusalem, when the rabbis were searching for equivalents to the sacrifices that could no longer take place, the offering of Isaac was taken up and interpreted as having anticipated future sacrifices.[b] It was held to count for those sacrifices which could no longer be offered. This change in emphasis (brought about by the fall of Jerusalem) explains why those parts of the New Testament which were written before the fall of Jerusalem referred to the offering of Isaac, *not* as a prototype of the Crucifixion (and sacrificial death) of Christ, but as an example of faith (Heb. xi. 17 ff., Jas. ii. 21). Attempts to find the offering of Isaac (with a sacrificial emphasis) in Paul are probably reading into the text rather than out of it.

There is a discussion of the binding of Isaac and its importance in Jewish and Christian thought in G. Vermes, *Scripture and Tradition . . .*, ch. viii, but Vermes made no reference to the possible difference made by the fall of Jerusalem and the cessation of sacrifice. A more detailed survey has been made by R. le Déaut, *La Nuit Pascale*, and he is far more balanced and cautious in his conclusions (see especially pp. 202–8, 'Conclusions pour le N.T.', and pp. 374–6). But here again, not enough

---

[a] Isaac is one example among many. Similarly in Wisdom x. 5 there is no emphasis on the sacrificial efficacy of Isaac's offering. Cf. also the straightforward account in Jub. xvii. 16–xviii. 19. Josephus, as is to be expected, reveals a half-way position (*Ant.* i. 233 f.). The nearest anticipation is in Philo, *de Abr.* xxxii–xxxv, particularly xxxiii. 177 and xxxv. 198; but the development of Philo's argument was much affected by his concern to refute the errors of child-sacrifice, and to find a more worthy motive for Abraham's action. Philo's own explanation follows in xxxvi. Elsewhere (*de Sacr.* xxxiii. 110) Philo referred to the 'Aqedah as a 'paradigm' ($\pi\alpha\rho\acute{\alpha}\delta\epsilon\iota\gamma\mu\alpha$) of certain sacrifices.

[b] A good example of this complete change in emphasis is to be found in Ps. Philo (Appendix 1). See also Ps. Jon. on Gen. xxii. 13–14.

consideration has been given to the possibility that Gen. xxii might have meant different things to different people, or that the fall of Jerusalem might have had an important effect on the way in which the 'Aqedah was used. Thus le Déaut concluded: 'Si la théologie juive de l'Aqeda est *pleinement développée* dans les écrits plus tardifs seulement, tous les éléments essentiels de cette théologie sont présents dans des écrits vierges de toute influence chrétienne et, pour la plupart, d'origine *palestinienne.*'[a] The mistake is to assume that the presence of sacrificial language automatically involves a conscious sacrificial theology. There is no doubt about the sacrificial setting of Gen. xxii, since it is already present in the original narrative. This means that any treatment of Gen. xxii is bound to use sacrificial language. But it is by no means certain that all exegetes of the chapter drew out of it specifically sacrificial implications; there were other, equally important, lessons to be derived. It would be fairer to say that since the chapter contains sacrificial elements, it was always open to an interpretation emphasising those elements; it is not that the interpretation *could* not have happened before the fall of Jerusalem, but that the fall of Jerusalem explains why it happened as it did in rabbinic Judaism. It is entirely possible that the sacrificial emphasis might have been developed in an earlier period, perhaps in areas far removed from the Temple, and it may be that the Targums rest on those early traditions. But the evidence to establish this needs to be handled with great care and discrimination.

On the 'Aqedah elsewhere in the Targums on the Pentateuch, see the Targums on Exod. xii. 42, Lev. xxii. 27.

9 See the Targum and notes on Gen. viii. 20, xxii. 2.

10 On the self-offering of Isaac, see the Targum and notes on Gen. xxii. 8. The speech of Isaac reflects a halakic[b] concern that his binding should conform to ritual requirements. For details, see R. le Déaut, *La Nuit Pascale*, p. 160.

The term *yeḥidim*, 'unique ones' (i.e. distinguished people) became technical in rabbinic terms. For a discussion of the status of the *yaḥid*, see B.Taan. 10*a*, *b*.

13 See the notes on Gen. ii. 2. 'The one ram'[c] replaces the preposition *'aḥar* (R.V. 'behind him'), and Ps. Jon. may therefore have read *'eḥad*. This reading is also found in LXX, Pesh., Sam. Pent. and T.O.

---

[a] *La Nuit Pascale*, p. 202 (italics le Déaut).
[b] On the meaning of *halakah* see pp. 43–8.   [c] *Ḥad.*

Rashi gives a convenient summary of Jewish thought on the efficacy of the binding of Isaac:

In the stead of his son: . . . At every sacrificial act which he performed on it, he prayed, saying: 'Let it be your will that this shall be as though it had been done with my son, as though my son were being slain, as though his blood were being sprinkled, as though he were being flayed, as though he were being burned and reduced to ashes.'

Compare also Rashi on Lev. xxvi. 42, and see J.Taan. ii. 4, Tanh.B. i. 115, Tanh. Vay. 23, Pes.K. xxiii. 9.

18 On 'merits' (*zekuth*), see the Targum and notes on Gen. xv. 6.

19 See the Targum and notes on Gen. ix. 27. The text of Genesis does not say that both Abraham *and* Isaac returned to the young men, so the Targum has suggested where Isaac was. See also Ps. Jon. and F.T. (Gins. p. 14, see also p. 78) on Gen. xxiv. 63.

20 The text of Genesis does not record that Abraham and Sarah ever met again after the offering of Isaac. In fact xxii. 9 says that Abraham was at Beer-sheba, xxiii. 2 says that Sarah died at Kiriath-arba, and xxiii. 2 then says, *Abraham 'came' to mourn for Sarah*. Ps. Jon. simply connected the two chapters more closely together. A less exaggerated story was repeated by Rashi:[a] 'The account of Sarah's death follows the binding of Isaac, because as a result of the news of the binding, that her son had been made ready for sacrifice and almost had been sacrificed, her soul gasped out of her (with shock) and she died.'

A fuller story was recorded in P.R.E. 32, where Sammael is enraged because his attempt to destroy Abraham's faith has been frustrated. See also Yalqut on Gen. §§98 and 99.

[a] On Gen. xxiii. 3.

GENESIS XXVI. 5

5 '... *because that Abraham obeyed* my word, *and kept* my word, *my commandments, my statutes, and my laws.*'

Notes on Genesis xxvi. 5

This verse formed a basis for the belief that Abraham kept the Law before the time of its revelation to Moses. Midr. Teh. on Ps. i. 13 recorded:

R. Samuel b. Naḥman said: 'Abraham's father did not instruct him and he had no teacher to instruct him, so from whom did he learn Torah?' He gave the answer of R. Simeon b. Joḥai: 'The Holy One, blessed be he, gave Abraham kidneys[a] like to overflowing containers filling him with wisdom and understanding throughout the night, as it is written, *Yea, my reins instruct me in the night season.*[b]

The belief arose at an early date because of the problem posed by the fact that Abraham was manifestly '*the friend of God*'[c] but Torah had not yet been revealed. How was he able to please God without observing the specific requirements of Torah? As early as Jubilees the theory was proposed that all the patriarchs observed Torah so far as God made it known to them.[d] It is said specifically of Abraham in xvi. 21, xxii. 1–4, xxxvi. 20; and in xxi. 1 ff. Abraham instructs Isaac in various laws. (In Test. Levi ix. 6 ff. the same instructions are attributed to Isaac.) The view that Abraham kept the Law before its time was stated by Philo commenting on Gen. xxvi. 5:

He did them, not taught by written words, but unwritten nature gave him the zeal to follow where wholesome and untainted impulse led him. And when they have God's promises before them what should men do but trust in them most firmly? Such was the life of the first, the founder of the nation, one who obeyed the Law, some will say, but rather, as our discourse has shown, himself a Law and an unwritten statute.[e]

---

[a] The kidneys were regarded as the seat or place of conscience.
[b] Ps. xvi. 7. The same appears in A.R.N. 37, Yalqut on Ps. xvi. 7.
[c] Isa. xli. 8, II Chron. xx. 7.
[d] Jub. xxxiii. 16; Charles' comment *ad loc.*, connecting the verse with Paul, does not represent the intention of the verse.
[e] *de Abr.* xlvi. 275 f.; cf. also *de Post. Cain.* li. 174.

Whether Ecclus. xliv. 20 implies the same view is difficult to say. It may simply have picked up Gen. xxvi. 5 without meaning anything very specific by it. The Hebrew text argues against it, reading, '... who kept the commandments (*miẓwoth*) of 'Elyon'. But it is at least significant that in a brief comment it isolated this particular aspect.

The belief was often expressed, but there was some doubt about how much of Torah Abraham observed. A minority view held that he kept only the seven Noachian precepts,[a] but the usual view was that he kept the whole of Torah because of his faithful relationship with God. Among many examples see M.Qid. iv. 14,[b] Ber.R. xlix. 2, lxiv. 3, xcv. 3, Tanḥ.B. i. 58, 71, 211, Tanḥ. Lek 1 f. B.Yom. 28*b*, B.A.Z. 3*a*, Yalqut on Prov. §932. Paul's discussion of Abraham and of law (both natural and revealed) is much illuminated in the context of these beliefs and the debate about them.

[a] The seven Noachian precepts according to the list in B.San. 56*a* are: social justice (usually taken to mean 'courts of law'), refraining from blasphemy, from idolatry, from adultery (or incest), from bloodshed, from robbery, and from eating flesh cut from a living animal. The precepts represent in Judaism a kind of 'natural law', binding on all men. For references to the Noachian precepts, see Ginzberg, *Legends*, v, 92 f.

[b] Emphatically: 'We find that Abraham our father observed the whole of Torah, all of it, while it was not yet given.'

GENESIS XXXVII

1 *And Jacob dwelt* in confidence *in the land of his father's sojournings in the land of Canaan.*

2 *These are the generations of Jacob. Joseph, being seventeen years old,* had come from the house of instruction, *and he was a lad* brought up *with the sons of Bilhah, and with the sons of Zilpah, his father's wives: and Joseph brought the evil report of them* that he had seen them eating flesh torn from living animals, the ears and the tails, and he came and told *their father.*

3 *Now Israel loved Joseph more than all his children, because* the appearance of Joseph was like his own appearance: *and he made him* an embroidered garment.[a]

(4–12 These verses follow the Hebrew.)

13 And at the appointed time of days *Israel said unto Joseph, 'Do not thy brethren feed the flock in Shechem?'* I am afraid lest the Hivites come and smite them because they smote Hamor and Shechem[b] and the inhabitants of the town. *Come, and I will send thee unto them.' And he said to him, 'Here am I'.*

14 *And he said to him, 'Go now, see whether it be well with thy brethren, and well with the flock; and bring me word again'. So he sent him* because of the profound advice spoken to Abraham in *Hebron,* and on that day began the captivity of Egypt. And Joseph arose, *and he came to Shechem.*

15 And Gabriel in the likeness of *a man found him, and behold he was wandering in the field: and the man asked him, saying, 'What seekest thou?'*

16 *And he said,'I seek my brethren: tell me, I pray thee, where they are feeding the flock'.*

17 *And the man said, 'They are departed hence: for I heard* from behind the veil[c] that, behold, from this day will begin the servitude in Egypt. And it was said to them in prophecy that the Hivites were seeking to draw

---

a *Pargod. Pargod* is a word particularly used of the curtain or veil in heaven: see, for example, B.Ḥag. 15 a, B.B.M. 49 a. T.O. has 'a tunic (*kituna,* as LXX) of stripes' or 'reaching to the hands and ankles', as Aq. Vulg. has 'of many threads', Sam. Pent. 'many coloured', Pesh. 'with long sleeves'.

b Gen. xxxiv.   c *Pargoda.*

up their battle order against them, therefore they said, *Let us go to Dothan.' And Joseph went after his brethren, and found them in Dothan.*

18 *And they saw him afar off, and before he came near unto them, they conspired against him to slay him.*

19 *And* Simeon and Levi, who were brothers[a] in conspiracy,[b] *said one to another, 'Behold this master of dreams[c] cometh.*

20 *Come now therefore, and let us slay him, and cast him into one of the pits, and we will say, An evil beast hath devoured him: and we shall see what will* be the interpretation *of his dreams.'*

21 *And Reuben heard it, and delivered him out of their hand; and said, 'Let us not* kill him that we may not become guilty of his blood'.[d]

22 *And Reuben said unto them, 'Shed no* innocent[e] *blood; cast him into this pit that is in the wilderness, but* the hand of murderers do not lay *upon him':* that he might deliver him out of their hand, to restore him to his father.*

23 *And it came to pass, when Joseph was come unto his brethren, that they stripped Joseph of his* embroidered garment, the figured[f] garment *that was on him;*

24 *and they took him, and cast him into the pit: and the pit was empty, there was no water in it,* but there were snakes and scorpions in it.

25 *And they sat down to eat bread: and they lifted up their eyes and looked, and, behold, a travelling company of* Arabs[g] *came from Gilead, with their camels bearing* wax and balsam and resin and ladanum[h] *going to carry it down to Egypt.*

26 *And Judah said unto his brethren, 'What profit* of wealth[i] *is it to us if we slay our brother and conceal his blood?*

27 *Come, and let us sell him to the* Arabs, *and let not our hand be upon him to kill him, for he is our brother, our flesh.' And his brethren hearkened unto him.*

28 *And there passed by Midianites, merchantmen; and they drew and lifted up Joseph out of the pit, and sold Joseph to the* Arabs *for twenty* me'ah[j] *of silver,* and they bought sandals with them. *And they brought Joseph into Egypt.*

---

[a] I.e. 'partners'. [b] On the basis of Gen. xxxiv.
[c] R.V. marg. [d] So also C.G.
[e] *Zakkai*; C.G. has the same. [f] Or 'shaped'.
[g] T.O. also has 'Arabs'; F.T. (Gins. pp. 19, 79, 100) and C.G. have 'Sarqi' (Sarqain).
[h] Cf. R.V. marg. [i] *Mammon.*
[j] 'Six me'ah of silver equals one denar' (T.B.B. v. 12). See also C.G.

29 *And Reuben returned unto the pit,* because he had not been eating[a] with them when they sold him, since he was sitting and fasting because he had disturbed his father's bed.[b] And he had gone and sat down in the mountains, that he might return to the pit and bring him up for his father, to see if he might win favour for himself. But when he returned and saw, *behold Joseph was not in the pit; and he rent his clothes.*

30 *And he returned unto his brethren, and said, 'The child is not; and I, whither shall I go?* And how can we see the look on my father's face?'[c]

31 *And they took Joseph's* embroidered garment, *and killed* a kid of the goats because its blood is like the blood of a man, *and dipped* the embroidered garment *in the blood.*

32 *And they sent* by the hand of the sons of Zilpah and by the hand of the sons of Bilhah the embroidered garment, *and they brought it to their father; and said, 'This have we found: know now whether it be thy son's* embroidered garment *or not'.*

33 *And he knew it, and said, 'It is my son's* embroidered garment; a wild beast *hath* not *devoured him,* and he has not been killed by the hand of the sons of men, but I have seen by means of[d] the holy spirit that an evil woman[e] is standing before him'.

34 *And Jacob rent his garments, and put sackcloth upon his loins, and mourned for his son many days.*

35 *And all his sons and all* the wives of his sons[f] *rose up* and came *to comfort him; but he refused to be comforted; and he said, 'For I will go down to* the house of *the grave to my son mourning'. And* Isaac *his father wept for him* as well.

36 *And the Midianites sold him into Egypt unto Potiphar, an officer of Pharaoh's, the* chief of the executioners.[g]

---

a See Gen. xxxvii. 25 *a.*

b The incident referred to is that of Gen. xxxv. 22; note that Ps. Jon. on that verse (as also B.Shab. 55 *b*) made the offence of Reuben much smaller.

c So also C.G. and Test. Zeb. iv. 5.

d Or 'in'.

e I.e. the wife of Potiphar in Egypt; see further F.T. on this verse, and Ps. Jon. on Gen. xxxix.

f He only had one daughter, hence the change: see further Ber.R. lxxxiv. 21.

g T.O., 'chief of the killers'; LXX, 'chief of the cooks', as also Jub. xxxiv. 11.

Selections from other Targums on Genesis xxxvii

3 F.T. (Gins. pp. 19, 79, 100): A figured[a] embroidered garment.
C.G. on Gen. xxxvii. 31 has a form of *kituna*, but in verse 32 it has *pergoda*.

7,9 F.T. (Gins. pp. 19, 100) has a few words.

20 F.T. (Gins. p. 100) has one word.

21,22 C.G.: see p. 238 nn. d and e.

25 F.T. and C.G.: see p. 238 n. g.

30 C.G.: see p. 239 n. c.

31 C.G. has the verse without the addition.

32 F.T. (Gins. p. 100) has two words.

33 F.T. (Gins. p. 19; see also pp. 79, 100): 'A wild *beast hath* not *devoured him*, and my son has certainly not been slain, but I have seen by means of[b] the holy spirit that an evil woman stands before him, the wife of Potiphar, an officer of Pharaoh, the chief of the executioners.'
C.G.: 'My son Joseph has certainly not been slain and *an evil beast hath* not *devoured him*. But what is really the case is that an evil woman is standing before him, and she is like a wild beast. Truly I trust in the master[c] of the world, the Lord, that he will rescue him from the hands of the woman, and will show me the countenance of Joseph, my son, in safety while I am still alive.'

36 T.O.: see p. 239 n. g.

Notes on Genesis xxxvii

1 The context of this chapter is the list of the kings of Edom and of the descendants of Esau, the great enemies of the Jews. Jacob might, therefore, have dwelt in fear.

R. Ḥunia said: 'This is like a man who was walking in the road when he saw a pack of dogs and was afraid of them, so he sat down among them.[d] So also when our father Jacob saw Esau and his warriors, he was afraid of them, so he dwelt in their midst.' R. Levi said: 'This is like a blacksmith who had his forge on one side of the street, while his son, a goldsmith, had his workshop on the other. He saw a huge pile of rubbish[e] being brought into the town, which made him say, "How terrible! this pile of rubbish will

---

a See Ps. Jon. on Gen. xxxvii. 23. b Or 'in'.
c *Rabbon.* d In order to conceal his fear.
e Lit. 'thorns'.

ruin the town". But a certain bystander said, "Why fear this? One spark from your forge and another from your son's and you will burn it up." So also when our father Jacob saw Esau and his warriors and was afraid, the Holy One, blessed be he, said: "Why fear them? One spark from you and another from your sons, and you will burn them all up. For it is written, *And the house of Jacob shall be a fire, and the house of Joseph a flame, and the house of Esau for stubble, and they shall burn among them . . ."*[a][b]

2   The accusation against the sons of Bilhah and Zilpah (which involved the breaking of the commands to Noah, as in Ps. Jon. on Gen. ix. 4) was also recorded in P.R.E. 38. It was based on Gen. xxxvii. 31, where the verb used of the killing of the he-goat is one that was used of ritual slaughter. See Ber.R. lxxxiv. 5, J.Pes. i. 1, Tanh.B. i. 180, Tanh.Vayesh. 7.

   Joseph was early and commonly known as *haZaddiq*, the righteous one. See, for example, IV Macc. ii. 2, A.R.N. 16, Ber.R. xciii. 7.

3 The same argument is applied to Joseph as was applied to Isaac; see the Targum and notes on Gen. xxi. 2. T.O. has: '. . . because he was a wise son'. Both Targums were avoiding the plain statement of Genesis that Joseph was the son of Jacob's old age, because that description properly belongs to Benjamin. Hence P.R.E. 38 asks: 'Was Joseph in fact the son of his old age? Was not Benjamin the son of his old age? It was because Jacob saw through his prophetic gift that Joseph would be a ruler in the future that he loved him more than his brothers.'

   On Joseph's likeness to Jacob, see Test. Joseph xviii. 4; but contrast Jub. xxxi. 9.

14 Hebron was not, according to Num. xiii. 22, in a valley, therefore Jacob could not have sent Joseph *out of the vale of Hebron*. Rashi therefore commented:

Was not Hebron on a hill, as it is said *And they went up by the South, and came unto Hebron?* It was a result of the profound[c] counsel of the righteous one[d] who is buried in Hebron,[e] so that what was spoken to Abraham between the pieces might be established, *thy seed shall be a stranger . . .*[f]

Joseph's journey to his brothers was the beginning of the sequence of events leading to their bondage in Egypt.

[a] Obad. verse 18.   [b] Ber.R. lxxxiv. 5.
[c] I.e. 'deep'.   [d] *Zaddiq.*
[e] I.e. Abraham.   [f] Gen. xv. 13.

15 This was also the identification of Tanhuma[a] on the basis of Dan. ix. 21: *Yea, while I was speaking in prayer, the man Gabriel whom I had seen . . .* See also P.R.E. 38.

It is just possible that Philo knew of the identification of the unknown 'man' with an angel. In *Quod Det.* viii. 22–8 he says that the 'man' is the inner voice of conscience, which he calls in 24 ἔλεγχος. The word is used elsewhere by Philo to apply to various things and people, including the angel of God. Josephus did not mention the incident at all.

19 This was derived from Gen. xlix. 5–6. See also Ber.R. xcix. 7, Tanh.B. i. 183, Tanh. Vayesh. 9.

24 'According to R. Kahana, R. Nathan b. Minyomi said in the name of R. Tanhum: "Why is it written, *And the pit was empty, there was no water in it*? If it says the pit was empty can I not presume that there was no water in it? There was no water, but there were snakes and scorpions." '[b] C.G. does not have the addition.

Test. Zeb. ii. 7 f. also noticed the tautology: 'Meanwhile Reuben arose and said: "Come, my brethren, let us not slay him, but let us cast him into one of these dry pits, which our fathers digged and found no water. For this cause the Lord forbade that water should rise up in them, in order that Joseph should be preserved." '

25 On the spices see Mek. Vayehi. 6.

28 This was based on Amos ii. 6: 'They have sold the righteous for silver, and the needy for a pair of shoes.' It is stated specifically in P.R.E. 38, and it appears also in Test. Zeb. iii. 2.

33 Why did God not immediately tell Jacob that they were lying? The Targums suggested that Jacob in fact saw through their plot. Rashi commented:

> The holy spirit was stirred within him that at some time the wife of Potiphar would assail Joseph. And why did not the Holy One, blessed be he, reveal it to him?[c] Because they had invoked the ban[d] and cursed anyone who should reveal it, and they had included the Holy One, blessed be he, with them.[e] In fact Isaac knew that Joseph was alive, but he said, 'How can I reveal it when the Holy One, blessed be he, does not wish to reveal it to him?'

See also Test. Naph. vii. 2–4.

35 Isaac was thought still to be alive despite the statement in Gen. xxxv. 29, *And Isaac gave up the ghost.* This is because of the principle expressed

---

[a] Tanh.B. i. 183, Tanh. Vayesh. 7.   [b] B.Shab. 22 a.
[c] That Joseph was still alive.   [d] Herem.
[e] This is the interpretation of Tanhuma.

by, for example, Rashi,[a] 'There is no earlier or later in Torah', which means that events are not always told in strict sequence but are sometimes anticipated if an earlier mention seems more appropriate. Thus Rashi continued, 'The selling of Joseph preceded the death of Isaac by twelve years'. This conclusion was reached by adding up the total of years actually mentioned in Genesis in different places.[b] Since Isaac knew that Joseph was alive[c] the *him* in this verse must have been taken by Ps. Jon. to refer to Jacob: Isaac wept to see Jacob's grief. The same interpretation was recorded by Kit. alMaj. 127 a: 'And Joseph was sold in the lifetime of Isaac and he was a companion to Jacob in his sorrow.' See also Ber.R. lxxxiv. 22.

36 See Ps. Jon. on Gen. xxxix. 1.

[a] On Gen. xxxv. 29.
[b] For the way in which it was done see Rashi, *loc. cit.*
[c] See the notes on verse 33.

GENESIS XXXIX

1 *And Joseph was brought down to Egypt; and Potiphar* bought him (because he saw that he was handsome, that he might practise sodomy with him, and at once a decree was issued against him, and his testicles dried up, and he became impotent; and he was *an officer of Pharaoh's,* the chief of the executioners, *an Egyptian*) with pledges from the Arabs *which had brought him down thither.*

2 *And* the word[b] *of the Lord was* for Joseph's help, *and he was a prosperous man; and he was in the house of his master, the Egyptian.*

3 *And his master saw that* the word[c] *of the Lord was* for his help, *and that the Lord made all that he did to prosper in his hand.*

4 *And Joseph found* mercies *in his sight, and he ministered unto him: and he made him overseer over his house, and all that he had he put into his hand.*

5 *And it came to pass from the time that he made him overseer in his house, and over all that he had, that the Lord blessed the Egyptian's house* because of the merit[d] of Joseph; *and the blessing of the Lord was upon all that he had, in the house and in the field.*

6 *And he left all that he had in Joseph's hand; and he knew not aught that was with him, save* his wife with whom he lay. And Joseph was *comely in appearance and well favoured* in looks.

(7-9 These verses follow the Hebrew, except that verse 8 adds, '... refused to come near her', and verse 10 ends, 'before the Lord', instead of 'against God'.)

10 *And it came to pass, as she spake to Joseph day by day, that he hearkened not unto her, to lie by her, or to be with her,* lest he be condemned with her in the day of the great judgement of the world to come.

11 *And it came to pass* on this day *that he went into the house* to reckon up the accounts of his reckoning. *And there was none of the men of the house there within* the house.

12 *And she caught him by his garment, saying, 'Lie with me': and he left his garment in her hand, and fled* outside.

ª Chapter xxxviii, the story of Judah, is an intrusion in the Joseph narratives, and for that reason it has not been translated here.
b So also T.O. and C.G.
c So also T.O.   d So also C.G.

₁₃ *And it came to pass, when she saw that he had left his garment in her hand, and was fled* outside,

₁₄ *that she* scattered beaten-up white of egg on the bed and *called unto the men of her house, and spake (unto them saying), 'See* the spilling of seed which this man, whom your master brought *unto us,* put forth, *an Hebrew to mock us; he came in unto me to lie with me, and I cried with a* high *voice'.*

₁₉ These verses follow the Hebrew.)

₂₀ *And Joseph's master* took counsel from the idol-priests who had examined it, that it was white of egg, so he did not kill him, but *put him into the prison, the place where the king's prisoners were bound: and he was there in the prison.*

₂₁ *But* the word of *the Lord was* for Joseph's help, *and shewed kindness unto him, and gave him favour in the sight of the keeper of the prison.*

₂₂ *And the keeper of the prison committed to Joseph's hand all the prisoners that were in the prison; and whatsoever they did there, he was the* orderer *of it.*

₂₃ *The keeper of the prison* had no need to watch over Joseph according to the way of all prisoners, because he did not see any fault in his hands at all; for the word of *the Lord was* for his help, *and that which he did, the Lord made it to prosper.*

Selections from other Targums on Genesis xxxix

₁ F.T. (Gins. p. 101): Chief of the executioners.
T.O.: ... the chief of the killers ...
C.G.: ... the chief of the executioners ...

₄ F.T. (Gins. p. 101): *And he made him overseer over his house.*

₆ C.G. has the verse without the interpretation.

₁₀ F.T. (Gins. p. 20): To sleep *with her* in this world so as not to be joined with her in Gehinnom in the world to come.
C.G. ... and Joseph *hearkened not unto her* to sin *with her* in this world, becoming worthy not to be joined with her in Gehinnom in the world to come.

₁₃, ₁₈ F.T. (Gins. p. 101) has the same word as Ps. Jon. for 'fled'; on verse 18, see also Gins. p. 20.

₂₂ F.T. (Gins. p. 101) has a few words.

₂₃ T.O.: *The keeper of the prison* did not see any fault in his hands at all; since the word of *the Lord* was for his help, *and that which he did....*

Notes on Genesis xxxix

1 The accusation against Potiphar was derived from the word in the Hebrew *seris* (R.V. 'officer') which means 'castrate'. Ps. Jon. took it as 'eunuch', and supplied the reason why be became so. Ber.R. lxxxvi. 3 recorded the same interpretation; see also B.Sot. 13*b*, Tanḥ.B i. 185.

That Potiphar asked for pledges from the Arabs was derived from the statement that he was *an Egyptian*: that might have been taken for granted, since the verse has already said that Joseph had been taken to Egypt. Why was it mentioned specifically? It was in order to show that Potiphar shared the outstanding characteristic of the Egyptians, their cunning. For example, Shem.R. xxii. 1 says:

> Scripture compares the four kingdoms[a] to wild animals, as it says, *And four great beasts came up from the sea*;[b] but it compares Egypt to a fox, because a fox is smaller than the wild animals and Egypt is smaller than the other kingdoms, as it says, *It shall be the basest of the kingdoms.*[c] R. Eleazar b. Simon said: 'The Egyptians are compared to foxes because of their cunning... What did they say? They said, "*Come, let us deal wisely with them.*[d] Let us deal cunningly with Israel devising a bondage for them which God will not be able to punish measure for measure.[e] If we bring a sword against them God can bring one against us, if we bring fire against them God can bring fire against us. But we know that he has sworn never again to bring a flood on the earth,[f] so let us persecute them with water[g] which he cannot bring against us." The Holy One, blessed be he, said to them, "It may be that I have sworn not to bring another flood on the earth, but this I can do to you: I can submerge each of you in his own flood".'

Potiphar shared this characteristic of cunning, and Ber.R. lxxxvi. 3 makes it clear how the argument proceeded:

> 'He was a man of cunning. In what way? He said: "Usually a white man sells a dark man, but here dark-skinned men are selling a white man. Is he a slave?" He said, "Bring me a pledge".'[h]

6 '*Except the bread:* that is his wife, but it speaks here by means of euphemism.'[i]

10 This was an extension of a common understanding of the phrase, 'to be *with her* in the world to come'.[j]

---

[a] Who oppressed Israel.
[b] Dan. vii. 3.
[c] Ezek. xxix. 15.
[d] Exod. i. 10.
[e] Cf. Ps. Jon. on Gen. xxxviii. 26 (not translated).
[f] Gen. ix. 11.
[g] Exod. i. 22.
[h] In case it turns out that he was abducted.
[i] Rashi *ad loc.*
[j] So Rashi *ad loc.*, Ber.R. lxxxvii. 6 and Jub. xxxix. 6.

11 The phrase in the Hebrew, 'like this day', is unusual, and it was taken to be a part of a statement of Potiphar's wife, that there was no day like this day for putting her plans into action. It was therefore further concluded that it was the day of an Egyptian festival, and that since Joseph refused to participate in idolatry he was working on his own in the house.[a]

20 See Ps. Jon. on Gen. xlvii. 22.

[a] This is the interpretation in Ber.R. lxxxvii. 7 and Tanḥ. *ad loc.*, and in Josephus, *Ant.* ii. 45.

GENESIS XL

1 *And it came to pass after these things, that* it was shown, saying, The chief of the butlers of *the king of Egypt and* the chief of the bakers *offended* and plotted to put deadly poison in his food and in his drink to kill their *lord the king of Egypt.*

2 *And Pharaoh* when he heard *was wroth against his two officers, against the chief of the butlers, and against the chief of the bakers.*

(3-4 These verses follow the Hebrew.)

5 *And they dreamed a dream both of them, each man his dream, in one night, each man* his own dream and *the interpretation of his* companion's dream, *the butler and the baker of the king of Egypt, which were bound in the prison.*

6 *And Joseph came in unto them in the morning, and saw them, and, behold, they were sad.*

7 *And he asked Pharaoh's officers that were with him in ward in his master's house, saying, 'Wherefore look ye worse today* than all the days you have been here so far?'

8 *And they said unto him, 'We have dreamed a dream, and there is none that can interpret it'.* And *Joseph said unto them,* 'Is not the interpretation of dreams from before the Lord? *Tell it me, I pray you.'*

(9-11 These verses follow the Hebrew, with slightly fuller phrasing.)

12 *And Joseph said unto him, 'This is the interpretation of it: the three branches* are the three fathers of the world, Abraham, Isaac and Jacob, the children of whose sons are going to be brought into servitude in Egypt, and after that they will be rescued by the hands of three shepherds.[a] And as you said, "I took the grapes and pressed them for the cup of Pharaoh, and gave the cup into the hand of Pharaoh", it is the vial of wrath which Pharaoh is going to drink in the end. But you, chief of the butlers, will receive a good reward in accordance with your good dream which you have dreamed. And the interpretation of it for yourself is this: the three branches are the *three days* until your release.

[a] The three shepherds were derived from Zech. xi. 8: 'And I cut off the three shepherds in one month.' B.Taan. 9a comments: 'Did they all die in one month? Surely Miriam died in Nisan, Aaron in Ab, Moses in Adar? This is to show that the three gifts which were given because of their merit were cancelled and made to disappear in one month.' For the names, see Mic. vi.4.

13 At the end of *three days* the remembrance of you will come before *Pharaoh*, and he will *lift up thine head* in honour, *and restore thee unto thine office: and thou shalt give Pharaoh's cup into his hand, after the former manner when thou wast his butler.'*

14 Joseph forsook his trust in heaven, and he put his trust in a son of man[a] and said to the chief butler, '*But have me in thy remembrance when it shall be well with thee, and shew kindness, I pray thee, unto me, and make mention of me* before *Pharaoh, and bring me out of this house of* imprisonment:

15 *for indeed I was stolen away out of the land of the Hebrews: and here also have I done nothing* evil *that they should put me into* the house of imprisonment.'

16 *When the chief baker saw that the interpretation was good,* for he had seen the interpretation of his companion's dream,[b] he began to speak in an angry voice, and *he said unto Joseph, 'I also was in my dream, and, behold, three baskets of white bread were on my head:*

17 *and in the uppermost basket there was of all manner of* delicacies *for Pharaoh* made by the baker; *and the birds did eat them out of the basket upon my head.'*

18 *And Joseph answered and said, 'This is the interpretation thereof; the three baskets are* the three enslavements with which the house of Israel is going to be enslaved, and you, the chief baker, will receive an evil reward in accordance with your evil dream which you have dreamed.' Now Joseph had interpreted to him what was pleasant in his view, but now he said to him, 'This is its interpretation for you: *the three baskets are three days* to your death;

19 at the end of *three days shall Pharaoh* with a sword *lift up thy head from off* your body, *and shall hang thee on a tree; and the birds shall eat thy flesh from off thee'.*

20 *And it came to pass the third day, which was Pharaoh's birthday, that he made a feast unto all his servants: and he lifted up the head of the chief butler and the head of the chief baker among his servants.*

21 *And he restored the chief butler unto his butlership again,* because he discovered that he had not been in that plot; *and he gave the cup into Pharaoh's hand:*

22 *but he hanged the chief baker* because he had plotted to kill him: *as Joseph had interpreted to them.*

a *Bar nash.* b See Ps. Jon. on Gen. xl. 5.

23 And because Joseph had abandoned the faithfulness of heaven and had put his trust in the chief of the butlers, in a mortal man, he transgressed.[a] Therefore *did not the chief butler remember Joseph, but forgat him* until the appointed time came from before the Lord for him to be released.

Selections from other Targums on Genesis xl

1, 2 F.T. (Gins. p. 101) has two words in each verse.

10 F.T. (Gins. p. 101) has part of the verse.

12 F.T. (Gins. pp. 20 f.; compare also pp. 80, 101):

And Joseph said unto him, 'This is the interpretation of the dream: the *three branches* are the three fathers of the world, the children of whose sons are going to be brought into servitude in the land of Egypt "in mortar and in brick",[b] and they are going to be rescued by the hand of three faithful leaders, by the hand of Moses and Aaron and Miriam, who are like the clusters.[c] And as you pressed them into the cup of Pharaoh and set the cup in Pharaoh's hand, it is the vial of great wrath which Pharaoh is going to drink in the end.' He said further: 'You, chief of the butlers, will receive a good reward for your good dream that you dreamed.' But Joseph had not explained the interpretation of the dream (as it applied) to him, so afterwards he asked Joseph to explain how[d] he interpreted for himself; so he said to him: 'This is the interpretation of the dream: the three branches are the *three days.'*

16, 17 F.T. (Gins. pp. 80, 101) has a few words.

18 F.T. (Gins. p. 21; compare with this p. 80):

And Joseph answered and said, 'This is the interpretation of the dream: *the three baskets are* the three terrible enslavements with which Israel is going to be enslaved in the land of Egypt "in clay and in brick, and in all manner of service in the field".[e] And Pharaoh, the king of Egypt, is going to issue decrees against Israel, and throw their sons into the river,[f] but the end[g] of Pharaoh and his servants and his hosts is that they will be destroyed, and Israel will go forth with head uncovered. And you, chief of the bakers, will receive an evil reward, for this dream is an evil dream.' But the interpretation of the dream Joseph did not explain to him. And Joseph gave him the interpretation because he had not made it known to him. Afterwards Joseph told him and said, '*This is the interpretation . . .'*

23 F.T. (Gins. p. 21; see also p. 80): And Joseph abandoned the faithfulness above and the faithfulness below which had accompanied him from

---

[a] By putting confidence in human flesh and blood; it does not mean that the flesh is prone to sin, as F.T. might be taken to imply; see S. Zeitlin, *J.Q.R.* XLVIII (1957), p. 83.　　[b] Exod. i. 14.　　[c] Gen. xl. 10.
[d] Or 'what'.　　[e] Exod. i. 14　　[f] Exod. i. 22.
[g] *Sopha*, an anticipatory play of words on *Yam Suph.*

his father's house, and put his trust in the chief of the butlers. He put his trust in flesh which passes away, and in flesh which will taste the cup of death. He did not remember the scripture where it is written, '*Cursed is the man that trusteth in man, and maketh man his trust* . . . and *blessed is the man that trusteth* in the name of the word of the Lord, and the word of the Lord is his trust'.[a] Therefore *did not the chief butler remember Joseph* . . .

Notes on Genesis xl

₅ This translation was made necessary by verse 16: Joseph at that point has interpreted the butler's dream, but the baker sees that *the interpretation was good*. How could he know that the interpretation of the other dream was right if he had not already seen it in his own dream? This translates the Hebrew as, 'They dreamed the dream of both of them'. This is also the translation in xli. 11. See also Ber.R. lxxxviii. 4, B. Ber. 55 b.

₁₂ The double interpretation of these dreams was extremely common, though the ways in which they were applied to Israel's history varied greatly. There are summaries of various suggestions in Ber.R. lxxxviii. 5–6, and B.Ḥull. 92 a.

₁₄ This interpretation was extremely common, and it supplied a reason why Joseph was not released at the same time as the butler. See Ber.R. lxxxix. 2, 3, Tanḥ.B. i. 189, 190, Tanḥ. Vayesh. 9, Midr. Teh. on Ps. cv. 19. See also Ps. Jon. on xl. 23.

₁₆ The imputation of anger came from a double translation of the word '*aph*. It means 'also', but it can mean 'anger'. R. Ḥama observed further:

Four began with '*aph* (also) and were destroyed in '*aph* ('anger'). They were the serpent, the chief baker, the congregation of Korah, and Haman. The serpent, as in *Yea, hath God said . . . ?*;[b] the baker, as here; the congregation of Korah, as in, *Moreover thou hast not brought us into a land flowing with milk and honey . . .*;[c] Haman, as in, *Yea, Esther the queen . . .*[d].[e]

₂₃ In this interpretation a reason was given why Joseph stayed in prison a further two years. At the same time it may well have been added to give both warning and encouragement to Jews in situations of danger and persecution.

---

[a] Jer. xvii. 5, 7.
[b] Gen. iii. 1; Ps. Jon. has, 'Has the Lord God in truth said?'
[c] Num. xvi. 14. [d] Esther v. 12. [e] Ber.R. lxxxviii. 6.

1 *And it came to pass at the end of two full years, that* the remembrance of Joseph came before the word of the Lord, and *Pharaoh dreamed: and, behold, he stood by the river.*

(2-8 a These verses follow the Hebrew.)

8 b . . . *But there was none that could interpret them unto Pharaoh,* because it was brought about from before the Lord, since the time had arrived for Joseph to come out of the prison house.

9 *Then spake the chief butler before Pharaoh, saying, 'I do remember my faults this day:*

10 It was brought about from before the Lord that *Pharaoh was wroth with his servants, and put me in ward in the house of the captain of the guard, me and the chief baker:*

11 *and we dreamed a dream in one night, I and he;* we dreamed each man his dream and the interpretation of his companion's dream.'

(12-15 These verses follow the Hebrew.)

16 *And Joseph answered Pharaoh, saying, 'It is not* from *me:* it is not man that interprets dreams, but from before the Lord is given the peace of Pharaoh'.

(17-37 These verses follow the Hebrew, except that the beginning of verse 36 is made clearer: 'And provisions will be stored in a cave[a] in the ground, to be drawn on in *the seven years of famine . . .*')

38 *And Pharaoh said unto his servants, 'Can we find such a one as this, a man in whom* is the spirit of prophecy from before the Lord?'

39 *And Pharaoh said unto Joseph, 'Forasmuch as God hath shewed thee all this, there is none so discreet and wise as thou.*

40 *Thou shalt be* overseer *over my house, and according* to the decree of the *word* of your mouth *shall all my people* be nourished: *only in the* king's *throne will I be greater than thou.'*

41 *And Pharaoh said unto Joseph, 'See, I have set thee* as ruler *over all the land of Egypt.*

42 *And Pharaoh took off his signet ring from his hand, and put it upon Joseph's hand, and arrayed him in vestures of fine linen, and put a gold chain about his neck;*

---

[a] *Ma'arta,* used especially of a burial cave; see, for example, B.B.B. 58 a of the cave where Abraham was buried.

43 *And he made him to ride in the second chariot which he had; and they cried before him,* 'This is the father of the king, great in wisdom, tender in years':[a] *and he set him* as ruler *over all the land of Egypt.*

44 *And Pharaoh said unto Joseph,* 'I am Pharaoh the king, and you are second ruler,[b] *and without* your word *shall no man lift up his hand* to take up arms, *or his foot* to mount a horse *in all the land of Egypt*'.

45 *And Pharaoh called Joseph's name,* The man who reveals hidden things.[c] *And he gave him to wife Asenath,* whom Dinah had borne to Shechem and whom the wife *of Poti-phera,* the ruler of Tanis, had brought up. *And Joseph went out* as officer in charge *over the land of Egypt.*

46 *And Joseph was thirty years old when he stood before Pharaoh king of Egypt. And Joseph went out from the presence of Pharaoh and went* as ruler and officer in charge *throughout all the land of Egypt.*

47 *And in the seven plenteous years the earth brought forth* so that every ear of corn made two *handfuls* until all the stores were filled.

(48-51 These verses follow the Hebrew, except that verse 50 again changes the description of Asenath: '... *Asenath,* who had been brought up in the house *of Poti-phera,* ruler of Tanis ...')

52 *And the name of the second called he Ephraim: for* he said: 'The Lord has established me *in the land of my affliction,* just as he is going to establish the house of my father here in their affliction.'

(53-7 These verses follow the Hebrew, though verse 55 emphasises the severity of the famine by adding that the seed-corn itself was barren.)

Selections from other Targums on Genesis xli

1 F.T. (Gins. pp. 80, 101) has a few words.

2 F.T. (Gins. p. 101) has part of the verse.

8, 10 C.G. has these verses without the interpretations.

16 T.O.: ...'*It is not* from my wisdom but from before the Lord that is given the peace of Pharaoh.'
C.G.: ... '*It is not* from *me*: the word of the Lord will answer the peace of Pharaoh.'

23 F.T. (Gins. p. 101) has two words.

34 F.T. (Gins. pp. 80, 101) has a few words.

---

[a] See also F.T. on Gen. xlix. 22.   [b] Lit. *alqaphta*: see Jastrow 73 *b*.
[c] Josephus, 'Discoverer of Secrets' (*Ant.* ii. 91); so also Pesh., T.O. and Arab. Vers.

38 T.O.: *And Pharaoh said unto his servants, 'Can we find such a one as this, a man in whom* is the spirit of prophecy from before the Lord?'

40 T.O.: '. . . *and according unto thy word shall all my people* be nourished . . .'

43 F.T. (Gins. p. 21; see also p. 101): *And they cried before him,* saying, 'This is the father of the king, great in wisdom, tender in years'.

T.O.: . . . 'This is the father of the king.'

45 F.T. (Gins. pp. 21, 101): The ruler of Tanis.

T.O.: . . . *the daughter of Potiphera the ruler*[a] *of On* . . . .

Notes on Genesis xli

11 See Ps. Jon. on Gen. xl. 5.

43 The word in the Hebrew is *abrek* (R.V. *Bow the knee*; marg. 'Abrech, probably an Egyptian word, similar in sound to the Hebrew word meaning "to kneel" '). There were several attempts to explain it, of which Rashi summarised three:

Abrek: according to the Targum,[b] This is the father[c] of the king; Rek in Latin[d] means 'king'[e] . . . In the words of Haggadah R. Judah explained it: 'Abrek is Joseph who was a father[f] in wisdom and tender[g] in years.'[h] R. Jose, son of a Damascus woman, said to him, 'How long will you distort the scripture for us? Abrek is nothing but the word "knees",[i] because all who came and went were under his hand, exactly as it is said, *And he set him over all the land of Egypt.*'[j]

Jubilees[k] has: 'A herald proclaimed before him, God, God, the mighty one of God.' LXX also has, 'A herald proclaimed before him', but omits any word proclaimed. Pesh. has, 'and proclaimed before him, Father and prince, and he set him over all the land of Egypt'.

45 There were many interpretations of the name, of which Ber.R. xc. 4 recorded some typical examples:

R. Johanan said: 'The name means that he reveals hidden things[l] easily.' Hezekiah said: 'He reveals hidden things with his understanding, and

---

a So also in verse 50.
b I.e. Onqelos.   c *Ab.*
d Accepting *romi* as the intended reading in Rashi.
e *Rex*; see also B.B.B. 4*a*.   f *Ab.*
g *Rek.*
h This interpretation was recorded in Sifre.   i *Birkayim.*
j Gen. xli. 43*b*.
k xl. 7.   l *Zefuroth.*

brings peace to troubled hearts.' Our rabbis said: 'It is "foreseer",[a] "re-deemer",[b] "prophet",[c] "supporter",[d] "interpreter",[e] "wise",[f] "dis-criminating",[g] "seer".[h] R. Aḥa said: 'It means, " You have come to reveal the woman that was hidden here".'

The last suggestion is a reference to the story that Dinah, having borne a son to Shechem, was driven out by Jacob. She had a mark of identification as did Hagar when she was driven out by Abraham.[i] It meant, of course, that Joseph did not marry a non-Jew.[j] P.R.E. 38 says:

What did Jacob do? He wrote the name on a gold disc and hung it round her neck and sent her away. She went, but everything is revealed before the Holy One, blessed be he, so Michael went down and took her and led her into Egypt to the house of Poti-phera, because she was appointed to become the wife of Joseph. Poti-phera's wife was barren, so Asenath grew up with her as a daughter, and when Joseph came down into Egypt he married her.

Compare also Yalqut on Gen. §146. In Test. Jos. xviii. 3, On was identified as Heliopolis.

[a] *Zopheh*; the interpretation is by *notariqon*; see p. 318.
[b] *Podeh.* [c] *Nabi.* [d] *Tomek.*
[e] *Pother.* [f] *'Arum.* [g] *Nabon.*
[h] *Ḥozeh.*
[i] See Ps. Jon. on Gen. xxi. 14.
[j] Contrast Jub. xl. 10: '. . . the daughter of Potiphar, the daughter of the priest of Heliopolis'.

GENESIS XLII

1 *Now Jacob saw that* provisions could be bought, and *corn* brought down from *Egypt, and Jacob said unto his sons,* '*Why* are you afraid to go down to Egypt?'

(2-3 These verses follow the Hebrew.)

4 *But Benjamin, Joseph's brother, Jacob sent not with his brethren; for he said,* 'Behold, he is young, and I fear lest death *befall him.*

5 *And the sons of Israel came* each one by one gate, lest the evil eye should have power over them, since they went together to buy among the Canaanites who went to buy, *for the famine was in the land of Canaan.*

6 *And Joseph was the governor over the land,* and he knew that his brothers had come to buy, because he had put overseers in the gates of the city to record, of everyone who came there that day, his name and his father's name. *He it was that sold* corn *to all the people of the land: and Joseph's brethren came,* and they searched in the camps and open places and brothels, but they did not find him, and they went to his house, *and bowed down themselves to him with their faces to the earth.*

7 *And Joseph saw his brethren, and he knew them, but made himself* in their eyes as a stranger, *and spake roughly with them; and he said unto them,* '*Whence come ye?' And they said, 'From the land of Canaan to buy food*'.

8 *And Joseph knew his brethren,* because when he parted from them they had the mark of their beards, *but they knew not him,* because he had not had the mark of a beard, but at this time he did have.

9 *And Joseph remembered the dreams which he dreamed of them, and said unto them,* '*Ye are spies; to see the nakedness* of the prostitutes[a] *of the land ye are come*'.

(10-13*a* These verses follow the Hebrew.)

13*b* '. . . *and one* went out from us, and we do not know what happened to him in the end.'[b]

(14-22 These verses follow the Hebrew.)

23 *And they knew not that Joseph understood* the language of the Temple, because Manasseh was acting as *an interpreter between them.*

[a] So also in verse 12.
[b] Or 'in his end', so also in verse 32.

24 *And he turned himself about from them, and wept; and he returned to them, and spake to them, and took Simeon from among them,* because he had advised them to kill him, *and bound him before their eyes.*

25 *Then Joseph commanded his servants to fill*[a] *their vessels with corn, and to restore every man's money into his sack, and to give them provision for the way: and thus it was done unto them.*

26 *And they laded their asses with corn, and departed thence.*

27 *And* Levi, who had been left on his own without Simeon his close companion, *opened his sack to give his ass provender in the lodging place, and he espied his money; and, behold, it was in the mouth of his sack.*

28 *And he said unto his brethren, 'My money is restored; and, lo, it is even in my sack': and their heart failed them, and they turned trembling one to another, saying, 'What is this that* the Lord *hath done unto us,* not corresponding with our sin?'

29-35a These verses follow the Hebrew.)

35b *... they were afraid,* because of Simeon who had been left there.

36 *And Jacob their father said unto them, 'Me have ye bereaved of* Joseph— you said, An evil beast has devoured him—and Simeon—you said, The king of the land has bound him; *and ye will*[b] *take Benjamin away,* and it rests on me to raise up *all* the twelve tribes'.

37 *And Reuben spake unto his father, saying, 'Slay my two sons* with a curse, *if I bring him not to thee: deliver him into my hand, and I will bring him to thee again'.*

38 *And he said, 'My son shall not go down with you; for his brother is dead, and he only is left* of his mother; *and if* death *befall him by the way in the which ye go, then shall ye bring down my gray hairs with sorrow to the* house of the *grave'.*

Selections from other Targums on Genesis xlii

1 F.T. (Gins. p. 22): *Now Jacob saw* by means of[c] the holy spirit *that there was* provision of[d] *corn in Egypt, and Jacob said unto his sons, 'Why should you show yourselves satisfied among the starving?'*

4, 8, 9 F.T. (Gins. p. 101) has a few words from each of these verses.

13 F.T. (Gins. p. 22): And we do not know what happened to him in the end.[e]

---

[a] Ginsburger, 'and they filled'.   [b] I.e. 'seek'.

[c] Or 'in'.   [d] So also T.O.   [e] Or 'in his end'.

21 F.T. (Gins. p. 101) has a few words.

23 F.T. (Gins. p. 22; see also p. 80) has the same interpretation with slightly different wording.

35 F.T. (Gins. p. 101) has one word.

36 F.T. (Gins. p. 22; see also p. 80): *And Jacob their father said unto them,* 'Me have ye bereaved of Joseph; since the time I sent him to you to Dothan I have not known what happened to him in the end. You said of him, A wild beast has devoured him; and Simeon, in the hour that I sent Reuben to Egypt I have not known what happened to him in the end. You said, The ruler of the land imprisoned him; *and ye will take Benjamin away,* so that to my credit[a] twelve tribes will not be reckoned.'

38 F.T. (Gins. p. 101) has one word.

Notes on Genesis xlii

1 The Hebrew says, *Why do ye look one upon another?* It was usually taken to mean that they were looking at each other in alarm, since the word for 'look' suggested the word for 'fear': so Sam. Pent., Pesh. and Vulg. LXX took it as meaning that they hesitated because they were lazy. In Ber.R. xci. 2 it was taken to mean, 'Do not make yourselves conspicuous': 'Jacob said to them, "Do not go out with a piece of bread in your hands, do not crowd through a single gate for fear of the (evil) eye".'[b]

For the interpretation of F.T. see B.Taan. 10*b*.

5 See Ber.R. xci. 2, quoted in the notes on xlii. 1; and see also Tanḥ.B. i. 193–5, Tanḥ. Miq. 8, Yalqut on Gen. §148, Midr. haGad. i. 635.

5 This interpreted the phrase 'Joseph's brethren' to mean that they retained their brotherly affection, and were therefore hoping to find Joseph and redeem him. 'R. Benjamin b. Levi said: "*And Joseph's ten brethren;*[c] why does it specify ten?[d] To show that ten parts of their intention was love, one part was to buy corn." '[e]

For Joseph's decrees, by means of which he found out when his brothers arrived, see Ber.R. xci. 6, Qoh.R. ix. 15. 3, Tanḥ.B. i. 194, 202, Tanḥ. Miq. 8.

a Lit. 'against me'.
b See also Ber.R. xci. 6, with slight variants.   c Gen. xlii. 3.
d The number could have been inferred.   e Ber.R. xci. 2.

8 Josephus[a] also expanded the reason why Joseph was not recognisable, but simply said it was because Joseph had grown older. See also Ber.R. xci. 7, B.Yeb. 88 a.

23 Manasseh was Joseph's first-born son (Gen. xli. 51). The same identification was made by Ber.R. xci. 8.

24 Compare Tanh. Vayig. 4.

27 Simeon and Levi were specified because it was thought that Joseph would wish to separate them, in order to prevent them from plotting a second time together to kill him.[b]

38 'Harm' is identified with death in Mek. Nez. 8, but only as a possibility.

[a] *Ant.* ii. 97.   [b] See Rashi *ad loc.*

GENESIS XLIII

(1-13) These verses follow the Hebrew.)

14 '*And God Almighty give you mercy before the man, that he may release unto you your other brother and Benjamin. And* as for me, I have long ago been told by the holy spirit *that if I be bereaved of* Joseph I shall be *bereaved* of Simeon and Benjamin.'

15 *And the men took that present, and they took double money in their hand, and they took Benjamin; and rose up, and went down to Egypt, and stood before Joseph.*

16 *And when Joseph saw Benjamin with them, he said to* Manasseh, whom he had appointed overseer[a] *of his house, 'Bring the men into the house, and* open the slaughter house, and remove the sinew which shrank,[b] and prepare meat before them, *for the men shall dine with me at* the time of the *noon*-day meal'.

(17-31) These verses follow the Hebrew, except that verse 23 adds, *Peace be to you* from my Lord . . .; verse 25 adds, *For they heard* from him . . .)

32 *And they set on for him by himself, and for them by themselves, and for the Egyptians, which did eat with him, by themselves: because* it was not right for the Egyptians to *eat bread with* the Jews, because the animals which the Egyptians worship the Jews eat.

33 *And they sat before him, the first-born[c] according to his birthright, and the youngest according to his youth,* for he had taken the silver cup in his hand, and striking it to make it ring as though divining, he set the sons of Leah in order on one side, and the sons of Zilpah one one side, and the sons of Bilhah on one side, and Benjamin, the son of Rachel, he put beside himself, *and the men marvelled one with another.*

34 *And he took* portions from his table, and they set them forth *unto them from before him: but Benjamin's portion was five times so much as any of theirs,* one part being his own part, one part from Joseph, and one part from his wife, two parts from his two sons. *And they drank, and were merry with him,* since from the day they had been parted from him neither he nor they had drunk wine until that day.

[a] So also in Ps. Jon. on Gen. xliv. 1, 4.
[b] See Gen. xxxii. 32.   [c] Lit. 'the oldest'.

Selections from other Targums on Genesis xliii

8-11 F.T. (Gins. pp. 22, 80, 102) has various words from each of these verses.

14 F.T. (Gins. p. 22): 'And as for me, if I have not been *bereaved* of Joseph my son, so also I will not be *bereaved* of Simeon or of Benjamin.'
C.G.: 'And as for me, if I am not bereaved of Joseph my son, I will not be bereaved of Simeon or of Benjamin.'

16, 19, F.T. (Gins. pp. 22 and 102) has part of these verses.
30, 31

32 T.O.: ... *because* the Egyptians are not able *to eat bread with the Hebrews*, because the animals which the Egyptians worship the Hebrews eat.
C.G. has a slightly different form of the same.

Notes on Genesis xliii

14 The same interpretation will be found in Ber.R. xcii. 2.

16 See Ps. Jon. on Gen. xlii. 23, T.d.E. 131, B.Ḥull. 91 a, Tanḥ.B. i. 197, 202.

32 Polemic against Egyptian animal worship was common. For example the Sibylline Oracles[a] say, 'There is one God, who rules alone...self-begotten, the unseen seer of all things...You do not worship him, nor do you fear him: you wander in error worshipping snakes and sacrificing to cats and dumb idols and images of men carved in stone.'
Compare also Justin, *Apol.* i. 24. 2:

> We only are hated for the name of Christ; and when doing no ill, are put to death as criminals; whilst other men, in other places, worship trees and rivers, mice, cats, crocodiles, and almost all other irrational animals ... for the same animals are considered by some to be gods; by others, to be wild beasts; and by others still, to be sacrificial victims, as you well know.[b]

33 No reason is actually stated in the original narrative why the men should have marvelled. Ps. Jon. suggested that they marvelled because he apparently knew how to divide the family according to their mothers. The same explanation will be found in Ber.R. xcii. 5; see also Rashi (quoting Tanḥuma)[c] for a slightly different version.

34 The first addition answered the question why 'five' precisely was specified; the second covered the brothers against the accusation of excess.

[a] iii. 14. 30. [b] Trans. G. J. Davie, *Lib. of the Fathers.*
[c] Vayesh. 4.

GENESIS XLIV

(1-12 These verses follow the Hebrew (though see p. 260 n. a for verses 1 and 4.)

13 *Then they rent their clothes, and* mighty[a] strength was given to them, and they *laded every man his ass, and returned to the city.*

(14-15 These verses follow the Hebrew.)

16 *And Judah said, 'What shall we say unto my lord* concerning the former money, and *what shall we speak* concerning the second money? *or how shall we* be innocent[b] concerning the cup? From before the Lord *hath been found out the iniquity of thy servants; behold, we are my lord's bondmen, both we, and he also in whose hand the cup is found.'*

17 *And he said, 'God forbid that I should do so: the man in whose hand the cup is found, he shall be my bondman; but as for you, get you up in peace unto your father.'*

18 *Then Judah came near unto him, and said, 'Oh my lord, let thy servant, I pray thee, speak a word in my lord's ears, and let not thine anger burn against thy servant: for* at the hour when we came to you, you said to us: "I fear the Lord."[c] But now your judgements are made as the judgements of *Pharaoh.'*

(19-34 These verses follow the Hebrew, except that verse 21 adds, '... *set mine eyes upon him* for good'; and verse 29 is interpreted in the same way as xlii. 38.)

Selections from other Targums on Genesis xliv

5, 12, 15 F.T. (Gins. pp. 22, 80, 102) has a few words from these verses.

18 F.T. (Gins. p. 22; see also pp. 73, 80, 102):[d] '*For* from the first time when we came to you did you not say to us "I fear[e] the Lord"? But now your judgements are like the judgements of *Pharaoh* your master. But I

---

a Or 'miraculous'.

b From *zky*; so also C.G., which has only a small part of the interpretation.

c Lit. 'from before the Lord I fear'.

d There are important variants in this section, many of which are listed in Ginsburger, pp. 22, 73, 80.

e Lit. 'from before the Lord I fear'.

am a man of honour like you, and my father is a man of honour like Pharaoh your master of whom you say, By him I swear.[a] I can swear by the life of my father's head, just as you can swear by the life of the head of Pharaoh your master, that if I draw my sword from its sheath I will not return it to its sheath until we have filled all the land of Egypt with the dead, and until we have made all the land of Egypt empty of the sons of men, beginning with you and ending with Pharaoh your master. Has it not been told you, and has it not reached you, what my two brothers Simeon and Levi did in the town of Shechem, when they entered it while they were at peace, and killed every man in the place according to the law of war because of their defilement of Dinah our[b] sister?[c] How much more will it be because of Benjamin, included among us in the dividing of the land among the tribes, who received a portion and inheritance in the dividing of the land. And as for me, my strength is more adamant than both of theirs, since I vouched for the boy before my father, saying, "If I do not bring him to you and set him before you I will be guilty before you and banned from your greeting of peace for ever". Has it not been told you and has it not reached you that we are kings and rulers like you in the land of Canaan?' Now when Joseph saw that the temper of Judah his brother had risen, and that the hairs of his chest[d] came forth,[e] and that they tore his clothes, at that moment Joseph beckoned to Manasseh his first-born, and he stamped with his feet in the midst of the palace, and they trembled. Judah reckoned[f] in his heart and said, 'This strength is from my father's house'. He therefore began to be more moderate in his speech, and said, (19) '*My lord asked his servants...*'

C.G. also provides a variant form of this speech.

29, F.T. (Gins. pp. 80, 102) has some words in each of these verses.
34

a The reference is to Gen. xlii. 15, on which see Ber.R. xci. 7, Tanh.B. i. 203.

b Some MSS, 'their'.

c Cod. 75 adds: 'who has not been reckoned with us among the tribes and has not received a portion, nor shared with us in the dividing of the land'.

d Lit. 'heart'.

e 'R. Ḥanin said: "When Judah was filled with anger, the hairs from his chest would go right through his clothes and out the other side, and he would put bars of iron between his teeth, and grind them like powder." ' (Ber.R. xciii. 6.) Cf. also Midr. haGad. i. 664 f., Tanh. Vayig. 3.

f So Gins. text; but probably redivide: 'and it trembled. And Judah . . .'

Notes on Genesis xliv

13 Ber.R. xcii. 8 has: 'Each man took his own baggage in one hand and loaded it on his ass.' Both of these comments took literally the Hebrew, which is in the singular: *Each man loaded his ass.*

16 Each of the three questions in the Hebrew has been given a precise reference, as also in Ber.R. xcii. 9, Tanh.B. i. 198 ,Tanh. Miq. 10.

18 From the fact that Judah said to Joseph, 'Let not thine anger burn . . .',[a] it was inferred that Judah spoke in a way likely to provoke anger. What did he say, and in what sense did he state that Joseph was 'even as Pharaoh'? Ber.R. xciii. 6 recorded several suggestions, including those offered by F.T.:

Let thy servant, I pray thee, speak a word in my Lord's ears: He said, 'Let my words enter your ears, because . . . two of us went up to a great town and destroyed it. That was because of a woman,[b] this will be because of a man . . . *For thou art even as Pharaoh:* just as Pharaoh issues decrees but does not stick to them, so do you; just as Pharaoh lusts after men, so do you;[c] just as Pharaoh is a king and you are second to him in the land of Egypt, so my father is a king in Canaan and I am second to him; if I draw my sword I will start with you and finish with Pharaoh your master.'[d] If he had said, 'I will start with Pharaoh and finish with you', Joseph would have done nothing.[e] But since he said, 'I will start with you', he beckoned to Manasseh and he stamped on the floor and the palace trembled. Judah said, 'But this can only be from my father's house'. And when he saw how things were he began to speak more moderately.[f]

[a] Gen. xliv. 18.   [b] Dinah.

[c] I.e. he infers that that was the reason why Joseph wanted to keep Benjamin; so also Tanh.B. i. 205.

[d] This translates the phrase as, 'You and Pharaoh will be alike'.

[e] I.e. he might well have allowed Judah to kill the Egyptians and would then have revealed himself when he was about to become the final victim.

[f] For a detailed analysis of this verse in the Jewish tradition see G. Vermes, *Scripture and Tradition*, ch. i.

GENESIS XLV

1 *Then Joseph could not refrain himself* so as not to weep *before all them that stood by him; and he* said, *'Cause every man to go out from me'. And there stood no man with him, while Joseph made himself known unto his brethren.*

2-7 These verses follow the Hebrew, except that verse 4 adds, *'Come near to me, I pray you,* and see the place of my circumcision'; and verse 5 changes 'to preserve life' to 'to establish you'.)

8 *'So now it was not you that sent me hither, but* the event was brought about before the Lord, *and he hath made me a* lord^a *to Pharaoh, and lord of all his house, and ruler over all the land of Egypt.'*

9-13 These verses follow the Hebrew, except that verse 12 adds, '. . . *that speaketh unto you* in the language of the Temple'.)

14 *And he fell upon his brother Benjamin's neck, and wept* because the Temple was going to be built in the portion of Benjamin, and was going to be destroyed twice; *and Benjamin wept upon* Joseph's *neck* because he saw that the Tabernacle of Shiloh was going to be in the portion of Joseph, and was going to be destroyed.

15 *And he kissed all his brethren, and wept upon them* because he saw that they would be brought into servitude among the nations: *and after that his brethren talked with him.*

16-23 These verses follow the Hebrew, except that verse 19 adds that Joseph is to arrange things for his father's honour, and that the waggons are to be drawn by oxen; verse 23 adds *'ten asses laden* with wine and *with the good things of Egypt'.)

24 *So he sent his brethren away, and they departed: and he said unto them,* 'Do not dispute about my having been sold, lest those who pass *by the way* become angry at you'.

25 *And they went up out of Egypt, and came unto the land of Canaan unto Jacob their father.*

26 *And they told him, saying, 'Joseph is yet alive, and he is ruler over* all the land of Egypt'. *And his heart* was divided, *for he believed them not.*

27 *And they told him all the words of Joseph, which he had said unto them: and when he saw the waggons which Joseph had sent to carry him, the*

^a Probably a mistake for 'father'.

spirit of prophecy returned which had gone up from him at the time when Joseph was sold, and it rested over *Jacob their father.*

28 *And Israel said,* 'Many good things the Lord has done with me: he rescued me from the hands of Esau and from the hands of Laban and from the hands of the Canaanites who pursued after me; and many consolations have I seen and expect to see, but I never expected that *Joseph my son* would *yet be alive: I will go* now *and see him before I die'*.

Selections from other Targums on Genesis xlv

2, 8 F.T. (Gins. pp. 23, 102) has some words from these verses.

12 T.O.: '. . . that I am speaking with you in your language.'

16 F.T. (Gins. pp. 80, 102) has two words.

26 F.T. (Gins. p. 80): Was divided.

T.O.: . . . And these words were weak in *his heart.*

27 T.O.: . . . And the holy spirit rested on *Jacob their father.*

28 F.T. (Gins. p. 23; see also pp. 80, 102): 'Many good things and consolations I had expected to see, but I had not expected that Joseph would *yet be alive: I will go and see him before I die.'*

Notes on Genesis xlv

12 This verse (together with Exod. ii. 14, v. 3, Gen. xiv. 13) was taken by Mek. Pisḥa. 5 to prove that the patriarchs always spoke Hebrew.

14 The Hebrew word for 'neck' is plural in form; Ber.R. therefore asked:[a]
'Did Benjamin have two necks? R. Eleazar said: "Joseph saw by the holy spirit that two temples were going to be built in the part belonging to Benjamin and that they would both be destroyed." '

23 'Wine' is an explanatory gloss. Rashi commented:
'It says in the Talmud[b] that he sent him old wine, which old people like greatly. Midrash[c] interprets, "split beans".[d]'

24 No reason is given in the Hebrew why they should 'fall out' on their way. See also B.Taan. 10*b*.

27 A fuller version is given in P.R.E. 38:
When the brothers found Joseph alive they released themselves from their oath;[e] so Jacob heard that Joseph was alive and his soul and his spirit revived.

[a] xciii. 12; cf. also B.Meg. 16*b*.   [b] B.Meg. 16*b*.   [c] Ber.R. xciv. 2.
[d] They were thought to encourage sleep.
[e] Lit. 'ban'; they had sworn not to tell Jacob what had happened to Joseph.

Had his spirit died so that it needed to be revived? In fact the holy spirit had left him because of the oath, but when they released themselves from the oath the holy spirit rested on him as in the beginning.

See also Midr. Teh. on Ps. xxiv. 1,[a] Tanh. Vayesh. 2, A.R.N. 30.

28 The Hebrew simply says *rab*, 'enough' or 'much'. The Targums took the single word as an abbreviation.

[a] Midr. Teh. refers to T.O. W. G. Braude's note (*The Midrash on Psalms*, II, 460), to the effect that extant editions of the Targum do not support what Midr. Teh. says, is wrong.

1 *And Israel took his journey with all that he had, and came to Beer-sheba, and offered sacrifices unto the God of his father Isaac.*

2 *And God spake unto Israel in* a prophecy *of the night, and said, 'Jacob, Jacob'. And he said, 'Here am I'.*

3 *And he said, 'I am God, the God of thy father: fear not to go down into Egypt* on account of the servitude which I decreed with Abraham, *for I will there make of thee a great nation:*

4 *I am he who, in my word, will go down with thee into Egypt;* and I will see the affliction of your children, and my word will bring you in there, *and I will also* cause your descendants to come out from there, but *Joseph shall put his hand upon thine eyes'.*

(5-11 These verses follow the Hebrew, except that verse 10 added, '*Shaul,* who is Zimri, who acted like[a] the Canaanites in Shittim'.)

12 *And the sons of Judah; Er, and Onan, and Shelah, and Perez and Zerah: but Er and Onan died* because of their evil works *in the land of Canaan.* And Shelah and Zerah did not beget sons in the land of Canaan, *and the sons of Perez* who went down into Egypt *were Hezron and Hamul.*

13 *And the sons of Issachar,* wise and masters of reckoning, *Tola, and Puvah, and Iob and Shimron.*

14 *And the sons of Zebulun,* travelling traders and merchants, providing for their brothers, the sons of Issachar, and receiving a reward like theirs; and their names were *Sered, and Elon, and Jahleel.*

15-17a These verses follow the Hebrew.)

17b ... *and Serah their sister* who was taken while still alive to the garden of Eden, because she told Joab that Joseph was still alive. It was she who rescued the inhabitants of Abel from the sentence of death in the days of Jacob. *And the sons of Beriah* who went down into Egypt, *Heber, and Malchiel.*

(18-20 These verses follow the Hebrew, except that Asenath is interpreted as in Gen. xli. 45.)

21 *And the sons of Benjamin* were ten, and their names according to the wonderful deeds of Joseph his brother were: *Bela,* he was swallowed up from him; *Becher,* he was the first-born[b] of his mother; *Ashbel,* he

---

[a] Lit. 'worked the work of'.   [b] Or perhaps 'the beloved'.

went into captivity; *Gera*, he became a sojourner in a strange land; *Naaman*, he was gracious and honourable; *Ehi*, for he was his brother, the son of his mother; *Rosh*, he was head of his father's house; *Muppim*, he was sold in Muph; *Huppin*, at the time when he was separated from him he was eighteen years old and was ready for the marriage bed; *Ard*, he went down to Egypt.

22 *These are the sons of Rachel, which were born to Jacob: all the souls were fourteen.*

23 *And the sons of Dan*, industrious and traders, and there is no end to their number.

(24-6 These verses follow the Hebrew.)

27 *And the sons of Joseph, which were born to him in Egypt, were two souls;* Joseph, who was already in Egypt, and Jochebed, the daughter of Levi, who was born at the moment when they entered Egypt between the walls. The total of *all the souls of the house of Jacob, which came into Egypt, were threescore and ten.*

28 *And he sent Judah before him unto Joseph, to shew the way before him,* and to subdue the inhabitants of the land, and to prepare before him a dwelling house in *Goshen; and they came into the land of Goshen.*

29 *And Joseph made ready his chariot, and went up to meet Israel his father, to Goshen;* and before he recognised him, his father bowed down to him, and he was condemned to have his years shortened, and so it was. And he was seen by him, and he *fell on his neck, and wept on his neck a good while* because he had bowed down to him.

30 *And Israel said unto Joseph,* 'Even if I die at this moment I have been consoled, for with the death which the righteous die I shall die after I have seen the brightness[a] of your face, *because thou art yet alive*'.

(31-4 These verses follow the Hebrew.)

Selections from other Targums on Genesis xlvi

20 F.T. (Gins. p. 102): Ruler of Tanis.

28 F.T. (Gins. p. 23; see also p. 80): And to prepare for him a dwelling house in *Goshen*.

30 F.T. (Gins. p. 23) has a similar interpretation.

T.O.: . . . 'If I were to die at this moment I would be consoled, after I have seen your face, because *thou art yet alive.*'

a Or 'appearance'.

Notes on Genesis xlvi

3 This was based on Gen. xv. 13.

4 In Mek. Shir 4 it is stressed that God goes down and brings them up again. It was in the same way that P.R.E. 39 solved the problem of Gen. xlvi. 27 (*q.v.*): God himself made the number up to 70.

10 Shaul is identified with 'Zimri, the son of Salu', who was the offending Israelite in the story in Num. xxv. For the name, see Num. xxv. 14 and for a discussion of the whole chapter in Numbers, see B.San. 82 *a–b*.

12 The reference to 'their evil works' is to Gen. xxxviii. 7 ff.; the comment on Shelah and Zerah is an argument from silence.

13 See Ps. Jon. on Gen. xlix. 14.

17 The reference is to the story in II Sam. xx. 14 ff. On Serah bringing the news to Jacob, see Ps. Jon. on Num. xxvii. 46. But elsewhere Ps. Jon. recorded the view that Naphtali, the swift messenger, brought the news: see Ps. Jon. on Gen. xlix. 21.

21 The interpretations were derived from roots which were thought to underlie the names. The names and the interpretations correspond in Aramaic.

23 The word 'Hushim' means 'leaves'.

27 There is a discrepancy in the numbers in Genesis: 66 in verse 26, plus 2 in verse 27, makes 68; but verse 27 says the total was 70. Joseph, being already in Egypt, brought the number up to 69. Jochebed was supplied from Num. xxvi. 59: ... *Jochebed, the daughter of Levi, who was born to Levi in Egypt.* Hence Ber.R. xciv. 9 comments:

> R. Levi said in the name of R. Samuel b. Naḥman: 'Can a man give his friend 66, then 3, then call them 70? But the extra one is Jochebed, who brought the number up in Egypt ... Jochebed was conceived in Canaan but born in Egypt ... She was born at the gates of Egypt.'

LXX, by adding more descendants born in Egypt, raised the total to 75, hence Acts vii. 14; compare also Jub. xliv. 12–33, Jos. *Ant.* ii. 176–83.

29 Ps. Jon supplied a reason why Joseph should have wept so greatly: Joseph should not have accepted honour and obeisance from his father.

GENESIS XLVII

(1-6 These verses follow the Hebrew, except that in verse 2, the *five men* are specified as Zebulon, Dan, Naphtali, Gad and Asher.)

7 *And Joseph brought in Jacob his father, and set him before Pharaoh: and Jacob blessed Pharaoh* and said, 'May it be the will of God that the waters of the Nile overflow and that the famine leaves the world in your days'.

8 *And Pharaoh said unto Jacob, 'How many are the days of the years of thy life?'*

9 *And Jacob said unto Pharaoh, 'The days of the years of my pilgrimage are an hundred and thirty years: few and evil have been the days of the years of my life,* for when I was young I fled from before Esau my brother and stayed in a land which was not my own, and now in my old age I have come down to stay here, *and* my days *have not attained unto the days of the life of my fathers in the days of their pilgrimage*'.

10-20 These verses follow the Hebrew, except that in verse 11 Rameses is identified as Pilusin,[a] and verse 13 adds 'the inhabitants of' Egypt, and of Canaan.)

21 *And as for the people* of a town he moved them to a city, and the people of a city he moved to a town for the sake of Joseph's brothers: in order that they should not be called 'homeless', he caused the people to be moved from one end of Egypt to the other.

22 *Only the land of the priests bought he not* because they had considered him to be innocent[b] at the time when his master was wanting to kill him, and they had rescued him from the judgement of death: *for* a portion he had said should be given to them *from Pharaoh, and they did eat their portion which Pharaoh gave them; wherefore they sold not their land.*

(23-6 These verses follow the Hebrew.)

27 *And Israel dwelt in the land of Egypt* and they built for them houses of study and large houses *in the land of Goshen,* and they inherited there inheritances of fields and vineyards, *and were fruitful, and multiplied exceedingly.*

---

a As also in F.T. (Gins. p. 102); Arab. Vers. has Ain Shams, perhaps thinking of On, Heliopolis.　　b *Zekutha.*

28 *And Jacob lived in the land of Egypt seventeen years: so the days of Jacob, the years of his life, were an hundred forty and seven years.*

29 *And the time drew near that Israel must die: and he called his son Joseph, and said unto him, 'If now I have found grace in thy sight, put, I pray thee, thy hand* on the place of my circumcision, *and deal kindly and truly with me; bury me not, I pray thee, in Egypt:*

30 *but when I sleep with my fathers, thou shalt carry me out of Egypt, and bury me in their burying place'.* But because he was his son he did not put his hand (there), but *he said, 'I will do as thou hast said'.*

31 *And he said, 'Swear unto me': and he sware unto him.* And at once the glory of the Shekina of the Lord was revealed upon him. *And Israel bowed himself upon the bed's head.*

Selections from other Targums on Genesis xlvii

21 F.T. (Gins. pp. 80, 102): He enslaved them.[a]

24, 31 F.T. (Gins. pp. 80, 102) has a few words from these verses.

Notes on Genesis xlvii

2 The number 'five' in the Hebrew seemed to demand comment. The five singled out by Ps. Jon. were selected from those included in the blessing of Moses in Deut. xxxiii. 2–29. They needed the blessing because they were the weakest.[b] Rashi gave a different list:

Some of the weakest of them in strength, who did not look strong, because if Pharaoh saw that they were strong he would make them men of his army; and they were Reuben, Simeon, Levi, Issachar and Benjamin: it was these whose names Moses did not repeat when he blessed them, but the names of the strong ones he did repeat... That is the version of Bereshith Rabba, which is a haggadah of the land of Israel.[c] But in our Babylonian Talmud[d]

[a] So also LXX, Pesh., Vulg.

[b] For an argument as to why these were included in the blessing and not the others, see B.B.Q 92a; see also Ber. xcv. 4.

[c] I.e. a Palestinian midrash. The compilation of Ber.R. was traditionally ascribed to R. Hoshaiah, one of the Palestinian Amoraim of the third century (see p. 79). The formula was sometimes given (for example, by Menaḥen b. Solomon in his commentary on Genesis and Exodus, Sekel Tob) in the form, 'The men of the holy city said...'

[d] B.B.Q. 92a.

we find that those whose names Moses repeats were the weaker,[a] and he brought them before Pharaoh ... In the Boraita in Sifre on, *And this is the blessing*,[b] the interpretation is like the Talmud.

7 Rashi commented:

And Jacob blessed: after the manner of all who leave the presence of princes, blessing them and leaving them with the wish of Peace. And what was his actual blessing? That the Nile waters might rise to his feet, because Egypt does not drink[c] rain water, but the Nile rises and waters it. So when Jacob had blessed him, whenever Pharaoh came to the Nile the waters rose to meet him and watered the land.[d]

9 Ps. Jon. specified why his days had been 'few and evil'.

22 See Ps. Jon. on Gen. xxxix. 20. According to Philo, *de Jos.* x. 52, Joseph's innocence was proved by the fact that his garment was torn at the back, not the front.

27 These are all signs of permanency.

30 This is an argument from silence.

---

[a] I.e. they were repeated because they were weaker.
[b] Deut. xxxiii. 1.   [c] I.e. absorb.
[d] Quoted from Tanḥuma.

1 *And it came to pass after these things, that* it was said *to Joseph, 'Behold, thy father is* lying *sick': and he took with him his two sons, Manasseh and Ephraim.*

(2-6 These verses follow the Hebrew, except that in verse 3 *appeared* becomes 'was revealed', and verse 5 adds, *Ephraim and Manasseh . . .* are reckoned *as mine.*)

7 *'And as for me,* I beg of you to bury me with my fathers. *When I came from Padan, Rachel died* suddenly *by me in the land of Canaan in the way, when there was still* much ground before reaching *Ephrath,* and I was not able to take her to bury her in the double cave,[a] *and I buried her there in the way to Ephrath (the same is Beth-lehem).'*

8 *And Israel beheld Joseph's sons, and said, 'Who are these?'*

9 *And Joseph said unto his father, 'They are my sons, whom* the word of the Lord *hath given me* according to the marriage contract,[b] on the basis of which I took Asenath the daughter of Dinah, your daughter, to be my wife'. *And he said, 'Bring them, I pray thee, unto me, and I will bless them'.*

(10-14 These verses follow the Hebrew.)

15 *And he blessed Joseph, and said,* 'The Lord *before whom my fathers Abraham and Isaac did walk,* the Lord *which hath fed me, all my life long unto this day,*

16 may it be pleasing before you that *the angel* whom you appointed for me to rescue me from all evil, *may bless the lads; and let my name be named on them, and the name of my fathers Abraham and Isaac; and* as the fish of the sea are greatly multiplied in the water, so may the sons of Joseph *grow into a multitude in the midst of the earth'.*

(17-19 These verses follow the Hebrew.)

20 *And he blessed them that day, saying, 'In thee,* Joseph my son, shall the house of *Israel bless* the child on the day of circumcision, *saying,* The Lord *make thee as Ephraim and as Manasseh;* and in the reckoning of the tribes the ruler of Ephraim shall be reckoned before the ruler of Manasseh': *and he set Ephraim before Manasseh.*

[a] See Ps. Jon. on Gen. xxiii. 9.
[b] *Ketuba,* perhaps simply 'writing' or 'document'; see Gen. xli. 45.

21 *And Israel said unto Joseph, 'Behold,* my end comes to *die,* the word of the Lord will be for your help, *and bring you again unto the land of your fathers.*

22 *Moreover I have given to thee* the town of Shechem, *one portion* for a gift *above thy brethren, which I took out of the hand of the Amorite* at the time when they went into the midst of it, and I arose and helped you *with my sword and with my bow.'*

Selections from other Targums on Genesis xlviii

14 F.T. (Gins. p. 102) has several words.

20 C.G.: ...'*In thee* shall they bless in Israel each man his neighbour, *saying,* The Lord *make thee as Ephraim and Manasseh'; and* he made the order of blessing *Ephraim before Manasseh.*

21 T.O.: ... 'The word of the Lord will be for your help ...'

C.G.: ... '*Behold,* I am now about to be gathered, and the word of the Lord will be for your help ...'

22 F.T. (Gins. p. 24; see also pp. 80, 103): '*Moreover I have given to thee one portion above thy brethren,* the garment of Adam of old, which was given to Abraham, and he gave it to Isaac, my father. And Isaac, my father, gave it to Esau, my brother, and I did not take it from him *with my sword and with my bow* but with my merit[a] and my good works.'

Some texts[b] of T.O.: '... by my prayer and by my pleading'.

Notes on Genesis xlviii

7 Ps. Jon. was trying to explain why Jacob failed to take Rachel to the ancestral grave.

16 For the guardian angel see p. 185. The comparison with the fish was derived from a play on the Hebrew word *dag.* C.G. also has 'fish', but with a different word; otherwise it remains close to the Hebrew. The same play on words was made in T.O. See also the addition in Ps. Philo iii. 11 (Appendix I) to the promises to Noah.

a *Zekuth.* In Ber.R. c (xcvii) 6 one of the interpretations of the phrase is, 'with acts of mercy and with good deeds'.
b Sperber, J, G, Vc.

22   The word for 'portion' in the Hebrew is *'shechem'*, hence the identification made here, as also in LXX, Ber.R. xcvii. 6, B.B.B. 123 *a*. For the garment of Adam see the Targum and notes on Gen. iii. 20. For the legend of Jacob's wars, see Jub. xxxiv. 1–8.

For a summary of other interpretations of the verse, see A. Neher, 'Rabbinic Adumbrations to Non-Violence', in *Studies in Rationalism* . . . (ed. R. Loewe, 1966), pp. 185–8.

GENESIS XLIX

1 *And Jacob called unto his sons, and said:* 'Purify yourselves from uncleanness, and I will show you hidden secrets and unknown ends, the recompense of the reward of the just, and the retribution of the wicked, and the security of Eden, what it is.' The twelve tribes of Israel gathered themselves as one around the golden bed on which he lay: and after the glory of the Shekina of the Lord had been revealed to him,[a] the time when the king, Messiah, was going to come was concealed from him; and then he said, 'Come, *that I may tell you that which shall befall you in the latter days.*

2 *Assemble yourselves, and hear, ye sons of Jacob; and* receive instruction from *Israel your father.*

3 *Reuben, thou art my first-born,* the *beginning* of the *might* of my generation and the first outpouring[b] of my imagination full of desire. To you belonged the birthright and the chief priesthood and the kingdom, but because you sinned, my son, the birthright has been given to Joseph, the kingdom to Judah, and the priesthood to Levi.

4 I will liken you to a small garden into which enter torrents rushing and strong, and it is not able to endure them, and it is swamped. So you have been carried away, Reuben, my son; in that you have sinned, do not do so again, and your sin will be forgiven you; for it is reckoned to you as though you went to the woman with whom your father had lain, at the time when you disturbed my *bed*, when you went to it.

5 *Simeon and Levi are brethren* alike in every way.[c] Sharp weapons for violence, it is this by which they may be recognised.[d]

6 In their counsel *my soul* has taken no pleasure, and in their gathering to destroy Shechem my honour was not involved; *for in their anger they* killed the king and rulers, and of their own freewill they split open the fortified wall[e] of their enemy.

---

a See Ps. Jon. on Gen. xlvii. 31.

b Or 'loosing'.   c Lit. 'twins'.

d Ps. Jon. offered here two alternative explanations of *mekeyrotheyhem*, R.V. *their swords.* The word does not occur elsewhere in the O.T.

e Ps. Jon. retained here the Hebrew word *shor*; the root letters can mean either 'an ox' or 'a wall'; in the sense of 'ox' it was sometimes applied to Joseph because of the reference in Deut. xxxiii. 17.

7 Jacob said, 'The stronghold of Shechem was *cursed* when they entered it to destroy it in their anger which was relentless, and (cursed) their hatred against Joseph, because it was adamant'. Jacob said, 'If both of them dwell together as one, there is no king or ruler who can stand before them. *I will divide* the inheritance of the sons of Simeon into two parts. One part shall come from the inheritance of the sons of Judah, one part shall be among the rest of the tribes of *Jacob*, and I will *scatter* the tribe of Levi among all the tribes of *Israel*.

8 *Judah*, you acknowledged what happened with Tamar, therefore your brothers shall acknowledge you, and they shall be called Jehudain after your name. Your hands will take revenge for you on your enemies, shooting arrows at them when they turn their necks before you.[a] And *thy father's sons* will be ever quick to give you their greeting in advance of your own.

9 I will liken you, Judah my son, to a *whelp*, the young one of lions, because from the killing of Joseph my son your soul departed, and from the judgement of Tamar you will be saved. He is at ease and rests in confidence *as a lion*, and like a strong lion when he is resting *who shall rouse him up?*

10 Kings and rulers shall not cease *from* the house of *Judah*, nor scribes teaching the law from his seed, until the time when the king, Messiah, shall *come*, the youngest of his sons;[b] and because of him *the peoples* shall flow together.[c]

11 How noble is the king, Messiah, who is going to rise from the house of Judah. He has girded his loins and come down, setting in order the order of battle with his enemies and killing kings with their rulers (and there is not a king or a ruler who shall stand before him),[d] reddening the mountains with the blood of their slain. With his garments dipped in blood, he is like one who treads grapes in the press.[e]

12 More noble are the *eyes* of the king, Messiah, like sparkling[f] *wine*, than to see the uncovering of nakedness and the shedding of innocent[g]

[a] Derived from II Sam. xxii. 41; see Rashi on Gen. xlix. 8.
[b] See T.O. on Deut. xxviii. 57.
[c] Or 'shall melt away'; but cf. Aquila σύστημα.
[d] The last part of this sentence is probably added by mistake from verse 9.
[e] For extravagant versions of the exploits of Judah, see Test. Jud. ii–vii. With this verse, see also Isa. lxiii. 1 ff., which is frequently given an eschatological interpretation in rabbinic writings. For a brief summary, see Targ. Is. *ad loc.*
[f] Or 'clear'.   [g] *Zakkai.*

blood; his *teeth* are cleaner than *milk*, not for eating the torn or the stolen. And thus his mountains are red, and his press red from wine, and his hills are white from the corn and from the tents of the flocks.[a]

13 *Zebulun shall dwell* on the shores *of the sea*, and he will have authority over the harbours, subduing the domains of the sea with *ships; and his border* will extend as far as *Zidon*.[b]

14 *Issachar* longs for[c] the law. He is a strong tribe knowing the determined times,[d] and he lies down *between the* borders of his brothers.

15 *And he saw* the *resting place* of the world to come, *that it* is *good*, and the portion of the land of Israel, that it is pleasant, therefore he bent his shoulders to labour in the law, and to him shall his brothers offer gifts.

16 From the house of *Dan* there is going to arise a man who will *judge his people* with the judgement of truth; *as one* the tribes of Israel will listen to him.

17 He will be a chosen man, and he will arise from the house of *Dan*, being like the venomous snake which lies at the parting of *the way*, and like the head of the *serpent* which hides on *the path* and *biteth the horse* in its *heel*, and it falls. And in his terror *his rider* is thrown off *backward* on his back. So will Samson the son of Manoah kill all the mighty men of the Philistines, both horsemen and men on foot, and he will hamstring their horses and throw their riders on to their backs.'

18 Jacob, when he saw Gideon the son of Joash, and Samson the son of Manoah, who were established to be deliverers,[e] said: 'I do not await the deliverance of Gideon, and I do not look out for the deliverance of Samson, because their salvation, being temporal, will not last.[f] But I wait for your *salvation*, and look out for it, O Lord, because your salvation is eternal.[g]

19 The tribes of *Gad*, well-armed, will cross, with the rest of the tribes, the streams of Arnon, and they will subdue before them the inhabitants

---

a The last sentence is an alternative explanation.
b Or 'in the direction of'; cf. Sam. Pent., LXX, Pesh. and Vulg.
c This interprets M.T. *ḥamor* as *ḥamid*, as does LXX (ἐπεθύμησεν); but Tanḥ. and Rashi have the same explanation on a different basis: 'He bears Torah like a strong ass on which a heavy load is placed.'
d I Chron. xii. 32.
e Or 'saviours'.   f Lit 'will be for an hour'.
g This verse and its possible relevance to the New Testament is discussed by M. McNamara, *The New Testament and the Palestinian Targum . . .*, pp. 243–5.

of the land.[a] And they will return armed at the end with great riches, and they will dwell securely beyond the crossing of the Jordan. For as they desire, so will it be to them, and they will receive their possession.

20 Happy is *Asher*, how rich are his fruits! His land produces spices and the roots of frankincense, and his border will produce the delicacies of kings, and he utters thanks and praises for them before the Lord of the universe.

21 *Naphtali* is a swift messenger, like *a hind* which runs on the tops of the mountains, bringing good news. He brought the news that Joseph was still alive. He went at speed to Egypt and brought the title deed of the field of the double cave, in which Esau has no part.[b] And when he opens his mouth in the company[c] of Israel to praise, his voice will be chosen out of all voices.

22 My son, whom I brought up, *Joseph*, you my son who became great and strong: the end was upon you[d] to be strong and to subdue your inclination[e] in the case of your mistress and in the case of your brothers. I will liken you to a ▾ine planted by streams of water which sends out its roots and splits the sharp rocks, and with her branches subdues[f] all the barren trees. Even so, Joseph my son, you subdued by your wisdom and by your good deeds all the sorcerers of Egypt. And when praises were sung before you, the daughters of the rulers walked on the walls and threw before you rings[g] and necklaces of gold to make you raise your eyes to them, but you did not raise your eyes to (any) one of them to be united with them in the day of great judgement.

23 And all the sorcerers of Egypt were bitter and angry against him, so they brought information to Pharaoh hoping to bring him down from (his place of) honour. They spoke against him slanderously,[h] which is as wounding as arrows.

24 And the *strength* of his member reverted (through penitence)[i] to its former state so as not to lie with his mistress, and *his hands* were strengthened from the imagining of seed, and he subdued his inclina-

---

[a] The same phrase is used by Ps. Jon. on Gen. xlvi. 28.

[b] See Ps. Jon. on Gen. l. 13.   [c] *Kenishta*.

[d] I.e. it was foreordained; but perhaps read *tubh* with Ginsburger.

[e] *Yeẓer*.

[f] I.e. supplants.   [g] Or 'chains'.

[h] Lit. 'talk about third persons'.

[i] See B.Sot. 36*b*; Joseph began to succumb to temptation, but through repentance was saved from actual offence.

tion[a] because of the firm training which he received from *Jacob*. And for that reason he became worthy[b] to be a leader and to have his name engraved with theirs on the stones *of Israel*.

25 From the word[c] of the *God of thy father* will be your *help*, and he who is called '*Almighty*'[d] *shall bless thee, with blessings* which come down from the dew of heaven from above, and from the good *blessings* of the streams[e] *of the deep* which come up and make the plant grow from below. Blessed are *the breasts* from which you were suckled and *the womb* in which you lay.[f]

26 *The blessings of thy father* will be added to *the blessings* by which my fathers Abraham and Isaac blessed me, which the princes of this world, Ishmael and Esau and all the sons of Qeturah, desired. All these blessings will be united and be made a diadem of majesty for *the head of Joseph, and on the crown* of the man who became a chief man and a ruler in Egypt, and attentive to the glory of his *brethren*.

27 *Benjamin is* a strong tribe like *a wolf* with his prey. In his land the Shekina of the ruler of the world will dwell, and in his possession will be built the house of the sanctuary. *In the morning* the priests will offer the lamb regularly until the fourth hour *and at even*[g] they will offer the second lamb and in the evening they will *divide* what is left, the remainder of the offerings, and they will eat each man his own part.

28 *All these are the twelve tribes of Israel*, all of them righteous as one: *and this is it that their father spake unto them and blessed them; everyone according to his blessing he blessed them.*

29-33 These verses follow the Hebrew.)

Selections from other Targums on Genesis xlix

1 F.T. (Gins. p. 24; see also p. 80): *And Jacob called unto his sons, and said: 'Gather yourselves* and I will show you what will happen to you, the recompense of the reward for the just, and the retribution which is going to come to the wicked at the time when they will be gathered together at the end of days.' For he was revealing to them all that was

---

[a] *Yezer.* [b] *Zeka.* [c] *Memar.*
[d] *Shaddai.* [e] Or 'fountains'.
[f] This verse and its possible application to Luke vi. 36 are discussed by M. McNamara, *The New Testament and the Palestinian Targum*, pp. 131–3.
[g] Lit. 'between the suns'.

going to come about after the footprints of the Messiah.[a] After it was revealed to him it was concealed from him; and Jacob rose up and blessed them; each man according to the substance of his blessing he blessed them. When the twelve tribes of Jacob were gathered, and there appeared the golden bed on which Jacob our father was lying, they expected him to show them the time of redemption, but it was concealed from him.[b] Jacob answered and said to them: 'From Abraham, my father's father, came a worthless issue in Ishmael and in the sons of Qeturah. From Isaac my father came a worthless issue, Esau my brother, and I fear lest there should be among you a man who may attach some of the sons of his brothers to worshipping before idols.'[c] The twelve tribes of Jacob answered with a single voice,[d] 'Hear, O Israel; the Lord our God the Lord is One'.[e]

3-4 F.T. (Gins. p. 24; see also p. 81): *Reuben, thou art my first-born, my might, and the beginning of* my sorrow. To you it might have been to receive three parts above your brothers, the birthright and the kingdom and the high priesthood. (4) But because you have offended, Reuben, the birthright has been given to Joseph, the kingdom to Judah and the high priesthood to the sons of the tribe of Levi.

T.O.: *Reuben, thou art my first-born, my might, and the beginning of my strength.* To you it might have been to receive three parts, the birthright, the priesthood and the kingdom. (4) But because you have walked blindly like spilled water you will not benefit, a good part you will not receive; for you *went up* to the place where your father sleeps, then defiled my bed, my son, when you *went up*.

5-7 F.T. (Gins. p. 24, verse 7; see also pp. 81, 103): *Simeon and Levi are brethren* alike in every way; they are masters of sharp *weapons*, they fought from their youth up. In the land of their enemy they achieved victories in war. (6) In their counsel *my soul* has taken no pleasure, and in their gathering to destroy Shechem they did not respect my honour; *for in their anger they* killed kings in their sovereignty, and of their own freewill they sold Joseph their brother like *an ox*. (7) The

[a] See M.Sot. ix. 15. The phrase is based on Ps. lxxxix. 51 (52).

[b] Cf. also the longer variant: 'After the secret was made known to him it was hidden from him, and after the door was opened to him it was closed against him.'

[c] Or (Gins. emend.): 'who may adhere to the sons of my brother, to worship before idols'.   [d] Lit. 'heart'.

[e] The *Shema' Israel*, the fundamental confession of faith.

town of Shechem was *cursed* when Simeon and Levi rose up against it to destroy it in *their anger*, for it was relentless, and in their hatred, for it was adamant.' And our father Jacob said, 'If these two, Simeon and Levi, dwell together as one, no people and kingdom will stand before them. *I will divide* the sons of the tribes of Simeon to be scribes and teachers of the law of the sons of the company[a] of Jacob; and I will *scatter* the sons of the tribe of Levi in the house of instruction[b] of the sons of Israel.'

T.O.: *Simeon and Levi are brethren*, mighty men; in the land where they settled they did a mighty deed.[c] (6) *My soul* was not in their secret, I did not come down from my honour to join their gathering together; *for in their anger* they killed a killing, and of their own freewill they shattered the wall[d] of their enemy. (7) *Cursed be their anger*, for it is relentless, and their hatred, for it is adamant. *I will divide them in Jacob, and scatter them in Israel.*

8-9 F.T. (Gins. pp. 24 f.; see also p. 81): *Judah*, all your brothers shall acknowledge you and they shall be called Jehudai after your name. Your hands will take revenge for you on your enemies. All *thy father's sons* will be ever quick to give you their greeting in advance of your own. (9) I will liken you, *Judah*, to a *whelp* of lions, on account of the (intended) killing of Joseph my son, when you were sparing to him, and on account of the judgement of Tamar, when you said, She is innocent,[e] more than I. You are at ease and dwell in the city *as a lion* or *lioness*. There is no kingdom which shall stand before you.

T.O.: *Judah*, you are praise and not shame, your brothers shall acknowledge you. Your hand will be strong against your enemies, your enemies will be scattered. Their neck will be turned back before you, *thy father's sons* will be ever quick to give you their greeting in advance of your own. (9) A ruler[f] he will be in the beginning,[g] and in the end a

---

[a] *Kenishta.* [b] *Bet midrasha.*

[c] T.O. perhaps changed *mekeyrotheyhem* to *megureyhem*; but more probably it took *mekorothayik* (Ezek. xvi. 3, translated as 'thine habitation') as being the same word. See Rashi *ad loc.* [d] Or 'the ox'; see above, p. 277.

[e] *Zakkaah.* Compare Jub. xli. 23 ff.: 'And Judah acknowledged that the deed which he had done was evil . . . and he began to lament and supplicate before the Lord because of his transgression. And we told him in a dream that it was forgiven him, because he supplicated earnestly, and lamented, and did not again commit it.' [f] Or 'dominion'.

[g] David began humbly but ended in splendour. The reference is to II Sam. v. 2; see Rashi on Gen. xlix. 9.

king will be established in strength from the house of Judah, because from the sentence of death, my son, your soul you have caused to escape.[a] He will be at ease, he will rest in confidence *as a lion* and like a strong lion, and there is not a kingdom which shall trouble him.

10-12 F.T. (Gins. p. 25; see also pp. 81, 103): Kings and rulers shall not cease *from* the house of *Judah*, nor scribes teaching the law from his children's children, until the time when the king, Messiah, shall come, whose is the kingdom, and to him all the kingdoms of the earth are going to be in servitude. (11) How noble is the king, Messiah, who is going to arise from the house of Judah. He has girded his loins, he has gone forth to fight against his enemies, killing kings with their rulers, and making the mountains red with the blood of their slain and the hills white with the fat of their mighty men. His garments are dipped in blood. (12) More noble are the *eyes* of the king, Messiah, than sparkling *wine:* they will not look on the uncovering of nakedness or on the shedding of innocent blood. His *teeth* are used according to the law, and not in eating things torn or stolen. His mountains are *red with* vines and his presses with wine, and his hills are *white with* corn and with flocks of sheep.

T.O.: There will not ever pass away a ruler[b] *from* the house of *Judah* nor a scribe from his children's children for ever, until Messiah shall come, whose is the kingdom, and to him peoples shall be in servitude.[c] (11) Israel will go round about his towns, the people will build his temple, the just will be round about him and be observant of the law under his instruction. Of finest purple will be his garment, and his raiment of wool dyed brightly and coloured. (12) His mountains will be *red with* vineyards and his presses will flow with *wine*. His valleys will be *white with* corn and with the flocks of sheep.

13 T.O. *Zebulun shall dwell* on the shore of the seas, and he will subdue the harbours of the sea with ships, and he will eat the good of the sea, and his boundary will extend as far as *Zidon*.

14-15 F.T. (Gins. p. 25; see also p. 81): *Issachar is a strong* tribe, and his border will be set *between* two borders. (15) *And he saw* the house of the sanctuary (which is called 'the place of rest'),[d] *that it was good, and the land* of Israel, *that* its fruits are abundant, *and he bowed his*

---

[a] Lit. 'go up'.   [b] Or 'dominion'.
[c] Or 'peoples will obey him'.
[d] *Menuḥa*, based on Deut. xii. 9, *For ye are not as yet come to the rest and to the inheritance . . ..*

shoulder to labour in the law, and to him shall all his brothers offer tribute.

T.O.: *Issachar*, rich in possessions, his inheritance will be *between* borders.[a] (15) *And he saw* his portion, *that it was good, and the land that it* bears fruit; and he will subdue the territories of the peoples and scatter their inhabitants, and those among them who remain will be servants and bearers of tribute.

16-18 F.T. (Gins. p. 25; cf. p. 73, and see also pp. 81, 103): From the house of *Dan* will arise a deliverer and judge. *As one* the whole gathering *of the tribes* of the children *of Israel* will listen to him. (17) *Dan shall be* like *a serpent* lying *in the way*, and like the venomous snake hiding at the parting of the way. It bites the horse in its heel and makes it ill, and from terror *his rider* is overthrown and he falls on his back. Such is Samson, the son of Manoah, whose fear is on his enemies, and he goes out to fight against those that hate him, killing kings with their rulers. (18) Jacob our father said: 'My soul has not *waited* for the salvation of Gideon son of Joash, which lasts a short while,[b] and my soul has not waited for the salvation of Samson son of Manoah, which is a salvation of man,[c] but for the salvation about which you have said it will come to your people Israel, for this salvation I have waited, *O Lord*.'

T.O.: From the house of *Dan* will be chosen and will arise a man in whose days his people will be delivered and in whose time[d] *the tribes of Israel* will rest *as one*. (17) He will be a man who will be chosen and will arise from the house of *Dan*. His terror will be cast on the peoples, and his smiting will be relentless against the Philistines. Like a serpent, a venomous snake,[e] lying on *the way*, and like an adder hiding on *the path*, he will kill the warriors of the hosts of the Philistines, the horsemen with the men on foot. He will hamstring horses and chariots, and he will throw their riders on to their backs. (18) For your salvation I have hoped, *O Lord*.

19 F.T. (Gins. p. 25; see also p. 81): From the house of *Gad* will go forth hosts equipped with arms, and they will bring Israel over the Jordan, and make them possess the land of Canaan, and after that they will return in peace to their dwellings.

---

[a] So also Vulg.; Pesh. 'paths', but the Commentary of Ishodad is closer to the Targums. (See A. Levene, 'Remarques sur deux commentaires...', 1960.)

[b] Lit. 'for an hour'.   [c] Or 'passing away'.

[d] Lit. 'years'.

[e] Rashi took Hurman as a proper name.

T.O.: From the house of *Gad* armed hosts will cross the Jordan before their brothers to battle, and with much substance they will go back to their land.

20 F.T. (Gins. p. 25; see also p. 81): Happy is *Asher*, how rich is his land! His land will produce delicacies of the kingdoms for the children of Israel.

T.O.: *Of Asher* the land will be good and it will produce the delicacies of kings.

21 F.T. (Gins. p. 25; see also p. 81): *Naphtali is* a swift messenger bringing good news. He brought the news to our father Jacob first of all, that Joseph was still living.[a] And he went down to Egypt in a short time and brought the title deed of the field of the double cave. And when he opens his mouth in the assembly of Israel his talk flows with milk and honey.[b]

T.O.: *Naphtali*, his lot will be cast in a good land, and his possession will bear fruit. They will give thanks and praises for them.

22-4 F.T. (Gins. p. 26; see also pp. 81, 103): My son, whom I brought up, *Joseph*, you my son who became great and strong: you were indeed destined to be mighty. I will liken you, Joseph my son, to a vine planted by streams of water which sends its roots to the borders and splits the tops of all the stones and sends its branches out high and subdues[c] all the trees. So you, Joseph my son, subdued by your wisdom all the wise men of the Egyptians and all their sorcerers when you were set to ride in the second chariot of Pharaoh, and they praised you and said, 'Long live the father of the king, great in wisdom, tender in years'.[d] And the daughters of the kings and rulers crushed upon you from the windows and gazed upon you from the walls and they threw down upon you rings, bracelets, necklaces and ornaments that you might raise your face and look on one of them. But you, my son Joseph, did not in any way raise your face to look on one of them lest you might be joined with her in Gehinnom. And the daughters of the kings and the rulers said to each other, 'This is Joseph the faithful'[e] who does not go after the sight of his eyes nor after the lustful imagination of his heart'. For the sight of the eyes and the imagination of the heart make the son of man[f]

---

[a] But contrast Ps. Jon. on Gen. xlvi. 17.

[b] Naphtali is interpreted as *nofeth li*, 'a honeycomb to me'.

[c] I.e. supplants.   [d] See Ps. Jon. on Gen. xli. 43.

[e] Or 'upright, pious'.   [f] *Bar nasha*.

perish from the face of the earth. Therefore there will arise from you two tribes, Manasseh and Ephraim, and they will receive a possession with their brothers in the dividing of the land. (23) They were bitter against him and rose up to accuse him, and they brought information before Pharaoh the king of Egypt in order to bring him down from the throne of his kingdom, and they used to speak slander against him in the palace of Pharaoh, for they were as harsh against him as arrows. (24) And he put his trust in the Almighty, and he stretched out his hands and his arms, and begged mercies from *the Mighty One of* his father *Jacob*, and from beneath the arm of his strength, whence all the tribes of the children of Israel are led.

T.O.: My son who increases is *Joseph*, my son who is blessed like a vine planted by a spring of water. Two tribes will come forth from his sons, and they will receive a part and a possession. (23) The mighty men were bitter against him and took their vengeance and oppressed him, the men who are masters of strife. (24) And his prophecy settled with them, because he kept the law in secret and he put his trust in the Almighty. Therefore gold was placed on his arms, and he took possession of the kingdom and was strong. This was to him from before the almighty God *of Jacob*, who by his word[a] sustained the fathers and the children,[b] the seed of Israel.

25-6 F.T. (Gins. p. 26; see also pp. 81, 103): The word[c] of the God of your father will be for your *help*, and the God of heaven will *bless thee* from the good *blessings* of dew and rain which the *heaven* brings down from *above*, and from the *blessings of* the streams[d] of *the deep* which spring forth and come up from the earth from below, and from the blessings of your father and mother. (26) *The blessings of thy father* will be added to the blessings with which Abraham and Isaac blessed you, who are like mountains; and from the blessing of the four mothers who are like *hills*, Sarah and Rebecca and Rachel and Leah. All these blessings will come and make a diadem of majesty *on the head of Joseph, and on the crown* of the faithful man who became king and ruler of the land of Egypt, and a splendour in the glory of his father, and equally the diadem of majesty of *his brethren*.

---

a *Memra.*

b T.O. divided the word *'eben*, 'stone' into *ab ben*, 'father, son'.

c *Memar.*

d Or 'fountains'.

T.O.: The word[a] of the God of your father will be for your help, and it is *the Almighty*[b] who will *bless thee* with *the blessings* coming down from the dew of the heavens from *above*, with *the blessings* which spring up from the depths of the earth below, with the blessings of your father and your mother. (26) *The blessings of thy father* will be added to the blessings with which my father blessed me, which the mighty men who are of this world desired. They will all be *on the head of Joseph*, he who was more distinguished[c] than *his brethren*.

27 F.T. (Gins. p. 27; see also p. 81): *Benjamin is a* strong tribe. I will liken him to a ravening *wolf*. In his borders the house of the sanctuary will be built and in his possession the glory of the Shekina of the Lord will dwell. *In the morning* they will offer the regular lamb, *and at even*[d] will offer the lamb of the tamid, and in the evening they will offer a lamb as a burnt sacrifice, and the offerings, and they will *divide* what is left of the offerings of the children of Israel.

T.O. *Benjamin*, in his land the Shekina will dwell, and in his possession the sanctuary will be built. *In the morning* and in the evening[e] the priests will offer offerings, *and at even* they will *divide* what is left of their parts, the remainder of the holy things.

Notes on Genesis xlix

1 It was generally thought wrong that Jacob should have undertaken to reveal 'the latter days' without first gaining permission from God. B.Pes. 56a recorded the following version:

Jacob wished to reveal to his sons 'the end of days',[f] but the Shekina immediately left him. He said, 'Heaven forbid, but perhaps there is an unworthy one among my sons: from Abraham there came Ishmael, and from Isaac there came Esau. His sons replied, "Hear, O Israel; the Lord our God the Lord is One". At once Jacob cried out, "Blessed be the name of his glorious kingdom for ever and ever".'

The response of Jacob's sons was produced by taking the name 'Israel' in Deut. vi. 4[g] as being the name of Jacob.[h] Hence the sentence

---

[a] *Memar*.
[b] *Shaddai*.
[c] Or perhaps, 'he who was parted from'.
[d] Lit. 'between the suns'.
[e] *Panya*.
[f] Cf. Dan. xii. 13.
[g] *Hear O Israel: the Lord our God is one Lord*.
[h] Gen. xxxii. 28, xxxv. 10.

was turned into an address to Jacob. Ber.R. xcviii. 3 recorded the comment:

Eleazar b. Aḥwai said: 'From here Israel earned the right[a] to recite the Shemaʿ. When Jacob our father was about to leave the world, he summoned his twelve sons, and said to them, "Is the God of Israel, who is in the heavens, your father? Perhaps it is in your hearts to desert the Holy One, blessed be he?" They replied, "Hear, Israel, our father: as it is not in your heart to desert the Holy One, blessed be he, so it is not in ours to desert him; on the contrary, the Lord our God the Lord is One". He also cried out "Blessed be the name of his glorious kingdom for ever and ever". R. Berekiah and R. Ḥelbo in R. Samuel's name said: "This is why Israel says every morning and evening, Hear, Israel, our father, from the cave of Machpelah: what you commanded us, we still practise, the Lord our God the Lord is One."'

See also Sifre on Deut. §32, Midr. Tann. 24, Tanḥ. Vayeḥi 8.

3-4 See Ber.R. xcviii. 4, xcix. 6 and Rashi *ad loc.* for a summary of the ways in which these interpretations were derived. Pesh. has, 'You have flowed in all directions like water, you do not stand firm'. LXX, 'You have run out of control like water, do not overflow'. Sam. Pent., 'You are as swift as waters...' The word which caused uncertainty in the Hebrew was *pahaz*: on that word, see Ber.R. *op. cit.* and Judg. ix. 4, Zeph. iii. 4. See also Ps. Jon. on Gen. xxxv. 22.

5-7 Compare P.R.E. 38:

Cursed be their anger, for it was fierce; and he also cursed their swords in Greek, for he said, 'Weapons of violence are their swords'. All the kings of the earth trembled when they heard, saying, 'If two of Jacob's sons have done these mighty deeds, all of them banded together will be able to destroy the world'. And the fear of the Holy One, blessed be he, fell upon them, as it is written, *A great terror was upon the cities that were round about them, and they did not pursue after the sons of Jacob.*[b]

For the attempt to derive *mekeyrotheyhem* from the Greek *machaira* see also Ber.R. xcix. 7.

The particular interpretation of F.T., that Simeon and Levi were not entirely deprived of a blessing because their descendants would be scribes and teachers, is found elsewhere. It is of interest that Tertullian[c] and Hippolytus[d] knew the tradition that the Pharisees and the Scribes

---

[a] *Zaku.*
[b] Gen. xxxv. 5.
[c] *Adv. Marcion.* iii. 18; *Adv. Jud.* 10.   [d] On Gen. xliv. 5.

were descended from Simeon and Levi. See also Tanḥ.B. i. 218 f., Tanḥ. Vayeḥi 9, 10. Pes.R. 28 *a–b* also maintained that Reuben, Simeon and Levi received a blessing, although they were reprimanded for their offences. On the other hand sources like Ber.R.[a] held that the reproof was so severe that the younger sons tried to creep away before their turn came. T.O. took a position half-way between the two.

LXX has, 'they ended the violence of their nature,[b] . . . because in their anger they slew men, and in their passion they houghed an ox'. Pesh., 'instruments of violence are among them . . . in their violence they overthrew a wall'. Vulg. and Arab. Vers. also took it as 'a wall',[c] Sam. Pent., 'an ox'.

Rashi commented:

For in their anger they slew a man; that is Hamor and the men of Shechem. The men are reckoned together as 'a single man'[d] . . . That is its midrashic explanation. Its plain meaning[e] is that a group of men is called 'a man', each man on his own, because in their fury they slew each man with whom they were enraged[f] . . . *And in their selfwill they houghed an ox:* they wished to eliminate Joseph, who was called 'an ox', as it is said, *The firstling of his bullock, majesty is his.*[g]

Test. Levi v. 3 says that Simeon and Levi destroyed Shechem in obedience to a command from an angel, and are therefore not to be blamed. See also Test. Levi vi.

10–12 LXX has, 'A ruler will not depart from Judah, nor a leader from his thighs until the things stored up come to him; and he will be the hope of the nations'; Pesh. has, 'The sceptre shall not depart from Judah, nor a lawgiver from between his feet, until he come whose it is; and the nations expect him'. All these versions (except Ps. Jon.) took Shiloh as *shelloh*, equivalent in meaning to *asher lo*. The messianic interpretation of the verse is mentioned in B.San. 98 *b*. See also Ber.R. xcviii. 6–10, xcix. 8, Tanḥ. Vayeḥi 10, Midr. haGad. i. 735–9, Test. Jud. i. 6, *Bet haMidr.* vi. 84. On the verses in general, see Rashi *ad loc.*, especially on verses 11 and 12, where the derivations of many of the

---

[a] xcviii. 5, xcix. 8. Cf. also Sam. Pent.

[b] Reading the text as *killu ḥamas mekeyrotheyhem.*

[c] See also Aq. and Sym.

[d] But LXX and Pesh. changed the Heb. singular to the plural; Arab. Vers. has 'a nation'. Rashi compares Exod. xv. 1, Judg. vi. 16.

[e] *Peshuto.*

[f] Rashi compares Ezek. xix. 3.   [g] Deut. xxxiii. 17.

words are explained. Much of the imagery was supplied from Isa. lxiii. 1 ff.

13 Compare Ber.R. xcviii, 11, xcix. 9, Test. Zeb. vi. 1–3.

14-15 LXX also transformed the reproach of verse 15, translating it, 'and he became a man working on the land'. See also Ber.R. xcviii. 12, xcix. 10, Tanḥ. Vayeḥi 11, Test. Iss. v. 1–3.

16-18 The reference is to Samson (Judg. xiii. 2). See also Ber.R. xcviii. 13, 14, xcix. 11, Tanḥ. Vayeḥi 12.

19 On Gad being the first to reach the promised land, see Ber.R. xcviii. 15, xcix. 11, Rashi *ad loc.*

20 See also Ber.R. xcviii. 16, xcix. 12, Tanḥ. Vayeḥi 13.

21 The specific exclusion of Esau from the cave of Machpelah may perhaps be based on the tradition (recorded in Midr. Teh. on Ps. xviii. 41) that Judah killed Esau in the cave at the time of Isaac's burial; Esau slipped back into the cave to kill Jacob, but Judah struck first.

On the swiftness of Naphtali and his errands see Bem.R. xiv. 11, T.d.E. 51 and 59, Midr. haGad. i. 746 f. See also Ber.R. xcviii. 17 and (a brief mention) xcix. 12. Test. Naph. ii. 1 has: 'And I was swift on my feet like the deer, and my father Jacob appointed me for all messages, and as a deer did he give me his blessing.'

22 The story of the women trying to attract Joseph's attention occurs also in P.R.E. 39:

When he went out in his chariot riding throughout the land of Egypt, the women used to climb up on the walls because of him, and they threw gold rings at him to make him look at them, so that they could see his handsome figure... as it is written, *Joseph is a fruitful bough* ... (*his*) *daughters*[a] *run over the wall.*

A more elaborate version was recorded in Chron. Jer. xxxix. 2:

One day all the Egyptian women assembled together to see Joseph's beauty. When Joseph was brought before them to wait upon them, his mistress offered each of them an apple and knife to peel it; but when they started peeling their apples they all cut their hands, since they were so much captivated with Joseph's beauty that they could not take their eyes from him. She (Potiphar's wife) then said, 'If you do this after seeing him but for one hour, how much more should I be captivated who see him continually?'

See also Ber.R. xcviii. 18, Yashar xl, Qur'ān xii. 31 f.

[a] R.V. marg.

25-6 See also Ber.R. xcviii. 19, 20.

27 Since Jerusalem was known to have been in the territory of Benjamin the interpretation made here was almost inevitable. It is to be found in Mek. Vayehi. 6 and in a shorter form in Midr. Teh. on Ps. lxviii. 28. Ber.R. xcix. 3 ascribed the opinion to R. Phinehas: 'R. Phinehas said: "It refers to the altar: as a wolf seizes prey, so the altar seized sacrifices."' See also Test. Ben. ix. 2, xi. 1.

GENESIS L

1 *And Joseph* laid his father on a bed of ivory covered with fine gold, set with fine stones, and tied with linen cords. There they sprinkled mulled wines and there burned precious spices. There stood the mighty men from the house of Esau and the mighty men from the house of Israel.[a] There stood the lion of Judah, the mighty one of his brethren. He answered and said to his brothers, 'Come and let us establish over our father a high cedar whose top will reach to the summit of heaven, with its branches overshadowing all the inhabitants of the earth, and its roots descending into the depths of the earth. From him have arisen twelve tribes; from him are going to arise kings and rulers and priests in their divisions to offer offerings; from him also the Levites in their appointments for singing.' Then, behold, Joseph *fell upon his father's face, and wept upon him, and kissed him.*

2 *And Joseph commanded his servants the physicians to embalm his father: and the physicians embalmed Israel.*

3 *And forty days* from the embalming were *fulfilled for him; for so are fulfilled the days of embalming:* and the Egyptians wept for him threescore *and ten days,* saying, 'Come, let us weep for Jacob the faithful,[b] for because of his merit[c] famine was turned away from the land of Egypt'. It had been decreed that there should be famine for forty-two years, but because of the merit of Jacob forty years were held back from Egypt, and there was famine for two years only.

4 *And when the days of weeping for him were past, Joseph spake unto the* chiefs of the *house of Pharaoh, saying, 'If now I have found grace in your eyes, speak, I pray you, in the ears of Pharaoh . . .'*

(5-9 These verses follow the Hebrew.)

10 *And they came to* the laying-out room in the house *of Atad, which is beyond Jordan, and there they lamented with a very great and sore lamentation: and he made a mourning for his father seven days.*

11 *And when the inhabitants of the land, the Canaanites, saw the mourning in the* house of the laying-out room *of Atad,* they loosed the girdles of their loins in honour of Jacob and stretched out their hands, and *they*

---

a Ishmael? b Or 'upright, pious'.
c *Zekuth.*

said, 'This is a grievous mourning to the Egyptians': wherefore the name of it was called Abel-mizraim, which is beyond Jordan.

12 *And his sons did unto him according as he commanded them:*

13 and *his sons carried him into the land of Canaan*, and a report was heard by Esau the wicked, so he came from the mountain of Gabla with many legions, and he came to Hebron and would not allow Joseph to bury his father in the double cave. At once Naphtali went and ran down into Egypt and returned in a single day and brought the agreement which Esau had written for Jacob his brother in the dispute over the double cave. At once he signalled to Ḥushim, the son of Dan, who took a sword and cut off the head of Esau the wicked, and the head of Esau rolled into the middle of the cave until it came to rest on the chest of Isaac his father; and his body the sons of Esau buried in the double field, and later the son of Jacob buried him in the cave of the double field; *Abraham bought* the field *for a possession of a burying place* from *Ephron the Hittite, before Mamre.*

14 *And Joseph returned into Egypt, he, and his brethren, and all that went up with him to bury his father, after he had buried his father.*

15 *And when Joseph's brethren saw their father was dead*, and that he (Joseph) did not return to sit together with them to eat bread, *they said, 'It may be that Joseph will hate us, and will fully requite us all the evil which we did unto him'.*

16 *And* they instructed Bilhah to say *unto Joseph, 'Thy father did command before he died, saying* to you,

17 "*So shall ye say unto Joseph, Forgive, I pray thee now, the transgression of thy brethren, and their sin, for that they did unto thee evil: and now, we pray thee, forgive the transgression of the servants of the God of thy father".' And Joseph wept when they spake unto him.*

18 *And his brethren also went and fell down before his face; and they said, 'Behold, we be thy servants'.*

19 *And Joseph said unto them, 'Fear not: for* I will not do to you evil, but good, because I fear and am humble before the Lord.

20 *And as for you*, you reckoned *evil* reckonings against me, that when I did not join you in eating, it was because I kept enmity against you, but the word of the Lord reckoned concerning me *for good*, because my father put me at the head, and because of his glory[a] I was accepted: and now I am not accepted for the sake of my own worthiness[b] that I should

---

a Or 'honour'.   b √zky.

work for us deliverance this day to establish a mighty people from the house of Jacob.

21 *Now therefore fear ye not: I will nourish you and your little ones.' And he comforted them, and spake kindly unto them.*

22 *And Joseph dwelt in Egypt, he, and his father's house: and Joseph lived an hundred and ten years.*

23 *And Joseph saw Ephraim's children of the third generation: the children also of Machir the son of Manasseh* Joseph circumcised when they *were born.*

24 *And Joseph said unto his brethren, 'I die: but God will surely* remember *you, and bring you up out of this land unto the land which he sware to Abraham, to Isaac, and to Jacob'.*

25 *And Joseph took an oath of the children of Israel, saying* to their children, 'Behold, you will be brought into servitude in Egypt, but you shall not plan to go up from Egypt until the time when the two deliverers shall come and say to you, The Lord *surely* remembers you. And at the time when you go up *ye shall carry up my bones from hence.'*

26 *So Joseph died, being an hundred and ten years old: and they embalmed him* and adorned him and put him *in a coffin* and sank him in the middle of the Nile *in Egypt.*

Selections from other Targums on Genesis l

1 F.T. (Gins. p. 27: see also p. 81) has a similar expansion, but with slightly different phrases.

4 F.T. (Gins. p. 103) has two words.

16 F.T. (Gins. p. 27): *And* they instructed Bilhah, the handmaid of Rachel, to say (to Joseph), '*Thy father did command before he* was gathered, *saying'.*

19 F.T. (Gins. p. 27): *And Joseph said unto them, 'Fear not, for* the evil which you did to me has ended; are not the reckonings of the sons of men[a] always before the Lord?'

T.O.: ... '*Fear not, for* I am a fearer of the Lord.'

21 F.T. (Gins. p. 27) expands the end of the verse.

26 F.T. (Gins. pp. 27, 103) has several words.

[a] *Bene nasha.*

Notes on Genesis l

3 Speculations about the length of the famine were recorded in Ber.R. lxxxix. 9:

> R. Judah said: 'Pharaoh's dreams meant fourteen years.'[a] R. Nehemiah said: 'It was twenty-eight years of each, because he dreamt it, then told it to Joseph.'[b] The rabbis said: 'It was forty-two years, because Pharaoh dreamed it, then told it to Joseph and Joseph repeated them back.' R. Jose b. Ḥanina said: 'The famine lasted for two years, for as soon as Jacob went down to Egypt it stopped.'[c] So when did it continue? In the time of Ezekiel, as it is written, *And I will make the land of Egypt a desolation.*[d]

Compare also P.R.E. 48.

11 The full version of this is given in Ber.R. c. 6:

> R. Samuel b. Naḥman said: 'In the whole of scripture we have failed to find a place called Atad. Is there a threshing floor for thorns?[e] It refers in fact to the Canaanites who deserve to be trampled down like thorns. By what merit were they saved? By the merit of honouring Jacob.' How did they honour him? R. Eleazar said, 'By loosing the girdles of their loins'.

See also Tanḥ.B. i. 222, Tanḥ. Vayeḥi 17, J.Sot. i. 9, Pes.K. xi. 9.

13 The legend of Esau's death is old, and it passed through several different forms. In some versions it is Judah who killed Esau (as in J.Ket. i. 5, J.Git. v. 6, Sifre on Deut. §348). According to Jubilees,[f] Midr. Teh. on Ps. xviii. 41, and Test. Jud.[g] it was Jacob. In the later versions it is Ḥushim, as in Ps. Jon., and also in B.Sot. 13a and P.R.E. 39. Yashar gives the legend in even more elaborate form.

15 This addition was necessary because of a self-contradiction in Genesis: there is no record that Jacob in fact gave the order of verse 16. So Deb.R. xv. 5 recorded: 'Resh Laqish said, "Great is peace, because words which are not strictly true were written to make peace between Joseph and his brethren. When their father died they were afraid that he would take his revenge." ' See also Tanḥ. Told. 1.

19 Joseph's willingness to forgive his brothers was frequently held up as exemplary. See, for example, Test. Sim. iv. 3, 4, Test. Zeb. viii. 4–6.

---

[a] Fourteen years of famine and fourteen years of plenty, adding the two dreams together.
[b] I.e. four times seven.
[c] Cf. Gen. xlv. 6.   [d] Ezek. xxix. 12.
[e] Heb. *atad.*
[f] xxxviii. 2.   [g] ix. 3.

26 Two different traditions were recorded in Mek. Vayehi. 1:

And Moses took the bones of Joseph with him;[a] to make known the wisdom and faithfulness[b] of Moses. All Israel were taking care of the spoil, but Moses was taking care of the bones of Joseph. Of him it is written, *The wise in heart will receive commandments.*[c] But how did Moses know where the grave of Joseph was? It is said that Serah, the daughter of Asher, survived from that generation, and she showed Joseph's grave to Moses. She said to him: 'The Egyptians made a metal coffin for him which they sank in the middle of the Nile.' Moses went and stood on the bank: he took a gold tablet on which was carved the tetragrammaton,[d] and he threw it into the Nile crying out and saying, 'Joseph, son of Jacob, the oath which the Holy One, blessed be he, swore to Abraham our father, that he would redeem his children, is about to be fulfilled. If you come up, it is good; but if not, then we are free of your oath.'[e] At once the coffin of Joseph came up, and Moses took it[f] . . . R. Nathan said: 'In the necropolis of Egypt they buried him among the kings, as it is written, *And they embalmed him, and he was put in a coffin in Egypt.*[g] But how did Moses know where the coffin of Joseph was? Moses went and stood among the coffins. He cried out saying, "Joseph, Joseph, the oath which God swore to Abraham our father is about to be fulfilled" . . . Immediately Joseph's coffin began to move, so he took it and went away.'

Test. Sim. viii. 3–4 has a shorter version:

The bones of Joseph the Egyptians guarded in the tombs of the kings. For the sorcerers told them, that on the departure of the bones of Joseph there should be throughout all the land darkness and gloom, and an exceeding great plague to the Egyptians so that even with a lamp a man should not recognise his brother.

See also T. Sot. iv. 7, B. Sot. 13a, Tanḥ. Beshall. 2, Ps. Jon. on Exod. xiii. 19, and Shem.R. xx. 19.

[a] Exod. xiii. 19.
[b] Or 'piety'.
[c] Prov. x. 8.
[d] *Shem mephorash.*
[e] Gen. l. 25.
[f] Mek. then argued on the basis of *qal waḥomer* (from the less to the greater) that if Elisha could make iron float it is not surprising that Moses could also do so.
[g] Gen. l. 26.

APPENDICES
BIBLIOGRAPHY
INDEXES

APPENDIX I

THE BIBLICAL ANTIQUITIES OF PHILO: A TRANSLATION OF THE PASSAGES RELATED TO GENESIS[a]

I

1 The beginning of the world.[b] Adam begat three sons and one daughter, Cain, Noaba, Abel and Seth. (Like Chronicles, Pseudo-Philo opens with the genealogy of Adam, based on Gen. v, but with the addition of many names.[c] The whole of ch. i is devoted to this genealogy, in which a point of particular importance is the treatment of Enoch.)

15 And Enoch lived 165 years and begat Matusalam. And Enoch lived after he begat Matusalam 200 years, and he begat five sons and three daughters.[d]

16 But Enoch pleased God at that time and was not found because God translated him.[e]

II

1 Now Cain lived in the earth trembling as God decreed for him after he killed Abel his brother[f] and the name of his wife was Themech.

2 And Cain knew Themech his wife; she conceived and bore Enoch.[g]

3 Now Cain was fifteen years old when he did these things, and from that time he began to build cities, until he had founded seven cities.[h] And these are the names of the cities. The name of the first city took the name of his son Enoch, the name of the second city that of Maulli, and of the third

---

a On Ps. Philo see pp. 30f. The translation is included here because it is so often referred to in the notes on Ps. Jon., and because Ps. Philo is in any case of such obvious importance in the history of Jewish exegesis and traditions. It has been translated by M. R. James, but his translation is out of print and not readily available.

b *Initium mundi*, following the LXX title of Genesis.

c A feature of Ps. Philo is its elaboration of genealogies, perhaps because it took the book of Chronicles as its model. These lists of names have not been translated or transcribed in full, not least because they have been much corrupted in the course of transmission. Indication is given of where the lists occur.

d Gen. v. 21–3.

e *Placuit autem Enoch Deo in illo tempore et non inveniebatur quoniam transtulit illum Deus.* Note the addition of *in illo tempore*.

f Gen. iv. 14. g Gen. iv. 17. h Gen. iv. 17.

that of Leeth, and the name of the fourth city that of Teze, and the name of the fifth that of Jesca, the name of the sixth that of Celeth, and the name of the seventh that of Jebbath.

4 And Cain lived after he begat Enoch 715 years, and he begat three sons and two daughters. The names of his sons, Olad, Lezas, Fosal, and of his daughters Citha and Maac. And all the days of Cain were 730 and he died.

5 Then Enoch took a wife from the daughters of Seth, and she bore him Ciram and Cuut and Madab. And Ciram begat Matusael, and Matusael begat Lamech.

6 Now Lamech took for himself two wives. The name of one was Ada and the name of the other was Sella.[a]

7 And Ada bore Jobab, who was the father of all those who live in tents and pasture flocks. And again she bore him Jobal, who was the first to teach every musical song,[b] and began to play the lyre and lute,[c] and every instrument of sweet music.[d]

8 And at that time when the dwellers on earth began to work evil, each one with his neighbour's wife defiling them, and to corrupt the earth, God was angry.

9 Now Sella bore Tobel[e] and Miza and Theffa. And this is the Tobel who showed men skills in lead and tin and iron and copper and silver and gold. And then the dwellers on earth began to make images and worship them.

10 Then Lamech said to his two wives Ada and Sella: 'Hear my voice, O wives of Lamech, and give heed to my precept; for I have corrupted men for myself, and have taken away sucklings from the breast, that I might show my sons and the dwellers on earth how to work evil. And now vengeance shall be taken seven times of Cain, but of Lamech seventy times seven.'[f]

III

1 And it happened when men had begun to multiply on the earth, that beautiful daughters were born to them. And the sons of God saw the daughters of men, that they were very beautiful; they took wives for themselves of all that they had chosen.[g]

2 And God said: 'My spirit will not judge[h] among all these men for ever, because they are flesh; but their years will be 120'; at which he set the limits of life;[i] and in their hands the law[j] will not be extinguished.[k]

---

[a] Gen. iv. 19.
[b] Or 'instrument'; Latin, *psalmum organorum.*
[c] *Cyneram et cytheram.*   [d] Gen. iv. 21.   [e] Gen. iv. 22.
[f] Gen. iv. 23–4.   [g] Gen. vi. 1.   [h] *Non diiudicabit.*
[i] Or 'of the world', *terminos seculi.*
[j] Some texts, 'evil deeds'.
[k] Gen. vi. 5.

3 And God saw that among all the dwellers on earth evil works were put into effect, and since they thought about wickedness all their days, he said, 'I will destroy man and everything which has come to life in the earth, because it repents me that I have made him'.

4 But Noe found favour and pity[a] before the Lord; and these are his generations. Noe, who was a just man and undefiled[b] in his own generation, was pleasing to God. To him God said, 'The time of all men living on the earth has come, because their works are very evil. And now, make for yourself an ark of cedar wood, and thus shall you make it: its length shall be 300 cubits, and its width 50 cubits, and its height 30 cubits. And you shall enter into the ark, yourself and your wife and your sons and your sons' wives with you, and I will make my covenant with you, that I will destroy all the dwellers on earth. But of the clean animals and of the clean birds of the sky you shall take them seven by seven, male and female, that their seed may be able to bring life to the earth. Of the unclean animals and of the unclean birds you shall take them for yourself two by two, male and female. You shall take provision for yourself and for them.'[c]

5 So Noe did what God commanded him, and he entered into the ark, himself and all his sons with him. And it happened after seven days that the water of the flood began to be on the earth. And in that day all the depths were opened and the great fountain[d] and the cataracts of heaven, and there was rain on the earth for forty days and forty nights.[e]

6 It was then 1652 years since God had made heaven and earth, on the day when the earth was destroyed[f] together with its inhabitants because of the wickedness of their works.

7 And with the flood continuing 150[g] days on the earth, Noe alone was left, and those who were with him in the ark. And when God remembered Noe, he made the water diminish.

8 And it happened on the ninetieth day that God dried the earth and said to Noe: 'Go out of the ark, you and all who are with you, and increase and multiply in the earth.' So Noe went out of the ark, himself and his sons and his sons' wives, and all the beasts and reptiles and birds and cattle he brought out with him, just as God had commanded him. Then Noe built an altar to the Lord, and he took of all the clean animals and birds, and offered burnt offerings on the altar, and it was acceptable to the Lord as an odour of rest.[h]

9 And God said, 'I will not again curse the earth for man, since the image[i] of man's heart has left him from his youth; and therefore I will not again destroy all living things as I have done. But it will be that when the dwellers on earth have sinned, I will judge them by famine or sword or fire

---

[a] *Gratiam et misericordiam.*

[b] *Inmaculatus.*   [c] Gen. vi. 13–21.   [d] *Fons magnus.*

[e] Gen. vii. 5–11.   [f] Lit. 'corrupted'.   [g] One text, 140.

[h] Or 'cessation', *tamquam odor requietionis*; Gen. viii. 16–21.

[i] *Figura.*

or death, and there will be earthquakes, and they will be scattered to un-inhabited parts. But I will not again destroy the earth with a flood of water, and in all the days of the earth seed-time and harvest, cold and heat, summer and autumn, day and night will not cease, as long as I remember those who dwell on the earth, until the times are complete.[a]

10 But when the years of the world[b] are complete, then will light cease and darkness be extinguished, and I will give life to the dead, and I will raise up those who sleep from the earth. The nether world[c] will pay its debt, and destruction make good its part, that I may pay to each one according to his works and according to the fruit of his imaginings, as I judge between soul and body. And the world shall cease and death shall be extinguished, and the nether world shall close his mouth. And the earth will not be without birth, nor barren for those dwelling in it. And none shall be defiled once they have been justified in me.[d] And there will be another earth and another heaven, an everlasting habitation.'

11 And the Lord again spoke to Noe and his sons: 'Behold, I will make my covenant with you and with your seed after you, and I will not add again to destroy the earth with the water of a flood. And everything which moves and lives shall be for you as food. Nevertheless flesh with the blood of life[e] you shall not eat. For he who sheds the blood of man, at the hand of God his blood shall be shed, since God made man in his own image. But as for you, increase and multiply and fill the earth, as the multitude of fishes multiplying themselves in the waves.'[f]

IV

1–2 (Lists the sons of Noe who went out of the ark and gives further genealogies based on Gen. x.)

3 And these are the ones who were dispersed and dwelt in the earth among the Persians and Monidians, in the islands which are in the sea. And Farath, the son of Tudeni, went up and ordered ships of the sea to be made, and then was the third part of the earth divided.

4 Now Domereth and his sons took Ladeth, Magog and his sons took Besto, Juban and his sons took Ceel, Tubal and his sons took Feed, Misech and his sons took Nepthi, Iras and his sons took Jesca, Duodenin and his sons took Goda, Rizath and his sons took Bosorra, Tergoma and his sons took Futh, Elisa and his sons took Thabola, Thesis and his sons took Mare-cham, Cethim and his sons took Thoan, Duodennin and his sons took Caruba.

5 Then they began to work the earth and to sow on it. And when the earth was thirsty, its inhabitants cried out to the Lord. And God heard them and gave them rain abundantly. And it happened that when the rain fell on the earth, a bow appeared in the cloud. And the dwellers on earth saw a

---

[a] *Donec compleantur tempora.* [b] Or 'age', *seculi.*
[c] *Infernus.* [d] *In me iustificatus est.*
[e] *In sanguine anime.* [f] Gen. ix. 8–9, 11.

memorial of the covenant, and they fell on their faces and sacrificed, offering burnt offerings to the Lord.

6 Now the sons of Cham are Chus and Mestra and Funi and Chanaan. And these are the sons of Chus: Saba and Evila, Sabatha, Regma and Sabathaca.

The sons of Regma: Saba and Tudan.

And the sons of Funi: Zeleu, Tulup, Geluc, Lefuc.

And the sons of Chanaan: Sidona, Aendain, Racin, Simmin, Urum, Nemigin, Amathin, Nefin, Telaz, Elat, Cusin.

7 Now Chus begat Nembroth; he began to be proud[a] before the Lord. But Mestram begat Ludin and Niemigin and Labin and Latuin and Petrosorim and Cesluin. Thence came forth the Philistines and the Cappadocians.

8 And then as well they began themselves to build cities, and these are the cities which they built: Sidon and its environs, that is Resin, Beosomata, Gerras, Calon, Dabircamo, Tellun, Lachis, Sodom and Gomorra, Adam and Seboim.

(Verses 9 and 10 list the descendants of Shem, of Jeptam and of Phalech.)

11 But Ragau took as a wife for himself Melcha the daughter of Ruth, and she bore for him Seruch. And when the day of her delivery came she said: 'From him will be born in the fourth generation one who shall set his dwelling on high, and he will be called perfect and without stain,[b] and he will be a father of nations, and his covenant will not be dissolved, and his seed will be multiplied for ever.'

(Verses 12–14 trace the descent from Ragu through Seruch and Nachor to Tharam, adding the names of various other sons and daughters.)

15 And Thara lived seventy years and begat Abram and Nachor and Aran. And Aran begat Loth.

16 Then those who inhabit the earth began to star-gaze, and they started to prognosticate and make divinations from the stars, and to make their sons and daughters pass through fire. But Seruch and his sons did not walk in their way.

17 These are the generations of Noe in the earth, according to their tribes and languages, from which the races were divided on the earth after the flood.

V

1 Then the sons of Cham came and made Nembroth a ruler for themselves,[c] but the sons of Jafeth appointed Fenech as leader for themselves, but the sons of Sem assembled and made Jectam a ruler for themselves.

---

[a] *Superbus.* [b] *Perfectus . . . et inmaculatus.*

[c] Cf. P.R.E. 24: 'R. Aqiba said: "They threw off the kingdom of heaven and appointed Nimrod as their king, a slave, the son of a slave. Are not all the children of Ham slaves? Unhappy the land that has a slave for its king, as it is written, *For three things the earth doth tremble . . . For a servant when he is king . . .* (Prov. xxx. 21 f.)." '

2   And when they came these three into one they took counsel that they might make account of the people of their followers; and this was while Noe was still alive. And it happened that when they came together in one they dwelt without division and the earth was at peace.

3   Now in the 340th year after Noe went out of the ark, after God dried up the flood, the rulers took account of their people.

(The rest of ch. v is a record of this account, giving the strength of the various parties.)

VI

1ᵃ   Then those who had been divided, all the dwellers on earth, assembled after that and dwelt together. And they set forth from the East and found a plain in the land of Babylon, and, dwelling there, they said each to his neighbour:ᵇ 'See, it is going to come about that we shall be scattered, each from his own brother, and in the lastᶜ days we will be fighting one against another. Now, therefore, come, and let us build for ourselves a tower, whose top shall reach to heaven, and we shall make for ourselves a name and a glory on earth.'

2   And they said each one to his neighbour: 'Let us take bricksᵈ and write each of us our own names on the bricks and burn them with fire; and it will be that they will be thoroughly baked into clay and brick.'

3   So they took, each of them, their bricks, except for twelve men who refused to do so; and these are their names: Abraham, Nachor, Loth, Ruge, Tenute, Zaba, Armodat, Jobab, Esar, Abimahel, Saba, Ausin.

4   And the people of the land seized them, and brought them to their rulers and said to them: 'These are the men who have transgressed our plans and refuse to walk in our ways.' So the leaders said to them: 'Why have you refused to set out each one of you his brick with the people of the land?'

ᵃ This legend also appears in Chron. Jer. xxix.
ᵇ Gen. xi. 2–4.   ᶜ *Novissimis.*
ᵈ In view of what they did with them, *lapides* must here be 'bricks' not 'stones'. Cf. P.R.E. 24: 'R. Phineḥas said: "Since there were no stones in that place, what did they do? They baked bricks and burned them as builders do." ' Similarly Jub. x. 20 has: 'And they began to build, and in the fourth week they made brick with fire, and the bricks served them for stone, and the clay with which they cemented them together was asphalt which comes out of the sea, and out of the foundations of water in the land of Shinar.' The worship of a brick was a recognised form of idolatry. It is discussed in B.A.Z. 46a, and in B.San. 107b (uncensored) Jesus is accused of having set up a brick and worshipped it. Here it is derived from a literal interpretation of Gen. xi. 4, *Let us make us a name.* The passage in B.San. 107b has been discussed by H. J. Zimmels, 'Jesus and "Putting Up a Brick" '. He suggested that the word intended was 'fish', not 'brick', and then connected the passage with a proverb in B.B.M. 59b, 'If one has a person in his family who has been hanged, say not in his presence, 'Hang the fish up'''. But in view of the passage in Ps. Philo, that explanation seems improbable.

Then they answered saying to them, 'We do not set out bricks with you, nor do we join our intentions with yours. One God we know and him do we worship. Even if you set us in the fire with your bricks we will not consent to you.'

5   Then the angered leaders said, 'As they have spoken so do to them: it shall be that unless they consent with you in setting forth bricks, you shall consume them in fire with your bricks'.

6   Then Jectan, who was the first ruler of the leaders, replied: 'Not so; there shall be given them a space of seven days, and it shall be that if they turn away from their most evil decisions and are willing to set forth bricks with you, they shall live. But if not, they shall be burned according to your decision.' But he sought how he might save them from the hands of the people, since he was of their tribe, and served God.

7   With these words he took them and shut them up in the king's house.[a] And when evening was come he ordered fifty men, mighty in courage, to be called to him, and said to them: 'Go, and take those men tonight who are shut up in my house, and put provisions for them from my house on ten pack-animals, and bring those men to me; and take their provisions with the pack-animals to the mountains, and wait with them there. And understand that if anyone knows what I have said to you, I will burn you with fire.'

8   So the men went and did everything which their leader had commanded them. And they brought the men to his house by night, and taking their provisions they put them on pack-animals and led them to the mountains as he had ordered them.

9   Then the ruler called those twelve men to himself and said to them: 'Be of good courage and fear not, for you are not going to die. For God is strong in whom you trust, and therefore be firm in him, who will set you free and save you. And now understand, I have given orders to fifty men to lead you out, with provisions taken from my house. Go to the mountains and hide yourselves in a valley, and I will give you fifty other men to lead you out thither. So go and hide yourselves there in the valley, having water to drink flowing down from the rock, and keep yourselves there for thirty days, until the hatred of the people of the land abates and until God sends his wrath upon them and shatters them. For I know that the plan of wickedness which they have plotted to do will not endure, since their thinking is empty. And it shall be, when seven days have passed and they look for you, that I shall say to them: "The door of the prison, in which they were shut up, was broken, so they have gone out and have fled in the night, and I have sent a hundred men to look for them." And I will turn them away from their present fury.'

10   Then eleven of the men replied to him saying, 'Your servants have found favour in your eyes, because we have been set free from the hands of these proud men'.

[a] *In domo regia.*

11   But Abraham alone was silent, so the leader said to him: 'Why do you not reply to me, Abraham, servant of God?' Abraham replied and said: 'Suppose I flee today to the mountains: if I escape the fire, wild animals may emerge from the mountains and come and devour us, or our food may run out and we shall die of hunger; and we shall be found fleeing before the people of the earth and falling in our sins. And now, as he lives in whom I trust, I will not move from my place in which they have put me. And if there be any sin of mine so that I am utterly consumed (in the fire), God's will be done.' Then the leader said to him: 'Your blood be on your own head if you are unwilling to go with them. But if you are willing to go you will be free. So if you wish to stay, stay as you will.' Then Abraham said, 'I will not go, here I will stay'.

12   Then the leader took the eleven men and sent fifty others with them, and gave them orders saying, 'Wait as well in the mountains for fifteen days with those fifty who have been sent on ahead, and when you come back, say, We did not find them, just as I have told the earlier men. And know that if anyone disobeys any of these words which I have spoken to you he shall be burned with fire.' So when the men had gone, he took Abraham alone and shut him up where he had been imprisoned before.

13   After seven days had gone by the people assembled and spoke to their leader saying, 'Hand over to us the men who refused to join in our plans and we will burn them with fire'. And they sent authorities to bring them, and they found none except Abraham. And the whole assembly said to their leaders, 'The men whom you imprisoned have fled, eluding our intention'.

14   Then Fenech and Nembroth said to Jectan: 'Where are the men whom you imprisoned?' He said: 'They completely broke their bonds in the night. But I have sent a hundred men to look for them, not only shall they burn them with fire but they shall give their bodies to the birds of the air, and thus shall they destroy them.'

15   At that they said to him, 'Then let us burn this one who was found'. And they took Abraham, and led him to their leaders; and they said to him, 'Where are those who were with you?' And he said, 'I was sleeping soundly one night; when I woke I could not find them'.

16   So they took him and built a furnace and set it alight. And they put bricks burnt with fire into the furnace. Then Jectan, stupefied, took Abraham and put him with the bricks in the fire of the furnace.

17   But God caused a great earthquake, and the fire, leaping up from the furnace, burst into flames and sparks of flame, and it burnt up all those standing around in sight of the furnace. And all those who were burnt up in that day were 83,500. But on Abraham there was not any sign of hurt in the burning of the fire.

18   So Abraham arose from the furnace and the fiery furnace fell down; and Abraham was saved, and he went to the eleven men who had hidden themselves in the mountains, and he told them everything that had happened

to him. And they came down with him from the mountains rejoicing in the name of the Lord, and no one met them to terrify them that day. And they called that place by the name of Abraham, and in the Chaldaean language Deli, which means God.

VII

1 And it happened after these things that the people of the land were not turned from their evil intentions, and they came together again to the leaders and said: 'The people will never be overcome: so let us now assemble and build for ourselves a city and a tower which will never be carried away.'[a]

2 And when they had begun to build it, God saw the city and the tower which the sons of men were building, and God said, 'Behold this is one people and their speech is one,[b] and this which they have begun to do the earth will not sustain nor heaven allow when it sees it. And it will be that if they are not hindered now they will dare everything which they take it in mind to do.

3 Therefore, behold, I will divide their speech[c] and I will scatter them in every region, and a man will not know his brother, nor will any man understand the language of his neighbour. And I will hand them over to the rocks, and they will build for themselves huts and reeds of straw; and they will dig out for themselves caves and dwell there like beasts of the field. And thus it will be in my sight for ever, that they may never devise these things. And I will reckon them as a drop of water and account them as spittle; and for some their end will come by water and others will be parched with thirst.

4 And before them all I will choose my child, Abraham, and I will bring him out from their land, and I will lead him into a land which my eye saw from the beginning when all the inhabitants of the earth sinned in my sight and I brought the water of the flood; and I did not exterminate it but preserved it. For the fountains of my wrath did not break forth in it, not did the water of my destruction come down upon it. Therefore there will I make my child Abraham to dwell, and I will make my covenant with him, and his seed will I bless, and I will be called his God for ever.'

5 But as for the dwellers on earth, when they had begun to build the tower God divided their languages and changed their appearances, and no one knew his brother, nor did anyone understand his neighbour's language. And so it happened that when the builders told their workmen to bring stones they brought water, and if they demanded water they brought straw, and thus their intention was broken down and they ceased to build the city. And God scattered them thence over the face of the whole earth. Therefore was the name of that place called Confusion, because there God confounded their languages and thence he scattered them over the face of the whole earth.[d]

[a] Gen. xi. 4.
[c] Gen. xi. 7.
[b] Gen. xi. 5–6.
[d] Gen. xi. 8–9.

VIII

1   But Abraham went forth from there and dwelt in the land of Canaan, and took with him Lot, his brother's son, and Sarai his wife.[a] And since Sarai was barren and had not conceived, Abraham took Agar her maidservant, and she bore for him Ishmael. And Ishmael had twelve sons.

2   Then Lot departed from Abram and dwelt in Sodom, but Abram dwelt in the land of Cham. And the men of Sodom were very wicked men and great sinners.[b]

3   And God appeared[c] to Abram saying: 'To your seed will I give this land, and your name will be called Abraham, and Sarai your wife will be called Sara.[d] And I will give you everlasting seed from her, and I will make my covenant with you.' And Abraham knew Sarah his wife, and she conceived and bore Isaac.[e]

4   Now Isaac took for himself a wife from Mesopotamia, the daughter of Batuel, and she bore for him Jacob and Esau.

5   Esau took as wives for himself Judin, daughter of Bereu, and Bassemech, daughter of Elom,[f] and Elibemam, daughter of Anan, and Manem, daughter of Samael, and she bore Adelifan for him, and the daughter of Danelifan, and the daughter of Elifan, Themar, Omar, Seffor, Getan, Zenaz, Amalech. And Judin bore Tenac, Isier, Vebemas; Bassemen bore Rugil. And the sons of Rugil were Naizar, Samaza. And Elibema bore Auzio, Ollam, Coromane, Tenethe, Chenatela.

6   Jacob took as wives for himself the daughters of Laban of Syria, Lia and Rachel, and two concubines Balam and Zelfam. And Lia bore for him Ruben, Symeon, Levi, Iudam, Ysachar, Zabulon and Dina their sister. And Rachel brought forth Joseph and Benjamin.

And Bala bore Dan and Neptali, and Zelfa bore Gad and Aser. These are the sons of Jacob, twelve in number, and one daughter.

7   So Jacob dwelt in the land of Canaan, and Sychem, the son of Emor the Correan, seized Dina his daughter and humiliated her. So the sons of Jacob, Symeon and Levi, attacked and slew their whole city with the edge of the sword, and they took Dina their sister and went away.[g]

8   After that Job[h] took her to wife and he begat by her fourteen sons and six daughters, that is, seven sons and three daughters before he was smitten with affliction, and afterwards, when he had been restored[i] (another) seven sons and three daughters. And these are their names: Elifac, Ermoe, Diasat,

[a] Gen. xii. 4–5.
[b] Gen. xiii. 12–13.
[c] *Visus est.*
[d] Gen. xiii. 15; xvii. 5, 15.
[e] *Ysaac.*
[f] Gen. xxvi. 34.
[g] Gen. xxxiv.
[h] Jobab (Gen. xxxvi. 33) was identified with Job; see Eusebius, *Praep. Ev.* ix. 25, and see also p. 15.
[i] *Salvus factus est.*

Philias, Diffar, Zellut, Thelon, and his daughters, Meru, Litaz, Zeli. And the names of the second group were the same as those of the first.

9 Now Jacob and his twelve sons dwelt in the land of Canaan. And they hated Joseph their brother, whom in fact they handed over into Egypt, to Potiphar, the chief of Pharaoh's cooks;[a] and he was with them for fourteen years.

10 And it happened, after the king of Egypt had seen a dream, that they told him about Joseph, and he unfolded the dreams to him. And it happened, after he had unfolded the dreams to him, that Pharaoh made him a ruler over all the land of Egypt. At that time there was a great famine in the earth, as Joseph had judged, and his brothers came down to buy food in Egypt, since only in Egypt was there any food. And Joseph recognised his brothers, but he was not known to them. And he did not treat them harshly but sent and called his father from the land of Canaan, and he came down to him.

(Verses 11–14 list the names of those who went down into Egypt, following roughly Gen. xlvi. 8 ff., but with some additions.)

XIII

6–10 Refers to creation and to the offence of Adam and Eve.

XVII

2–4 Compares the rod of Aaron[b] with the rods of Jacob 'while he was in Mesopotamia with Laban the Syrian'. Verse 4 reads: 'Therefore was the synagogue made like to a flock of sheep, and as the cattle brought forth according to the almond rods, so was the priesthood established by means of the almond rods.'

XVIII

5 Then God said to him (Balaam): 'Was it not of this people that I spoke to Abraham in a vision, saying, Your seed will be as the stars of heaven,[c] when I lifted him up above the firmament and showed him all the orderings of the stars[d] and asked for his son as a burnt-offering? He brought him and placed him on the altar, but I restored him to his father, and because he made no demur the offering was made acceptable in my sight, and I

---

a Pseudo-Philo has followed the mistaken LXX translation of Gen. xxxvii. 36.

b Num. xvii. 6, 8.

c Gen. xxii. 17.

d The legend that Abraham was taken up into heaven and shown around it is widespread in the Jewish tradition. See p. 291.

311

chose this people because of his blood.[a] Then said I to the angels who work cunningly,[b] Did I not say of him, I will reveal to Abraham everything that I do?[c]

6 And to Jacob also, his third son, whom I called the first-born: he, when he wrestled in the dust with the angel who takes charge of the praises,[d] did not let him go until he had blessed him. And now do you reckon to go with them that you may curse those whom I have chosen? . . .'

XIX

11 The rod of Moses is compared to the rainbow given as a sign of God's covenant with Noah, and it is said that it will be in God's sight as a remembrance.[e]

XXIII

4 Then Jesus[f] rose up in the morning and assembled all the people and said to them: 'Thus says the Lord: One rock was there, from which I dug out your father,[g] and the cutting of that rock begat two men whose names are these, Abraham and Nachor; and from the hewing out of that place two women were born whose names were Sara and Melcha, and they dwelt together across the river. And Abraham took Sara, and Nachor Melcha.

5 And when the inhabitants of the land were led astray, each one after his own presumption, Abraham believed in me and was not led astray with them. And I rescued him from the fire and took him and led him into the land of Canaan, and I said to him in a vision, I will give this land to your seed. And he said to me, But look, you have given me a wife and she is barren, so how shall I have seed from a womb shut up?

6 Then I said to him, Take for me a calf of three years old, and a she-goat of three years and a ram of three years, a turtle dove also and a pigeon.[h] And he took them as I commanded. But I sent a sleep on him and surrounded him with fear,[i] and put before him the place of fire in which are avenged[j] the works of those who do evil against me, and I showed him the torches of fire by which the just who have believed in me[k] shall be illuminated.

7 Then I said to him, These will be for a witness between me and you that I will give you seed from a womb shut up. And I will liken to the dove the city which you have taken to be mine, which your sons begin to build in my sight. But the turtle-dove I will liken to the prophets which are to be born from you, and I will liken the ram to the wise men who are to be enlightened from you, and I will liken the calf to the multitude of people who are to be

---

[a] *Pro sanguine eius elegi istos.*
[b] Or 'watch closely'? *Minute.*
[c] Gen. xviii. 17.
[d] *Cum angelo qui stabat super ymnos.*
[e] *In commemorationem.*
[f] I.e. Joshua.
[g] Isa. li. 1, 2.
[h] Gen. xv. 9–10.
[i] *Pavore.*
[j] *Expientur.*
[k] *Iusti qui crediderunt mihi.*

multiplied through you, and I will liken the she-goat to the women whose wombs I will open, and they will bring forth. And these things will be a witness between us that I will not break my words.

8 And I gave Isaac to him and formed him in the womb of her who bore him, and I ordered it to give him up quickly in the seventh month, and for this reason every woman who brings forth in the seventh month, the child shall live, because I have declared my glory over him.'

XXXII

1 Then Deborra and Barach the son of Abino and all the people together sang a hymn to the Lord in that day[a] saying: 'Behold from on high the Lord has shown his glory, just as he did in the earlier places, sending out his voice to confound the languages of men. And he chose our race, and plucked out of the fire Abraham our father, and he chose him before all his brothers, and guarded him from the fire and set him free from the bricks of building. And he gave him a son in the latest days of his old age bringing him out of a barren womb. And all the angels[b] were jealous of him, and the disposers of the hosts were envious of him.

2 So it happened, when they were jealous of him, that God said to him, Kill the fruit of your loins for my sake, and offer to me in a sacrifice that which was given to you from me. Abraham did not demur but set out at once. And as he went, he said to his son, Behold, now I am offering you as a burnt-offering to God, and I am delivering you into the hands of him who gave you to me.

3 Then the son said to his father, Hear me, father. If a lamb from the flock is accepted for an offering to the Lord for an odour of sweetness,[c] and for the iniquities of men sheep are appointed for slaughter, but man is set to inherit the world, then how do you now say to me, Come and inherit an unthreatened life,[d] and time without measure? If I had not been born in the world, I would not be offered as a sacrifice to him who made me. But my blessedness[e] will be above that of every man, because there will not be anything other;[f] and with respect to me generations will announce, and through me peoples will make known, that God has accounted the soul of man fit[g] for sacrifice.

4 Then when the father offered the son on the altar and bound his feet to kill him, the Most Mighty made haste and sent his voice from on high

[a] Josh. v. 1 ff.
[b] In Jub. xvii. 16 it is the prince Mastema who comes and tells God that Abraham loves Isaac more than he loves God. See the Targum and notes on Gen. xxii. 1.
[c] *In odorem suavitatis*, the phrase used by the Vulgate to describe the sacrifice of Noah.
[d] *Securam vitam.*
[e] *Beatitudo.*
[f] *Quia non erit aliud.*
[g] *Dignificavit.*

saying, You shall not kill your son, nor destroy the fruit of your loins. For now I have made manifest, that you may appear to those who know you not, and I have shut up the mouth of those who continually speak evil against you. And the remembrance of you[a] will be in my sight for ever, and your name and his will endure from generation to generation.

5 And he gave Isaac two sons, those also from wombs that were closed, and their mother was then in the third year of her marriage; and it will not be so with any other woman, nor shall she glorify herself so, who approaches her husband in the third year. And Esau and Jacob were born. And God chose Jacob, but Esau he hated because of his works.

6 And it happened that in the old age of their father Jacob blessed Isaac and sent him to Mesopotamia, and he begat there twelve sons. And they went down into Egypt and dwelt there.'

XL

2 (Jephthah's daughter tries to comfort her father who is bound to sacrifice her in obedience to a vow):[b] 'Who is it that is said to die when a people is set free? Or have you forgotten what happened in the days of our fathers, when a father gave his son for a burnt-offering, and he did not demur to him but agreed to it gladly, so that he who was being offered was prepared and he who was offering was rejoicing?'

[a] *Memoria tua.*   [b] Judg. xi. 29 ff.

APPENDIX II

THE SEVEN AND THIRTEEN RULES
OF INTERPRETATION

Biblical interpretation gradually evolved its own rules and methods. Two sets of rules were particularly respected, the seven rules (or *middoth*) of Hillel, and the extension of them in the thirteen *middoth* of Ishmael.

The seven *middoth* of Hillel are listed in A.R.N. 37, the introduction to Sifra 3*a*, and T.San. vii. 11. The *middoth* are:

1. *Qal waḥomer:* what applies in a less important case will certainly apply in a more important case.

2. *Gezerah shawah:* verbal analogy from one verse to another; where the same words are applied to two separate cases it follows that the same considerations apply to both.

3. *Binyan ab mikathub 'eḥad:* building up a family from a single text; when the same phrase is found in a number of passages, then a consideration found in one of them applies to all of them.

4. *Binyan ab mishene kethubim:* building up a family from two texts; a principle is established by relating two texts together; the principle can then be applied to other passages.[a]

5. *Kelal upherat:* the general and the particular; a general principle may be restricted by a particularisation of it in another verse; or conversely, a particular rule may be extended into a general principle.

6. *Kayoẓe bo bemaqom 'aḥer:* as is found in another place; a difficulty in one text may be solved by comparing it with another which has points of general (though not necessarily verbal) similarity.

7. *Dabar halamed me'inyano:* a meaning established by its context.

Exactly how these rules are related to Hillel is difficult to determine. Most of them are a matter of common sense, and it seems probable that they

---

[a] The fourth *middah* of Hillel is very uncertain. Some texts of Sifra omit it altgether, and thus state that there are seven *middoth* but then list only six. Other texts of Sifra read simply *shene kethubim*, 'two texts'; A. Schwarz (*Die hermeneutische Antinomie* . . .) took that to equal the thirteenth *middah* of Ishmael, *shene kethubim hamakḥishim* . . .: where two texts contradict each other a third text must be found to reconcile them. The argument is supported by the fact that the texts of T.San. also vary in their statement of this *middah*, which perhaps suggests that it was elaborated from the brief form *shene kethubim*. If Schwarz is right, it means that one of two similar *middoth* would be removed and an independent (and important) principle of exegesis would appear in the earliest formulation of exegetical rules.

315

existed before his time. No doubt they were attributed to Hillel because of the well-known story of how Hillel rose to prominence in Jerusalem: it was a consequence of his success in an exegetical debate with the bene Bathyra[a] in which Hillel used some of the seven *middoth*. There are three slightly different versions of the story, in J.Pes. vi. 1, T.Pes. iv. 1–3, B.Pes. 66a. Basically, an uncertainty arose when Nisan 14 fell on a sabbath: could the Passover offering be slaughtered on the sabbath or did the rules of sabbath observance take precedence? The bene Bathyra were told: 'There is a man

---

[a] The bene Bathyra (lit. Beteyra) occur frequently in Rabbinic literature, but it is difficult to be sure exactly who they were. Almost certainly the name was applied to different groups or at least to a changing group, which makes identification all the harder. The most important references to Bathyrans are as follows:

(i) In the first century B.C. they appear as a group (or family?) with considerable authority in religious matters. When Hillel came from Babylon he entered into dispute with them (T.Pes. iv. 12, J.Pes. vi. 1, B.Pes. 66a). He gained the ascendancy in Jerusalem by winning them over to his side.

(ii) Herod the Great wanted to strengthen his army against the Trachonites, and when he learned that 'a Jew from Babylonia (later named as Zamaris) had crossed the Euphrates with five hundred horsemen' he offered them tax-free land and settled them in Bathyra (*Ant.* xvii. 23–8). It would be hard to connect them with a religious group except for the fact that Josephus also says, 'There came to him many men—and from all parts—who were devoted to the ancestral customs of the Jews'.

(iii) The bene Bathyra appear as opponents of Rn. Joḥanan b. Zakkai in his attempts to reorganise Judaism at Yavneh. See, for example, B.R.H. 29b.

(iv) At least two Tannaim called Judah b. Bathyra lived in Nisibis. Nisibis was an important centre of Judaism in Mesopotamia, being almost exactly mid-way between Jerusalem and Yavneh (the centre of Palestinian Judaism) and Nehardea, the centre of Babylonian Judaism. J. Neusner argued (*A History of the Jews in Babylonia*, 1, 43–9) that the presence of a 'powerful and loyal adherent' of Pharisaism in Nisibis at an early date points to Nisibis being a staging-post in the transmission of tannaitic Judaism to Babylonia.

It is hard to say how many of these Bathyrans are connected. Hillel's *floruit* is usually placed c. 30 B.C., which would mean that (i) and (ii) might be unconnected; but Neusner (*op. cit.* p. 40 n. 1) argued that Hillel's prominence would have come late in his career and that his success in controversy with the Bathyrans is more credible on the assumption that Herod imported some of Zamaris' adherents and gave them influential positions in Jerusalem. On the other hand, S. B. Hoenig (*The Great Sanhedrin*, 1950) argued that there is no connection between (i) and (ii), and suggested that Hillel's opponents are not Bathyrans at all; the Tosefta calls them *bene Pathyra*, and if that is taken from *pathar* the meaning would be 'interpreters of scripture'. In addition to the works mentioned above see also L. Finkelstein, *Pharisees and Men of the Great Assembly*, J. Neusner, *A Life of Rabban Yoḥanan ben Zakkai*.

from Babylon, Hillel the Babylonian, who studied under the two greatest men of their generation;[a] he will know whether or not Passover takes precedence over Sabbath.' They sent for Hillel and he answered that the Passover offering *can* be slaughtered on the sabbath. According to J.Pes. and T.Pes. he proved this with three arguments, only two of which appear in the seven *middoth*. All three are specifically named in J.Pes., but only *qal waḥomer* is named in T.Pes.:

1. *Heqesh*: straightforward analogy; *tamid* (the daily sacrifice) is a whole-offering, a communal sacrifice, so is the Passover lamb. Since *tamid* takes precedence over sabbath, so too does the slaughtering of the Passover lamb.

2. *Qal waḥomer*: the omission of *tamid* does not carry the penalty of being 'cut off',[b] yet it takes precedence over sabbath; omission of passover *does* carry that penalty and is therefore a more important sacrifice, therefore it must take precedence over sabbath.

3. *Gezerah shawah*: the phrase 'at its appointed time' is used of *tamid* (Num. ix. 3) and of Passover (Num. xxviii. 2). Therefore what applies to *tamid* will apply also to the Passover lamb.

According to J.Pes. those arguments were rejected by the bene Bathyra, but when Hillel appealed to the authority of Shemaiah and Abtalion his argument prevailed.

According to B.Pes. Hillel produced only two arguments, (2) and (3), and these arguments were immediately accepted.

The contradictions in these accounts in fact suggest a possible picture of how the seven *middoth* emerged: several rules of exegesis gradually emerged, of which Hillel certainly used some, though they did not entirely coincide with the seven *middoth* as they were later formulated (J.Pes. included *heqesh*). As the rules began to establish themselves they became crystallised in the seven *middoth*. They were ascribed to Hillel because he was known to have used at least some of them, particularly in his debate with the bene Bathyra. Thus although he only used three on that occasion (B.Pes. made it two by omitting *heqesh*, no doubt because it was aware that *heqesh* was not one of the seven *middoth*) all seven were said in the later accounts to have been expounded to the bene Bathyra. A.R.N. 37 concludes, 'These are the seven *middoth* which Hillel the elder gave to the bene Bathyra', and T.San. vii. 11 says: 'Hillel expounded the following rules to the bene Pathyra[c] ...'

The thirteen *middoth* of R. Ishmael are extensions of the seven *middoth*, and they are printed (and translated) in the Jewish Daily Prayer Book.[d] There are also references to rules formulated by R. Ishmael's exegetical rival, R. Aqiba,[e]

[a] Shemaiah and Abtalion.
[b] Num. ix. 13.
[c] *Sic.*
[d] *The Authorised Daily Prayer Book* (1957), pp. 13–14; (1962), pp. 14–15.
[e] B.Gitt. 67a, Sifre on Num. xxv. 1. On the rivalry see p. 54.

and finally there are thirty-two rules of exegesis ascribed to R. Eliezer ben Jose haGelili.[a]

For a further discussion of the rules see especially W. Bacher, *Die Exegetische Terminologie* . . .; A. Schwarz (several works on rabbinic hermeneutics; see the bibliography); I. Sonne, *The Schools of Shammai and Hillel* . . .; D. Daube, 'Rabbinic Method of Interpretation and Hellenistic Rhetoric'; J. V. Doeve, *Jewish Hermeneutics* . . ., pp. 52–90; S. Zeitlin, 'Hillel and the Hermeneutic Rules'.

[a] Those rules are much later; they are transliterated and explained in H. L. Strack, *Introduction to the Talmud and Midrash*, pp. 95–8; for references pointing to the late date of the thirty-two Rules, see R. Loewe, 'The "Plain" Meaning of Scripture . . .', p. 152; and see also the Bibliography under H. G. Enelow. In addition to rules of exegesis there were of course many techniques and methods of extracting meaning from the text, some paying minute attention to each single letter. Four techniques of particularly common occurrence are *gematria* (adding up the numerical value of the letters), *notariqon* (taking the letters of a word as the initial letters of an acrostic), *ziruf* or *hiluf* (anagram) and *temurah* (substituting one letter for another).

APPENDIX III

THE RECOGNISED VARIANTS IN THE SEPTUAGINT

Certain passages were recognised as having been changed by the LXX translators for legitimate reasons. B.Meg. 9 *a–b* recorded the variants as follows:

' "God created in the beginning";[a] "I shall make man in image and likeness";[b] "And God completed his works which he had made, on the sixth day, and he rested from his works ... on the seventh day";[c] "Male with female parts[d] he created him";[e] "Now I will descend and there confound their tongues";[f] "And Sarah laughed among her relatives";[g] "For in their anger they slew an ox, and in their wrath they tore up a stall";[h] "And Moses took his wife and his sons, and made them ride on a carrier of man";[i] "And the sojourning of the children of Israel which they sojourned in Egypt and in other lands was four hundred (and thirty) years";[j] "And he sent the elect of the children of Israel";[k] "And against the elect of the children of Israel he put not forth his hand";[l] "I have taken not one valuable of theirs";[m] "Which the Lord thy God distributed to give light unto all the peoples";[n] "And he went and served other gods ... which I commanded the nations should not be served";[o] they also wrote for Ptolemy,[p] "and the slender-footed"[q] instead of "the hare", because Ptolemy's wife was called "Hare",[r] and he might have said, "They are mocking me by putting her name in Torah".'

[a] Gen. i. 1.
[b] Gen. i. 26.
[c] Gen. ii. 2.
[d] Or 'male and female'.
[e] Gen. v. 2.
[f] Gen. xi. 7.
[g] Gen. xviii. 12; Abraham also 'laughed inwardly', but not in public.
[h] Gen. xlix. 6.
[i] Exod. iv. 20; this sounds more dignified than 'an ass'.
[j] Exod. xii. 40; according to the Bible the stay in Egypt was only 210 years.
[k] Exod. xxiv. 5.
[l] Exod. xxiv. 11.
[m] Num. xvi. 15.
[n] Deut. iv. 19.
[o] Deut. xvii. 3.
[p] According to tradition, he commissioned the LXX; see the Introduction, p. 4.
[q] Lev. xi. 6; but since it is representing LXX δασύποδα, it should probably be 'covered with hair'.
[r] I.e. λαγώς (*lagus*); in fact, it was the name of Ptolemy's father; or perhaps because the Queen's name was Arnebeth, the Heb. for 'hare' in this verse.

In Mek. Pisḥa 14 the list is almost the same, but Exod. xxiv. 5 and 11 are not included, and the change in Exod. xii. 40 is different. Mekilta reads: 'Now the sojourning of the children of Israel, which they sojourned in Egypt and in the land of Canaan and in the land of Goshen, was four hundred and thirty years.'[a]

Mek. Amal. 1 also discusses Gen. xlix. 6–7 and suggests that it could be read: 'In their anger they slew a man[b] and in their self-will they hewed oxen that were cursed.'

The list of variants is also given in J.Meg. i. 5, Mas. Sof. i. 7 f.

[a] The conflict between Gen. xv. 13 and xv. 16, and between Gen. xv. 13 and Exod. xii. 40 is discussed by the Mekilta in the immediately preceding passage.

[b] Or 'men'.

APPENDIX IV

THE DOTTED WORDS IN GENESIS

A.R.N. 34 summarises the ten dotted words in the Pentateuch, of which five come in Genesis. In origin the placing of dots above particular letters was perhaps meant to indicate that the scribe had made a mistake, or that the reading was uncertain, or that some of the letters might perhaps be changed, but A.R.N. took them as implying something of exegetical importance:

'*The Lord judge between me and thee.*[a] The letter *y* is dotted to show that Sarah spoke to Abraham about Hagar alone; some say it refers to those who provoke arguments "beween me and you".

And they said unto him, Where is Sarah thy wife?[b] That is to show that they really knew where she was but still asked for her.

And he knew not when she lay down, nor when she arose.[c] That is to show that he did not know only when the younger daughter arose.

And Esau ran to meet him, and embraced him, and fell on his neck, and kissed him.[d] That is to show that he did not kiss him with all his heart. Rabbi Simeon ben Eleazar said that he did on this occasion, but that whenever else he kissed he did not.

And his brethren went to feed his father's flock in Shechem.[e] That is to show that they did not go to feed the flock, but to eat, drink and be merry.'

The other passages are: Num. iii. 39, ix. 10, xxi. 30, xxix. 15, and Deut. xxix. 28. On the dotted words see also L. Blau, *Masoretische Untersuchungen*, pp. 6–34; S. Liebermann, *Hellenism in Jewish Palestine*, pp. 43 ff.; S. Zeitlin, 'Some Reflections on the Text of the Pentateuch', *J.Q.R.* LI (1961), 321–4.[f]

a The *y* in the middle of 'and between thee' (*ubeyneyka*) is dotted, but the comment in A.R.N. makes it clear that what caused uncertainty was the suffix. A.R.N. recorded two suggestions: first, that it should have been, 'between me and *her* (i.e. Hagar); second, that it should have been, 'between me and them' (i.e. those who have tried to create dissension): Gen. xvi. 5.

b Gen. xviii. 9. The letters in *unto him* are all dotted. It is possible that the dots indicate that the words *unto him* are superfluous. There is no one else they could have been talking to. For other explanations see Ber.R. xlviii. 15.

c Gen. xix. 33. The letter *waw* in the middle of *when she arose* is dotted.

d Gen. xxxiii. 4. The letters in *and he kissed him* are dotted. Again, the word is superfluous, since the text already says that Esau embraced him.

e Gen. xxxvii. 12. The letters in the particle, *'eth*, which indicates the accusative, are dotted.

f See also Mas. Sof. vi. 3, Bem.R. iii. 13, Sifre on Num. ix. 10.

APPENDIX V

THE TRACTATES IN THE MISHNAH

The following is an alphabetical list of the tractates (*massektoth*) of the Mishnah. The number following each tractate shows in which of the six orders (*sedarim*) it is to be found. 1 = Zeraim, 2 = Moed, 3 = Nashim, 4 = Neziqin, 5 = Qodashim, 6 = Tohoroth.[a] The abbreviations used in references to the tractates usually take the first three or four letters or, in the case of a title made up of two separate words, the initial letter of each word; thus M.A.Z. = Mishnah Abodah Zarah.

Abodah Zarah (4)	Kilaim (1)	Rosh haShanah (2)
Aboth; also Pirqe	Maaseroth (1)	Sanhedrin (4)
Aboth (4)	Maaser Sheni (1)	Shabbath (2)
Arakin (5)	Makkoth (4)	Shebiith (1)
Baba Bathra (4)	Makshirin (6)	Shebuoth (4)
Baba Mezia (4)	Megillah (2)	Sheqalim (2)
Baba Qamma (4)	Meilah (5)	Sotah (3)
Bekoroth (5)	Menahoth (5)	Sukkah (2)
Berakoth (1)	Middoth (5)	Taanith (2)
Bezah (= Yom Tob) (2)	Miqwaoth (6)	Tamid (5)
Bikkurim (1)	Moed Qatan (2)	Tebul Yom (6)
Demai (1)	Nazir (3)	Temurah (5)
Eduyyoth (4)	Nedarim (3)	Terumoth (1)
Erubin (2)	Negaim (6)	Tohoroth (6)
Gittin (3)	Niddah (6)	Uqzin (6)
Hagigah (2)	Oholoth (6)	Yadaim (6)
Hallah (1)	Orlah (1)	Yebamoth (3)
Horayoth (4)	Parah (6)	Yoma (2)
Hullin (5)	Peah (1)	Yom Tob (= Bezah) (2)
Kelim (6)	Pesahim (2)	Zabim (6)
Kerithoth (5)	(K) Qiddushin (3)	Zebahim (5)
Ketuboth (3)	(K) Qinnim (5)	

[a] For the meaning of these terms, see p. 60.

APPENDIX VI

RABBINIC GENERATIONS

Rabbis are dated by the generations in which they lived—their actual dates are rarely known (see pp. 49, 53); it follows that dates are usually approximate. The rabbis are divided into three groups, pre-Tannaim (to A.D. 10), Tannaim (A.D. 10 to 220), and Amoraim. The Tannaim are divided into six generations, perhaps because there were six descendants or successors of Hillel:[a]

T1	10–80
T2	80–120
T3	120–140
T4	140–65
T5	165–200
T6	200–20

The Amoraim are divided into countries (Palestine and Babylonia) as well as into generations. The division into generations varies in different systems, and the classifications of the *Jewish Encyclopedia* and of the *Rabbinic Anthology* are both given here.

Jewish Encyclopedia

PA1	219–79	BA1	219–57
PA2	279–320	BA2	257–320
PA3	320–59	BA3	320–75
		BA4	375–427
		BA5	427–68
		BA6	468–500

Rabbinic Anthology

PA1	Ḥiyya (mid second century)	BA1	Huna I (*c.* 260)
PA2	Joḥanan (d. 279)	BA2	Ḥisda (d. 309)
PA3	Ammi (third century)	BA3	Rabbah b. Naḥmani (d. 339)

[a] The six are: (1) Simeon (B.Shab. 15a). (2) Rn. Gamaliel I (T1) (Acts v. 34). (3) Rn. Simeon I b. Gamaliel I. (4) Rn. Gamaliel II. (5) Rn. Simeon II b. Gamaliel II. (6) Rabbi, R. Judah haNasi. A slightly different system of dating the Tannaitic generations (followed, e.g., by R. le Déaut) divides them into five generations as follows: T1, 10–90; T2, 90–130; T3, 130–60; T4, 160–200; T5, 200–20.

PA 4   Mana (fourth century)
PA 5   Tanḥuma b. Abba (fourth
        century)

BA 4   Raba (d. 352)

BA 5   Papa (d. 375)
BA 6   Mar Zutra (d. 417)
BA 7   Rabina b. Huna (d. 499)

The Index to the Soncino Talmud indicates the century, *not* the generation, to which each rabbi belonged.

APPENDIX VII

CAIRO GENIZA FRAGMENTS

Published in P. Kahle, *Masoreten des Westens* II, part 2.

Genesis iv. 4–16	pp. 6–7
vi. 18–vii. 15	pp. 30–1
vii. 17–viii. 8	pp. 15–16
ix. 5–23	pp. 31–2
xxviii. 17–xxxi. 35	pp. 33–42
xxxi. 38–54	pp. 8–9
xxxii. 13–30	pp. 10–11
xxxiv. 9–25	pp. 11–12
xxxv. 7–15	pp. 12–14
xxxvii. 20–34	pp. 16–17
xxxviii. 16–26	pp. 18–19
xxxviii. 16–xxxix. 10	pp. 42–5
xli. 6–26	pp. 45–6
xliii. 7–xliv. 23 (3 fragments)	pp. 19–22 (only parts of these verses occur)
xliii. 23–xliv. 5	pp. 47–8
xlviii. 11–20	pp. 22–3

On other biblical books: Exod. v. 20–vi. 10, vii. 10–22, ix. 21–33, xv, xix. 1–xx. 23, xx, xxi. 1–xxii. 27; Lev. xxii. 26–xxiii. 44; Num. xxviii. 16–31; Deut. v. 19–26, xxvi. 18–xxvii. 11, xxviii. 15–18, 27–9, xxxiv. 5–12.

BIBLIOGRAPHY

Details of texts and translations of rabbinic and other works have been given in the Introduction, and for reasons of space they are not repeated separately but are included in the general bibliography. For ease of reference an alphabetical list of the main works is given here, together with the page of the Introduction where they are discussed and where references to the general bibliography will be found.

I. Main works cited

II. Reference Works

Berlin, M. and Zevin, S. Y. (ed.). *Encyclopedia Talmudit*, i–x, Jerusalem, 1946 *et seq.*

Brederek, E. *Konkordanz zum Targum Onkelos*, Giessen, 1906.

Buxtorf, J. (ed. B. Fischer). *Lexicon Chaldaicum, Talmudicum et Rabbinicum . . .*, 2 vols. Leipzig, 1869, 1875.

Dalman, G. H. *Aramäisch-neuhebräisches Handwörterbuch zu Targum, Talmud und Midrasch*, second edn. Frankfurt, 1922.
Grammatik des jüdisch-palästinischen Aramäisch nach den Idiomen des palästinischen Talmud, des Onkelostargum und Prophetentargum und der Jerusalemischen Targume, second edn. Leipzig, 1905.
Encyclopaedia Judaica (10 vols. only)
Goldschmidt, L. *Subject Concordance to the Babylonian Talmud* (ed. R. Edelmann), Copenhagen, 1959.
Horovitz, A. M. *Thesaurus Midrasi Rabbae* (A only), Jerusalem, 1939.
Hyman, A. *Beit Vaad leHekamim*, London, 1902.
Jastrow, *A Dictionary of the Targumim, the Talmud Babli and Yerushalmi, and the Midrashic Literature*, 2 vols. repr. New York, 1950.
Jeiteles, B. *Ozar Tannaim veAmoraim*, I, Manchester, 1961.
The Jewish Encyclopedia
Kassovsky, H. J. *Ozar Lashon haTosefta*, I–VI, Jerusalem, 1912 et seq.
Ozar Lashon haTalmud, I–XI, Jerusalem, 1954 et seq.
Ozar Lashon haMishnah, I–IV, Jerusalem, 1957 et seq.
Concordance to the Targum Onqelos, Jerusalem, 1947.
Kiriyat Sefer, Bibliogr. Quarterly, 1924– (Hebr.).
Kittel, G. *et al. Theologisches Wörterbuch zum Neuen Testament.*
Krauss, S. *Griechische und Lateinische Lehnwörter in Talmud, Midrasch und Targum*, Berlin, 1898.
Levy, J. *Chaldäisches Wörterbuch uber die Targumim . . .*, repr. 1959.
Margoliouth, M. (ed.). *Encyclopedia of Talmudic and Geonic Literature*, Tel Aviv, 1946.
Margolis, M. L. *A Manual of the Aramaic Language of the Babylonian Talmud*, München, 1910.
Mayer, L. A. *Bibliography of the Samaritans*, suppl. to *Abr Nahraim*, no. 1, 1964 (ed. D. Broadribb).
Neumann, D. *Motif-Index of Talmudic-Midrashic Literature* (photogr. repr. of thesis, Michigan, 1954).
Pauly–Wissowa, *Realencyclopädie der Klassischen Altertumswissenschaft. Real-encyclopädie für Bibel und Talmud.*
Sambatyon, M. *An Encyclopaedic Dictionary of the Talmud . . .*, I, Tel Aviv, 1955.
Segal, M. H. *A Grammar of Mishnaic Hebrew*, Oxford, 1927.
Stevenson, W. B. *Grammar of Palestinian Jewish Aramaic*, Oxford, 1924, new edn. 1962.
Strack, H. L. and Billerbeck, P. *Kommentatar zum Neuen Testament aus Talmud und Midrasch*, 1922–8.

III. General Bibliography

Abel, F. M. *Histoire de la Palestine depuis la conquête d'Alexandre jusqu'à l'invasion arabe*, 2 vols. Paris, 1952.

Abelson, J. *The Immanence of God in Rabbinical Literature*, London, 1912. *Jewish Mysticism*, London, 1913.

Abrahams, I. *Studies in Pharisaism and the Gospels*, 2 vols. Cambridge, 1917, 1924.

Aicher, G. *Das Alte Testament in der Mischna*, Freiburg, 1906.

Albeck, H. (Ch.). *Untersuchungen über die Redaktion der Mischna*, Berlin, 1923.

'Die Herkunft des Tosefta-materials', *M.G.W.J.* LXIX, 1925.

Untersuchungen über die halakischen Midraschim, Berlin, 1927.

'Apocryphal Halakah in the Palestinian Targums and the Aggadah', in *Jub. Vol. to B. M. Lewin*, Jerusalem, 1940, 93–104.

'On the Editing of the Talmud Babli', *Tarbiz*, XV, 1943, 14–26.

Mehqarim baBaraita uvaTosefta, Jerusalem, 1954 (Hebr.).

Mabo laMishnah, Jerusalem, Tel Aviv, 1959 (Hebr.).

Shishah Sidrei Mishnah, 6 vols. Jerusalem, 1953–9 (Hebr.).

Midrash Bereshit Rabba (second edn. with corrections by H. Albeck), Jerusalem, 1965 (with J. Theodor, *q.v.*).

Alon, G. *Toledoth ha Yehudim be'Erez Yisrael biTekufat haMishnah weha-Talmud*, 2 vols. Tel Aviv, 1952–5 (Hebr.).

Mehqarim beToledoth Yisrael . . ., 2 vols. Tel Aviv, 1957–8 (Hebr.).

'Studies in the Halakah of Philo', *Tarbiz*, V, 1933, 28–36; 1934, 241–6; VI, 1934, 30–7; 1935, 452–9 (Hebr.).

'Some Early Tannaitic Halakoth', *Tarbiz*, IX, 1938, 278–83 (Hebr.).

'The Halakah in the Epistle of Barnabas', *Tarbiz*, XI, 1939, 23–38 (Hebr.).

Altmann, A. (ed.). *Biblical Motifs*, Harvard, 1966.

Amir, J. 'Philo's Homilies on Fear and Love and their Relation to the Palestinian Midrashim', *Zion*, XXX, 1965, 47–60 (Hebr.).

Aptowitzer, V. 'Das Schriftwort in der rabbinischen Literatur', I–V, 1906–15.

'La chute de Satan et des Anges', *R.E.J.* LIV, 59–63.

Kain und Abel in der Agada, den Apokryphen, der hellenistischen, christlichen und muhammedanischen Literatur, Leipzig, 1922.

Parteipolitik der Hasmonäerzeit im rabbinischen und pseudepigraphischen Schrifttum, Wien, 1927.

Arzt, M. 'The Teacher in Talmud and Midrash', *M. M. Kaplan Jubilee Volume*, New York, 1953.

Baars, W. 'A Targum on Exod. xv. 7–21 from the Cairo Geniza', *V.T.* XI, 1961, 340–2.

Bacher, W. *Die Agada der babylonischen Amoräer*, Strassburg, 1878, second edn. Frankfurt, 1913.

Die Agada der Tannaiten, 2 vols. Strassburg, 1884–90.

Bacher, W. (*cont.*)
Die Agada der palästinischen Amoräer, 3 vols. Strassburg, 1892–9.
Terminologie der Tannaiten, Leipzig, 1899.
Terminologie der Amoräer, Leipzig, 1905.
Die exegetische Terminologie der jüdischen Traditions-literatur, 2 vols. Leipzig, 1899, 1905 (collective reference to above vols.).
Die Proömien der alten jüdischen Homilie, Leipzig, 1913.
'Satzung vom Sinai', in *Studies . . . in honour of K. Kohler*, Berlin, 1913.
Tradition und Tradenten in den Schulen Palästinas und Babyloniens, Frankfurt, 1914.
Rabbanan, die Gelehrten der Tradition, Budapest, 1914.
Erkhe Midrash, Tel Aviv, 1923 (Hebr.).
Baer, Y. 'The Ancient Hasidim in Philo's Writings and in Hebrew Tradition', *Zion*, XVIII, 1953, 91–108 (Hebr.).
'The Book of Josippon the Jew', *Benzion Dinaburg Festschrift*, 1949, pp. 178–205 (Hebr.).
Bamberger, B. J. *Proselytism in the Talmudic Period*, Cincinnati, 1939.
'Revelations of Torah after Sinai', *H.U.C.A.* XVI, 1941, 97–113.
'The dating of Aggadic Materials', *J.B.L.* LXVIII, 1949.
Bardtke, H. 'Der Traktat der Schreiber (Sopherim)', W.Z. d. Karl Marx-Univ. Leipzig, III, 1953–4.
Barnstein, H. *The Targum Onkelos to Genesis . . .*, London, 1896.
Baron, S. W. *A Social and Religious History of the Jews*, 8 vols. Philadelphia, 1952.
Bassfreund, J. 'Das Fragmententhargum zum Pentateuch, sein Ursprung und Charakter und sein Verhältniss zu den anderen pentateuchischen Targumim', Breslau, 1896 (from *M.G.W.J.* XL, 1896).
Baumstark, A. 'Neue orientalistische Probleme biblischer Textgeschichte', *Z.D.M.G.* LXXXIX, 1935, 89–118.
Belkin, S. *Philo and the Oral Law*, H.S.S. XI, 1940.
'On the Question of the Sources of the Commentary of Philo of Alexandria', *Horeb*, IX, 1946, 1–20 (Hebr.).
'The Interpretation of Names in Philo', *Horeb*, XII, 1956, 3–61 (Hebr.).
'Philo and the Midrashic Tradition of Palestine', *Horeb*, XIII, 1958, 1–60 (Hebr.).
'Philo of Alexandria's Questions and Answers on Genesis and Exodus and their Relation to the Palestinian Midrash', *Horeb*, XIV, 1960, 1–74 (Hebr.).
'The Philonic Exposition of the Torah in the Light of the Ancient Rabbinic Midrashim', *Sura*, IV, 1964, 1–68 (Hebr.).
Bergman, J. *Jüdische Apologetik im neutestamentlichen Zeitalter*, Berlin, 1908.
Das Judentum in der hellenistisch-römischen Zeit, Giessen, 1927.
Berliner, A. *Die Masorah zum Targum Onkelos nach Handschriften und unter Benutzung*, Leipzig, 1877.
Targum Onkelos, Berlin, 1884.
Beiträge zur Geographie und Ethnographie im Talmud und Midrasch, Berlin, 1884.

Bernhardt, K. H. 'Zu Eigenart und Alter der messianisch-eschatologischen Zusätze im Targum Jeruschalmi I', in *Gott und die Götter*, Berlin, 1958, 68–83.

Bikermann, E. J. 'La chaîne de la tradition pharisienne', *R.B.* LIX, 1952, 44–54.

'The Septuagint as a Translation', *P.A.A.J.R.* XXVIII, 1959.

Bin-Gorion, E. *Shebile Agada*, Jerusalem, 1950 (Hebr.).

Bin-Gorion, M. J. *Die Sagen der Juden*, 5 vols., second edn. Berlin, 1935.

Birkeland, H. 'The Language of Jesus', *A.N.V.A.* 1954.

Black, M. *An Aramaic Approach to the Gospels and Acts*, second edn. Oxford, 1954; third edn. 1967.

'Die Erforschung der Muttersprache Jesu', *T.L.* 1957, 663 ff.

Blackman, P. *Mishnayoth...*, 7 vols., second edn. London, New York, 1951–63.

Blau, L. 'Tosefta, Mischna et Baraita', *R.E.J.* LXVII, 1914, 1–23.

Das altjüdische Zauberwesen, second edn. 1928.

Masoretische Untersuchungen, Strassburg, 1891.

Bloch, J. *On the Apocalyptic in Judaism*, *J.Q.R.* Monograph no. 2, 1952.

Bloch, R. 'Ecriture et tradition dans le judaïsme', *Cahiers Sioniens* VIII, 1, 1954.

'Note méthodologique pour l'étude de la littérature rabbinique', *R.S.R.* XLIII, 1955, 194–227.

'Note sur l'utilisation des fragments de la Geniza du Caire pour l'étude du Targum palestinien', *R.E.J.* XIV, 1955, 5–35.

'Quelques aspects de la figure de Moïse dans la tradition rabbinique', in *Moïse l'Homme de l'Alliance*, Paris, 1955.

'Ezéchiel xvi: exemple parfait du procédé midrashique dans la Bible', *Cahiers Sioniens*, 1955.

'Midrash', *Dict. de la Bible*, suppl. V, Paris, 1957.

Boismard, M.-E. 'Les citations targumiques du quatrième évangile', *R.B.* LXVI, 1959, 374–8.

Bokser, B. Z. *Pharisaic Judaism in Transition*, New York, 1935.

Bonsirven, J. *On the Ruins of the Temple*, London, 1931.

Le Judaïsme palestinien au temps de Jésus-Christ, 2 vols. Paris, 1934–5.

Textes rabbiniques des deux premiers siècles chrétiens pour servir à l'intelligence du Nouveau Testament, Rome, 1955.

Bowker, J. W. 'Intercession in the Qur'ān and the Jewish Tradition', *J.S.S.* XI, 1966, 69–82.

'Speeches in Acts: a Study in Proem and Yelammedenu Form', *N.T.S.* XIV, 1967, 96–111.

'Haggadah in the Targum Onqelos', *J.S.S.* XII, 1967, 51–65.

Bowman, J. 'The Pharisees', *Evang. Quart.* XX, 1948.

'Prophets and Prophecy in Talmud and Midrash', *Evang. Quart.* XXII, 1950.

Braude, W. G. *Jewish Proselytizing in the First Five Centuries of the Common Era*, Brown Univ. Studies, 1940.
'Overlooked Meanings of Certain Editorial Terms in the Pesikta Rabbati', *J.Q.R.* LII, 1962, 264–72.
The Midrash on Psalms, Yale Judaica Series, 1959.
Brayer, M. 'The Pentateuchal Targum attributed to Jonathan benUziel, a Source for Unknown Midrashim', in *Abraham Weiss Memorial Volume*, 201–31 (Heb.).
Brownlee, W. H. 'The Habakkuk Midrash and the Targum of Jonathan', *J.J.S.* VII, 1956, 169–86.
Buber, S. *Lekaḥ-Tob on Genesis and Exodus*, 1880 (completed by A. M. Padwa on Lev., Num. and Deut., Wilna, 1884).
Midrasch Tanchuma, 3 (4) vols. Wilna, 1885.
Midrasch Tehillim, Trier, 1892.
Midrasch Mishle, Wilna, 1893.
Midrasch Samuel, Cracow, 1893, Second edn. Wilno, 1924.
Midrasch Aggadah, Vienna, 1894.
Midrasch Zuta on Megilloth, Berlin, 1894, second edn. Wilno, 1925.
Aggadath Esther, Cracow, 1897, second edn. Wilno, 1925.
Ekah Rabbati, Wilna, 1899.
Yalkut Makiri, 2 vols. Berdyczew, 1899.
Midrasch Sechel-Tob, Berlin, 1900–1.
Aggadath Bereshith, Cracow, 1902, second edn. Wilno, 1925.
Pesiqta von Rab Kahana, second edn. Wilno, 1925.
Büchler, A. *Der galiläische Am haAreẓ des zweiten Jahrhunderts*, Vienna, 1906.
'Learning and Teaching in the Open Air in Palestine', *J.Q.R.* IV, 1913–14, 485–91.
The Economic Conditions of Judaism after the Destruction of the Second Temple, London, 1912.
Types of Jewish-Palestinian Piety . . ., London, 1922.
Studies in Sin and Atonement in the Rabbinic Literature of the First Century, London, 1928.
Chajes, Z. H. *The Student's Guide Through the Talmud*, Eng. trans. London, 1952.
Charles, R. H. (ed.). *The Apocrypha and Pseudepigrapha of the Old Testament in English*, Oxford, 1913 (repr. 1963).
Churgin, P. *Targum Jonathan to the Prophets*, New Haven, 1927.
'The Targum and the Septuagint', *A.J.S.L.* L, 1933–4, 41–65.
The Targum to the Hagiographa, 1945 (Hebr.).
Clark, K. W. 'Worship in the Jerusalem Temple after A.D. 70', *N.T.S.* VI, 1960, 269 ff.
Cohen, A. ed. *The Minor Tractates of the Talmud*, London, 1965.
Cohen, B. *Mishna and Tosefta: a comparative study*, I. Shabbat, New York, 1935.
(ed.) *The Saadia Anniversary Volume*, Texts and Studies, II, New York, 1943.

Corré, A. D. 'The Spanish Haftara for the Ninth of Ab', *J.Q.R.* XLVIII, 1957, 13–34.

Cowling, G. J. 'New Light on the New Testament? The Significance of the Palestinian Targum', *T.S.F. Bulletin*, 1968.

Dalbert, P. *Die Theologie der hellenistisch-jüdischen Missions-literatur* ..., Hamburg, 1954.

Dalman, G. *Aramäische Dialektproben*, 1927, repr. 1960 with *Grammatik* ... (see reference works).

Danby, H. trans. *Tractate Sanhedrin, Mishnah and Tosefta*, London, 1919. *The Mishnah*, Oxford, 1933.

Daniélou, J. *The Theology of Jewish Christianity*, Eng. trans. 1964.

Daube, D. Review of S. Belkin, *B.O.* v, 1948, 64–5.
'Rabbinic Method of Interpretation and Hellenistic Rhetoric', *H.U.C.A.* XXII, 1949, 239–64.
'Alexandrian Methods of Interpretation and the Rabbis', *Festschrift H. Lewald*, Basel, 1953.
The New Testament and Rabbinic Judaism, London, 1956.

Davies, W. D. *Torah in the Messianic Age and/or the Age to Come*, *J.B.L.* monogr. 7, 1952.
Paul and Rabbinic Judaism, London, second edn. 1953.
Christian Origins and Judaism, London, 1962.
The Setting of the Sermon on the Mount, Cambridge, 1964.

Déaut, R. le. 'Le Targum de Gen. xxii. 8 et I Pet. i. 20', *R.S.R.* XLIX, 1961, 103–6.
'Traditions targumiques dans le Corpus paulinien?', *Bibl.* XLII, 1961, 28–48.
La Nuit Pascale, Rome, 1963.
Liturgie juive et Nouveau Testament, Rome, 1965.
Introduction à la littérature targumique, Rome, 1966.

Dias, J. R. 'Ediciones del Targum samaritano', *E.B.* xv, 1956.
'Palestinian Targum and New Testament', *N.T.* VI, 1963, 75–80.

Diez-Macho, A. A complete bibliography appears in 'Magister-Minister' (see below). A few of the most important works are listed here:
'Nuevos fragmentos del Targum palestinense', *Sefarad*, xv, 1955.
'Nuevos fragmentos de Tosefta Targúmica', *Sefarad*, xvi, 1956.
'Nuevos manuscritos importantes, bíblicos et litúrgicos, en hebreo ó arameo', *Sefarad*, xvi, 1956.
'Una copia de todo el Targum Jerosolimitano ...', *E.B.* xv, 1956.
'The Recently Discovered Palestinian Targum: its Antiquity ...', suppl. to *V.T.* VII, 1960.
'Magister-Minister' (correspondence with Paul Kahle relating to the Targums, including a bibliography of Diez Macho's publications) in *Recent Progress in Biblical Scholarship* (ed. M. P. Hornik, Lincombe Lodge, 1965), 13–53.
'Targum', art. in *Enc. Bib.* VI, 1965, 865–81.

Doeve, J. V. *Jewish Hermeneutics in the Synoptic Gospels and Acts*, Assen, 1954.
'Le rôle de la tradition orale dans la composition des 'Evangiles synoptiques', in *La Formation des Evangiles*, Louvain, 1957.

Dor, Z. 'The Original Forms of some Statements of the First Palestinian Amoraim', *Tarbiz*, xxvi, 1957 (Hebr.).

Doubles, M. C. 'Towards the Publication of the Extant Texts of the Palestinian Targum(s)', *V.T.* xv, 1965, 16–26.

Drazin, N. *History of Jewish Education, 515 B.C.E.–220 C.E.*, Baltimore, 1940.

Dünner, J. H. *Die Theorien über Wesen und Ursprung der Tosephta kritisch dargestellt*, Amsterdam, 1874.

Edelmann, R. 'Features in Arabic Translations of the Pentateuch', *Melilah*, v, 1955, 45–50 (Hebr.).

Edersheim, A. *The Life and Times of Jesus the Messiah*, London, 1901.

Eisenstein, J. D. *Ozar Midrashim*, 2 vols. New York, 1915 (Hebr.).
Ozar Derushin Nibharim, New York, 1918.

Eissfeldt, O. 'Zur Kompositionstechnik des pseudo-philonischen Liber Antiquitatum Biblicarum', *Mélanges Mowinckel*, 1955, 53–71.
The Old Testament, an Introduction, Eng. trans. Oxford, 1965.

Elbogen, I. *Der jüdische Gottesdienst in seiner geschichtlichen Entwicklung*, third edn. Frankfurt, 1931.

Enelow, H. G. *The Mishnah of R. Eliezer, or The Midrash of the Thirty-two Hermeneutic Rules*, New York, 1933.

Epstein, A. *Midrash Tadshe...*, Vienna, 1887.

Epstein, I. (ed.). *The Talmud Babli*, 35 vols. Soncino Press, 1935–52 (reissued in 18 vols. 1961).

Epstein, J. N. 'On the Mishnah of R. Judah', *Tarbiz*, xv, 1943, 14–26 (Hebr.).
Mekilta deR. Simeon b. Johai, Jerusalem, 1955.
Mebooth leSifruth haTannaim, Jerusalem, Tel-Aviv, 1957 (ed. E. Z. Melamed) (Hebr.).
Mebooth leSifruth haAmoraim, Jerusalem, 1962 (ed. E. Z. Melamed) (Hebr.).
Mabo leNosah haMishnah, second edn. Tel-Aviv, 1964 (Hebr.).

Epstein, L. M. *Marriage Laws in Bible and Talmud*, Cambridge, Mass., 1942.

Etheridge, J. W. *The Targums of Onkelos and Jonathan ben Uzziel on the Pentateuch*, 2 vols. London, 1862–5.

Farmer, W. R. *Maccabees, Zealots, and Josephus*, New York, 1956.

Feldman, A. *The Parables and Similes of the Rabbis, Agricultural and Pastoral*, second edn. Cambridge, 1927.

Feldman, L. H. *Studies in Judaica*, Yeshiva Univ., n.d.
'The Orthodoxy of the Jews in Hellenistic Egypt', *J. Soc. Stud.* xxii, 1960, 215–37.

Feuillet, A. 'Les sources du livre Jonas', *R.B.* liv, 1947, 162–7.

Fiebig, P. *Die Gleichnisreden Jesu im Lichte der rabbinischen Gleichnisse des neutestamentlichen Zeitalters*, Tübingen, 1912.
Der Tosephtatraktat Rosh ha Shanah..., Bonn, 1914.
Jesu Bergpredigt..., Göttingen, 1924.
Der Erzählungsstil der Evangelien im Lichte des rabbinischen Erzählungsstils untersucht..., Leipzig, 1925.
Die Umwelt des Neuen Testamentes..., Göttingen, 1926.
Der Talmud, seine Entstehung, sein Wesen, sein Inhalt..., Leipzig, 1929.
Rabbinische Formegeschichte und Geschichtlichkeit Jesu, Leipzig, 1931.
Finch, R. G. *The Synagogue Lectionary and the New Testament*, London, 1939.
Finkel, A. *The Pharisees and the Teacher of Nazareth*, Leiden, 1964.
Finkelstein, L. 'The Book of Jubilees and the Rabbinic Halakah', *H.T.R.* XVI, 1923, 39–61.
Akiba, Scholar, Saint and Martyr, New York, 1936.
'Introductory Study to Pirqe Abot', *J.B.L.* LVII, 1938, 13–50.
'The Transmission of the Early Rabbinic Traditions', *H.U.C.A.* XVI, 1941, 115–35.
The Pharisees, 2 vols. Philadelphia, 1946.
HaPerushim weAnshe Keneset haGedolah, New York, 1950 (Hebr.).
Mabo leMassektot Abot weAbot deRabbi Nathan, New York, 1950 (Hebr.).
(ed.) *The Jews*, 2 vols. New York, 1960.
Finkelstein, M. L. 'Midrash, Halakot, and Haggadot', in *Sefer haYobal* (presented to Y. Baer), Jerusalem, 1960, 28–47.
Fisch, S. 'The Midrash Haggadol: its Author, Date and Place, and its Importance in Rabbinic Literature', *Melilah*, I, 1944, 129–41 (Hebr.).
Midrash Haggadol on the Pentateuch: Numbers..., Manchester, 1940; London, 1957 (Hebr.).
Fitzmyer, J. A. *The Genesis Apocryphon of Qumran Cave I*, Rome, 1966.
Flusser, D. 'The Author of the Book of Josippon', *Zion*, XVIII, 1953, 109–26 (Hebr.).
Frankel, Z. *Darke haMishnah*, Leipzig, 1859, repr. Israel, 1959.
Mabo haYerushalmi, Breslau, 1870.
Zu dem Targum der Propheten, Breslau, 1872.
Freedman, H. and Simon, M. (ed.). *The Midrash Rabbah*, 10 vols. Soncino Press, 1939.
Friedländer, G. *Rabbinic Philosophy and Ethics*..., London, 1912.
Pirke deRabbi Eliezer, London, 1916, repr. Hermon Press, 1965.
Friedmann, M. *Sifre on Deuteronomy*..., Vienna, 1864.
Mechilta deRabbi Ismaël..., Vienna, 1870.
Pesikta Rabbati, Vienna, 1880.
Onkelos und Akylas, Vienna, 1896.
Seder Eliahu rabba und Seder Eliahu Zuta..., Vienna, 1902.
Gandz, S. 'The Calendar of the Seder Olam', *J.Q.R.* XLIII, 1952, 177–92; 1953, 249 ff.

Gaster, M. *The Chronicles of Jerahmeel*, Oriental Translation Fund, IV, 1899.
The Exempla of the Rabbis, Cambridge, 1924.
Geiger, A. *Urschrift und Übersetzungen der Bibel*, second edn. Frankfurt, 1928.
Gerhardsson, B. *Memory and Manuscript*, Uppsala, 1961.
Tradition and Transmission in Early Christianity, Copenhagen, 1964.
Gerkan, A. von. 'Zur Hauskirche von Dura-Europos', in *Mullus: Festschrift Theodor Klauser*, ed. A. Stuiber and A. Hermann, Münster, 1964.
Ginsberg, H. L. (ed.). *Rashi Anniversary Volume*, Texts and Studies, I, New York, 1941.
Ginsburger, M. 'Die Anthropomorphismen in den Targumim', *Z.P.T.* 1891, 262–80, 430–58.
Das Fragmententhargum, Berlin, 1899.
'Die Fragmente des Thargum jeruschalmi zum Pentateuch', *Z.D.M.G.* LVII, 1903, 67–80.
Thargum Jonathan ben Usiël zum Pentateuch, Berlin, 1903.
'Les introductions araméennes à la lecture du Targum', *R.E.J.* LXXIII, 1921, 14–26, 186–94.
Ginzberg, L. *The Legends of the Jews*, 7 vols. Philadelphia, 1911–38.
'Tamid the Oldest Treatise of the Mishnah', *J.J.L.P.* I, 1919.
'The Religion of the Jews at the Time of Jesus', *H.U.C.A.* I, 1924.
(ed.) *Geniza Studies in Memory of Dr S. Schechter, I, Midrash and Haggadah*, New York, 1928.
'Jewish Folklore, East and West', in *Independence, Thought and Art*, Cambridge, Mass., 1937, 89–108.
A Commentary on the Palestinian Talmud . . ., 3 vols. New York, 1941 (Hebr.).
Glatzer, N. N. *Geschichte der Talmudischen Zeit*, Berlin, 1937.
'A Study of Talmudic Interpretation of Prophecy', *J.R.* XXVI, 1946, 115 ff.
Hillel the Elder . . ., New York, 1956.
'Hillel the Elder in the Light of the Dead Sea Scrolls', in *The Scrolls and the New Testament*, ed. K. Stendahl, New York, 1957.
Goldberg, A. M. *The Mishnah Treatise Oholoth*, Jerusalem, 1955 (Hebr.).
'Purpose and Method in R. Judah haNasi's Compilation of the Mishnah', *Tarbiz*, XXVIII, 1959, 260–9 (Hebr.).
'Die spezifische Verwendung des Terminus Schekhinah im Targum Onkelos als Kriterium einer relativen Datierung', *Judaica*, XIX, 1963, 43–61.
Goldin, J. *The Fathers according to Rabbi Nathan*, Yale Judaica Series, X, 1955.
'The Three Pillars of Simeon the Righteous', *P.A.A.J.R.* XXVII, 1957, 43 ff.
Goldschmidt, L. *Sepher Jeṣirah . . .*, Frankfurt, 1894.
Der Babylonische Talmud . . ., 12 vols. repr. Berlin, 1965.

Goodenough, E. R. *The Jurisprudence of the Jewish Courts in Egypt . . .*, New Haven, 1929.

By Light, Light . . ., New Haven, 1935.

Review of H. A. Wolfson, *J.B.L.* LXVII, 1948, 87–109.

Jewish Symbols in the Greco-Roman Period, 12 vols. New York, 1953–65.

Gordon, C. H. 'Leviathan, Symbol of Evil', in A. Altmann (ed.), *Biblical Motifs*, Harvard, 1966, 1–9.

Goshen-Gottstein, M. H. *Text and Language in Bible and Qumran*, 1960.

Targumei haMiqra haAramiim, Jerusalem, 1963 (Hebr.).

Gottlieb, W. 'The Translation of Jonathan b. Uzziel of the Torah', *Melilah*, I, 1944, 26–34 (Hebr.).

Graetz, H. *History of the Jews*, 1891–.

Grayzel, S. *A History of the Jews*, Philadelphia, 1947.

Greenberg, M. 'The Stabilization of the Text of the Hebrew Bible . . .', *J.A.O.S.* LXXVI, 1956, 157–67.

Greenup, A. W. *The Targum on the Book of Lamentations*, Sheffield, 1893.

Grelot, P. 'Une Tosephta targoumique sur Genèse xxii dans un manuscrit liturgique de la Geniza du Caire', *R.E.J.* XVI, 1957, 5–26.

'Les Targums du Pentateuque, étude comparative d'après Genèse iv. 3–16', *Semitica*, IX, 1959, 59–88.

Grünbaum, M. *Gesammelte Aufsätze zur Sprach- und Sagenkunde*, Berlin, 1901.

Neue Beiträge zur semitischen Sagenkunde, Leiden, 1893.

Grünhut, L. *Midrasch Shir haShirim . . .*, Jerusalem–Jaffa, n.d.

Guignebert, C. A. H. *Le Monde Juif vers le Temps de Jésus*, Paris, 1935, Eng. trans. 1939.

Guilding, A. *The Fourth Gospel and Jewish Worship*, London, 1957.

Gutmann, M. *Zur Einleitung in die Halacha*, 2 vols. Budapest, 1909–13.

'Zur Entstehung des Talmuds', *Entwicklungsstufen der jüdischen Religion*, Giessen, 1927.

Guttmann, A. *Das redaktionelle und sachliche Verhältnis zwischen Mischna und Tosephta*, Breslau, 1928.

'Akiba, "Rescuer of the Torah" ', *H.U.C.A.* XVII, 1942–3, 395–421.

'The Significance of Miracles for Talmudic Judaism', *H.U.C.A.* XX, 1947, 363–406.

Guttmann, J. A. 'Tractate Abot: its place in Rabbinic literature', *J.Q.R.* XLI, 1950, 181–93.

Guttmann, T. *The Mashal in the Tannaitic Period*, Frankfurt, 1924; also in Hebr. trans. with additions.

Habermann, A. M. *Megillot Midbar Yehuda*, Israel, 1959.

Hallevy, E. E. *Midrash Rabbah*, 8 vols. Tel Aviv, 1956–63.

Hamp, V. *Der Begriff 'Wort' in den aramäischen Bibelübersetzungen*, München, 1938.

Harding, G. L. 'Recent Discoveries in Jordan', *P.E.Q.* XC, 1958, 7–18.

Hasida, N. Z. *Midrash Haggadol on Deut. i–xxiii. 3, Hassegullah*, nos. 1–78, Jerusalem, 1934–42.

Hausdorff, L. 'Zur Geschichte der Targumim nach talmudischen Quellen', *M.G.W.J.* XXXVIII, 1894, 203–13.

Heinemann, I. *Philons griechische und jüdische Bildung* . . ., Breslau, 1932.
Darke haAggadah, Jerusalem, 1950 (Hebr.).

Heinemann, J. 'The Triennial Cycle and the Calendar', *Tarbiz*, XXXIII, 1964, 362–8 (Hebr.).
Review of G. Vermes, *Tarbiz*, XXXV, 1965, 84–94 (Hebr.).
Prayer in the Period of the Tannaim and the Amoraim . . ., Jerusalem, 1964 (Hebr.).

Helfgott, B. W. *The Doctrine of Election in Tannaitic Literature*, New York, 1954.

Heller, B. 'Tendances et idées juives dans les contes hébreux', *R.E.J.* LXXVII, 1923, 97–126.

Hengel, M. *Die Zeloten*, Leiden, 1961.

Hennecke, E. *New Testament Apocrypha*, 2 vols. Eng. trans. 1963, 1965.

Herford, R. T. *Christianity in Talmud and Midrash*, London, 1903.
Talmud and Apocrypha: a Comparative Study of the Jewish Ethical Teaching in the Rabbinical and Non-Rabbinical Sources . . ., London, 1933.

Heschel, A. *Torah min haShamaim*, Soncino, 1962.

Higger, M. *The Seven Minor Tractates*, New York, 1930.
The Additional Tractates, New York, 1931.
Massekoth Derek Erez, Pirqe ben Azzai, Tosefta Derek Erez, New York, 1935.
Pirqe Rabbi Eliezer, Horeb, VIII, 1944–X, 1948.

Hill, H. E. *Messianic Expectation in the Targum to the Psalms*, Yale (Dissertation), 1955.

Hirsch, W. *Rabbinic Psychology; beliefs about the soul in Rabbinic literature of the Talmudic period*, London, 1947.

Hoenig, S. B. *The Great Sanhedrin*, New York, 1953.
'Historical Inquiries: 1. Heber Ir. 2. City-Square', *J.Q.R.* XLVIII, 1957, 123–39.
Review of A. M. Habermann, *J.Q.R.* LI, 1960, 72–8.
'What is the explanation for the term, "BeTalmud" in the Scrolls?', *J.Q.R.* LIII, 1963, 274–6.
'Circumcision: the Covenant of Abraham', *J.Q.R.* LIII, 1963, 322–34.
'The Suppositious Temple-Synagogue', *J.Q.R.* LIV, 1963, 115–31.

Hoffmann, D. *Die erste Mischna und die Controversen der Tannaim*, Berlin, 1882.
Zur Einleitung in die halachischen Midraschim, Berlin, 1886–7.
'Zur Einleitung in Mechilta deRabbi Simeon b. Yoḥai', *J.J.G.L.* III, 1900, 191–205.
Mechilta deRabbi Simeon b. Johai, ein halachischer und haggadischer Midrasch . . ., Frankfurt, 1905.
Midrasch ha-gadol zum Buche Exodus, Berlin, 1913.
Midrash Tannaim, Berlin, 1908–9.

Hornik, M. P. (ed.). *Recent Progress in Biblical Scholarship*, Lincombe Lodge, 1965.

Horowitz, H. S. and Rabin, I. A. *Sifre on Numbers and Sifre Zuta*, Leipzig, 1917.

Mekilta deRabbi Ishmael, Frankfurt, 1931.

Sifre on Deuteronomy, Berlin, 1939.

Hruby, K. 'La synagogue dans la littérature rabbinique', *L'Orient Syrien*, IX, 1964, 473–514.

Humbert, P. *Le Messie dans le Targum des Prophètes*, Lausanne, 1911 (*R.T.P.* XLIV, 5–46).

Hunzinger, C.-H. 'Aus der Arbeit an den unveröffentlichten Texten von Qumran', *T.L.* LXXXV, 1960, 151.

Hyman, A. *Toledoth Tannaim weAmoraim*, 3 vols. London, 1910 (Hebr.).

Jacobs, L. 'The Economic Conditions of the Jews in Babylon in Talmudic Times Compared with Palestine', *J.S.S.* II, 1957, 349–59.

Studies in Talmudic Logic and Methodology, London, 1961.

James, M. R. *The Biblical Antiquities of Philo*, London, 1917.

The Lost Apocrypha of the Old Testament, London, 1920.

Jansma, T. *Twee Haggada's uit de Palestijnse Targum van de Pentateuch*, Leiden, 1950.

Jellicoe, S. 'The Occasion and Purpose of the Letter of Aristeas; a re-examination', *N.T.S.* XII, 1966, 144–50.

Jellinek, A. *Bet haMidrasch. Sammlung kleiner Midraschim und vermischter Abhandlungen aus der älteren jüdischen Literatur*, 6 vols. Leipzig, 1853–77.

Jeremias, J. *Jerusalem zur Zeit Jesu*, Göttingen, 1958.

Juster, J. *Les Juifs dans l'Empire romain*, 2 vols. Paris, 1914.

Kadari, M. Z. 'The Use of d- Clauses in the Language of Targum Onkelos', *Textus*, III, 1963, pp. 36–59.

'Studies in the Syntax of Targum Onkelos', *Tarbiz*, XXXII, 1963, 232–51 (Hebr.).

Kadushin, M. *The Theology of Seder Eliahu*, New York, 1932.

The Rabbinic Mind, New York, 1952; second edn. 1965.

Kahle, P. *Textkritische und lexicalische Bemerkungen zum samaritanischen Pentateuchtargum*, Leipzig, 1898.

Der Masoretische Text des Alten Testaments nach der Überlieferung der babylonischen Juden, Leipzig, 1902.

Masoreten des Ostens, Leipzig, 1913.

Masoreten des Westens, I–II, Stuttgart, 1927–30.

'The Targums', *Melilah*, III, 1950, pp. 70–7.

'Das palästinische Pentateuchtargum und das zur Zeit Jesu gesprochene Aramäisch', *Z.N.W.* XLIX, 1958, 100–16.

The Cairo Geniza, second edn. Oxford, 1959.

Kahn, J.-G. 'Did Philo know Hebrew? The Testimony of the Etymologies', *Tarbiz*, XXXIV, 1965, 337–45 (Hebr.).

Kalisch, I. *Sefer Yezira*, New York, 1877.

Kaminka, A. 'Septuaginta und Targum zu Proverbia', *H.U.C.A.* VIII, 1931–2, 169–91.

Meḥkarim beMiqra ubaTalmud, Tel Aviv, 1951 (Hebr.).

Kanowitz, I. *Rabbi Aqiba . . .*, Jerusalem, 1956 (Hebr.).

Kaplan, J. *The Redaction of the Babylonian Talmud*, New York, 1933.

Katz, B. Z. *Pharisees, Sadducees, Zealots, and Christians*, Tel Aviv, 1947 (Hebr.).

Kaufmann, J. *Midrashe Geulah . . .*, second edn. Jerusalem, 1954.

Kenyon, F. S. *Our Bible and the Ancient Manuscripts*, rev. edn. London, 1958.

King, E. G. *The Yalkut on Zechariah*, Cambridge, 1882.

Kisch, G. *Pseudo-Philo's Liber Antiquitatum Biblicarum*, Notre Dame, Indiana, 1949.

'A Note on the New Edition of Pseudo-Philo's Biblical Antiquities', *Hist. Jud.* XII, 1950, 153–8.

'Postlegomena to the New Edition', *H.U.C.A.* XIII, 1950–1, 81–93.

'The Editio Princeps of Pseudo-Philo's Liber Antiquitatum Biblicarum', *A. Marx Jub. Vol.* 1950, 125–46.

Kittel, G. (ed.). *Rabbinische Texte, Die Tosefta*, Stuttgart, 1934–.

Klijn, A. J. F. 'The Letter of Aristeas and the Greek Translation of the Pentateuch in Egypt', *N.T.S.* XI, 154–8.

Komlos, Y. 'Nosaḥ haTargum al Qeriat Yam-Suf', *Sinai*, 1959, 223–8 (Hebr.).

'The Aggadah in the Targumim of Jacob's Blessing', *Ann. of Bar Ilan Univ.* I, 1963, 195–206 (Hebr.).

Kraeling, C. H. *The Synagogue: The Excavations at Dura-Europos . . .*, Final Report, VIII, pt. 1, New Haven, 1956.

Krauss, S. *Talmudische Archaeologie*, 3 vols. Leipzig, 1910–12.

'Etudes de terminologie talmudique: (1) Rabban et Rabbi', *R.E.J.* LXVII, 1914, 170–3.

Kuhn, K. G. *Der tannaitische Midrasch Sifre zu Numeri*, Stuttgart, 1959.

Künstlinger, D. *Die Petihot der Pesiqta de Rab Kahana*, Krakau, 1912.

Die Petihot des Midrasch rabba zu Leviticus, 1913.

Die Petihot des Midrasch rabba zu Genesis, 1914.

Kutsch, E. 'Miqra', *Z.A.W.* LXV, 1953, 247–55.

Kutscher, E. Y. 'Das zur Zeit Jesu gesprochene Aramäisch', *Z.N.W.* LI, 1960, 46–54.

Lachs, S. T. 'Prolegomena to Canticles Rabba', *J.Q.R.* LV, 1965, 235–55.

'The Proems of Canticles Rabba', *J.Q.R.* LVI, 1966, 225–39.

Lagarde, P. de. *Prophetae Chaldaice*, Leipzig, 1872.

Hagiographa Chaldaice, Leipzig, 1873.

Lauterbach, J. Z. *Mekilta deRabbi Ishmael*, 3 vols. Philadelphia, 1933–5.

'Rashi the Talmud Commentator', *C.C.A.R. Yearbook*, L, 1940.

Rabbinic Essays, H.U.C.P. 1951.

Leon, H. J. *The Jews of Ancient Rome*, Philadelphia, 1960.

Levene, A. *The Early Syrian Fathers on Genesis*, London ('Taylor's Foreign Press), 1951.

Levertoff, P. P. *Midrash Sifre on Numbers: selections . . . translated*, London (Translation of Early Documents), 1926.

Lévi, I. 'Le prosélytisme juif', *R.E.J.* 1905–7, L, 1–9; LI, 1–31; LIII, 56–66. 'Le Martyre des sept Macchabées. . .', *R.E.J.* LIV, 138–41.

Lewis, J. P. *A Study of the Interpretation of Noah and the Flood. . .*, Leiden, 1968.

Lichtenstein, H. *Megillath Taanith*, Cincinnati, 1931–2 (repr. from *H.U.C.A.* VIII, 1931–2, 318–51).

Liebermann, S. *Debarim Rabbah*, Jerusalem, 1940.
Greek in Jewish Palestine, New York, 1942.
Hellenism in Jewish Palestine, New York, 1950.
The Tosefta and Tosefta Kifshuta: Seder Zeraim, 3 vols. New York, 1956; *Seder Moed*, 4 vols. New York, 1962.
Midrash Debarim Rabbah, second edn. Jerusalem, 1964.

Loewe, R. 'Apologetic Motifs in the Targum to the Song of Songs', in A. Altmann (ed.), *Biblical Motifs*, 159–96.
'The "Plain" Meaning of Scripture in Early Jewish Exegesis', in J. G. Weiss (ed.), *Papers of the Institute of Jewish Studies*, I, 1964, 140–85.

Lohse, E. *Die Ordination im Spätjudentum und im Neuen Testament*, Göttingen, 1951.

Lukyn Williams, A. *Tractate Berakoth, Mishnah and Tosefta*, London, 1921.

Mach, R. *Der Zaddik in Talmud und Midrasch*, Leiden, 1957.

Malter, H. 'A Talmudic Problem and Proposed Solutions', *J.Q.R.* II, 1911–12, 75–95.

Mandelbaum, B. *Pesiqta deRab Kahana*, 2 vols. New York, 1962.

Mann, J. 'Rabbinic Studies in the Synoptic Gospels', *H.U.C.A.* I, 1924.
The Bible as Read and Preached in the Old Synagogue, I, Cincinnati, 1940; II, 1966 (ed. I. Sonne).

Mansoor, M. *The Dead Sea Scrolls, A College Textbook and a Study Guide*, Leiden, 1964.

Mantel, H. *Studies in the History of the Sanhedrin*, *H.S.S.* XVII, 1961.

Margolioth, M. *Midrash Haggadol on Genesis*, Jerusalem, 1947.
Midrash Vayyikra Rabbah, 5 vols. Jerusalem, 1953–60.
Midrash Haggadol on Exodus, Jerusalem, 1956.

Margolis, M. L. *History of the Jewish People* (with A. Marx), Philadelphia, 1927.

Marmorstein, A. 'Les "Epicuriens" dans la littérature Talmudique', *R.E.J.* LIV, 1907, 181–93.
Studien zum Pseudo-Jonathan Targum, Pozsony, 1905.
'La réorganisation du doctorat en Palestine au troisième siècle', *R.E.J.* LXVI, 1913, 44–53.
The Doctrine of Merits in Old Rabbinical Literature, Jews' College Publications, no. 7, London, 1920.
'The Background of Haggadah', *H.U.C.A.* VI, 1929; repr. in *The A. Marmorstein Memorial Volume*, London, 1950.

Marmorstein, A. (*cont.*)

The Old Rabbinic Doctrine of God, 2 vols. 1927–37.

'Einige vorläufige Bemerkungen zu den neuentdeckten Fragmenten des jerusalemischen . . . Targums', *Z.A.W.* XLIX, 1931, 231–42.

Martin, M. F. 'The Babylonian Tradition and Targum', in *Le Psautier*, ed. R. de Langhe, Louvain, 1962, 425–51.

'The Palaeographical Character of Codex Neofiti I', *Textus*, III, 1963, 1–35.

Marx, A. 'Strack's Introduction to the Talmud and Midrash', *J.Q.R.* XIII, 1922–3.

McNamara, M. 'The New Testament and the Palestinian Targum to the Pentateuch', *Verbum Domini*, XLIII, 1965, 288–300.

'Some Early Rabbinic Citations and the Palestinian Targum to the Pentateuch', *Riv. d. Stud. Orient.* XLI, 1966, 1–15.

The New Testament and the Palestinian Targum to the Pentateuch, Rome, 1966.

Meechan, H. G. *The Letter of Aristeas*, Manchester, 1935.

Melamed, E. Z. 'Tannaitic Controversies over the Interpretation and Text of Older Mishnayoth', *Tarbiz*, XXI, 1950, 137–64 (Hebr.).

Melamed, R. H. *The Targum to Canticles* . . ., Philadelphia, 1921.

Metzger, B. M. 'The Formulas Introducing Quotations of Scripture in the N.T. and the Mishnah', *J.B.L.* LXX, 1951, 297–307.

Meyer, R. 'Der Am ha-Ares; Ein Beitrag zur Religionssoziologie Palästinas im ersten und zweiten nachchristlichen Jahrhundert', *Judaica*, III, 1947, 169–99.

Mez, A. *Die Bibel des Josephus untersucht für Buch v–vii der Archäologie*, Basel, 1895.

Mielziner, M. *Introduction to the Talmud*, third edn. New York, 1925.

Mihaly, E. 'A Rabbinic Defense of the Election of Israel', *H.U.C.A.* XXXV, 1964, 103–43.

Mingana, A. 'Syriac Versions of the Old Testament', *J.Q.R.* VI, 1915–16, 385–98.

Mirsky, S. K. *HaDerashah Bitqufath haMishnah wehaTalmud*, Horeb, 1943 (Hebr.).

'Types of Lectures in the Babylonian Academies', in *Essays . . . Presented to S. W. Baron*, New York, 1959.

Montefiore, C. G., and Loewe, H. *A Rabbinic Anthology*, London, 1938.

Moore, G. F. *Judaism in the First Centuries of the Christian Era*, 3 vols. Cambridge, Mass., 1927–30.

Mordell, P. 'Letters and Numerals in Sefer Yeẓirah', *J.Q.R.* II, 1911–12, 557–83; III, 1912–13, 517–44.

Murmelstein, B. 'Spuren altorientalischer Einflüsse im rabbinischen Schrifttum: der rebellische Mond (Gen. i. 16)', *Z.A.W.* LXXI, 1959, 136–50.

Murtonen, A. *Materials for a non-Masoretic Grammar*, 3 vols. 1958–64.

Neubauer, A. *La Géographie du Talmud*, Paris, 1868.

Medieval Jewish Chronicles, Oxford, 1887.

Neuman, A. A. 'Josippon: History and Pietism', *A. Marx Jub. Vol.* 1950, 637–67.

'A Note on John the Baptist and Jesus in Josippon', *H.U.C.A.* XXIII, 1950–1, 137–49.

'Josippon and the Apocrypha', *J.Q.R.* XLIII, 1952, 1–26.

Neusner, J. *Life of Rabban Yoḥanan ben Zakkai*, Leiden, 1962.

'Studies on the Problem of Tannaim in Babylonia, *c.* 130–160 C.E.', *P.A.A.J.R.* XXX, 1962.

'Judaism at Dura-Europos', *Hist. of Rel.* IV, 1964, 81–102.

A History of the Jews in Babylonia, I, The Parthian Period, Leiden, 1965.

Newman, J. *Semikhah-ordination; a Study of its Origin, History and Function in Rabbinic Literature*, Manchester, 1950.

Nickels, P. *Targum and New Testament, a Bibliography*, Rome, 1967.

Noah, M. M., trans. *Sefer haYashar* . . ., New York, 1840.

Odeberg, H. *III Enoch, or the Hebrew Book of Enoch*, Cambridge, 1928.

The Aramaic Portions of Bereshit Rabba . . ., Lund, Leipzig, 1939.

Olmstead, O. M. 'Could an Aramaic Gospel be written?', *J.N.E.S.* I, 1942, 41–70.

Ostrow, J. 'Tannaitic and Roman Procedure in Homicide', *J.Q.R.* XLVIII, 1958, 352–70; LII, 1961, 160–7; LII, 1962, 245–63.

Parzen, H. 'The *Ruaḥ haQodesh* in Tannaitic Literature', *J.Q.R.* XX, 1929, 51–76.

Pautrel, R. 'Les canons du mashal rabbinique', *R.S.R.* XXVI, 1936.

Peters, C. 'Targum und Praevulgata des Pentateuchs', *Or. Chr.* IX, 1934, 49–54.

'Peschitta und Targumim des Pentateuchs', *Museon*, XLVIII, 1935, 1–54.

'Vom palästinischen Targum und seiner Geschichte', *Heil. Land*, II, 1940, 9–22.

Ploeg, J. van der. *Le Targum de Job de la Grotte II de Qumran*, *M.A.A.* (new series), XXV, 1962.

Podro, J. *The Last Pharisee, The Life and Times of Rabbi Joshua ben Hananyah* . . ., London, 1959.

Porter, F. C. 'Judaism in New Testament Times', *Journ. Rel.* VIII, 1928, 30–62.

Praetorius, F. *Das Targum zu Joshua in jemenischer Überlieferung*, 1899.

Targum zum Buch der Richter in jemenischer Überlieferung, 1900.

Prijs, L. *Jüdische Tradition in der Septuaginta*, Leiden, 1948.

Rabbinowitz, J. *Mishnah Megillah*, Oxford, 1931.

Rabinowitz, E. N. *Midrash Haggadol on Leviticus*, New York, 1932.

Rankin, O. S. *Jewish Religious Polemic of early and later Centuries*, Edinburgh, 1956.

Rappaport, S. *Aggada und Exegese bei Flavius Josephus*, Frankfurt, 1930.

Ratner, B. *Seder Olam Rabba* (*Die Grosse Weltchronik*), Wilna, 1894–7.

Reinach, T. (ed.). *Œuvres complètes de Flavius Josephus*, Paris, 1900.

Rengstorf, K. H. (ed.). *Rabbinische Texte: Die Tosefta*, Stuttgart, 1934/60.

(ed.). *Tannaitische Midrashim*, Stuttgart, 1933/59.

Revel, B. 'An Inquiry into the Sources of Karaite Halakah', *J.Q.R.* II, 1911–12, 517–44; III, 337–96.

Roberts, B. J. *The Old Testament Text and Versions*, Cardiff, 1951.

Rosenbaum, M. and Silbermann, A. M. *Pentateuch with Targum Onkelos, Haphtaroth and Prayers for Sabbath and Rashi's Commentary*, 2 vols. London, 1946.

Rosenblatt, S. *The Interpretation of the Bible in the Mishna*, Baltimore, 1935.

Rosenthal, F. *Die Aramäistische Forschung . . .*, Leiden, 1939.

Rosenthal, L. A. *Über den Zusammenhang, die Quellen und die Entstehung der Mischna*, 3 vols. Berlin, 1891–1918.

Russell, D. S. *The Method and Message of Jewish Apocalyptic*, London, 1964.

Safrai, S. 'Teaching of Pietists in Mishnaic Literature', *J.J.S.* XVI, 1965, 15–33.

Sandmel, S. 'Abraham's Knowledge of the Existence of God', *H.T.R.* XLIV, 1951, 137–9.

Philo's Place in Judaism: a Study of Conceptions of Abraham in Jewish Literature, Cincinnati, 1956.

'Parallelomania', *J.B.L.* LXXXI, 1962, 1–13.

Sarfatti, G. B. 'Pious Men, Men of Deeds and the Early Prophets', *Tarbiz*, XXVI, 1956, 126–53 (Hebr.).

'Notes on the Genesis Apocryphon', *Tarbiz*, XXVIII, 1959, 254–9 (Hebr.).

'Talmudic Cosmography', *Tarbiz*, XXXV, 1965, 137–48 (Hebr.).

Schachter, M. *The Babylonian and Jerusalem Mishna Textually Compared*, Jerusalem, 1959.

Schechter, S. *Aboth deRabbi Nathan*, Vienna, 1887.

Agadath Shir haShirim, Cambridge, 1896.

Midrash haGadol, Cambridge, 1902.

Studies in Judaism, 3 vols. Philadelphia, 1945.

Aspects of Rabbinic Theology, Macmillan, 1909; p.b. 1961.

Schelbert, G. 'Exodus xxii. 4 im Palästinischen Targum', *V.T.* VIII, 1958, 253–63.

Schlatter, A. *Die Theologie des Judentums nach dem Bericht des Josefus*, Gütersloh, 1932.

Schmerter, B. *Sefer Ahabat Yehonatan*, Bilgaray, 1932 (Hebr.).

Schoenfelder, J. M. *Onkelos und Peschitto*, Munich, 1869.

Schoeps, H. J. *Theologie und Geschichte des Judenchristentums*, Tübingen, 1919. *Paulus*, Tübingen, 1959 (also in Eng. trans.).

Scholem, G. G. *Major Trends in Jewish Mysticism*, New York, 1941.

Jewish Gnosticism, Merkabah Mysticism, and Talmudic Tradition, New York 1960.

Schreckenberg, H. *Bibliographie zu Flavius Josephus*, Leiden (in preparation)

Schulz, S. 'Die Bedeutung der neuen Targumsforschung für die synoptische Tradition', in *Abraham unser Vater*, Leiden, 1963, 425–36.

Schürer, E. *A History of the Jewish People in the Time of Jesus Christ*, Eng. trans. 1897.

Schwab, M. *Le Talmud de Jérusalem*, 11 vols. Paris, 1871–89, repr. 1960.

Schwartz, J. 'Note sur la famille de Philon d'Alexandrie', *A.I.P.O.* 591–602.

Schwarz, A. *Die Controversen der Schammaiten und der Hilleliten*, Vienna, 1893.

Die hermeneutische Analogie in der Talmudischen Litteratur, Vienna, 1897.

Die hermeneutische Syllogismus in . . ., Karlsruhe, 1901.

Die hermeneutische Induktion in . . ., Leipzig, 1909.

Die hermeneutische Antinomie in . . ., Vienna, 1913.

Die hermeneutische Quantitätsrelation in . . ., Wien, 1916.

Die hermeneutische Kontext in . . ., Wien, 1921.

Seeligmann, I. L. 'Voraussetzungen der Midraschexegese', *V.T.* suppl. I, 1953, 150–81.

Segal, M. H. 'The Promulgation of the Authoritative Text of the Hebrew Bible', *J.B.L.* LXXII, 1953, 35–47.

Shanks, H. 'Is the Title "Rabbi" Anachronistic in the Gospels?', *J.Q.R.* LIII, 1962–3, and a reply by S. Zeitlin, *ibid.* 315–19.

Shereshevsky, E. 'The Significance of Rashi's Commentary on the Pentateuch', *J.Q.R.* LIV, 1963–4, 58–79.

Sibinga, J. S. *The Old Testament Text of Justin Martyr. I. The Pentateuch*, Leiden, 1963.

Silverstone, A. E. *Aquila and Onkelos*, Manchester, 1931.

Simon, C. *Les sectes juives au temps de Jésus*, 1960.

Singer, S. *Onkelos und das Verhältniss seines Targums zur Halacha*, Berlin, 1881.

(Singer, S.) *The Authorised Daily Prayer Book*, many editions.

Sjöberg, E. *Gott und die Sünder im palästinischen Judentum nach dem Zeugnis der Tannaiten und der apokryphisch-pseudepigraphischen Literatur*, Stuttgart, 1938.

'Wiedergeburt und Neuschöpfung im palästinischen Judentum', *S.T.* IV, 1950, 44–85.

Smith, M. *Tannaitic Parallels to the Gospels*, *J.B.L.* monogr. 6, 1951.

'The Image of God: notes on the Hellenization of Judaism . . .', *B.J.R.L.* XL, 1958, 473 ff.

Sonne, I. 'The Schools of Shammai and Hillel Seen from Within', *Louis Ginzberg Memorial Volume*, New York, 1945, 275–91.

Spanier, A. *Die Toseftaperiode in der tannaitischen Literatur*, Berlin, 1922.

Speier, S. 'Beiträge zu den Targumim', *S.Th.U.* XX, 1950, 52–61.

Sperber, A. *The Bible in Aramaic*, 4 vols. London, 1959–.

Spiro, A. 'Samaritans, Tobiads, and Judahites in Pseudo-Philo', *P.A.A.J.R.* XX, 1951, 279–355.

'Pseudo-Philo's Saul and the Rabbis' Messiah ben Ephraim', *P.A.A.J.R.* XXI, 1952, 119–37.

'The Ascension of Phinehas', *P.A.A.J.R.* XXII, 1953, 91–114.

Staerk, D. W. *Altjüdische liturgische Gebete*, Bonn, 1910.

Stauffer, E. 'Der Methurgeman des Petrus', in *Fest. Joseph Schmid*, 1963, 283–93.

Stearns, W. N. *Fragments of Graeco-Jewish Writers*, Chicago, 1908.
Stein, E. 'Die allegorische Exegese des Philo aus Alexandria', *Z.A.T.W.* LI, 1929.
Philo und Midrasch ..., Giessen, 1931.
Stein, S. 'The Dietary Laws in Rabbinic and Patristic Literature', *Stud. Patr.* II, 1957.
Stenning, J. F. *The Targum of Isaiah*, Oxford, 1949.
Stern, M. 'Sympathy for Judaism in Roman Senatorial Circles in the Period of the Early Empire', *Zion*, XXIX, 1964, 155–67.
Strack, H. L. *Introduction to the Talmud and Midrash*, Eng. trans. 1931, repr. 1959.
Stummer, F. 'Beiträge zu dem Problem "Hieronymus und die Targumim"', *Bibl.* XVIII, 1937, 174–81.
Sukenik, E. L. *The Ancient Synagogue of el-Ḥammeh* ..., Jerusalem, 1935.
Swete, H. B. *An Introduction to the Old Testament in Greek*, Cambridge, 1902.
Tcherikover, V. *Hellenistic Civilization and the Jews*, Eng. trans. Philadelphia, 1959.
The Jews in Egypt in the Hellenistic-Roman Age ..., Jerusalem, 1963.
Tcherikover, V., Fuks, A. and Stern, M. *Corpus Papyrorum Judaicarum*, 3 vols. Cambridge (Mass.), 1957–64.
Tchernowitz, Ch. *Toledoth haHalakah*, 4 vols. New York, 1934–50.
Teicher, J. L. 'A Sixth-Century Fragment of the Palestinian Targum', *V.T.* I, 1951, 125–9.
'Ancient Eucharistic Prayers in Hebrew', *J.Q.R.* LIV, 1963, 99–109.
Theodor, J. 'Die Midraschim zum Pentateuch und der dreijährige palästinische Cyclus', *M.G.W.J.* XXXIV, 1885–.
Bereschit Rabba mit kritischem Apparat und Kommentar, 4 vols. Berlin, 1903–36 (with H. Albeck, *q.v.*).
Thieme, K. [Hermann, A., and Glässer, E.]. *Beiträge zur Geschichte des Dolmetschens*, München, 1956.
Urbach, E. E. 'The Derasha as a Basis of the Halakah and the Problem of the Soferim', *Tarbiz*, XXVII, 1958, 166–82 (Hebr.).
Vermes, G. *Scripture and Tradition in Judaism*, Leiden, 1961.
The Dead Sea Scrolls in English, Pelican, 1962.
'Haggadah in the Onkelos Targum', *J.S.S.* VIII, 1963, 159–69.
'The Targumic Version of Gen. iv. 3–36', *Ann. of Leeds Univ. Orient. Soc.* IV, 1965, 13–53.
Vööbus, A. *Peschitta und Targumim des Pentateuchs*, Stockholm, 1958.
Vries, B. de. 'The Older Form of some Halakoth', *Ozar haHayyim*, II, 1932; *Hammaor*, 1935; *Tarbiz*, V, 1934, 247–56; XXII, 1951, 153–6; XXIV, 1955, 392–405; XXV, 1956, 369–84 (Hebr.).
'The Mishnah and Tosefta of Baba Mezia', *Tarbiz*, XX, 1950, 79–83 (Hebr.).
'The Mishnah and Tosefta of Makkoth', *Tarbiz*, XXVI, 1957, 255–61 (Hebr.).

'The Problem of the Relationship of the Two Talmuds to the Tosefta', *Tarbiz*, XXVIII, 1959, 158–70 (Hebr.).

'The Mishnah and Tosefta of Meilah', *Tarbiz*, XXIX, 1960, 229–49 (Hebr.).

Toledoth haHalakah haTalmudit, Tel Aviv, 1962 (Hebr.).

Review of H. Albeck, *Mabo laMishnah*, in *J.J.S.* X, 1959, 173–81.

Wächter, L. 'Der Einfluss platonischen Denkens auf rabbinische Schöpfungsspekulationen', *Z.R.G.* XIV, 1962, 36–56.

Wallis Budge, E. A. *The Book of the Cave of Treasures*, London, 1927.

Weil, G. E. 'Le Codex Neophiti I—à propos de l'article de M. F. Martin', *Textus*, IV, 1964, 225–9.

Weill, J. (trans.). *Œuvres Complètes de Flavius Josephus (Ant. i–v)*, ed. T. Reinach, Paris, 1900.

Weinberg, J. *LeToledot haTargumim*, New York, 1964 (Hebr.).

Weingreen, J. 'The Rabbinic Approach to the Study of the Old Testament', *B.J.R.L.* XXXIV, 1951–2, 166–90.

Weiss, A. *LeHeqer haTalmud*, New York, 1954.

Weiss, J. G. (ed.). *Papers of the Institute of Jewish Studies, London*, I, Jerusalem, 1964.

Weiss, J. H. *Sifra on Leviticus*, Vienna, 1862.

Dor Dor weDorshaw, 4 vols. fourth edn. Vilna, 1904.

Weiss, P. R. *Mishnah Horayoth, Its History and Exposition*, Manchester, 1952.

Welles, C. B. *et al. The Parchments and Papyri: The Excavations at Dura-Europos*, Final Report, V, pt. 1, New Haven, 1959.

Werblowsky, R. J. Z. 'Philo and Zohar', *J.J.S.* X, 1959, 25–44, 113–35.

Wernberg-Møller, P. Some Observations on the Relationship of the Peshitta Version of the Book of Genesis to the Palestinian Targum Fragments . . ., and to Targum Onkelos', *S.T.* XV, 1961, 128–80.

'An Inquiry into the Validity of the Text-critical Argument for an Early Dating of the Recently Discovered Palestinian Targum', *V.T.* XII, 1962, 312–31.

'Prolegomena to a Re-examination of the Palestinian Targum Fragments published by P. Kahle and their relationship to the Peshitta', *J.J.S.* VII, 1962, 253–66.

Widengren, G. 'Tradition and Literature in Early Judaism and the Early Church', *Numen*, X, 1963, 42–83.

Wieder, N. 'The Habakkuk Scroll and the Targum', *J.J.S.* IV, 1953, 14–18.

'The Old Palestinian Ritual, New Sources', *J.J.S.* IV, 1953, 30–7, 65–73.

Wiesenberg, E. 'Observations on Method in Talmudic Studies', *J.S.S.* XI, 1966, 16–36.

Wikgren, A. P. 'The Targums and the New Testament', *Journ. Rel.* XXIV, 1944, 89–95.

Wilnai, Z. *Jerusalem-Birath Yisrael*, Jerusalem, 1960 (Hebr.).

Windfuhr, D. 'Paulus als Haggadist', *Z.A.W.* III, 1926, 327–30.

(trans.) *Die Tosefta*, 2 vols. Stuttgart, 1960–5.

Winter, P. 'Luke. ii. 49 and Targum Yerushalmi', *Z.N.W.* XLV, 1954, 145–79.
'The Proto-Source of Luke i', *Nov. Test.* I, 1956, 184–99.
'Eine vollständige Handschrift des Palästinischen Targums aufgefunden', *Z.N.W.* XLVIII, 1957, 192.
Wohl, S. *Das Palästinische Pentateuch-Targum*, Bonn dissertation, 1935.
Wolfson, H. A. *Philo*, I–II, second edn. Cambridge, Mass., 1948.
Woude, A. S. van der. 'Das Hiobtargum aus Qumran-Höhle XI', *V.T.* suppl. IX, 1963, 322–31.
'Melchisedek als himmlische Erlösergestalt in den neugefundenen eschatologischen Midraschim aus Qumran-Höhle XI', in כה (Oudtestamentische Studiën, XIV), Leiden, 1965.
Wünsche, A. *Midrasch Rabba*, Leipzig, 1880–2.
Midrasch Tehillim . . ., Trier, 1892.
Wynkoop, J. D. 'A Peculiar Kind of Paronomasia in the Talmud and Midrash', *J.Q.R.* II, 1911, 1–23.
Yadin, Y. *Masada*, London, 1966.
Young, R. *Christology of the Targums* . . ., Edinburgh, 1848.
Zeitlin, S. 'The Semikah Controversy between the Zugoth', *J.Q.R.* VII, 1916–17, 499–517.
'Megillath Taanith as a Source', *J.Q.R.* IX, 71–102; X, 49–80.
'The Origin of the Synagogue', *P.A.A.J.R.* 1931.
'An Historical Study of the Canonization of the Hebrew Scriptures', *P.A.A.J.R.* 1932, 152 ff.
'Midrash, a historical study', *J.Q.R.* XLIV, 1953, 21–36.
'The Tosefta', *J.Q.R.* XLVII, 1957, 382–99.
'The Titles High Priest and the Nasi of the Sanhedrin', *J.Q.R.* XLVIII, 1957, 1–5.
'The Temple and Worship', *J.Q.R.* LI, 1961, 209–41.
'Some Reflections on the Text of the Pentateuch', *J.Q.R.* LI, 1961, 321–4.
'The Pharisees, a Historical Study', *J.Q.R.* LII, 1961, 97–129.
The Rise and Fall of the Jewish State, I, Philadelphia, 1962.
'There was no Synagogue in the Temple', *J.Q.R.* LIII, 1962, 168 f.
'Josippon', *J.Q.R.* LIII, 1963, 277–97.
'Hillel and the Hermeneutic Rules', *J.Q.R.* LIV, 1964, 161–73.
'The Tefillah, the Shemoneh Esreh', *J.Q.R.* LIV, 1964, 208–49.
'The Takkanot of Rn. Johanan b. Zakkai', *J.Q.R.* LIV, 1964, 288–310.
Ziegler, I. *Die Königsgleichnisse des Midrasch beleuchtet durch die römische Kaiserzeit*, Breslau, 1903.
Zimmels, H. J. 'Jesus and "Putting Up a Brick"', *J.Q.R.* XLIII, 1953, 225–8.
Zuckermandel, M. S. *Tosefta, Mischna und Boraitha in ihrem Verhältnis zu einander* . . ., 2 vols. and suppl. Frankfurt, 1908–10.
Zunz, L. *Die gottesdienstlichen Vorträge der Juden historisch entwickelt*, revised edn. 1892, translated into Hebrew by M. A. Jacque, 1950, with notes by Ch. Albeck.

INDEXES

I. REFERENCES

The references are indexed in the following order:

Biblical
   Old Testament
   Biblical Apocrypha
   New Testament
Versions
Targums
Apocrypha and Pseudepigrapha
Syriac Commentary and Commentary of
   Ishodad

Dead Sea Scrolls
Christian Writers
Qur'ān
Papyri and Inscriptions
Hellenistic Writers
Josephus
Philo
Rabbinic Works[1]
Commentators: Rashi

BIBLICAL
(in the order of the *English* Bible)

OLD TESTAMENT

Genesis

i. 1: 319
i. 11: 81
i. 12: 115
i. 20: 108
i. 26: 115, 185, 319
i. 27: 185
i. 31: 120, 198
ii. 2: 5, 118, 319
ii. 4: 139, 214
ii. 5–7: 115
ii. 17: 120
ii. 22: 143
iii. 1: 251
iii. 8: 119
iii. 15: 101
iii. 18 f.: 128
iii. 22: 107
iii. 24: 42
iv. 6: 115
iv. 7: 122
iv. 14: 301
iv. 16: 118, 139
iv. 17: 301
iv. 19: 302

iv. 22: 139, 302
iv. 23: 24, 138, 139, 302
iv. 26: 180
v. 1: 51, 139
v. 2: 117, 319
v. 3: 136
v. 21–3: 301
v. 22: 159
v. 32: 156
vi. 1: 141, 180, 302
vi. 5: 120, 302
vi. 6: 163, 302
vii. 4: 156
vii. 5–11: 302
vii. 6: 156
vii. 10: 156
vii. 12: 17, 216
vii. 19: 170
viii. 1: 95, 163
viii. 6: 154
viii. 14: 164
ix. 11: 246
ix. 13 f.: 114
ix. 15: 154
ix. 20: 169
ix. 27: 198
x: 17

x. 8: 141, 180
x. 10: 101
x. 21: 129
x. 25: 179, 224
xi. 1: 3
xi. 2–4: 306
xi. 4–9: 309
xi. 5: 185
xi. 6: 180
xi. 7: 185, 319
xi. 10: 156
xi. 28: 9
xii. 1: 229
xii. 4–5: 310
xii. 6: 224
xii. 10 ff.: 204, 229
xii. 17: 205
xiii. 12 f.: 310
xiii. 13: 87
xiii. 15: 310
xiv: 229
xiv. 1: 83, 188
xiv. 13: 266
xiv. 17–24: 229
xv. 2: 191
xv. 5: 224, 231
xv. 6: 229

[1] The Babylonian and Palestinian Talmuds are in the alphabetical order of these works under Talmud; the Additional Tractates follow after the Babylonian Talmud, *except* for Aboth de Rabbi Nathan, which is listed as a separate work under A.

VERSIONS

TARGUMS

(N.B.: references in the ordinary sequence of the translation and commentary are not repeated here.)

DEAD SEA SCROLLS

CHRISTIAN WRITERS

QUR'ĀN

PAPYRI AND INSCRIPTIONS

HELLENISTIC WRITERS

RABBINIC WORKS

---

[1] References to the Mekilta (as mentioned briefly on p. 71) are usually made, either to the present divisions of Exodus in the Hebrew Bible, or to the Tractates of the Mekilta, or to a combination of both. For ease of reference the Hebrew divisions of Exodus are given here, together with the Mekilta Tractates (in italics). The square brackets indicate those divisions of Exodus not covered by the Mekilta:

[Shemoth: Exod. i–vi. 1]
[Va'era: vi. 2–ix]
Bo: x–xiii. 16
    Pisha: xii. 1–xiii. 16
Beshallah: xiii. 17–xvii
    Vayehi: xiii. 17–xiv. 31
    Shirata: xv. 1–21
    Vayassa': xv. 22–xviii. 7
    'Amalek: xvii. 8–16

Yitro: xviii–xx
    'Amalek (cont.): xviii. 17–27
    Bahodesh: xix. 1–xx. 26 (23)
Mishpatim: xxi–xxiv
    Neziqin: xxi. 1–xxii. 24 (23)
    Kaspa: xxii. 25 (24)–xxiii. 19
[Terumah: xxv–xxvii. 19]
[Tezavveh: xxvii. 20–xxx. 10]
Ki tissah: xxx. 11–xxxiv.
    Shabbata: xxxi. 12–17, xxxv. 1–3.

COMMENTATORS

II. GREEK WORDS

Ἀδαμ, 116
ἀνδρόγυνος, 143
αὐτομόλησις, 180
γίγαντες, 158
δασύποδα, 319
δικαιοσύνη, 202

εἰκών, 97
ἔλεγχος, 242
ἐπεθύμησεν, 279
θύννος, 97
λαγώς, 319
μάχαιρα, 289

μισόξενοι, 192
παράδειγμα, 232
παραδίδονται, 158
σύστημα, 278
τετραγώνων, 159

III. SEMITIC WORDS AND PHRASES

ab bet din, meaning of, 56
abrek, 254
agen, 162
'aggadah, see haggadah
alqaphta, 253
'am(me) haArez, 160
anderoginos, 143
'aph, double meaning of, 251
appey hilkatha, meaning of, 58
appiqorsin, 147
'aqedah, 227
  see also Subject index, 'Aqedah
'arummim, 120
auwthan, 187

baraita, meaning of, 62
bar nash, 99, 135, 249, 286
bas, 114
bath qol, 227
  meaning of, 44 f.
bayit, 177
beishteutha, 175
bene elohim, 153
bene nash(a), 95, 295
bereshith, 99
  meaning of, 100
bet din, 186
  heavenly, 186
  meaning of, 56
bet haMidrash, 178, 237, 271, 283
  meaning of, 49
bet sefer, meaning of, 49
binyan ab mikathub 'ehad, 315
binyan ab mishene kethubim, 315

dabar halamed me'inyano, 315
dag, 275
delator, 121
demey, 139
demuth, 99
derek qezerah, meaning of, 51
deyokan, 97
dibbur, 124
dibre soferim, meaning of, 54
dilma, meaning of, 216
din, 154 f., 204

fada, 230

gemara, 66, 67
  meaning of, 64 f.
gematria, 318
gezerah shawah, 315, 317
gezeroth
  meaning of, 41
  Sadducean, 42
goy, 158

haftarah, 38
  meaning of, 13, 73
haggadah, 13, 41, 57, 89, 129
  meaning of, 40, 43, 69
hakamim, 82, 177
  meaning of, 38, 55
halakah, 41, 52, 53 f., 55, 57, 59 f., 61, 69
  meaning of, 40, 43–8
  'ways of', 58
hamid, 112, 279
hanaph, 147
haruzin, meaning of, 74

hashab, 201
hehel, 179 f.
heqesh, 317
herem, 242
hesed, 137, 153
hiluf, 318
hug, 104
huhal, 141

'ir, 184

ka'et hayyah, 211
kayoze bo bemaqom 'aher, 315
kelal
  examples of, 46, 51
  meaning of, 51
kelal upherat, 315
kenesset, meaning of, 10
kenishta, 280, 283
ketubim, meaning of, 5
  see also Hagiographa

le'athid, 128

ma'amadoth, meaning of, 9
ma'arta, 252
ma'aseh 'abot siman labanim, meaning of, 92
ma'aseh bereshith, 10, 85, 99, 100, 139
ma'aseh merkabah, 85
  meaning of, 38
mammon, 190, 238
massektoth, 322
  meaning of, 60
mekeyrotheyhem, 277, 283, 289
memar, 98, 113, 122, 124, 200, 281, 287, 288

366

IV. PLACES

V. NAMES AND DATES OF RABBIS

(The *generation* of each rabbi is given in parentheses after his name; see also Appendix VI)

VI. MODERN AUTHORS

VII. GENERAL SUBJECT INDEX

Mishnah, 12 f., 14, 19, 22 f., 43, 45, 47, 50, 53, 55, 65, 81, 87; abbreviations, 61; anonymous, 57, 60; basis of study, 53, 64; date of, 49, 56 ff.; described, 53–61; first, 57, 59; formation of, 56 ff.; order of, 50 ff., 59 f.; Orders of, 26, 60 f.; text of, 61; tractates of, 322; translations of, 61; ways of referring to, 61; written, 52, 53, 56; see also Semitic word index

Mnemonic techniques, 51

Moon, 103, 119; less than sun, 96, 99,105

Moriah, Mount, 123, 131

Moses, 7, 11, 41, 47, 165, 178; blessing of, 272; proto-prophet, 145; rod of (pre-created), 113 f.; tomb of (pre-created), 114

Moses, Chronicle of, see Chronicle of Moses

R. Moses haDarshan, 81

Mourning, 163, 293 f.

Muhammad, wives of, 26

Mystery, 13, 49

Mysticism, 38 f., 85; see also Semitic word index, merkabah

Naphtali: blessing on, 280, 286; messenger, 270, 280, 286, 291, 294

Narrative midrashim, 6, 8, described, 85

haNasi, see R. Judah the Prince

Natural law, see Law, natural

Neofiti I, 25, 26; date of, 16 ff.; described, 16 ff.; relation of to N.T., 20

Nephilim, 157 f.

New Testament, 17, 20

New Year, 165 f.

Nicolas of Damascus, 168

Niddah, 66

Nimrod, 86, 130, 304 ff.; and Amraphel, 188 f.; derivation of name, 179; sinful character of, 179 f., 204

Noachian precepts, 236, 241

Noah, 157, 165, 193, 241; altar of, 225; precepts of, 236, 241; righteousness of, 151, 153, 159, 161; vineyard of, 169, 172 f., 174 f.

Notariqon, see Semitic word index

Og, spared from flood, 193–5

Olives, Mount of, 167, 170

Onqelos, Targum of, 18 f., 21, 22–6; interpretation in, 23 f.; language of, 22 f.; relationship to other Targums, 24

Oral Torah, see Torah, oral; Semitic word index, torah shebe'al peh

Parable, 103; examples of, 102, 116, 138, 201, 240 f.

Passover, 75, 132, 193, 211, 316 f.

Paul, 232, 235, 236; and merkabah mysticism, 38

Pelitith, 208, 212 f.

Pereq haShalom, 68

Pesiqta deRab Kahana, 74–6, 79, 83

Pesiqta Rabbati, 74, 76, 79

Pharisees, 7, 40 f., 55; emergence of, 54; and Sadducees, 42; and Scribes, 54

Pharisaism, 8, 11, 37 f., 42

Philo, 6, 11, 29 f., 36 f., 48

Phylacteries, 68

Pilpul, see Semitic word index

Pirqe Aboth, see Aboth, Pirqe

Pirqe deRabbi Eliezer, 39, 85

Pishon, 111, 160; precious stone of, 152, 159 f.

Pointing, varieties of described, 22 f.

Prayer, 115, 136, 154, 195, 213–15, 220, 222 f.; the Daily, 68 f., 215; house of, 10; a principle of, 220; replaces sacrifice, 214

Priesthood, of Melchizedek, 196–9

Priests, 196 ff., 214; blessing of, 19

Proem homilies, see Homilies, proem

Prophecy, cessation of, 44

Prophets, 5, 7; reading of, 13, 73

Proselytes, 5, 69, 173, 178, 210, 222 f.

Proverbs, Midrash on, see Midrash on Proverbs

Psalms, Midrash on, see Midrash Tehillim

Pseudepigrapha, 32

Pseudo-Jonathan, 18, 24, 25, 85; described, 26 f.; name explained, 27; index of passages translated from, 94

Pseudo-Philo, 6, 8, 30–1, 85

Purim, 84

Qardon, 167, 168 f.

Qinnim, 62, 66; date of, 58

Qoheleth Rabbah, 84

Rabbenu haQodesh, 56

Rabbi, Rabbis: authority of, 36 f., 38, 43 f., 53, 317; Babylonian, 79, 80; dates of, 49, 50, 53, 323 f.; emergence of name, 56; example of, 65; generations of, 323 f.; Palestinian, 75, 79, 80, 84, 88; rivalries of, 54, 57, 69 f.; sayings of, 52; successors of Pharisees, 36, 42; see also Judaism, rabbinic

Rabbi (Judah haNasi), 56 ff.

Rabbinic Judaism, see Judaism, Rabbinic